IT Strategy in Action

IT Strategy in Action

James D. McKeen
Queen's University

Heather A. Smith
Queen's University

Upper Saddle River, New Jersey 07458

Library of Congress Cataloging-in-Publication Data

McKeen, James D.

   IT strategy in action / James D. McKeen, Heather A. Smith.—1st ed.

     p. cm.

   ISBN–13: 978-0-13-603631-9

   ISBN–10: 0-13-603631-7

   1. Information technology—Management.   I. Mckeen, James D.

    II. Smith, Heather A.

   HD30.2.M3987 2008

   004.068—dc22

2007048123

AVP/Executive Editor: Bob Horan
VP/Editorial Director: Sally Yagan
Product Development Manager:
  Ashley Santora
Project Manager, Editorial: Kelly Loftus
Marketing Manager: Anne Falhgren
Marketing Assistant: Susan Osterlitz
Senior Managing Editor: Judy Leale
Project Manager, Production:
  Ana Jankowski
Permissions Project Manager:
  Charles Morris

Senior Operations Specialist:
  Arnold Vila
Operations Specialist: Carol O'Rourke
Cover Design: Suzanne Behnke
Creative Director: Jayne Conte
Cover Illustration/Photo:
  Getty Images, Inc.
Composition/Full-Service Project
  Management: Aptara, Inc./
  Puneet Lamba
Printer/Binder: Edwards Brothers
Typeface: 10/12 Palatino Roman

Credits and acknowledgments borrowed from other sources and reproduced, with permission, in this textbook appear on appropriate page within text.

Pearson Education Ltd., London
Pearson Education Singapore, Pte. Ltd
Pearson Education Canada, Inc.
Pearson Education–Japan
Pearson Education Australia PTY,
  Limited

Pearson Education North Asia Ltd.,
  Hong Kong
Pearson Educación de Mexico, S.A. de C.V.
Pearson Education Malaysia, Pte. Ltd.
Pearson Education Upper Saddle River,
  New Jersey

10 9 8 7 6 5 4 3 2 1
ISBN 13: 978-0-13-603631-9
ISBN 10:   0-13-603631-7

TABLE OF CONTENTS

PREFACE

Today, with information technology (IT) driving constant business transformation, overwhelming organizations with information, enabling 24/7 global operations, and undermining traditional business models, the challenge for business leaders is not simply to *manage* IT, it is to *use* IT *to deliver business value.* Whereas until fairly recently, decisions about IT could be safely delegated to technology specialists *after* a business strategy had been developed, IT is now so closely integrated with business that, as one CIO explained to us, "We can no longer deliver business solutions in our company without using technology."

All too often, in our efforts to prepare future executives to deal effectively with the issues of IT strategy and management, we lead them into a foreign country where they encounter a different language, different culture, and different customs. Acronyms (e.g., SOA, FTP/IP, PKI, ITIL), buzzwords (e.g., asymmetric encryption, proxy servers, mailer-daemons), and the widely adopted practice of abstraction (e.g., Is a software monitor a person, place, or thing?) present formidable "barriers to entry" to the technologically uninitiated, but more important, they obscure the importance of teaching students how to make *business* decisions about a key organizational resource. By taking a critical issues perspective, *IT Strategy in Action* treats IT as a tool to be leveraged to save and/or make money or transform an organization—not as a study by itself.

This book combines the experiences and insights of many senior IT managers from leading-edge organizations with thorough academic research to bring important issues in IT management to life and demonstrate how *IT strategy is put into action* in contemporary businesses. Designed around some of the most critical real-world issues in IT management today, such as creating value with IT, effective IT governance, using IT for innovation, and developing strong IT capabilities, it introduces students to the challenges of making IT decisions that will have significant impacts on how businesses function and deliver value to stakeholders.

IT Strategy in Action focuses on how IT is changing and will continue to change organizations as we now know them. However, rather than learning concepts "free of context," students are introduced to the complex decisions facing real organizations by means of a number of minicases. These provide

> ### Key Features of this Book
>
> - A focus on IT *management* issues as opposed to *technology* issues
> - Critical IT issues explored within their organizational contexts
> - Readily applicable models and frameworks for implementing IT strategies
> - Minicases to animate issues and focus classroom discussions on real-world decisions, enabling problem-based learning
> - Proven strategies and best practices from leading-edge organizations
> - Useful and practical advice and guidelines for delivering value with IT
> - Extensive teaching notes for all minicases

an opportunity to apply the models/theories/frameworks presented and help students integrate and assimilate this material. By the end of the book, students will have the confidence and ability to tackle the tough issues regarding IT management and strategy and a clear understanding of their importance in delivering business value.

A DIFFERENT APPROACH TO TEACHING IT STRATEGY

The real world of IT is one of issues—critical issues—such as the following:

- How do we know if we are getting value from our IT investment?
- What specific IT functions should we seek from external providers?
- How do we build the IT leadership team?
- How do we enhance IT capabilities?
- How do we improve our budgeting/planning procedures?
- How do we improve project selection?

However, the majority of management information systems (MIS) textbooks are organized by system *category* (e.g., supply chain, customer relationship management, enterprise resource planning), by system *component* (e.g., hardware, software, networks), by system *function* (e.g., marketing, financial, human resources), by system *type* (e.g., transactional, decisional, strategic), or by a combination of these. Unfortunately, such organization does not promote an understanding of IT management in practice.

IT Strategy in Action tackles the real-world challenges of IT management. First, it explores a set of the most important issues facing IT managers today, and second, it provides a series of minicases that present these critical IT issues within the context of real organizations. By focusing the text as well as the minicases on today's critical issues, the book naturally reinforces problem-based learning.

IT Strategy in Action includes twelve minicases—each based on a real company presented anonymously.[1] Minicases are *not* simply abbreviated versions of standard, full-length business cases. They differ in two significant ways:

1. *A horizontal perspective.* Unlike standard cases that develop a single issue within an organizational setting (i.e., a "vertical" slice of organizational life), minicases take a "horizontal" slice through a number of coexistent issues. Rather than looking for a *solution* to a specific problem, as in a standard case, students analyzing a minicase must first *identify and prioritize* the issues embedded within the case. This mimics real life in organizations where the challenge lies in "knowing where to start" as opposed to "solving a predefined problem."
2. *Highly relevant information.* Minicases are densely written. Unlike standard cases, which intermix irrelevant information, in a minicase, each sentence exists for a reason and reflects relevant information. As a result, students must analyze each case very carefully so as not to miss critical aspects of the situation.

---

[1]We are unable to identify these leading-edge companies by agreements established as part of our overall research program (described later).

Teaching with minicases is, thus, very different than teaching with standard cases. With minicases, students must determine what is really going on within the organization. What first appears as a straightforward "technology" problem may in fact be a political problem or one of five other "technology" problems. Detective work is, therefore, required. The problem identification and prioritization skills needed are essential skills for future managers to learn for the simple reason that it is not possible for organizations to tackle all of their problems concurrently. Minicases help teach these skills to students and can balance the problem-solving skills learned in other classes. Best of all, detective work is fun and promotes lively classroom discussion.

To assist instructors, extensive teaching notes are available for all minicases. Developed by the authors and based on "tried and true" in-class experience, these notes include case summaries, identify the key issues within each case, present ancillary information about the company/industry represented in the case, and offer guidelines for organizing the classroom discussion. Because of the structure of these minicases and their embedded issues, it is common for teaching notes to exceed the length of the actual minicase!

This book is most appropriate for MIS courses where the goal is to understand how IT delivers organizational value. These courses are frequently labeled "IT Strategy" or "IT Management" and are offered within undergraduate as well as MBA programs. For undergraduate juniors and seniors in business and commerce programs, this is usually the "capstone" MIS course. For MBA students, this course may be the compulsory core course in MIS, or it may be an elective course.

Each chapter and minicase in this book has been thoroughly tested in a variety of undergraduate, graduate, and executive programs at Queen's School of Business.[2] These materials have proven highly successful within all programs because we adapt how the material is presented according to the level of the students. Whereas undergraduate students "learn" about critical business issues from the book and minicases for the first time, graduate students are able to "relate" to these same critical issues based on their previous business experience. As a result, graduate students are able to introduce personal experiences into the discussion of these critical IT issues.

ORGANIZATION OF THIS BOOK

One of the advantages of an issues-focused structure is that chapters can be approached in any order because they do not build on one another. Chapter order is immaterial; that is, one does not need to read the first three chapters to understand the fourth. This provides an instructor with maximum flexibility to organize a course as he or she sees fit. Thus, within different courses/programs, the order of topics can be changed to focus on different IT concepts.

Furthermore, because each minicase includes multiple issues, they, too, can be used to serve different purposes. For example, the minicase "Information Management at Homestyle Hotels" can be used to focus on issues of governance, vendor selection,

---

[2]Queen's School of Business full-time MBA program was ranked number one in the world outside the United States by *BusinessWeek* in 2006. The school consistently ranks among the top schools in the world for its full-time MBA, Executive MBA, and Executive Development Programs.

organizational structure, and/or change management just as easily as information management. The result is a rich set of instructional materials that lends itself well to a variety of pedagogical applications, particularly problem-based learning, and that clearly illustrates the reality of IT strategy in action.

The book is organized into four sections, each emphasizing a key component of developing and delivering effective IT strategy:

• **Section 1: Delivering Value with IT** is designed to examine the complex ways that IT and business value are related. Over the past twenty years, researchers and practitioners have come to understand that "business value" can mean many different things when applied to IT. Chapter 1 (Developing and Delivering on the IT Value Proposition) explores these concepts in depth. Unlike the simplistic value propositions often used when implementing IT in organizations, this chapter presents "value" as a multilayered business construct that must be effectively managed at several levels if technology is to achieve the benefits expected. Chapter 2 (Developing IT Strategy for Business Value) examines the dynamic interrelationship between business and IT strategy and looks at the processes and critical success factors used by organizations to ensure that both are well aligned. Chapter 3 (Linking IT to Business Metrics) discusses new ways of measuring IT's effectiveness that promote closer business-IT alignment and help drive greater business value. Finally, Chapter 4 (Managing Perceptions of IT) addresses the persistent challenge of dealing with the negative perceptions of IT value within business. It suggests that there is a hierarchy of business needs for IT that must be understood before IT can deliver true business value.

In the minicases associated with this section, the concepts of delivering value with IT are explored in a number of different ways. We see new CIO Richard Fanning at MaxTrade wrestle with how to produce value in an organization where business strategy is constantly changing, IT morale is at rock bottom, and everybody hates IT. In "Investing in TUFS," CIO Martin Drysdale watches as all of the work his IT department has put into a major new system fails to deliver value. And the ModMeters minicase follows CIO Brian Smith's efforts to create a strategic IT plan that will align with business strategy, keep IT running, and *not* increase IT's budget.

• **Section II: IT Governance** explores key concepts in how the IT organization is structured and managed to effectively deliver IT products and services to the organization. Chapter 5 (IT in the New World of Corporate Governance Reforms) describes the impact of an ever-more-stringent regulatory environment on the IT function and its management, practices, and processes, as a result of both direct legislation (e.g., privacy laws) and the indirect regulation of companies (e.g., the Sarbanes-Oxley Act). Chapter 6 (Creating and Evolving a Technology Roadmap) examines the challenges IT managers face in implementing new infrastructure, technology standards, and types of technology in their real-world business and technical environments, which is composed of a huge variety of hardware, software, applications, and other technologies, some of which date back more than thirty years. Chapter 7 (The IT Budgeting Process) describes the "evil twin" of IT strategy, discussing how budgeting mechanisms can significantly undermine effective business strategies and suggesting practices for addressing this problem while maintaining traditional fiscal accountability. Chapter 8 (Information Management: The Nexus of Business and IT) describes how new organizational needs for more useful and integrated information are driving the development of new business-oriented functions within IT that focus specifically on information and knowledge, as opposed to applications and data. And Chapter 9 (IT in 2010) discusses how IT as a function is changing within organizations, positioning emerging trends within the context of IT's development over the past fifteen years. In particular, it describes IT's evolving role and responsibilities in the enterprise and suggests how these will affect the ways and means whereby decisions about IT strategy will be made in the future.

The minicases in this section examine the difficulties of managing complex IT issues when they intersect substantially with important business issues. In "Building Shared Services at RR Communications," we see an IT organization in transition from a traditional divisional structure and governance model to a more centralized enterprise model, and the long-term challenges experienced by CIO Vince Patton in changing both business and IT practices to support this new approach. The AgCredit minicase explores how an organization is transforming itself from a functionally based structure to a process-based one and explores the related business and IT challenges establishing the appropriate governance and structure to manage them. In addition, both minicases describe issues associated with information management and delivery—information ownership at RR and information integration at AgCredit—and illustrate how these can affect what an organization can accomplish strategically and technically.

- **Section III: IT-enabled Innovation** discusses some of the ways technology is being used to transform organizations. Chapter 10 (Strategic Experimentation with IT) looks at the processes and practices organizations are using to investigate new ways of using IT, particularly to change business models, value chains, and processes. Chapter 11 (Enhancing the Customer Experience with Technology) examines the new "outside-in" strategies that many organizations are adopting to drive internal transformation. In the process, it describes how technology is forcing organizations to become more customercentric and to consider how IT can be used to extend their reach into the "market-space." Chapter 12 (Information Delivery: IT's Evolving Role) examines the fresh challenges IT faces in managing the exponential growth of data and digital assets; privacy and accountability concerns; and new demands for access to information on an anywhere, anytime basis. Chapter 13 (Digital Dashboards) discusses this innovative management tool for decision support and identifies some of the best practices used for designing and implementing them to give managers at different levels a real-time view of the organization. Finally, Chapter 14 (Managing Electronic Communications) discusses the rapidly developing technical, legal, and ethical minefields associated with managing the ever-increasing volume and types of electronic communication, both within an organization and externally.

The minicases in this section focus on the key challenges companies face in innovating with IT. "Information Management at Homestyle Hotels" presents some of the obstacles IT managers must overcome to deliver an integrated information strategy to the business. At Acme Consulting, senior consultant Josh Stein wrestles with the cultural, behavioral, and political dimensions of knowledge management in an organization that just wants to plug in technology and not make any other changes to how it works. In "CRM at Minitrex," we see some of the internal technological and political conflicts that result from a strategic decision to become more customercentric. And at Genex Fuels, we follow CIO Nick Devlin trying to implement enterprise-wide technology for competitive advantage in an organization that has been limping along with obscure and outdated systems.

- **Section IV: Reinventing IT Capabilities** looks at how the IT function must transform itself to be able to deliver business value effectively. Chapter 15 (Developing IT Capabilities) provides an overview of the core IT capabilities needed in a modern organization and presents a framework for identifying, improving, managing, and maturing them. Chapter 16 (IT Sourcing) describes the challenges involved in managing IT when many functions are being performed by external service providers, some halfway around the globe. Chapter 17 (Delivering IT Functions: A Decision Framework) describes the variety of strategies, such as insourcing, outsourcing, and partnerships, that IT departments are using to deliver functionality to the organization and how they decide where and when to use these strategies. Chapter 18 (Building Better IT Leaders from the Bottom Up) tackles the increasing need for improved leadership skills in all IT staff and examines the expectations of the business for strategic and innovative guidance from IT. And Chapter 19 (Developing IT Professionalism) discusses the personal responsibilities of every IT staff member for the quality, effectiveness, and value of their work.

The minicases associated with this section describe many of these themes embedded within real organizational contexts. In the SleepSmart minicase, CIO Greg Danson works with multiple vendors to completely revamp his company's outdated technology to develop enhanced IT capabilities in a short period of time. CIO Monique Lalonde at CanCredit examines the reasons for outsourcing certain IT functions and must defend the pros and cons of her decision. Finally, "Project Management at MM" shows how a top-priority, strategic project can take a wrong turn when project management skills are ineffective.

SUPPLEMENTARY MATERIALS

Online Instructor Resource Center

The following supplements are available online to adopting instructors:

- PowerPoint Lecture Notes
- Image Library (text art)
- Mini-Cases Teaching Notes
- Test Item File
- TestGen test generating software with WebCT- and Blackboard-ready conversions.

For detailed descriptions of all of the supplements listed above, please visit: www.prenhall.com/irc.

CourseSmart eTextbooks Online

CourseSmart is an exciting new choice for students looking to save money. As an alternative to purchasing the print textbook, students can purchase an electronic version of the same content and save up to 50% off the suggested list price of the print text. With a CourseSmart etextbook, students can search the text, make notes online, print out reading assignments that incorporate lecture notes, and bookmark important passages for later review. www.coursesmart.com.

THE GENESIS OF THIS BOOK

Since 1990 we have been meeting quarterly with a group of senior IT managers from a number of leading-edge organizations (e.g., Eli Lilly, Honda, HP, IBM, Sears, Bell Canada, and Sun Life) to identify and discuss critical IT management issues. This focus group represents a wide variety of industry sectors (e.g., retail, manufacturing, pharmaceutical, banking, telecommunications, insurance, media, food processing, government, and automotive). Originally, it was established to meet the companies' needs for well-balanced, thoughtful, yet practical information on emerging IT management topics, about which little or no research was available. However, we soon recognized the value of this premise for our own research in the rapidly evolving field of IT management. As a result, it quickly became a full-scale research program in which we were able to use the focus group as an "early warning system" to document new IT management issues, develop case studies around them, and explore more collaborative approaches to identifying trends, challenges, and effective practices in each topic area.[3] As we shared our materials with our business students, we realized that this issues-based approach resonated strongly with them, and we began to incorporate more of our research into the classroom.[4] This book is the result of our many years' work with senior IT managers, in organizations, and with students in the classroom.

Each issue in this book has been selected collaboratively by the focus group after debate and discussion. As facilitators, our job has been to keep the group's focus on IT management issues, not technology per se. In preparation for each meeting, focus group members researched the topic within their own organization, often involving a number of members of their senior IT management team as well as subject matter experts in the process. To guide them, we provided a series of questions about the issue, although members are always free to explore it as they see fit. This approach provided both structure for the ensuing discussion and flexibility for those members whose organizations are approaching the issue in a different fashion.

The focus group then met in a full-day session, where all aspects of the issue at hand were discussed by the members. Many also shared corporate documents with the group. We facilitated the discussion, in particular pushing the group to achieve a common understanding of the dimensions of the issue and seeking examples, best practices, and guidelines for dealing with the challenges involved. Following each session, we wrote a report based on the discussion, incorporating relevant academic and practitioner materials where these were available. (Because topics are "bleeding edge," there is often little traditional IT research available on them.)

---

[3]This now includes best practice case studies, field research in organizations, multidisciplinary qualitative and quantitative research projects, and participation in numerous CIO research consortia.

[4]Through our two previous books for practitioners, *Management Challenges in IS: Successful Strategies and Appropriate Action* (Wiley, 1996) and *Making IT Happen: Critical Issues in IT Management* (Wiley, 2003).

Each report has three parts:

1. A description of the issue and the challenges it presents for both business and IT managers
2. Models and concepts derived from the literature to position the issue within a contextual framework
3. Near-term strategies (i.e., those that can be implemented immediately) that have proven successful within organizations for dealing with the specific issue

Each chapter in this book focuses on one of these critical IT issues. We have learned over the years that the issues themselves vary little across industries and organizations, even in enterprises with unique IT strategies. However, each organization tackles the same issue somewhat differently. It is this diversity that provides the richness of insight in these chapters. Our collaborative research approach is based on our belief that when dealing with complex and leading-edge issues, "everyone has part of the solution." Every focus group, therefore, provides us an opportunity to explore a topic from a variety of perspectives and to integrate different experiences (both successful and otherwise) so that collectively, a thorough understanding of each issue can be developed and strategies for how it can be managed most successfully can be identified.

ABOUT THE AUTHORS

James D. McKeen (jmckeen@business.queensu.ca) is a professor of MIS at the School of Business, Queen's University at Kingston, Canada, and is the founding Director of the Monieson Centre, which conducts multiuniversity, collaborative research focused on generating value through knowledge in organizations. Jim received his Ph.D. in business administration from the University of Minnesota. He has been working in the field of MIS for many years as a practitioner, researcher, and consultant and is a frequent speaker at business and academic conferences. His research has been widely published in various journals including *MIS Quarterly*, *Knowledge Management Research and Practice*, the *Journal of Information Technology Management*, the *Communications of the Association of Information Systems*, *MIS Quarterly Executive*, the *Journal of Systems and Software*, the *International Journal of Management Reviews*, *Information and Management*, *Communications of the ACM*, *Computers and Education*, *OMEGA*, the *Canadian Journal of Administrative Sciences*, the *Journal of MIS*, *KM Review*, the *Journal of Information Systems Technology*, and *Database*. Jim is a coauthor of two books on IT management with Heather Smith—the most recent being *Making IT Happen* (Wiley, 2003). He currently serves on a number of editorial boards.

Heather A. Smith (hsmith@business.queensu.ca) was named North America's most published researcher on IT and knowledge management issues in 2006 by the *Communications of the Association for Information Systems*. A senior research associate with Queen's University School of Business, she is the coauthor of three books: the award-winning *Management Challenges in IS: Successful Strategies and Appropriate Action*, *Making IT Happen: Critical Issues in IT Management*, and *Information Technology and Organizational Transformation: Solving the Management Puzzle*. A former senior IT manager, she is currently codirector of the IT Management Forum and the CIO Brief, which facilitate interorganizational learning among senior IT executives. She is also a senior research associate with the American Society for Information Management's Advanced Practices Council and a research associate with the Lac Carling Congress on E-Government. In addition, she consults, presents, and collaborates with organizations worldwide, including British Petroleum, TD Bank, Canada Post, Ecole des Hautes Etudes Commerciales, the OPP, Boston University, the Institute for Citizen-Centred Service, and Farm Credit Canada. Her research is published in a variety of journals and books including *MIT Sloan Management Review*, *MIS Quarterly Executive*, the *Communications of the Association of Information Systems*, *Knowledge Management Research and Practice*, the *Journal of Information Systems and Technology*, the *Journal of Information Technology Management*, *Information and Management*, *Database*, *CIO Canada*, and the *CIO Governments Review*.

ACKNOWLEDGMENTS

The work contained in this book is based on numerous meetings with many senior IT managers. We would like to acknowledge our indebtedness to the following individuals who willingly shared their insights based on their experiences "earned the hard way":

Lynn Anderson, Maricon Aquino, Sergei Beliaev, Matthias Benfey, Steve Boily, Ray Brennan, Dave Bruyea, Gary Charlton, Michael Cole, Mark Collins, Tony D'Allesandro, Nick Danchuk, Tim Dinesen, Ken Dschankilic, Michael East, Reg Elliott, Bryan Good, Ian Graham, Maureen Hall, Karen Hilton, Tom Hopson, Gerry Kestenberg, Martin Kriho, Konstantine Liris, Lena McDonell, Farzaan Nusserwanji, Mark O'Gorman, Terry O'Toole, Brian Patton, Mark Pearlman, Pat Sadler, Robert Sandercott, Stewart Scott, Andy Secord, Linda Siksna, Andrea Stager, Bruce Thompson, Vanda Vicars, and Ted Vincent.

We would also like to recognize the contribution of Queen's School of Business to this work. The school has facilitated and supported our vision of better integrating academic research and practice and has helped make our collaborative approach to the study of IT management and strategy an effective model for interorganizational learning.

Kingston, Ontario
March 2008

James D. McKeen
Heather A. Smith
School of Business
Queen's University

Chapter

1

Developing and Delivering on the IT Value Proposition[1]

It's déjà vu all over again. For at least twenty years, business leaders have been trying to figure out exactly how and where IT can be of value in their organizations. And IT managers have been trying to learn how to deliver this value. When IT was used mainly as a productivity improvement tool in small areas of a business, this was a relatively straightforward process. Value was measured by reduced head counts—usually in clerical areas—and/or the ability to process more transactions per person. However, as systems grew in scope and complexity, so unfortunately did the risks. Very few companies escaped this period without making at least a few disastrous investments in systems that didn't work or didn't deliver the bottom-line benefits executives thought they would. Naturally, fingers were pointed at IT.

With the advent of the strategic use of IT in business, it became even more difficult to isolate and deliver on the IT value proposition. It was often hard to tell if an investment had paid off. Who could say how many competitors had been deterred or how many customers had been attracted by a particular IT initiative? More recently, many companies have been left with a substantial investment in e-business and little to show for it. While over the years there have been many improvements in where and how IT investments are made and good controls have been established to limit time and cost overruns, we are still not able to accurately articulate and deliver on a value proposition for IT when it comes to anything other than simple productivity improvements or cost savings.

Problems in delivering IT value can lie with how a value proposition is conceived or in what is done to actually implement an idea; that is, selecting the right project and doing the project right (Cooper, Edgett, and Kleinschmidt 2000; McKeen and Smith 2003). As well, while most firms attempt to calculate the expected payback of an IT investment before making it, few actually follow up to ensure that value has

---

[1]Smith, H. A., and J. D. McKeen, "Developing and Delivering on the IT Value Proposition," *Communications of the Association of Information Systems* 11 (April 2003): 438–50 (reproduced by permission of the Association of Information Systems).

been achieved or to question what needs to be done to make sure that value *will be* delivered.

This chapter first looks at the nature of IT value and "peels the onion" into its different layers. Then it examines the three components of delivering IT value: value identification, conversion, and value realization. Finally, it identifies five general principles for ensuring IT value will be achieved.

PEELING THE ONION: UNDERSTANDING IT VALUE

Thirty years ago the IT value proposition was seen as a simple equation: deliver the right technology to the organization, and financial benefits will follow (Cronk and Fitzgerald 1999; Marchand, Kettinger, and Rollins 2000). In the early days of IT, when computers were most often used as direct substitutes for people, this equation was understandable, even if it rarely worked this simply. It was easy to compute a bottom-line benefit where "technology" dollars replaced "salary" dollars.

Problems with this simplistic view quickly arose when technology came to be used as a productivity support tool and as a strategic tool. Under these conditions, managers had to decide if an IT investment was worth making if it saved people time, helped them make better decisions, or improved service. Thus, other factors, such as how well technology was used by people or how IT and business processes worked together, became important considerations in how much value was realized from an IT investment. These issues have long confounded our understanding of the IT value proposition, leading to a plethora of opinions (many negative) about how and where technology has actually contributed to business value over the past fifteen years. Stephen Roach (1989) made headlines with his macroeconomic analysis showing that IT had had absolutely no impact on productivity in the services sector. More recently, many companies feel they have been sold a bill of goods by the promise of e-business and have been lured into spending millions on Web sites and online shopping with very little payback (Earle and Keen 2000).

These perceptions, plus ever-increasing IT expenditures, have meant business managers are taking a closer look at how and where IT delivers value to an organization (Ginzberg 2001). As they do this, they are beginning to change their understanding of the IT value proposition. While, unfortunately, "silver bullet thinking" still predominates (i.e., plug in technology and deliver bottom-line impact), increasingly, IT value is seen as a multilayered concept, far more complex than it first appeared. This suggests that before an IT value proposition can be identified and delivered, it is essential that managers first "peel the onion" and understand more about the nature of IT value itself (see Figure 1.1).

What Is IT Value?

Value is defined as the worth or desirability of a thing (Cronk and Fitzgerald 1999). It is a subjective assessment. Although many believe this is not so, the value of IT depends very much on how a business and its individual managers choose to view it. Different

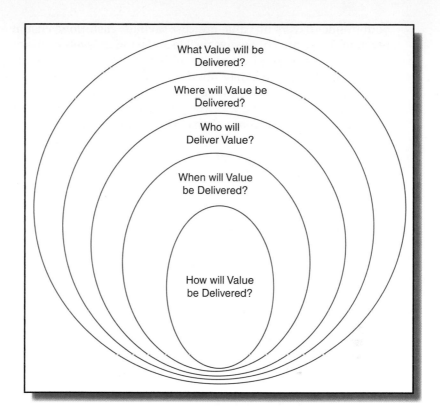

Figure 1.1
IT Value Is a
Many-Layered
Concept

What Value will be Delivered?

Where will Value be Delivered?

Who will Deliver Value?

When will Value be Delivered?

How will Value be Delivered?

companies and even different executives will define it very differently. Strategic positioning, increased productivity, improved decision making, cost savings, or improved service are all ways *value* could be defined. Today most businesses define *value* broadly and loosely, not simply as a financial concept (Ginzberg 2001). Ideally, it is tied to the organization's business model because adding value with IT should enable a firm to do its business better. In the focus group, one company sees value resulting from all parts of the organization having the same processes; another defines value by return on investment (ROI); still another measures it by a composite of key performance indicators. In short, there is no single agreed measure of IT value. As a result, misunderstandings about the definition of *value* either between IT and the business or among business managers themselves can lead to feelings that value has not been delivered. Therefore, a prerequisite of any IT value proposition is that everyone involved in an IT initiative agree on what value they are trying to deliver and how they will recognize it.

Where Is IT Value?

Value may also vary according to where one looks for it (Davern and Kauffman 2000). For example, value to an enterprise may not be perceived as value in a work group or by an individual. In fact, delivering value at one level in an organization may actually conflict with optimizing value at another level. Decisions about IT value are often made to optimize firm or business process value, even if they cause difficulties for business units or individuals. As one manager explained, "At the senior levels, our bottom-line drivers of value are cost savings, cash flow, customer satisfaction, and revenue. These are not always visible at the lower levels of the organization." Failure to consider value implications at all levels can lead to a value proposition that is counterproductive and may not deliver the value that is anticipated. Many executives take a hard line with these value conflicts. However, it is far more desirable to aim for value that is not a win-lose proposition, but is a win-win at all levels. This can leverage overall value many times over (Chan 2000).

Who Delivers IT Value?

Increasingly, managers are realizing that it is the *interaction* of people, information, and technology that delivers value, not IT alone.[2] Recent studies have confirmed that strong IT practices *alone* do not deliver superior performance. It is only the combination of these with an organization's skills at managing information and people's behaviors and beliefs that leads to real value (Ginzberg 2001; Marchand, Kettinger, and Rollins 2000). In the past, IT has borne most of the responsibility for delivering IT value. Today, however, there is a growing willingness on the part of business managers to share responsibility with IT to ensure value is realized from the organization's investments in technology. Most companies now expect to have an executive sponsor for any IT initiative and some business participation in the development team. However, many IT projects still do not have the degree of support or commitment from the business that IT managers feel is necessary to deliver fully on a value proposition (Thorp 1999).

When Is IT Value Realized?

Value also has a time dimension. It has long been known that the benefits of technology take time to be realized (Chan 2000). People must be trained, organizations and processes must adapt to new ways of working, information must be compiled, and customers must realize what new products and services are being offered. Companies are often unprepared for the time it takes an investment to pay off. Typically, full payback can take between three and five years and can have at least two spikes as a business adapts to the deployment of technology. Figure 1.2 shows this "W" effect, named for the way the chart looks, for a single IT project. Initially, companies spend a considerable amount in deploying a new technology. During this twelve-to-sixteen-month period, no benefits occur. Following implementation, some value is realized as companies achieve initial efficiencies. This period lasts for about six months. However, as use increases, complexities also grow. Information overload can occur and costs increase. At this stage, many can lose faith in the initiative. This is a dangerous period. The final set of benefits can occur only by making the business simpler and applying technology, information, and people more effectively. If a business can manage to do this, it can achieve sustainable, long-term value from its IT investment (Chatterjee and Seagars 2002). If it can't, value from technology can be offset by increased complexity.

---

[2]These interactions in a structured form are known as *processes*. Processes are often the focus of much organizational effort in the belief that streamlining and reengineering them will deliver value. In fact, new research shows that without attention to information and people, very little value is delivered (Chatterjee and Seagars 2002). In addition, attention to processes in organizations often ignores the informal processes that contribute to value.

Figure 1.2 The 'W' Effect in Delivering IT Value (after Chatterjee and Seagars 2002)

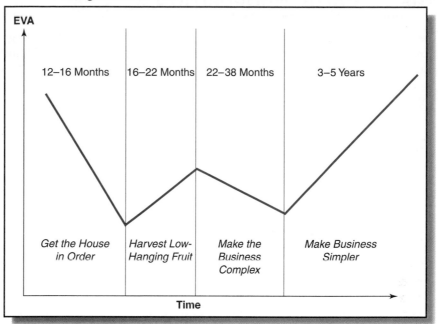

Time also changes perceptions of value. Many IT managers can tell stories of how an initiative is initially vilified as having little or no value when first implemented, only to have people say they couldn't imagine running the business without it a few years later. Similarly, most managers can identify projects where time has led to a clearer understanding of the potential value of a project. Unfortunately, in cases where anticipated value declines or disappears, projects don't always get killed (Cooper, Edgett, and Kleinschmidt 2000).

Clarifying and agreeing on these different layers of IT value is the first step involved in developing and delivering on the IT value proposition. All too often, this work is forgotten or given short shrift in the organization's haste to answer this question: How will IT value be delivered? (See next section.) As a result, misunderstandings arise and technology projects do not fulfill their expected promises. It will be next to impossible to do a good job developing and delivering IT value unless and until the concepts involved in IT value are clearly understood and agreed on by both business and IT managers.

Best Practices in Understanding IT Value

- Link IT value directly to your business model.
- Recognize value is subjective, and manage perceptions accordingly.
- Aim for a value "win-win" across processes, work units, and individuals.
- Seek business commitment to all IT projects.
- Manage value over time.

THE THREE COMPONENTS
OF THE IT VALUE PROPOSITION

Developing and delivering an IT value proposition involves addressing three components. First, potential opportunities for adding value must be identified. Next, these must be converted into effective applications of technology. Finally, value must be realized by the organization. Together, these comprise the fundamentals of any value proposition (see Figure 1.3).

Identification of Potential Value

Identifying opportunities for making IT investments has typically been a fairly informal activity in most organizations. Very few companies have a well-organized means of doing research into new technologies or strategizing about where these technologies can be used (McKeen and Smith 2003). More companies have mechanisms for identifying opportunities within business units. Sometimes a senior IT manager will be designated as a "relationship manager" for a particular unit with responsibility for working with business management to identify opportunities where IT could add value (Agarwal and Sambamurthy 2002). Many other companies, however, still leave it up to business managers to identify where they want to use IT. There is growing evidence that relegating the IT organization to a passive role developing systems according to business instructions is unlikely to lead to high IT value. Research is beginning to show that involving IT in business planning can have a direct and positive influence on the development of successful business strategies using IT (Ginzberg 2001; Marchand, Kettinger, and Rollins 2000). This suggests that organizations should establish joint business-IT mechanisms to identify and evaluate both business and technical opportunities where IT can add value.

Once opportunities have been identified, companies must then make decisions about where they want to focus their dollars to achieve optimal value. Selecting the right projects for an organization always involves balancing three fundamental factors: cash, timing, and risk (Luehrman 1997). In principle, every company wants to undertake only high-return projects. In reality, project selection is based on many different factors. For example, pet or political projects or those mandated by the government or competitors are often part of a company's IT portfolio (Carte, Ghosh, and Zmud 2001). Disagreement at senior levels about which projects to undertake can arise because of a lack of a coherent and consistent mechanism for assessing project value. All organizations need some formal mechanism for prioritizing projects. Without

Figure 1.3 The Three Components of the IT Value Proposition

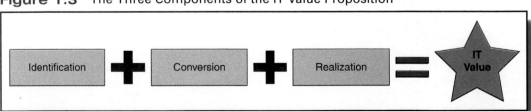

one, it is very likely that project selection will become highly politicized and, hence, ineffective at delivering value. There are a variety of means to do this, ranging from using strictly bottom-line metrics, to comparing balanced scorecards, to adopting a formal value-assessment methodology. However, while these help to weed out higher cost–lower return projects, they are not a foolproof means of selecting the right projects for an organization. Using strict financial selection criteria, for example, can exclude potentially high-value strategic projects that have less well-defined returns, longer payback periods, and more risk (Cooper, Edgett, and Kleinschmidt 2000). Similarly, it can be difficult getting important infrastructure initiatives funded even though these may be fundamental to improving organizational capabilities (Byrd 2001).

Therefore, increasingly, organizations are taking a portfolio approach to project selection. This allocates resources and funding to different types of projects, enabling each type of opportunity to be evaluated according to different criteria (McKeen and Smith 2003). One company has identified three different classes of IT—infrastructure, common systems, and business unit applications—and funds them in different proportions. In other companies, funding for strategic initiatives is allocated in stages so their potential value can be reassessed as more information about them becomes known (Luehrman 1997). Almost all companies have found it necessary to justify infrastructure initiatives differently than more business-oriented projects. In fact, some remove these types of projects from the selection process altogether and fund them with a "tax" on all other development (McKeen and Smith 2003). Other companies allocate a fixed percentage of their IT budgets to a technology renewal fund.

Best Practices in Identifying Potential Value

- Joint business-IT structures to recognize and evaluate opportunities
- A means of comparing value across projects
- A portfolio approach to project selection
- A funding mechanism for infrastructure

Organizations have come a long way in formalizing where and how they choose to invest their IT dollars. Nevertheless, there is still considerable room for judgment based on solid business and technical knowledge. It is, therefore, essential that all executives involved have the ability to think strategically and systematically as well as financially about project identification and selection.

Effective Conversion

"Conversion" from idea/opportunity to reality has been what IT organizations have been all about since their inception. A huge amount of effort has gone into this central component of the IT value proposition. As a result, many IT organizations have become very good at developing and delivering projects on time and on budget. Excellent project management, effective execution, and reliable operations are a critical part of IT value. However, they are not, in and of themselves, sufficient to convert a good idea into value or to deliver value to an organization.

Today both managers and researchers are recognizing that there is more involved in effective conversion than good IT practices. Organizations can set themselves up for failure by not providing adequate and qualified resources. Many companies start more projects than they can effectively deliver with the resources they have available. Not having enough time or resources to do the job means that people are spread too thin and end up taking shortcuts that are potentially damaging to value (Cooper, Edgett, and Kleinschmidt 2000). Resource limitations on the business side of a project team can be as damaging to conversion as a lack of technical resources. "[Value is about] far more than just sophisticated managerial visions . . . Training and other efforts . . . to obtain value from IT investments are often hamstrung by insufficient resources" (Chircu and Kauffman 2000). Inadequate business resources can lead to poor communication and ineffective problem solving on a project (Ginzberg 2001). Companies are beginning to recognize that the number and quality of the staff assigned to an IT project can make a difference to its eventual outcome. They are insisting that the organization's best IT and businesspeople be assigned to critical projects.

Other significant barriers to conversion that are becoming more apparent now that IT has improved its own internal practices include the following:

- *Organizational barriers.* The effective implementation of IT frequently requires the extensive redesign of current business processes (Chircu and Kauffman 2000). However, organizations are often reluctant to make the difficult complementary business changes and investments that are required (Carte, Ghosh, and Zmud 2001). "When new IT is implemented, everyone expects to see costs come down," explained one manager. "However, most projects involve both business and IT deliverables. We, therefore, need to take a multifunctional approach to driving business value." In recognition of this fact, some companies are beginning to put formal change management programs in place to help businesses prepare for the changes involved with IT projects and to adapt and simplify as they learn how to take advantage of new technology.

Best Practices in Conversion

- Availability of adequate and qualified IT and business resources
- Training in business goals and processes
- Multifunctional change management
- Emphasis on higher-level learning and knowledge management

- *Knowledge barriers.* Most often new technology and processes require employees to work differently, learn new skills, and have new understanding of how and where information, people, and technologies fit together (Chircu and Kauffman 2000). While training has long been part of new IT implementations, more recently, businesses are recognizing that delivering value from technology requires a broader and more coordinated learning effort (Smith and McKeen 2002). Lasting value comes from people and technology working *together* as a system rather than as discrete entities. Recent research confirms that high-performing organizations not only have strong IT practices, but also have people who have good information management practices and who are able to effectively use the information they receive (Marchand, Kettinger, and Rollins 2000).

Realizing Value

The final component of the IT value proposition has been the most frequently ignored. This is the work involved in actually realizing value *after* technology has been implemented. Value realization is a proactive and long-term process for any major initiative (Thorp 1999). All too often, after an intense implementation period, a development team is disbanded to work on other projects, and the business areas affected by new technology are left to sink or swim. As a result, a project's benefits can be imperfectly realized. Technology must be used extensively if it is to deliver value. Poorly designed technology can lead to high levels of frustration, resistance to change, and low levels of use (Chircu and Kauffman 2000).

Resistance to change can have its root cause in an assumption or an action that doesn't make sense in the everyday work people do. Sometimes this means challenging workers' understanding of work expectations or information flows. At other times it means doing better analysis of where and how a new process is causing bottlenecks, overwork, or overload. As one manager put it, "If value is not being delivered, we need to understand the root causes and do something about it." His company takes the unusual position that it is important to keep a team working on a project until the expected benefits have been realized. This approach is ideal but can also be very costly and, therefore, must be carefully managed. Some companies try to short-circuit the value management process by simply taking anticipated cost savings out of a business unit's budget once technology has been implemented, thereby forcing it to do more with less whether or not the technology has been as beneficial as anticipated. However, most often organizations do little or no follow-up to determine whether or not benefits have been achieved.

Best Practices in Realizing Value

- Plan a value-realization phase for all IT projects.
- Measure outcomes against expected results.
- Look for and eliminate root causes of problems.
- Assess value realization at all levels in the organization.
- Have provisions for acting on new opportunities to leverage value.

Measurement is a key component of value realization (Thorp 1999). After implementation, it is essential that all stakeholders systematically compare outcomes against expected value and take appropriate actions to achieve benefits. In addition to monitoring metrics, there must also be a thorough and ongoing assessment of value and information flows at all levels of analysis—individual, team, work unit, and enterprise. Efforts must be taken to understand and improve aspects of process, information, and technology that are acting as barriers to achieving value.

A significant problem with not paying attention to value recognition is that areas of unexpected value or opportunity are also ignored. This is unfortunate because it is only after technology has been installed that many businesspeople can see how it could be leveraged in other parts of their work. Realizing value should, therefore, also include provisions to evaluate new opportunities arising through serendipity.

FIVE PRINCIPLES FOR DELIVERING VALUE

In addition to clearly understanding what value means in a particular organization and to ensuring that the three components of the IT value proposition are addressed by every project, five principles have been identified that are central to developing and delivering value in every organization.

Principle 1. Have a Clearly Defined Portfolio *Value* Management Process

Every organization should have a common process for managing the overall value being delivered to the organization from its IT portfolio. This would begin as a means of identifying and prioritizing IT opportunities by potential value relative to each other. It would also include mechanisms to optimize *enterprise* value (e.g., through tactical, strategic, and infrastructure projects) according to a rubric of how the organization wants to allocate its resources.

A portfolio value management process should continue to track projects as they are being developed. It should ensure not only that projects are meeting schedule and budget milestones, but also that other elements of conversion effectiveness are being addressed (e.g., business process redesign, training, change management, information management, and usability). A key barrier to achieving value can be an organization's unwillingness to revisit the decisions made about its portfolio (Carte, Ghosh, and Zmud 2001). Yet this is critically important for strategic and infrastructure initiatives in particular. Companies may have to approve investments in these types of projects based on imperfect information in an uncertain environment. As they develop, improved information can lead to better decision making about an investment. In some cases this might lead to a decision to kill a project; in others, to speed it up or to reshape it as a value proposition becomes clearer.

Finally, a portfolio value management process should include an ongoing means of ensuring that value is realized from an investment. Management must monitor expected outcomes at appropriate times following implementation and hold someone in the organization accountable for delivering benefits (Thorp 1999).

Principle 2. Aim for Chunks of Value

Much value can be frittered away by dissipating IT investments on too many projects (Marchand, Kettinger, and Rollins 2000). Focusing on a few key areas and designing a set of complementary projects that will really make a difference is one way companies are trying to address this concern. Many companies are undertaking larger and larger technology initiatives that will have a significant transformational and/or strategic impact on the organization. However, unlike earlier efforts, which often took years to complete and ended up having questionable value, these initiatives are aiming to deliver major value through a series of small, focused projects that, linked together, will result in both immediate short-term impact and long-term strategic value. For example, one company has about three hundred to four hundred projects under way linked to one of a dozen major initiatives.

Principle 3. Adopt a Holistic Orientation to Technology Value

Because value comes from the effective interaction of people, information, and technology, it is critical that organizations aim to optimize their ability to manage and use them together (Marchand, Kettinger, and Rollins 2000). Adopting a systemic approach to value, where technology is not viewed in isolation and interactions and impacts are anticipated and planned, has been demonstrated to contribute to perceived business value (Ginzberg 2001). Managers should aim to incorporate technology as an integral part of an overall program of business change rather than dealing with people and information management as afterthoughts to technology (Thorp 1999). One company has done this by taking a single business objective (e.g., "increase market penetration by 15 percent over five years") and designing a program around it that includes a number of bundled technology projects.

Principle 4. Aim for Joint Ownership of Technology Initiatives

This principle covers a lot of territory. It includes the necessity of strong executive sponsorship of all IT projects. "Without an executive sponsor for a project, we simply won't start it," explained one manager. It also emphasizes that all people involved in a project must feel they are responsible for the results. "These days it is very hard to isolate the impact of technology," said another manager, "therefore, there must be a 'we' mentality." This perspective is reinforced by research that has found that the quality of the IT-business relationship is central to the delivery of IT value. Mutual trust, visible business support for IT and its staff, and IT staff who consider themselves to be part of a business problem-solving team all make a significant difference in how much value technology is perceived to deliver (Ginzberg 2001).

Principle 5. Experiment More Often

The growing complexity of technology, the range of options available, and the uncertainty of the business environment have each made it considerably more difficult to determine where and how technology investments can most effectively be made. Executives naturally object to the risks involved in investing heavily in possible business scenarios or technical gambles that may or may not realize value. As a result, many companies are looking for ways to firm up their understanding of the value proposition for a particular opportunity without incurring too much risk. Undertaking pilot studies is one way of doing this (Thomke 2001). Such experiments can prove the value of an idea, uncover new opportunities, and identify more about what will be needed to make an idea successful. They provide senior managers with a greater number of options in managing a project and an overall technology portfolio and enable potential value to be reassessed and investments in a particular project to be reevaluated and rebalanced against other opportunities more frequently. In short, experimentation enables technology investments to be made in chunks and makes "go/no go" decisions at key milestones much easier to make.

CONCLUSION

This chapter has explored the concepts and activities involved in developing and delivering IT value to an organization. In their efforts to use technology to deliver business value, IT managers should keep the maxim "value is in the eye of the beholder" clearly in mind. Because there is no single agreed-on notion of business value, it is important to make sure that both business and IT managers are working to a common goal. This could be traditional cost reduction, process efficiencies, new business capabilities, improved communication, or a host of other objectives. While each organization or business unit approaches value differently, increasingly this goal includes much more than the simple delivery of technology to a business unit. Today technology is being used as a catalyst to drive many different types of organizational transformation and strategy. Therefore, IT value can no longer be viewed in isolation from other parts of the business, namely people and information. Thus, it is no longer adequate to focus simply on the development and delivery of IT projects in order to deliver value. Today delivering IT value means managing the entire process from conception to cash.

REFERENCES

Agarwal, R., and V. Sambamurthy. "Organizing the IT Function for Business Innovation Leadership." Society for Information Management Advanced Practices Council Report, Chicago, September 2002.

Byrd, T. A. "Information Technology: Core Competencies, and Sustained Competitive Advantage." *Information Resources Management Journal* 14, no. 2 (Apr–Jun 2001): 27–36.

Carte, T., D. Ghosh, and R. Zmud. "The Influence of IT Budgeting Practices on the Return Derived from IT Investments." CMISS White Paper, November 2001.

Chan, Y. "IT Value: The Great Divide between Qualitative and Quantitative and Individual and Organizational Measures." *Journal of Management Information Systems* 16, no. 4 (Spring 2000): 225–61.

Chatterjee, D., and A. Seagars. Presentation to the SIM Advanced Practices Council, Chicago, September 2002.

Chircu, A., and R. J. Kauffman. "Limits to Value in Electronic Commerce-related IT Investments." *Journal of Management Information Systems* 17, no. 2 (Fall 2000): 59–80.

Cooper, R., S. Edgett, and E. Kleinschmidt. "New Problems, New Solutions: Making Portfolio Management More Effective." *Research Technology Management* 43, no. 2 (Mar/Apr 2000): 18–33.

Cronk, M., and E. Fitzgerald. "Understanding 'IS Business Value': Derivation of Dimensions." *Logistics Information Management* 12, no. 1–2 (1999): 40–49.

Davern, M., and R. Kauffman. "Discovering Potential and Realizing Value from Information Technology Investments." *Journal of Management Information Systems* 16, no. 4 (Spring 2000): 121–43.

Earle, N., and P. Keen. *From .com to .profit: Inventing Business Models that Deliver Value and Profit.* San Francisco: Jossey-Bass, 2000.

Ginzberg, M. "Achieving Business Value through Information Technology: The Nature of High Business Value IT Organizations." Society for Information Management Advanced Practices Council Report, Chicago, November 2001.

Luehrman, T. A. "What's It Worth? A General Manager's Guide to Valuation." *Harvard Business Review* May–June (1997): 131–41.

Marchand, D., W. Kettinger, and J. Rollins. "Information Orientation: People, Technology and the Bottom Line." *Sloan Management Review* Summer (2000): 69–80.

McKeen, J., and H. Smith. *Making IT Happen.* Chichester, England: John Wiley and Sons, 2003.

Roach, S. "The Case of the Missing Technology Payback." Presentation at the Tenth International Conference on Information Systems, Boston, December 1989.

Smith, H., and J. McKeen. "Instilling a Knowledge Sharing Culture." Presentation at the KM Forum, Queen's School of Business, Kingston, Ont., 2002.

Thomke, S. "Enlightened Experimentation: The New Imperative for Innovation." *Harvard Business Review* February (2001): 67–75.

Thorp, J. "Computing the Payoff from IT." *Journal of Business Strategy* 20, no. 3 (May/Jun 1999): 35–39.

Chapter 2

Developing IT Strategy for Business Value[1]

Suddenly, it seems, executives are "getting" the strategic potential of IT. Instead of being relegated to the back rooms of the enterprise, IT is now being invited to the boardrooms and is being expected to play a leading role in delivering top-line value and business transformation (Venkatramen and Henderson 1998). Thus, it can no longer be assumed that business strategy will naturally drive IT strategy, as has traditionally been the case. Instead, different approaches to strategy development are now possible and sometimes desirable. For example, the capabilities of new technologies could shape the strategic direction of a firm (e.g., e-business, wireless). IT could enable new competencies that would then make new business strategies possible (e.g., just-in-time inventory). New options for governance using IT could also change how a company works with other firms (think Wal-Mart or Dell Computer). Today new technologies coevolve with new business strategies and new behaviors and structures (see Figure 2.1). However, whichever way it is developed, if IT is to deliver business value, IT strategy must always be closely linked with sound business strategy.

Ideally, therefore, business and IT strategies should complement and support each other relative to the business environment. Strategy development should be a two-way process between the business and IT. Yet unfortunately, poor alignment between them remains a perennial problem (Frohman 1982; McKeen and Smith 1996; Rivard et al. 2004). Research has already identified many organizational challenges to effective strategic alignment. For example, if their strategy-development processes are not compatible (e.g., if they take place at different times or involve different levels of the business), it is unlikely that the business and IT will be working toward the same goals at the same time (Frohman 1982). Aligning with individual business units can lead to initiatives that suboptimize the effectiveness of corporate strategies

---

[1]Smith, H. A., J. D. McKeen, and S. Singh, "Developing IT Strategy for Business Value," *Journal of Information Technology Management* XVIII, no. 1 (June 2007): 49–58 (reproduced by permission of the Association of Management).

Figure 2.1 Business and IT Strategies
Coevolve to Create New Capabilities

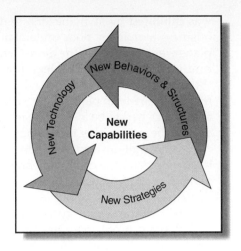

(McKeen and Smith 1996). Strategy implementation must also be carefully aligned to ensure the integration of business and IT efforts. Finally, companies often try to address too many priorities, leading to an inadequate focus on key strategic goals.

However, strategic *alignment* is only one problem facing IT managers when they develop IT strategy. With IT becoming so much more central to the development and delivery of business strategy, much more attention is now being paid to strategy *development* than in the past. What businesses want to accomplish with their IT and how IT shapes its own delivery strategy is increasingly vital to the success of an enterprise. This chapter explores how organizations are working to improve IT strategy development and its relationship with business strategy. It looks first at how our understanding of business and IT strategies has changed over time and at the forces that will drive even further changes in the future. Then it discusses some critical success factors for IT strategy development about which there is general consensus. Next it looks at the different dimensions of the strategic use of IT that IT management must address. Finally, it examines how some organizations are beginning to evolve a more formal IT strategy–development process and some of the challenges they are facing in doing so.

BUSINESS AND IT STRATEGIES: PAST, PRESENT, AND FUTURE

At the highest level, a strategy is an approach to doing business (Gebauer 1997). Traditionally, a competitive business strategy has involved performing different activities from competitors or performing similar activities in different ways (Porter 1996). Ideally, these activities were difficult or expensive for others to copy and, therefore, resulted in a long-term competitive advantage (Gebauer 1997). They enabled firms to charge a premium for their products and services.

Until recently, the job of an IT function was to understand the business's strategy and figure out a plan to support it. However, all too often, IT's strategic contribution was inhibited by IT managers' limited understanding of business strategy and by business managers' poor understanding of IT's potential. Therefore, most *formal* IT plans were focused on the more tactical and tangible line of business needs or opportunities for operational integration rather than on supporting enterprise strategy (Burgelman and Doz 2001). And projects were selected largely on their abilities to affect the short-term bottom line rather than on delivering top-line business value. "In the past IT had to be a strategic incubator because businesspeople simply didn't recognize the potential of technology," said a member of the focus group.

As a result, instead of looking for ways to be different, in the past decade, much business strategy became a relentless race to compete on efficiencies with IT as the primary means of doing so (Hitt, Keats, and DeMarire 1998; Porter 1996). In many industries, companies' improved information-processing capabilities have been used to drive down transaction costs to near zero, threatening traditional value propositions and shaving profit margins. This is leading to considerable disruption as business models (i.e., the way companies add value) are under attack by new, technology-enabled approaches to delivering products and services (e.g., the music industry, book-selling). Therefore:

> Strategists [have to] honestly face the many weaknesses inherent in [the] industrial-age ways of doing things. They [must] redesign, build upon and reconfigure their components to radically transform the value proposition. (Tapscott 1996)

Such new business strategies are inconceivable without the use of IT. Other factors, also facilitated by IT, are further influencing the relationship between the business and IT strategy. Increasingly, globalization is altering the economic playing field. As countries and companies become more deeply interrelated, instability is amplified. Instead of being generals plotting out a structured campaign, business leaders are now more likely to be participating in guerilla warfare (Eisenhardt 2002). Flexibility, speed, and innovation are, therefore, becoming the watchwords of competition and must be incorporated into any business or IT strategy–development process (Hitt, Keats, and DeMarire 1998).

These conditions have dramatically elevated the business's attention to the value of IT strategy (Ross and Beath 2002). As a result, business executives recognize that it was a mistake to consider technology projects to be solely the responsibility of IT. There is, thus, a much greater understanding that business executives have to take leadership in making technology investments in ways that will shape and/or complement business strategy. There is also recognition at the top of most organizations that problems with IT strategy implementation are largely the fault of leaders who "failed to realize that adopting . . . systems posed a business—not just a technological—challenge" and didn't take responsibility for the organizational and process changes that would deliver business value (Ross and Weill 2002, 6).

Changing value models and the development of integrated, cross-functional systems have elevated the importance of both *corporate* strategy and a technology strategy that crosses traditional lines of business. Many participants remarked that their executive teams at last understand the potential of IT to affect the top line. "IT recently added some new distribution channels, and our business has just exploded," stated one manager. Others are finding that there is a much greater emphasis on IT's ability to grow revenues, and this is being reflected in how IT budgets are allocated and projects prioritized. "Our executives have finally recognized that business strategy is not only enabled by IT, but that it can provide new business opportunities as well," said another manager. This is reflected in the changing position of the CIO in many organizations over the past decade. "Today our CIO sits on the executive team and takes part in all business strategy discussions because IT has credibility," said a group member. "Our executives now want to work closely with IT and understand the implications of technology decisions," said another. "It's not the same as it was even five years ago." Today CIOs are valued for their insights into business opportunities, their perspectives across the entire organization, and their abilities to take the long view.

However, this does not mean that organizations have become good at developing strategy or at effectively integrating business and IT strategies. "There are many inconsistencies and problems with strategy development," said a participant. Organizations have to develop new strategy-making capabilities to cope in the future competitive environment. This will mean changing their current top-down method of developing and implementing strategy. If there's one thing leading academics agree on, it's that future strategy development will have to become a more dynamic and continuous process (Eisenhardt 2002; Kanter 2002; Prahalad and Krishnan 2002; Quinn 2002; Weill, Subramani, and Broadbent 2002). Instead of business strategy being a well-crafted plan of action for the next three to five years, from which IT can devise an appropriate and supportive technology strategy, business strategy must become more and more evolutionary and interactive with IT. IT strategy development must, therefore, become more dynamic itself and focused on developing strategic *capabilities* that will support a variety of changing business objectives. In the future, managers will not align business strategy and IT at particular points in time, but will participate in an organic process that will address the need to continually evolve IT and business plans in concert with each other (Prahalad and Krishnan 2002).

FOUR CRITICAL SUCCESS FACTORS

While each focus group member had a different approach to developing IT strategy, there was general agreement that four factors had to be in place for strategy development to be effective.

1. *Revisit your business model.* The worlds of business and IT have traditionally been isolated from each other, leading to misaligned and sometimes conflicting strategies. Although there is now a greater willingness among business managers to understand the implications of technology in their world, it is still IT that must translate their ideas and concepts into business language. "IT must absolutely understand and focus on the business," said a participant.

Similarly, it is essential that all managers thoroughly understand how their business as a whole works. While this sounds like a truism, almost any IT manager can tell "war stories" of business managers who have very different visions of what they think their enterprise should look like. Business models and strategies are often confused with each other (Ross and Beath 2002). A business model explains how the different pieces of a business fit together. It ensures that everyone in an organization is focused on the kind of value a company wants to create. Only when the business model is clear can strategies be developed to articulate how a company will deliver that value in a *unique* way that others cannot easily duplicate (Ross and Beath 2002).

2. *Have strategic themes.*   IT strategy used to be about individual projects. Now it is about carefully crafted *programs* that focus on developing specific business capabilities. Each program consists of many smaller, interrelated business and IT initiatives cutting across several functional areas. These are designed to be adapted, reconfigured, accelerated, or canceled as the strategic program evolves. Themes give both business and IT leaders a broad yet focused topic of interest that challenges them to move beyond current operations (Kanter 2002). For example, one retail company decided it wanted to be "a great place to work." A bank selected e-banking as a critical differentiator. Both firms used a theme to engage the imaginations of their employees and mobilize a variety of ideas and actions around a broad strategic direction. By grouping IT and business programs around a few key themes, managers find it easier to track and direct important strategic threads in an organization's development and to visualize the synergies and interdependencies involved across a variety of projects spread out across the organization and over time.

3. *Get the right people involved.*   One of the most important distinguishing factors between companies that get high business value from their IT investment and those that don't is that senior managers in high-performing companies take a leadership role in IT decision making. Abdication of this responsibility is a recipe for disaster (Ross and Weill 2002). "In the past it was very hard to get the right people involved," said a focus group member. "Now it's easier." Another noted, "You don't send a minion to an IT strategy meeting anymore; it's just not done." In this type of organization, the CIO typically meets regularly with the president and senior business leaders to discuss both business and IT strategies.

   Getting the right people involved also means getting business managers and other key stakeholders involved in strategy as well. To do this, many companies have established "account manager" positions in IT to work with and learn about the business and bring opportunities for using technology to the table. Research shows that the best strategies often stem from grassroots innovations, and it is, therefore, critical that organizations take steps to ensure that good ideas are nurtured and not filtered out by different layers of management (Kanter 2002). "We have two levels of strategy development in our organization," said a focus group participant. "Our account managers work with functional managers and our CIO with our business unit presidents on the IT steering committee." This company also looks for cross-functional synergies and strategic dependencies by holding regular meetings of IT account managers and between account managers and infrastructure managers.

4. *Work in partnership with the business.*   Successful strategy demands a true partnership between IT and the business, not just use of the term. Strategy decisions are best made with input from both business and IT executives (Ross and Weill 2002). The focus group agreed. "Our partnerships are key to our success,"

stated a manager. "It's not the same as it was a few years ago. People now work very closely together." Partnership is not just a matter of "involving" business leaders in IT strategy or vice versa or "aligning" business and IT strategies. Effective strategizing is about continuous and dynamic synchronization of capabilities (Prahalad and Krishnan 2002). "Our IT programs need synchronizing with business strategy—not only at a high level, but right down to the individual projects and the business changes that are necessary to implement them properly," explained another participant.

THE MANY DIMENSIONS
OF IT STRATEGY

One of the many challenges of developing effective IT strategy is the fact that technology can be used in so many different ways. The opportunities are practically limitless. Unfortunately, the available resources are not. Thus, a key element of IT strategy is determining how best to allocate the IT budget. This issue is complicated by the fact that most businesses today require significant IT services just to operate. Utility and basic support costs eat up between 30 and 70 percent of the focus group members' budgets. That's just the cost of "keeping the lights on"—running existing applications, fixing problems, and dealing with mandatory changes (e.g., new legislation). IT strategy, therefore, has two components: how to do more with less (i.e., driving down fixed costs) and how to allocate the remaining budget toward those projects that will support and further the organization's business strategy.

With occasional exceptions, CIOs and their teams are mostly left alone to determine the most cost-effective way of providing the IT utility. This has led to a variety of IT-led initiatives to save money, including outsourcing, shared services, use of active server pages (ASPs), global sourcing, and partnerships. However, it is the way that IT spends the rest of its budget that has captured the attention of business strategists. "It used to be that every line of business had an IT budget and that we would work with each one to determine the most effective way to spend it," said a manager. "Now there is much more recognition that the big opportunities are at the enterprise level and cut across lines of business."

Focus group members explained that implementing a strategic program in IT will usually involve five types of initiatives. Determining what the balance among them will be is a significant component of how IT strategy delivers business value. Too much or too little emphasis on one type of project can mean a failure to derive maximum value from a particular strategic business theme:

1. *Business improvement.* These projects are probably the easiest to agree on because they stress relatively low-risk investments with a tangible short-to-medium-term payback. These are often reengineering initiatives to help organizations streamline their processes and save substantial amounts of money by eliminating unnecessary or duplicate activities or empowering customers/suppliers to self-manage transactions with a company. Easy to justify with a business case, these types of projects have traditionally formed the bulk of IT's discretionary

spending. "Cost-reduction projects have and always will be important to our company," stated one member. "However, it is important to balance what we do in this area with other types of equally important projects that have often been given short shrift."

2. *Business enabling.* These projects extend or transform how a company does business. As a result, they are more focused on the top-line or revenue-growing aspects of an enterprise. For example, a data warehouse could enable different parts of a company to "mine" transaction information to improve customer service, assist target marketing, better understand buying patterns, or identify new business opportunities. Adding a new Web-based channel could make it easier for customers to buy more or attract new customers. A customer information file could make it more enjoyable for a customer to do business with a company (e.g., only one address change) and also facilitate new ways of doing business. Often the return on these types of projects is less clear, and as a result, it has been harder to get them on the IT priority list. Yet many of these initiatives represent the foundations on which future business strategy will be built. For example, one CIO described the creation of a customer information file as "a key enabler for many different business units. . . . It has helped us build bench strength and move to a new level of service that other companies cannot match" (Smith 2003, 3).

3. *Business opportunities.* These are small-scale, experimental initiatives designed to test the viability of new concepts or technologies. In the past these types of projects have not received funding by traditional methods because of their high-risk nature. Often it has been left up to the CIO to scrounge money for such "skunkworks." There is a growing recognition of the potential value of strategic experiments in helping companies to learn about and prepare for the future. In some companies the CEO and CFO have freed up seed money to finance a number of these initiatives. However, while there is considerably more acceptance for such projects, there is still significant organizational resistance to financing projects for which the end results are unpredictable (Quinn 2002). In fact, it typically requires discipline to support and encourage experiments, which, by definition, will have a high number of false starts and wrong moves (Kanter 2002). The group agreed that the key to benefiting from experiments is to design them for learning, incorporate feedback from a variety of sources, and make quick corrections of direction.

4. *Opportunity leverage.* A neglected but important type of IT project is one that operationalizes, scales up, or leverages successful strategic experiments or prototypes. "We are having a great deal of success taking advantage of what we have learned earlier," said one manager. Coming up with a new strategic or technological idea needs a different set of skills than is required to take full advantage of it in the marketplace (Charitou and Markides 2003). Some companies actually use their ability to leverage others' ideas to their strategic advantage. "We can't compete in coming up with new ideas," said the manager of a medium-sized company, "but we can copy other peoples' ideas and do them better."

5. *Infrastructure.* This final type of IT initiative is one that often falls between the cracks when business and IT strategies are developed. However, it is clear that

the hardware, software, middleware, communications, and data available will affect an organization's capacity to build new capabilities and respond to change. One study found that most companies feel their legacy infrastructure can be an impediment to what they want to do (Prahalad and Krishnan 2002). Research also shows that leading companies have a framework for making targeted investments in their IT infrastructure that will further their overall strategic direction (Weill, Subramani, and Broadbent 2002). Unfortunately, investing in infrastructure is rarely seen as strategic. As a result, many companies struggle with how to justify and appropriately fund it.

While each type of project delivers a different type of business value, typically IT strategy has stressed only those initiatives with strong business cases. Others are shelved or must struggle for a very small piece of the pie. However, there was a general recognition in the group that this approach to investment leads to an IT strategy with a heavy emphasis on the bottom line. As a result, all participating companies were looking at new ways to build a strategy-development process that reflects a more appropriate balance of all dimensions of IT strategy.

TOWARD AN IT STRATEGY-DEVELOPMENT PROCESS

Strategy is still very much an art, not a science, explained the focus group. And it is likely to remain so, according to strategy experts. Strategy will never again be a coherent, long-term plan with predictable outcomes—if it ever was. "Leaders can't predict which combinations [of strategic elements] will succeed [and] they can't drive their organizations towards predetermined positions" (Quinn 2002, 96). This situation only exacerbates the problem that has long faced IT strategists. That is, it is difficult to build systems, information, and infrastructure when a business's direction is continually changing. Yet this degree of flexibility is exactly what businesses are demanding (Prahalad and Krishnan 2002). Traditional IT planning and budgeting mechanisms done once a year simply don't work in today's fast-paced business environment. "We always seem to lag behind the business, no matter how hard we try," said a manager.

Clearly, organizations need to be developing strategy differently. How to do this is not always apparent, but several companies are trying ways to more dynamically link IT strategy with that of the business. While no one company in the focus group claimed to have *the* answer, they did identify several practices that are moving them closer to this goal:

- *"Rolling" planning and budget cycles.* All participants agreed that IT plans and budgets need attention more frequently than once a year. One company has created an eighteen-month rolling plan that is reviewed and updated quarterly with the business to maintain currency.
- *An enterprise architecture.* This is an integrated blueprint for the development of the enterprise—both the business and IT. "Our enterprise architecture includes business processes, applications, infrastructure, and data," said a member. "Our

EA function has to approve all business and IT projects and is helpful in identifying duplicate solutions." In some companies this architecture is IT initiated and business validated; in others it is a joint initiative. However, participants warned that an architecture has the potential to be a corporate bottleneck if it becomes too bureaucratic.

- *Different funding "buckets."* Balancing short-term returns with the company's longer-term interests is a continual challenge. As noted above, all five types of IT projects are necessary for an effective IT strategy (i.e., business improvement, business enabling, business opportunities, opportunity leverage, and infrastructure). In order to ensure that each different type of IT is appropriately funded, many companies are allocating predetermined percentages of their IT budget to different types of projects (Ross and Beath 2002). This helps keep continual pressure on IT to reduce its "utility costs" to free up more resources for other types of projects. "Since we implemented this method of budgeting, we've gone from spending 70 percent of our revenues on mandatory and support projects to spending 70 percent on discretionary and strategic ones," said a manager. This is also an effective way to ensure that IT infrastructure is continually enhanced. Leading companies build their infrastructures not through a few large investments, but gradually through incremental, modular investments that build IT capabilities (Weill, Subramani, and Broadbent 2002).

- *Account or relationship managers.* There is no substitute for a deep and rich understanding of the business. This is why many companies have appointed IT account managers to work closely with key lines of business. These managers help business leaders to observe their environments systematically and identify new opportunities for which IT could be effective. Furthermore, together, account managers can identify synergies and interdependencies among lines of business. One organization holds both intra- and interfunctional strategy sessions on a regular basis with business managers to understand future needs, develop programs, and design specific roadmaps for reaching business goals. "Our account managers have been a significant factor in synchronizing IT and business strategies," said its manager.

- *A prioritization rubric.* "We don't do prioritization well," said one participant. IT managers have long complained that it is extremely difficult to justify certain types of initiatives using the traditional business case method of prioritization. This has led to an overrepresentation of business improvement projects in the IT portfolio and has inhibited more strategic investments in general capabilities and business opportunities. This problem is leading some companies to adopt multiple approaches to justifying IT projects (Ross and Beath 2002). For example, business-enabling projects must be sponsored at a cross-functional level on the basis of the capabilities they will provide the enterprise as a whole. Senior management must then take responsibility to ensure that these capabilities are fully leveraged over time. Infrastructure priorities are often left up to IT to determine once a budget is set. One IT department does this by holding strategy sessions with its account and utility managers to align infrastructure spending with the organization's strategic needs. Unfortunately, no one has yet figured out a way to prioritize business opportunity experiments. At present this is typically left to the "enthusiasms and intuitions" of the sponsoring managers, either in IT or in the business (Ross and Beath 2002). "Overall," said a manager, "we need to do a better job of thinking through the key performance indicators we'd like to use for each type of project."

While it is unlikely that strategy development will ever become a completely formalized process, there is a clear need to add more structure to how it is done. A greater understanding of how strategy is developed will ensure that all stakeholders are involved and a broader range of IT investments are considered. While the outcomes of strategy will always be uncertain, the process of identifying new opportunities and how they should be funded must become more systematic if a business is going to realize optimum value from its IT resources.

CHALLENGES FOR CIOs

As often happens in organizations, recognition of a need precedes the ability to put it into place. IT leaders are now making significant strides in articulating IT strategy and linking it more effectively with business strategy. Business leaders are also more open to a more integrated process. Nevertheless, there are still important organizational barriers remaining that often inhibit strategy development.

A supportive governance structure is frequently lacking. "Now that so many strategies are enterprisewide, we need a better way to manage them," explained one manager. Often there are no formal structures to identify and manage interdependencies between business functions and processes. "It used to be that everything was aligned around organizational boundaries, but strategy is now more complex since we're working on programs with broader organizational scope," said another. Similarly, current managerial control systems and incentives are often designed to reward thinking that is aligned to a line of business, not to the greater organizational good. Enterprisewide funding models are also lacking. "Everything we do now requires negotiation for funding between the lines of business who control the resources," a third stated. Even within IT, the group suggested it is not always clear who in the organization is responsible for taking IT strategies and turning them into detailed IT plans.

Traditional planning and budgetary practices are a further challenge. This is an often-neglected element of IT strategy. "Our business and IT strategies are not always done in parallel or even around the same time," said a participant. As a result, it is not easy to stay aligned or to integrate the two sets of plans. Another commented, "Our business plans change constantly. It is, therefore, common for IT strategies to grow farther and farther apart over time." Similarly, an annual budgeting process tends to lock an organization into fixed expenditures that may not be practical in a rapidly changing environment. IT organizations, therefore, need both a longer-term view of their resourcing practices and the opportunity to make changes to it more frequently. While rolling budgets are becoming more acceptable, they are by no means common in either IT or the business world today.

- A governance structure for enterprisewide projects
- Enterprisewide funding models
- Parallel and linked processes for developing IT and business strategies
- Traditional budget cycles
- Balancing strategic and tactical initiatives
- Skills in strategizing

Both business and IT leaders need to develop better skills in strategizing. "We've gotten really good at implementing projects," said an IT manager. "Strategy and innovation are our least developed capabilities." IT is pushing the business toward better articulation of its goals. "Right now, in many areas of our business, strategy is not well thought through," said another manager. "IT is having to play the devil's advocate and get them to think beyond generalities such as, 'we are going to grow the business by 20 percent this year.'" With more attention to the process, it is almost certain to get better, but managers' rudimentary skills in this area limit the quality of strategy development.

Over and over, the group stressed that IT strategy is mainly about getting the balance right between conflicting strategic imperatives. "It's always a balancing act between our tactical and operational commitments and the work that builds our long-term capabilities," said a participant. Deciding how to make the trade-offs between the different types of IT work is the essence of effective strategy. Unfortunately, few businesses do this very well (Burgelman and Doz 2001). According to the focus group, traditional business thinking tends to favor short-term profitability, while IT leaders tend to take a longer-term view. Making sure some types of IT work (e.g., infrastructure, new business opportunities) are not underfunded while others (e.g., utility, business improvement) are not overfunded is a continual challenge for all IT and business leaders.

CONCLUSION

Effective strategy development is becoming vital for organizations. As the impact of IT has grown in companies, IT strategy is finally getting the attention it deserves in the business. Nevertheless, most organizations are still at the earliest stages of learning how to develop an effective IT strategy and synchronize it with an overall business strategy. Getting the balance right between the many different ways IT can be used to affect a business is a constant challenge for leaders and one on which they do not always agree. While there is, as yet, no well-developed IT strategy–development process, there appears to be general agreement on certain critical success factors and the key elements involved. Over time, these will likely be refined and better integrated with overall business strategy development. Those who learn to do this well without locking the enterprise into inflexible technical solutions are likely to win big in our rapidly evolving business environment.

REFERENCES

Burgelman, R., and Y. Doz. "The Power of Strategic Integration." *MIT Sloan Management Review* 42, no. 3 (Spring 2001): 28–38.

Charitou, C., and C. Markides. "Responses to Disruptive Strategic Innovation." *MIT Sloan Management Review* (Winter 2003): 55–63.

Eisenhardt, K. "Has Strategy Changed?" *MIT Sloan Management Review* 43, no. 2 (Winter 2002): 88–91.

Frohman, A. "Technology as a Competitive Weapon." *Harvard Business Review* January–February (1982): 80–94.

Gebauer, J. "Virtual Organizations from an Economic Perspective." *Communications of the ACM* 40 (September 1997): 91–103.

Hitt, M., B. Keats, and S. DeMarire. "Navigating in the New Competitive Landscape: Building Strategic Flexibility." *Academy of Management Executive* 12, no. 4 (1998): 22–42.

Kanter, R. "Strategy as Improvisational Theater." *MIT Sloan Management Review* (Winter 2002): 76–81.

McKeen, J., and H. Smith. *Management Challenges in IS: Successful Strategies and Appropriate Action.* Chichester, England: John Wiley & Sons, 1996.

Porter, M. "What Is Strategy?" *Harvard Business Review* November–December (1996): 61–78.

Prahalad, C., and M. Krishnan, "The Dynamic Synchronization of Strategy and Information Technology." *MIT Sloan Management Review* (Summer 2002): 24–33.

Quinn, J. "Strategy, Science, and Management." *MIT Sloan Management Review* (Summer 2002): 96.

Rivard, S., B. Aubert, M. Patry, G. Pare, and H. Smith. *Information Technology and Organizational Transformation: Solving the Management Puzzle.* New York: Butterworth Heinemann, 2004.

Ross, J., and C. Beath. "Beyond the Business Case: New Approaches to IT Investment." *MIT Sloan Management Review* (Winter 2002): 51–59.

Ross, J., and P. Weill. "Six IT Decisions Your IT People Shouldn't Make." *Harvard Business Review* (November 2002): 5–11.

Smith, H. A. "The Best of the Best: Part II." *CIO Canada* October 1 (2003).

Tapscott, D. *The Digital Economy: Promise and Peril in the Age of Networked Intelligence.* New York: McGraw-Hill, 1996.

Weill, P., M. Subramani, and M. Broadbent. "Building IT Infrastructure for Strategic Agility." *MIT Sloan Management Review* (Fall 2002): 57–65.

Venkatramen, N., and J. Henderson. "Real Strategies for Virtual Organizing." *Sloan Management Review* 40, no. 33 (Fall 1998).

Chapter 3

Linking IT to Business Metrics[1]

From the first time IT started making a significant dent in corporate balance sheets, the holy grail of academics, consultants, and business and IT managers has been to show that what a company spends on IT has a direct impact on its performance. Early efforts to do this, such as those trying to link various measures of IT input (e.g., budget dollars, number of PCs, number of projects) with various measures of business performance (e.g., profit, productivity, stock value) all failed to show any relationship at all (Marchand, Kettinger, and Rollins 2000). Since then, everyone has properly concluded that the relationship between what is done in IT and what happens in the business is considerably more complex than these studies first supposed. In fact, many researchers would suggest that the relationship is so filtered through a variety of "conversion effects" (Cronk and Fitzgerald 1999) as to be practically impossible to demonstrate. Most IT managers would agree. They have long argued that technology is not the major stumbling block to achieving business performance; it is the business itself—the processes, the managers, the culture, and the skills—that makes the difference. Therefore, it is simply not realistic to expect to see a clear correlation between IT and business performance at any level. When technology is successful, it is a *team* effort, and the contributions of the IT and business components of an initiative cannot and should not be separated.

Nevertheless, IT expenditures must be justified. Thus, most companies have concentrated on determining the "business value" that specific IT projects deliver. By focusing on a goal that matters to business (e.g., better information, faster transaction processing, reduced staff) then breaking this goal down into smaller projects that IT can affect directly, they have tried to "peel the onion" and show specifically how IT delivers value in a piecemeal fashion. Thus, a series of surrogate measures are usually used to demonstrate IT's impact in an organization. (See Smith and McKeen 2003 for more details.)

---

[1]Smith, H. A., and J. D. McKeen, and C. Street, "Linking IT to Business Metrics," *Journal of Information Science and Technology* 1, no. 1 (2004): 13–26 (reproduced by permission of the Information Institute).

More recently, companies are taking another look at business performance metrics and IT. They believe it is time to "put the onion back together" and focus on what really matters to the enterprise. This perspective argues that employees who truly understand what their business is trying to achieve can sense the right ways to personally improve performance that will show up at a business unit and organizational level. "People who understand the business and are informed will be proactive and . . . have a disposition to create business value every day in many small and not-so-small ways" (Marchand, Kettinger, and Rollins 2000). While the connection may not be obvious, they say, it is there nevertheless and can be demonstrated in tangible ways. The key to linking what IT does to business performance is, therefore, to create an environment within which everyone thoroughly understands what measures are important to the business and is held accountable for them. This point of view does not suggest that all the work done to date to learn how IT delivers value to an organization (e.g., business cases, productivity measures) has been unnecessary, only that it is incomplete. Without close attention to business metrics *in addition*, it is easy for IT initiatives and staff to lose their focus and become less effective.

This chapter looks at how these controversial yet compelling ideas are being pursued in organizations to better understand how companies are attempting to link IT work and firm performance through business metrics. The first section describes how business metrics themselves are evolving and looks at how new management philosophies are changing how these measures are communicated and applied. Next it discusses the types of metrics that are important for a well-rounded program of business measurement and how IT can influence them. Then it presents three different ways companies are specifically linking their IT departments with business metrics and the benefits and challenges they have experienced in doing this. This section concludes with some general principles for establishing a business measurement program in IT. Finally, it offers some advice to managers about how to succeed with such a program in IT.

BUSINESS MEASUREMENT: AN OVERVIEW

Almost everyone agrees that *the* primary goal of the business is to make money for its shareholders (Goldratt and Cox 1984; Haspeslagh, Noda, and Boulos 2001; Kaplan and Norton 1996). Unfortunately, in large businesses this objective frequently gets lost in the midst of people's day-to-day activities because profit cannot be measured directly at the level at which most employees in a company work (Haspeslagh, Noda, and Boulos 2001). This "missing link" between work and business performance leads companies to look for ways to bridge this gap. They believe that if a firm's strategies for achieving its goal can be tied much more closely to everyday processes and decision making, frontline employees will be better able to create business value. Proponents of this value-based management (VBM) approach have demonstrated that an explicit, firmwide commitment to shareholder value; clear communication about how value is created or destroyed; and incentive systems that are linked to key business measures will increase the odds of a positive increase in share price (Haspeslagh, Noda, and Boulos 2001).

> Measurement counts. What a company measures and the way it measures influence both the mindsets of managers and the way people behave. The best measures are tied to business performance and are linked to the strategies and business capabilities of the company. (Marchand, Kettinger, and Rollins 2000)

Although companies ascribe to this notion in theory, they do not always act in ways that are consistent with this belief. All too often, therefore, because they lack clarity about the links between business performance and their own work, individuals and even business units have to take "leaps of faith" in what they do (Marchand, Kettinger, and Rollins 2000).

Nowhere has this been more of a problem than in IT. As has been noted so often in the past, IT investments have not always delivered the benefits expected (Bensaou and Earl 1998; Holland and Sharke 2001). "Efforts to measure the link between IT investment and business performance from an economics perspective have . . . failed to establish a consistent causal linkage with sustained business profitability" (Marchand, Kettinger, and Rollins 2000). Value-based management suggests that if IT staff do not understand the business, they cannot sense how and where to change it effectively with technology. Many IT and business managers have implicitly known this for some time. VBM simply gives them a better framework for implementing their beliefs more systematically.

One of the most significant efforts to integrate an organization's mission and strategy with a measurement system has been Kaplan and Norton's (1996) balanced scorecard. They explain that competing in the information age is much less about managing physical, tangible assets and much more about the ability of a company to mobilize its intangible assets, such as customer relationships, innovation, employee skills, and information technology. Thus, they suggest that not only should business measures look at how well a company has done *in the past* (i.e., financial performance), but they also need to look at metrics related to customers, internal business processes, and learning and growth that position the firm to achieve *future* performance. While it is difficult putting a reliable monetary value on these items, they suggest that such nonfinancial measures are critical success factors for superior financial performance in the future. Research is showing that this is, in fact, the case. Companies that use a balanced scorecard tend to have a better return on investment than those that rely on traditional financial measures alone (Alexander 2000).

Today many companies use some sort of scorecard or "dashboard" to track a variety of different metrics of organizational health. However, traditionally, IT has not paid much attention to business results, focusing instead on its own internal measures of performance (e.g., IT operations efficiency, projects delivered on time, etc.). This has perpetuated the serious "disconnect" between the business and IT that often manifests itself in perceptions of poor alignment between the two groups, inadequate payoffs from IT investments, poor relationships, and finger-pointing (Bensaou and Earl 1998; Holland and Sharke 2001). All too often IT initiatives are conceived with little reference to major business results, relying instead on lower-level business value surrogates that are not always related to these measures. While IT organizations are getting much better at this "bottom up" approach to IT investment than in the past (Smith and McKeen 2003), undelivered IT value remains a serious concern in many organizations. One survey of CFOs found that only 49 percent felt that their ROI expectations for technology had been met (Holland and Sharke 2001). "Despite considerable effort, no practical model has been developed to measure whether a company's IT investments will definitely contribute to sustainable competitive advantage" (Marchand, Kettinger, and Rollins 2000). Clearly, in spite of significant efforts over many years, traditional IT measurement programs have been inadequate at assessing business value. Many IT organizations believe, therefore, that it is time for a different approach to delivering IT value, one that holds IT accountable to the same measures and goals as the rest of the business.

KEY BUSINESS METRICS FOR IT

No one seriously argues that IT has no impact on an organization's overall financial performance anymore. While there may be disagreement about whether it has a positive or a negative impact, technology is too pervasive and significant an expense in most firms for it not to have some influence on the corporate bottom line. However, as has been argued above, we now recognize that neither technology nor business alone is responsible for IT's financial impact. It is instead a joint responsibility of IT *and* the business. This suggests that they need to be held accountable *together* for its impact. While some companies have accepted this principle for individual IT projects (i.e., holding business and IT managers jointly responsible for achieving their anticipated benefits), few have extended it to an enterprise level. VBM suggests that this lack of attention to enterprise performance by IT is one reason it has been so hard to fully deliver business value for technology investments. Holding IT accountable for a firm's performance according to key financial metrics is, therefore, an important step toward improving its contribution to the corporate bottom line.

However, while financial results are clearly an important part of any measurement of a business's success today, they are not enough. Effective business metrics programs should also include nonfinancial measures, such as customer and employee satisfaction. As noted above, because such nonfinancial measures are predictive of future performance, they offer an organization the opportunity to make changes that will ultimately affect their financial success.

Kaplan and Norton (1996) state "the importance of customer satisfaction probably cannot be overemphasized." Companies that do not understand their customers' needs will likely lose customers and profitability. Research shows that merely adequate satisfaction is insufficient to lead to customer loyalty and ultimately profit. Only firms where customers are completely or extremely satisfied can achieve this result (Heskett et al. 1994). As a result, many companies now undertake systematic customer satisfaction surveys. However, in IT it is rare to find external customer satisfaction as one of the metrics on which IT is evaluated. While IT's "customers" are usually considered to be internal, these days technology can make a significant difference in how external customers perceive a firm and whether or not they want to do business with it. Systems that are not reliable or available when needed, cannot provide customers with the information they need, or cannot give the customers the flexibility they require are all too common. And with the advent of e-business, self-service systems are being designed to interface directly with external customers. It is, therefore, appropriate to include external customer satisfaction as a business metric for IT.

Another important nonfinancial business measure is employee satisfaction. This is a "leading indicator" of customer satisfaction. That is, employee satisfaction in one year is strongly linked to customer satisfaction and profitability in the next (Koys 2001). Employees' positive attitudes toward their company and their jobs lead to positive behaviors toward customers and, therefore, to improved financial performance (Rucci, Kirn, and Quinn 1998; Ulrich et al. 1991). IT managers have always watched their own employee satisfaction rate intently because of its close links to employee turnover. However, they often miss the link between IT employee satisfaction and customer satisfaction—both internal customer satisfaction, which leads to improved general employee satisfaction, and external customer satisfaction. Thus, only a few companies hold IT managers accountable for general employee satisfaction.

Both customer and employee satisfaction should be part of a business metrics program for IT. With its ever-growing influence in organizations, technology is just as likely to affect external customer and general employee satisfaction as many other areas of a business. This suggests that there are three different levels of measurement and accountability for IT:

1. *Enterprise measures.* These tie the work of IT directly to the performance of the organization (e.g., external customer satisfaction, corporate financial performance).
2. *Functional measures.* These assess the internal work of the IT organization as a whole (e.g., IT employee satisfaction, internal customer satisfaction, operational performance, development productivity).
3. *Project measures.* These assess the performance of a particular project team in delivering specific value to the organization (e.g., business case benefits, delivery on time).

Functional and project measures are usually well addressed by IT measurement programs today. It is the enterprise level that is usually missing.

DESIGNING BUSINESS METRICS FOR IT

The firms that hold IT accountable for enterprise business metrics believe this approach fosters a common sense of purpose, enables everyone to make better decisions, and helps IT staff understand the implications of their work for the success of the organization (Haspeslagh, Noda, and Boulos 2001; Marchand, Kettinger, and Rollins 2000). The implementation of business metrics programs varies widely among companies, but three approaches taken to linking IT with business metrics are distinguishable.

1. ***Balanced scorecard.*** This approach uses a classic balanced scorecard with measures in all four scorecard dimensions (see box). Each metric is selected to measure progress against the entire enterprise's business plan. These are then broken down into business unit plans and appropriate submetrics identified. Individual scorecards are then developed with metrics that will link into their business unit scorecards. With this approach, IT is treated as a separate business unit and has its own scorecard linked to the business plan. "Our management finally realized that we need to have everyone thinking in the same way," explained one manager. "With enterprise systems, we can't have people working in silos anymore." The scorecards are very visible in the organization with company and business unit scorecards and those of senior executives posted on the company's intranet. "People are extremely interested in seeing how we're doing. Scorecards have provided a common framework for our entire company." They also provide clarity for employees about their roles in how they affect key business metrics.

Sample Balanced Scorecard Business Metrics

- Shareholder value (financial)
- Expense management (financial)
- Customer/client focus (customer)
- Loyalty (customer)
- Customercentric organization (customer)
- Effectiveness and efficiency of business operations (operations)
- Risk management (operations)
- Contribution to firmwide priorities and business initiatives (growth)

Although scorecards have meant that there is better understanding of the business's drivers and plans at senior management levels, there is still considerable resistance to them at the lower levels in IT. "While developers see how they can affect our customers, they don't see how they can affect shareholder value, profit, or revenue, and they don't want to be held accountable for these things," stated the manager. She noted that implementing an effective scorecard program relies on three things: good data to provide better metrics, simplicity of metrics, and enforcement. "Now if someone's scorecard is not complete, they cannot get a bonus. This is a huge incentive to follow the program."

2. ***Modified scorecard.*** A somewhat different approach to a scorecard is taken by one company in the focus group. This firm has selected five key measures (see box) that are closely linked to the company's overall vision statement. Results are communicated to all staff on a quarterly basis in a short performance report. This includes a clear explanation of each measure, quarterly progress, a comparison with the previous year's quarterly results, and a "stretch" goal for the organization to achieve. The benefit of this approach is that it orients all employees in the company to the same mission and values. With everyone using the same metrics, there is much clearer alignment all the way through the firm, according to the focus group manager.

Modified Scorecard Business Metrics

- *Customer Loyalty Index*—the percent of customers who said they were very satisfied with the company and would recommend it to others
- *Associate Loyalty Index*—employees' perception of the company as a great place to work
- *Revenue Growth*—the percentage of this year's total revenues with last year's total revenues

- *Operating Margin*—the operating income earned before interest and taxes for every dollar of revenue
- *Return on Capital Employed*—earnings before interest and tax divided by the capital used to generate the earnings

In IT these key enterprise metrics are complemented by an additional set of business measures established by the business units. Each line of business identifies one or two key business unit metrics on which they and their IT team will be measured. Functional groups within IT are evaluated according to the same metrics as their business partners, as well as on company and internal IT team performance. For example, the credit group in IT might be evaluated on the number of new credit accounts the company acquires. Shared IT services (e.g., infrastructure) are evaluated according to an average of all of the IT functional groups' metrics.

The importance the company places on these metrics is reflected in the firm's generous bonus program (i.e., bonuses can reach up to 230 percent of an individual's salary) in which all IT staff participate. Bonuses are separate from an individual's salary, which is linked to personal performance. The percentage influence of each set of business measures (i.e., enterprise, business unit, and individual/team) varies according to the level of the individual in the firm. However, all staff have at least 25 percent of their bonus linked to enterprise performance metrics. No bonuses are paid to anyone if the firm does not reach its earnings-per-share target (which is driven by the five enterprise measures outlined in the box). This incentive system makes it clear that everyone's job is connected to business results and helps ensure that attention is focused on the things that are important to the company. As a result, there is a much stronger interest among IT staff about how the business is doing. "Everyone now speaks the same language," said the manager. "Project alignment is much easier."

3. *Strategic imperatives.* A somewhat different approach is taken by a third focus group company. Here the executive team annually evaluates the key environmental factors affecting the company then identifies a number of strategic imperatives for the firm (e.g., achieve industry-leading e-business capability, achieve 10–15 percent growth in earnings per share). These can vary according to the needs of the firm in any particular year. Each area of the business is then asked to identify initiatives that will affect these imperatives and to determine how they will be measured (e.g., retaining customers of a recent acquisition, increased net sales, a new product). In the same way, IT is asked to identify the

key projects and measures that will help the business to achieve these imperatives. Each part of the company, including IT, then integrates these measures into its variable pay program (VPP).

The company's VPP links a percentage of an individual's pay to business results and overall business unit performance. This percentage could vary from a small portion of one's salary for a new employee to a considerable proportion for senior management. Within IT, the weight that different measures are accorded in the VPP portion of their pay is determined by a measurement team and approved by the CIO and the president. Figure 3.1 illustrates the different percentages allocated to IT's variable pay component for a typical year. Metrics can change from year to year depending on where management wants to focus everyone's attention. "Performance tends to improve if you measure it," explained the manager. "Over the years, we have ratcheted up our targets in different areas. Once a certain level of performance is achieved, we may change the measure or change the emphasis on this measure."

An important difference from the scorecard approach is the identification of key IT projects. "These are not all IT projects, but a small number which are closely aligned with the strategic business imperatives," stated the manager. "Having the success of these projects associated with their variable pay drives everyone's behavior. People tend to jump in and help if there's a problem with one of them." The goal in this process is for everyone to understand the VPP measures and to make them visible within IT. Targets and results are posted quarterly, and small groups of employees meet to discuss ideas about how they can influence business and IT goals. "Some amazing ideas have come out of these meetings," said the manager. "Everyone knows what's important, and these measures get attention. People use these metrics to make choices all the time in their work."

Figure 3.1 Percentage Weightings Assigned to IT Variable Pay Components for a Particular Year

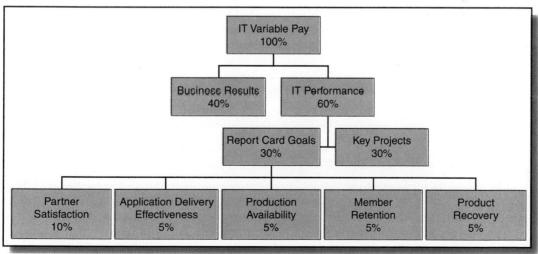

While each of these business measurement programs has been implemented somewhat differently, they all share several key features that could be considered principles of a good business metrics program for IT:

1. *Focus on overall business performance.* These programs all focus employees on both financial and nonfinancial enterprise performance and have an explicit expectation that everyone in the organization can influence these results in some way.

2. *Understanding is a critical success factor.* If people are going to be held accountable for certain business results, it is important that they understand them. Similarly, if the organization is worried about certain results, this must be communicated as well. Holding regular staff meetings where people can ask questions and discuss results is effective, as is providing results on a quarterly basis. Understanding is the goal. "If you can ask . . . a person programming code and they can tell you three to four of their objectives and how those tie into the company's performance and what the measures of achieving those objectives are, you've got it" (Alexander 2000).

3. *Simplicity.* Successful companies tend to keep their measures very simple and easy to use (Haspeslagh, Noda, and Boulos 2001). In each approach outlined above, a limited number of measures are used. This makes it very easy for employees to calculate their bonuses (or variable pay) based on the metrics provided, which further strengthens the linkage between company performance and individual effort.

4. *Visibility.* In each of the programs discussed above, metrics were made widely available to all staff on a quarterly basis. In one case they are posted on the company's intranet; in another they are distributed in a printed report; in a third they are posted in public areas of the office. Visibility encourages employee buy-in and accountability and stimulates discussion about how to do better or what is working well.

5. *Links to incentive systems.* Successful companies tend to include a much larger number of employees in bonus programs than unsuccessful ones (Haspeslagh, Noda, and Boulos 2001). Extending incentive schemes to all IT staff, not just management, is important to a measurement program's effectiveness. The most effective programs appear to distinguish between fair compensation for individual work and competencies and a reward for successfully achieving corporate objectives.

ADVICE TO MANAGERS

Our focus group had some final advice for other IT managers who are thinking of implementing a business metrics program:

- *Results will take time.* It takes time to change attitudes and behavior in IT, but it is worthwhile making the effort. Positive results may take from six months to a year to appear. "We had some initial pushback from our staff at the beginning," said one manager, "but now the metrics program has become ingrained in our attitudes and behaviors." Another manager noted, "We had a few bumps during our first year, but everyone, especially our executives, is getting better at the program now [that] we're in our third year. It really gets our staff engaged with the business." If there has been no dramatic difference within three years, management should recognize that it is either using the wrong measures or hasn't got employee buy-in to the program (Alexander 2000).

- *Have common goals.* Having everyone measured on the same business goals helps to build a strong team at all levels in the organization. It makes it easier to set priorities as a group and to collaborate and share resources, as needed.

- *Follow up on problem areas.* Companies must be prepared to take action about poor results and to involve staff in their plans. In particular, if companies are going to ask customers and employees what they think, they must be prepared to act on the results. All metrics must be taken seriously and acted on if they are to be used to drive behavior and lead to continuous improvement.

- *Be careful what you measure.* Measuring something makes people pay attention to it, particularly if it is linked to compensation. Metrics must, therefore, be selected with care because they will be a major driver of behavior. For example, if incentives are solely based on financial results, it is probable that some people may be so driven, they will trample on the needs and interests of others. Similarly, if only costs are measured, the needs of customers could be ignored. Conversely, if a metric indicates a problem area, organizations can expect to see a lot of ingenuity and support devoted to addressing it.

- *Don't use measurement as a method of control.* A business metrics program should be designed to foster an environment in which people look beyond their own jobs and become proactive about the needs of the organization (Marchand, Kettinger, and Rollins 2000). It should aim to communicate strategy and help align individual and organizational initiatives (Kaplan and Norton 1996). All managers should clearly understand that a program of this type should not be used for controlling behavior, but rather as a motivational tool.

CONCLUSION

Getting the most value out of IT has been a serious concern of the business for many years. In spite of considerable effort, measurement initiatives in IT that use surrogates of business value or that focus on improving internal IT behavior have not been fully successful in delivering results. What has not been tried until very recently is expecting IT to participate in achieving specific enterprise objectives—the same goals as the rest of the organization. This chapter has shown that there are significant benefits to holding IT accountable for key business metrics. Not only are there demonstrable financial returns, but there is also considerable long-term value in aligning everyone's behavior with the same goals; people

become more supportive of each other and more sensitive to the greater corporate good, and decisions are easier to make. A good business metrics program, therefore, appears to be a powerful component of effective measurement in IT. While IT employees may initially resist accountability for business results, the experiences of the focus group demonstrate that their objections are usually short lived. If a business measurement program is carefully designed, properly linked to an incentive program, widely implemented, and effectively monitored by management, it is highly likely that business performance will become an integral part of the mindset of all IT staff and ultimately pay off in a wide variety of ways.

REFERENCES

Alexander, S. "Business Metrics." *Computerworld* 34, no. 24 (2000): 64.

Bensaou, M., and M. Earl. "The Right Mind-set for Managing Information Technology." *Harvard Business Review* 76, no. 5 (Sept.–Oct. 1998): 110–28.

Cronk, M., and E. Fitzgerald. "Understanding 'IS Business Value': Derivation of Dimensions." *Logistics Information Management* 12, no. 1–2 (1999): 40–49.

Goldratt, E., and J. Cox. *The Goal: Excellence in Manufacturing* Croton-on-Hudson, NY: North River Press, 1984.

Haspeslagh, P., T. Noda, and F. Boulos. "Managing for Value: It's Not Just about the Numbers." *Harvard Business Review* July–August (2001): 65–73.

Heskett, J., T. Jones, G. Loveman, E. Sasser, and L. Schlesinger. "Putting the Service Profit Chain to Work." *Harvard Business Review* March–April (1994): 164–74.

Holland, W., and G. Sharke. "Is Your IT System VESTed?" *Strategic Finance* 83, no. 6 (Dec. 2001): 34–37.

Kaplan, R., and D. Norton. *The Balanced Scorecard.* Boston: Harvard Business School Press, 1996.

Koys, D. "The Effects of Employee Satisfaction, Organizational Citizenship Behavior, and Turnover on Organizational Effectiveness: A Unit-level, Longitudinal Study." *Personnel Psychology* 54, no. 1 (Spring 2001): 101–14.

Marchand, D., W. Kettinger, and J. Rollins. "Information Orientation: People, Technology and the Bottom Line." *Sloan Management Review* (Summer 2000): 69–89.

Rucci, A., S. Kirn, and R. Quinn. "The Employee-Customer-Profit Chain at Sears." *Harvard Business Review* 76 (January/February 1998): 82–97.

Smith, H. A., and J. D. McKeen. "Developing and Delivering on the IT Value Proposition." *Communications of the Association of Information Systems* 11, article 25 (April 2003): 438–50.

Ulrich, D., R. Halbrook, D. Meder, M. Stuchlik, and S. Thorpe. "Employee and Customer Attachment: Synergies for Competitive Advantage." *Human Resource Planning* 14 (1991): 89–103.

Chapter 4

Managing Perceptions of IT[1]

IT managers have struggled to deal with negative perceptions of IT's effectiveness and value for many years (Busch et al. 1991; McKeen and Smith 1996) and it is clear that IT is still wrestling with many of these same challenges. A 2005 survey of business leaders gave IT's value to the organization a rating of six out of ten (Overby 2005). Another survey found that while business leaders recognize the growing importance of IT as a fundamental driver of business, they still have doubts about the role of senior IT managers in developing strategy and concerns about IT's cost effectiveness and the value it adds (Willcoxson and Chatham 2004). Studies by McKinsey Associates and Gartner Group found similar results: "CIOs must do more to improve the perceptions of IT amongst CEOs and other business leaders" (Prewitt 2005). Other research shows that executives continue to have mixed feelings about IT, believing it is important but feeling that it is also a barrier to change (Flint 2004).

These findings demonstrate that IT still has some work to do in understanding business leaders' perceptions in order to address any misperceptions or problem perceptions. As a result, this chapter first looks at the concept of perceptions and why they are important for business and IT leaders to understand and manage. Next, it examines the nature of perceptions in the business-IT relationship and the factors that affect them. In the final two sections of this chapter, we discuss some of the root causes of perceptual problems and present some practical approaches for measuring and managing perceptions in this relationship.

---

[1]Smith, H. A., J. D. McKeen, and S. Singh, "Managing Perceptions of IS," *Communications of the Association of Information Systems* 20, article 47 (November 2007), 760–773 (reproduced by permission of the Association for Information Systems).

THE VALUE OF PERCEPTIONS

A perception is "a thought, belief, or opinion held by many people and based on appearances" (Overby 2005). At an organizational level, the collective and multidimensional perceptions of a variety of stakeholder groups constitute a firm's reputation (i.e., *brand* in marketing terms). A reputation is perceptual and includes not only facts and knowledge, but also emotions toward an organization. While a firm's reputation may vary with its different stakeholder groups, studies show that firms with good reputations are those that tend to align the interests of their various stakeholders (Martinez and Norman 2004). Unfortunately, there is no consistent definition about what a reputation is and how it should be measured.

It is interesting, therefore, that research shows that while perceptions are immediate, they are often more accurate than opinions based on large amounts of data. While no one really understands how perceptions work, our unconscious minds appear to be primed to make rapid, instinctive judgments based on very "thin slices" of exposure to a situation (Gladwell 2005). In short, perceptions are formed in our unconscious, are grounded in a variety of factual and emotional factors, and are the basis for establishing a more enduring reputation or brand.

The value and importance of perceptions have been recognized in marketing for some time. Understanding and addressing both favorable and unfavorable attitudes to a particular brand and the beliefs and feelings about it is an important step in the marketing process (Rossiter and Percy 1987). Most organizations also understand that their reputations are important intangible resources that must be carefully managed (Martinez and Norman 2004).

However, while the concepts of reputation, perceptions, and attitudes are also applied to IT by researchers and practitioners, how to manage them appropriately is much less well understood. Although many IT leaders believe that managing perceptions of IT is important, few feel that marketing is the way to deal with them (Pastore and Cosgrove 2005). Sometimes these efforts try to sell others in the organization on what IT wants *to be*, which can set up false expectations and further damage IT's reputation when they are not met (Schrage 2006). Typically, however, IT managers believe that "formal marketing should not be required since, if the product is good, it will sell itself" (McKeen and Smith 1996).

Nevertheless, *not* managing perceptions is dangerous for three important reasons. First, "understanding, shaping, and fulfilling the expectations of stakeholders is central to successful strategy execution" (Gold 2006). Expectations and perceptions drive stakeholders' behavior, which, in turn, influences the quality of the business-IT partnership and "ultimately how efficiently the resources that drive enterprise performance and strategy execution are used" (Gold 2006). Furthermore, *not* trying to change perceptions of IT's value may threaten the future success and influence of IT in the organization (Jaska and Hogan 2006). As a result, ignoring this issue will likely lead to missed opportunities and increased inefficiencies (Pastore and Cosgrove 2005). As well, better management of perceptions is seen to have a number of positive benefits for both IT and the organization, such as increased credibility, closer alignment, and improved teamwork (Pastore and Cosgrove 2005).

Second, even *within* IT there are perceptual problems that need to be better managed. "We must first understand how we perceive ourselves and present ourselves to our users," said one manager. "There's no one in IT who's responsible for how we are perceived." Another noted, "We need internal credibility and trust *inside* IT in order to build it outside."

These comments are supported by recent research showing that organizational citizenship behaviors (OCBs)—behaviors that promote effective organizational functioning that are discretionary and not recognized by the formal reward system—are much lower for IT workers than for others in organizations (Moore and Love 2005). OCBs tend to be higher when staff perceive they are treated fairly and with dignity and respect, and lower when management places unrealistic and arbitrary demands on them and there is a lack of resources. When OCBs are high, staff are more likely to see their work as a social exchange rather than as simply an economic relationship. The authors speculate that in high-pressure, deadline-driven work such as that in IT, staff may not have time to exhibit OCBs. This thought was echoed by a manager who stated, "We're so busy, we can't take time to work on how we are perceived." OCBs become increasingly important as individuals' jobs grow less clear, span organizational boundaries, and contain ambiguities (Moore and Love 2005). Thus, gaining political alignment and collaboration is an important reason for managing perceptions in today's organizational environment. At a time when IT staff are expected to be resourceful, proactive, and innovative, it is vital that managers ensure that the internal perceptions of IT staff toward IT are positive.

Third, perceptions can simply be wrong, and such misperceptions can result in improper judgments and poor decisions. Gladwell (2005) writes, "while our unconscious is a powerful force, it's fallible . . . our instinctive reactions have to compete with all kinds of other interests, emotions, and sentiments." The focus group agreed. "There are misperceptions of problems and real gaps. We need to distinguish between these." The good news is that people's perceptions can be trained to be more accurate, and this is where managing them becomes important.

PERCEPTIONS IN THE BUSINESS-IT RELATIONSHIP

Before looking at how perceptions in the business-IT relationship can be managed and measured, it is important to better understand how perceptions manifest themselves in this relationship. Deeper insights in this area will help IT managers learn how and where their efforts can have an impact.

The most obvious problem for IT in dealing with perceptions is that they vary significantly according to who you ask. There are a number of factors that may affect perceptions in the business-IT relationship:

- *The subfunction of IT with which the user deals.* As noted above, in many organizations, there is no single "brand" or identity that IT promotes. Therefore, it is not surprising that different parts of the business (and even different parts of IT) can have significantly different experiences with IT. Even if the business thinks of "IT" as a single entity, different parts of IT see themselves differently and have different strengths and weaknesses. For example,

IT operations can be very efficient and customercentric, but applications development or IT planning processes can be inadequate. One manager noted that his organization had a centralized IT function for shared services and planning, while the rest of IT was decentralized into the major business units. "We have a daily fight to keep our credibility and trust with the business unit leaders," said this business unit–focused IT manager, "because central IT keeps screwing up."

- *The needs and interests of business stakeholders.* Similarly, "the business" is not one entity. "There are significant cultural differences between our business units and what they want from us," explained a manager whose IT department was trying to serve three different businesses. "The vision of IT depends on who you ask." There are two common views of IT among business executives. The first is that IT is "table stakes" and a service; the second is that IT is a critical differentiator (Deloitte 2004). Clearly what different business leaders want from IT will affect their perceptions and result in different perspectives of how well IT achieves its goals (Jaska and Hogan 2006). Unfortunately, once a specific group of stakeholders is dissatisfied, its impressions can be hard to change (Martinez and Norman 2004).

- *Level in the corporate hierarchy.* The CEO and senior management team's views of IT are especially important because they contribute strongly to how IT is used in the organization. Positive attitudes toward IT are related to more progressive use of technology (Tallon, Kraemer, and Gurbaxani 2000). A number of surveys show that senior leaders in particular have mixed feelings about the role, importance, and value of IT (Anonymous 2002; Flint 2004; Prewitt 2005; Willcoxson and Chatham 2004). While almost all studies have found that senior leaders believe that IT is important to the business, its ability to add value, be responsive to business needs, and drive growth are questioned. The CEO-CIO relationship is particularly critical in setting the tone for how IT is viewed. One manager noted, "Our CEO is very hands-off with IT, so the different business units each do what they like." Unfortunately, CIOs appear to have different perceptions of their relationships than CEOs. One study found that, while most CIOs believe they are trusted and respected business leaders, their CEOs are significantly less likely to see them this way (Flint 2004).

- *The rising bar of expectations.* One of the biggest frustrations is that IT expectations are constantly shifting. While surveys show that there have been significant improvements in many aspects of IT's work, overall impressions of IT remain negative (Anonymous 2002; Willcoxson and Chatham 2004). One study noted that "at the micro level of individual service and communication, the IT-business relationship is much healthier than it was. However, considerable work needs to be done at the macro level in promoting understanding of IT's capacity and potential across the organization" (Anonymous 2002). The phenomenon that improvements in the business-IT relationship at the individual level are not necessarily reflected in overall perceptions of IT was first noted more than twenty years ago (Smith 1990).

Each of these factors suggests that the overall image or brand of IT is enduringly negative, in spite of ongoing efforts to improve it with individual stakeholders and groups. This reflects a wider principle of managing perceptions noted by the Reputation Institute (cited in Martinez and Norman 2004):

> . . . various stakeholders [can] have different images of the firm based on differing values, expectations, and experiences. In contrast, reputation is the **aggregate, overall attractiveness of the [function] to all constituents.** Notably, although experiences . . . may be most meaningful at the individual level, they cannot be aggregated at the stakeholder level. (emphasis added)

In short, it seems that the image of IT and its reputation in the organization arise from a set of *shared* perceptions among all stakeholder groups that exist over and above those at the individual level.

Therefore, it is important to understand and manage business's perceptions of IT *as a whole* and how IT *as a whole* perceives and presents itself to the business. The following are some common perceptions of the IT function as articulated by the focus group and various studies (Overby 2005):

- IT costs too much.
- IT takes too long to deliver.
- IT fails to deliver competitive differentiation.
- IT is not aligned with business strategy.
- IT doesn't do the right things.
- IT doesn't do things right.
- IT doesn't add value.
- IT is a barrier to change.
- IT is inflexible.

While these may or may not be valid, because people *act* on their perceptions, there are consequences to the organization (e.g., poor decisions, inefficiencies, and missed opportunities) if IT does not make an effort to address and manage existing perceptions of IT.

THE ROOT CAUSES OF PERCEPTIONS OF IT

In our earlier research into how IT is viewed by the rest of the organization, we suggested that an organization's needs for IT essentially parallel Maslow's hierarchy of needs (McKeen and Smith 1996). Maslow suggested that people are motivated by five sets of needs—(1) physiological, (2) safety, (3) love and belonging, (4) esteem, (5) and self-actualization—represented as a pyramid (Thierauf, Klekamp, and Geeding 1977). Only after lower-level needs are met can an individual concentrate on needs at the next highest level. Thus, physiological needs take priority over all others. The first four levels are "deficiency needs" meaning that the individual does not feel anything if they are met but feels anxious and increasingly frustrated if they are *not* met (Wikipedia 2007). Over time, these feelings can turn into hostility toward the source of frustration. The highest level, self-actualization, contains growth needs, which when fulfilled, do not go away but motivate the individual further. However, if lower-level needs cease being met (e.g., as in a natural disaster or a war), then the individual will stop striving to meet higher-level needs and will refocus on meeting survival needs (McKeen and Smith 1996).

We described a similar but simplified three-level pyramid for addressing the organization's IT needs:

- *Level I needs.* At the most basic level, organizations require a **competent** IT organization that delivers basic IT services to the business. In order to be considered competent, IT must demonstrate that it can consistently deliver cost-efficient services as well as essential security, reliability, and integrity of data.
- *Level II needs.* At the next level, organizations need a **credible** IT organization that delivers high-quality systems that meet real organizational goals on time and on budget.
- *Level III needs.* After credibility has been established, organizations need an IT **partner** to help guide and direct the organization's use of technology to achieve the organization's strategic objectives.

As with Maslow's hierarchy, we suggested that even if an IT organization is acting as a business partner, failure to meet lower-level needs will refocus the business on addressing those needs and could result in anxiety and frustration, which, in turn, could manifest itself in hostility toward IT (McKeen and Smith 1996). The focus group concurred that this analysis is still sound and that IT's failure to consistently address lower-level needs could be the source of many of the ongoing negative perceptions of IT. "They never forget that screw-up," said one manager. Another noted, "If nothing breaks, we're credible." "Everyone wants to be at level III," said a third, "but it's based on credibility; you must do what you say you will do."

More contemporary analysis of business needs at the first two levels shows that IT has made significant strides in being perceived as capable and credible in the past two decades (Anonymous 2002; Deloitte 2004; Overby 2005; Pastore and Cosgrove 2005). Service-level agreements, benchmarking, cost transparency, project management offices, and improved tools and technologies for system development have all helped to address many of the challenges that IT faced a decade ago. Unfortunately, important *new* challenges have helped undermine IT's image at these two layers. The advent of the Internet and online crime, heightened appreciation for security in a post-9/11 world, compliance laws and regulations, the increased visibility of IT errors when online systems fail, and the growing vulnerability of organizations because of their dependence on IT have all raised the bar on what is needed from a competent IT organization (Smith and McKeen 2006). Similarly, credibility involves a great deal more than it did ten years ago. Today's IT projects are considerably more complex than those of the past in that they involve many more elements, such as risk management; integration across multiple platforms and business units; anywhere, anytime access; customercentric services; information and content management; and adherence to numerous laws, regulations, and standards. Multiple stakeholder groups are typically involved as well, including different business units, outsourcers, various IT functions (e.g., architecture), and sometimes vendors or other third parties. At the same time, hardware, software, and development tools; methods; and practices are constantly changing.

The result is that staying a competent and credible IT function is a bit like walking along the shifting floors of a fun house; the ground keeps moving, and you're never sure what's going to jump out at you! Yet these are simply fundamentals for most IT organizations today. The real challenge is how to leverage the skills, capabilities, and investment the organization has in its IT department. Today competence and credibility are simply not enough to admit IT to the inner circle of business decision making.

Also, we now understand the nature of the business's higher-lever needs (i.e., partnership) in a much more nuanced fashion. There is now widespread recognition that business and IT need strong, positive interpersonal interactions before they can truly work together to make decisions for the organization (Jaska and Hogan 2006; Pastore and Cosgrove 2005; Tallon, Kraemer, and Gurbaxani 2000; Willcoxson and Chatham 2004). To paraphrase Maslow, the business needs to feel that IT is "part of the family" and will keep its best interests at heart. In turn, these relationships form the foundation on which trust is built. Corresponding to Maslow's "esteem layer," trust is a condition of mutual respect and confidence. As a result, competence, credibility, relationships, and trust are considered "deficiency needs" in that, when they are present, they are not noticed, but when absent, frustration, miscommunication, dysfunctional behavior, and ultimately negativity result. As one manager commented, "When things are going well, no one notices." Finally, there is a need for business value, or the self-actualization of the organization as characterized by innovation, the ability to learn from failures and mistakes, problem-solving, and proactiveness. Together, these suggest that the IT hierarchy of needs more closely parallels Maslow's than we previously thought (see Figure 4.1). Therefore, our original level III has been split into three new higher-level business needs, which are described in more detail below:

- *New level III need: relationship.* It is clear that IT is still not accepted as "part of the family" in many organizations. "We want to be loved, but we're still viewed as techies," said one manager. "The business views IT differently than other parts of the organization," said another. There is wide agreement that relationships are essential to changing perceptions. One researcher noted that IT managers are left out of decision making because of their naïveté about how relationships work at the highest levels of the business (Anonymous 2002). Experts point out the importance of a strong CIO-CEO relationship (Flint 2004; Prewitt 2005) and have noted that relationships are important because mutual understanding, interests, and expectations are formed and shaped during interpersonal interaction leading to business-IT alignment (Gold 2006). Often the need for relationship is described as a need for more communication to ensure that goals are fully understood and acted upon (Tallon, Kraemer, and Gurbaxani 2000). In general, there is a perception that IT and the business need to move closer together so they can act as a team (Pastore and Cosgrove 2005). Research shows that having a deep understanding of (and identification with) the organization is strongly associated with positive perceptions of the impact of IT (Jaska and Hogan 2006). This is why so many IT organizations have created roles for relationship managers whose job is to represent IT to the business, understand business needs, and ultimately to align the two (Young 2005). "It's all about relationships," said a manager. "We need to get out there with the business, have lunch, and talk with them. This really makes a difference."

Figure 4.1 The IT Hierarchy of Needs

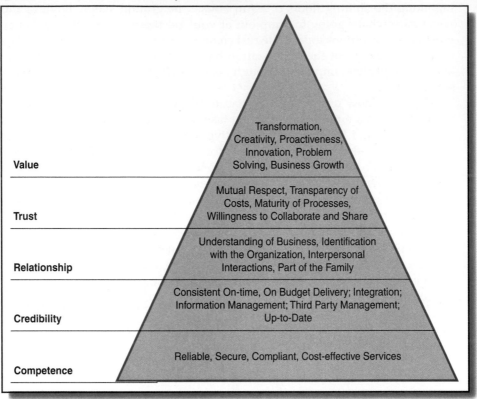

- *New level IV need: trust.* While relationships build interpersonal trust, trust in the IT function itself is also needed. At this level, both business and IT staff must trust IT's processes, leaders, and plans. One manager described an example of how a lack of trust is manifested in her organization: "There's a feeling that IT is self-serving. The users say, 'We did the package selection ourselves because we knew you wouldn't come up with it.'" IT's processes are notoriously convoluted and bureaucratic, leaving the business unsure of how to accomplish their business strategies with IT (McKeen and Smith 2001; Smith, McKeen, and Singh 2007). From strategy alignment to prioritization to budgeting and resourcing to delivering value to managing ongoing costs, it must be clear that what IT is doing is for the benefit of the enterprise, not itself. This is why so many experts recommend transparency of costs and improved communication about IT's value (Levinson and Pastore 2005; Overby 2005; Prewitt 2005). Similarly, developing more mature processes to carry out the work of IT and effective leadership is often cited as the precursor to delivering business value (Gerrard 2004; Young 2005). Before real value can be achieved, IT and the business must have mutual respect for each other's skills and abilities and be willing to defer to each other's area of expertise. It is a lack of trust that often leads business managers to question IT costs or to make "end runs" around IT. Trust is built on agreement on four elements: (1) the role of IT, (2) that it's doing things right, (3) that it's doing the right things, (4) and that it's positioning the organization well for the future (Deloitte 2004; McKeen and Smith 2003). Trust is also essential because of the increasing ambiguity, uncertainty, and complexity of IT work and the growing need for business-IT collaboration (Anonymous 2002; Mack 2006; Willcoxson and Chatham 2004).

• *New level V need: value.*   The goal of addressing the four "deficiency needs" is, of course, to get to the point where IT can deliver real business value to the organization. Researchers have found that business executives can pinpoint areas in the organization where IT is creating value and that these perceptual measures correlate strongly with more traditional objective measures (Apfel 2006; Tallon, Kraemer, and Gurbaxani 2000). Studies also show that CEOs want their IT organizations to deliver value more consistently (Prewitt 2005). Business is looking for IT to provide transformational leadership, to offer innovative and creative solutions to business problems, and to leverage existing investments in technology (Smith and McKeen 2006). Yet poor perceptions of how well IT delivers value often result in tentative IT investments and underuse of technology by the business, which, in turn, can further undermine an organization's competitive position (Gerrard 2004).

Addressing these three new layers of need while remaining competent and credible represents the crux of the challenge for IT in managing the business's perceptions. The next section will address some ways that IT functions can measure and work to change perceptions at these levels.

MANAGING PERCEPTIONS

"Managing perceptions is a daily challenge," one manager said with a sigh. "They always want to know what you've done for them lately." There is no shortage of suggestions about how to better manage poor business perceptions of IT and just as much disagreement about what should be done. What is clear is that managing perceptions actually consists of three steps: (1) understanding current perceptions, (2) addressing perceptual problems, and (3) monitoring perceptions on an ongoing basis. All IT organizations should, therefore, have strategies in place for dealing with each of these.

1. *Understanding current perceptions.*   It is often confusing to IT leaders that individual perceptions of IT appear to be good but overall perceptions remain negative (Anonymous 2002). As noted above, overall perceptions are not necessarily built one by one (although this won't hurt). Instead, IT needs mechanisms for understanding *aggregate* perceptions. While it may seem odd to some to measure overall perceptions, rather than use more objective measures, there are two important reasons for doing so. First, perceptions, whether accurate or not, *are* important because they guide behavior at a subconscious level (Gladwell 2005). Second, perceptions have been shown to be surprisingly accurate measures of actuality (Tallon, Kraemer, and Gurbaxani 2000).

   Current perceptions can be captured in both qualitative and quantitative ways, such as through surveys, focus groups, or interviews (Gold 2006). However,

IT managers tend to distrust formal surveys as not capturing meaningful dimensions of the business-IT relationship (Smith 2006). "I'm not convinced formal surveys touch on perceptions," said a manager. Another added, "The best indicator of how the business feels about you is how the users wave at you at night. Metrics simply don't get at perceptions."

A good starting point for understanding perceptions is often a simple assessment of overall feelings and beliefs based on a short set of "impressionistic" questions (McKeen and Smith 1996; McKeen and Smith 2003; Smith 2006). These can be supplemented with comments or interviews, if more detail is needed. Questions can be based on the "IT hierarchy of needs" outlined above, or they can relate to a set of categories identified by the organization (e.g., behaviors and attitudes, leadership, and execution excellence). Appendixes A and B provide two different samples of assessment tools, which have been successfully used by practitioners to get at perceptions in the business-IT relationship. Such tools can be used by IT alone, by pairs of IT and business managers, or by business managers alone. In all cases, however, for the reasons outlined above, it is essential to focus on overall impressions, rather than on individual relationships.

2. *Addressing perceptual problems.*   Once perceptions at this level are understood, they can be "educated, trained, and controlled" (Gladwell 2005). There is no single best way to do this. "We're each trying to hit the target and using a variety of approaches," said a manager. There are certainly many lists of activities IT should be doing to resolve negative perceptions (see Jaska and Hogan 2006; Mack 2006; Pastore and Cosgrove 2005 for some of these). However, participants suggested that generalized marketing programs have not been effective, and this belief is also borne out by practitioner surveys (Pastore and Cosgrove 2005). Three approaches for addressing perceptual problems were recommended:

   a. *Ensure that the IT function understands and practices a set of core IT values.* These should be established, communicated, and monitored by the IT leadership team, who should take accountability for IT's image in the rest of the organization. IT's brand should be consistent across the function and reflected in its leadership, daily activities, and processes.

   b. *Build from the bottom up.*   While all IT organizations want to deliver innovation, creativity, and business value, the business will not accept these types of initiatives unless IT is already addressing its lower-level needs. Efforts to address perceptions should, therefore, start from the bottom up, ensuring that IT is considered competent and credible, has good relationships, and is trusted as a function.

   c. *Use focused metrics and communication to retrain perceptions.*   IT organizations often err on the side of providing too many metrics and too much communication, which is why scorecards and dashboards have become so popular with business executives (Kaplan and Norton 1996; McKeen and Smith 2003; Smith, McKeen, and Street 2004). Once the IT leadership team has targeted a set of needs to address, more focused efforts can be employed. For example, if IT is not trusted as a function, internal initiatives can streamline processes and make costs and service levels more transparent. Communications and metrics may then be used to effectively correct misperceptions or clarify confusion. Education should also be used selectively, for example, to help business leaders better understand what IT is doing in this area. "We must be honest with our message," said a manager, "but we can use communication and education to interpret situations for the business."

3. *Monitor perceptions on an ongoing basis.* While value should always be the objective of all IT activities, we suggest that *perceptions* of the value IT adds will become increasingly positive as IT addresses lower-level business needs. To this end, IT should monitor perceptions of value with every new initiative (Apfel 2006). A key means of monitoring perceptions is with informal "check-ins" with business leaders. One participant stressed that IT managers should make regular opportunities to interact casually with their business colleagues. He believes "management by walking around" will help deal with many problem perceptions—both those that are real and those that are the result of faulty interpretations. Another informal indicator is "how much the CFO hassles us." More formal assessments of overall perceptions should be done annually, using one of the tools suggested above. These will help demonstrate trends and show where management efforts are working or need improvement. However they are monitored, perceptions should be assessed and discussed regularly by the IT management team and viewed as appropriate and valuable indicators of how well IT is serving the needs of the organization and delivering value.

CONCLUSION

In spite of significant achievements in its delivery of services, negative perceptions of IT persist. In addition, these perceptions tend to be undervalued by IT managers who, possibly because of their training, prefer harder and more objective assessments of their performance. This chapter has shown that positive perceptions of IT must be built by addressing four layers of business need: (1) competence, (2) credibility, (3) relationships, and (4) trust, in this order. Failing to meet these needs will likely reinforce existing negative perceptions and result in an inability to deliver real business value. Understanding and managing perceptions is, therefore, at least as important for IT managers as dealing with the "hard numbers" and should command more of their effort and attention than it has to date.

REFERENCES

Anonymous. "Senior IT People Excluded from IT Decision-making." *Career Development International* 7, no. 6/7 (2002): 377–78.

Apfel, A. "Findings: Perception Can Be Reality When It Comes to Forecasting the Business Value of IT." *Gartner Research* G00143472 (September 21, 2006).

Busch, E., S. Jarvenpaa, N. Tractinsky, and W. Glick. "External versus Internal Perspective in Determining a Firm's Progressive Use of Information Technology." Proceedings of the 12th International Conference on Information Systems, New York, 1991.

Deloitte Development. "Eliminating Roadblocks to IT and Business Alignment." *CIO Advertising Supplement* (2004).

Flint, D. "Senior Executives Don't Always Realize the True Value of IT." *Gartner Research* COM-22-5499 (June 21, 2004).

Gerrard, M. "Four Giant Steps to Maximize the Business Value of IT." *Gartner Research* G00124196 (December 22, 2004).

Gladwell, M. *Blink: The Power of Thinking without Thinking.* New York: Little Brown and Company, 2005.

Gold, R. "Perception *Is* Reality: Why Subjective Measures Matter, and How to Maximize Their Impact." *Harvard Business School Publishing Balanced Scorecard Report* July–August (2006).

Jaska, P., and P. Hogan. "Effective Management of the Information Technology Function." *Management Research News* 29, no. 8 (2006).

Kaplan, R., and D. Norton. *The Balanced Scorecard.* Boston: Harvard Business School Press, 1996.

Levinson, M., and R. Pastore. "Transparency Helps Align IT with Business." *CIO Magazine* (June 1, 2005).

Mack, R. "IT Organizations Must Build Four Cornerstones to Establish Credibility with Business Partners." *Gartner Research* G00142119 (September 20, 2006).

Martinez, R., and P. Norman. "Whither Reputation? The Effects of Different Stakeholders." *Harvard Business Review* September (2004): 25–32.

McKeen, J., and H. Smith. *Management Challenges in IS: Successful Strategies and Appropriate Action.* Chichester, England: John Wiley & Sons, 1996.

———. "IT Project Prioritization." *IT Management Forum* 11, no. 2 (2001).

———. *Making IT Happen: Critical Issues in IT Management.* Chichester, England: John Wiley & Sons, 2003.

Moore, J., and M. Love. "IT Professionals as Organizational Citizens." *Communications of the ACM* 48, no. 6 (June 2005).

Overby, S. "Turning IT Doubters into True Believers: IT Value." *CIO Magazine* (June 1, 2005).

Pastore, R., and L. Cosgrove. "Turning IT Doubters into True Believers: Executive Summary." *CIO Research Reports* (June 1, 2005).

Prewitt, E. "The Communication Gap." *CIO Magazine* (June 1, 2005).

Rossiter, J., and L. Percy. *Advertising and Promotion Management,* New York: McGraw-Hill, 1987.

Schrage, M. "The Right Question." *CIO Magazine* (August 15, 2006).

Smith, H. A. "The User/Information Systems Relationship: A Study of Power and Attitudes." *Journal of Information Technology Management* 1, no. 2 (1990).

———. "Business Partner Reviews." Presentation to the SIM Advanced Practices Council, Chicago, 2006.

Smith, H. A., and J. D. McKeen. "IT in 2010." *MIS Quarterly Executive* 5, no. 3 (September 2006): 125–36.

Smith, H. A., J. D. McKeen, and S. Singh. "Developing IT Strategy for Business Value." *Journal of Information Technology Management* XVIII, no. 1 (June 2007): 49–58.

Smith, H. A., and J. D. McKeen, and C. Street. "Linking IT to Business Metrics." *Journal of Information Science and Technology* 1, no. 1 (2004): 13–26.

Tallon, P., K. Kraemer, and V. Gurbaxani. "Executives' Perceptions of the Business Value of Information Technology: A Process-oriented Approach." *Journal of Management Information Systems* 16, no. 4 (Spring 2000): 145–73.

Thierauf, R., R. Klekamp, and D. Geeding. *Management Principles and Practices: A Contingency and Questionnaire Approach.* Santa Barbara: John Wiley & Sons, 1977.

Willcoxson, L., and R. Chatham. "Progress in the IT/Business Relationship: A Longitudinal Assessment." *Journal of Information Technology* 19, no. 1 (March 2004).

Wikipedia. "Abraham Maslow." http://en.wikipedia.org/wiki/Abraham_Maslow (accessed February 13, 2007).

Young, C. "Relationship Management Is More Than Critical, It's Pivotal." *Gartner Research* G00129613 (October 25, 2005).

Suggested Indicators of How Positively IT Is Perceived

Competence

IT services are considered reliable and high quality by the business.

Migration to new technology is managed effectively.

Our infrastructure supports our current business needs.

Our service levels are consistently high.

Credibility

IT provides technological leadership to the organization.

Our middle-level business managers are strong supporters of information systems.

The IT department consistently meets its commitments to users.

Project management is one of our core competencies.

Relationship

IT and line management share the responsibility for delivering IT projects.

The IT department is consulted about most business decisions.

IT staff understand the business well.

Employees from the IT department are actively recruited by other areas of the business.

Trust

IT plans are closely tied to the organization's strategic plans.

The IT leadership team has a unified vision of its mission and values.

The organization considers IT leadership to be strong.

The role of IT has been clearly articulated to the organization.

Value

IT investments are positioning the firm well for the future.

IT is actively involved in the organization's long-term planning activities.

Our CIO is a member of the organization's senior management team.

Top executives consider IT to be a source of strategic advantage.

Appendix B

Business Partner Review
(after Smith 2006)

These reviews are a facilitated dialogue between matched pairs of IT and business leaders and are designed to capture overall perceptions in the business-IT relationship. Each pair of leaders has a working relationship with each other, but as a group, different parts of the organization and different levels of the relationship are represented. The pair discusses a set of ten questions in a ninety-minute face-to-face conversation. Each question specifically relates to a mutual goal for the business-IT partnership, as determined through preliminary interviews (see below for a sample set of questions). Together, the pair must agree on a mutual grade (using a five-point scale) for each question. In addition, the facilitator captures any relevant comments. Results are rolled up and averaged to provide a rating for the relationship in each category, as well as an overall average and a summary of comments. Specific questions can change year by year, but the categories of perception stay the same.

Behaviors & Attitudes	• Do the business and IT effectively collaborate, sharing information, resources, and expertise to accomplish our objectives?
	• Do we effectively collaborate, sharing information, resources, and expertise to accomplish our objectives?
	• Do we display a "can-do attitude," sense of urgency, inclusion, and flexibility?
Technology Leadership	• Does IT demonstrate and apply insight into leading-edge technologies?
	• Does IT envision alternatives and introduce ideas that meet the needs of the business?
Execution Excellence	• Do we (the business and IT) assume joint accountability for arriving at solutions that meet both our needs?
	• Do we define the best mix of capability, cost, and schedule to maximize the value to the business?
	• De we appropriately staff our projects, using the right people with the right skills at the right level?
	• Do we communicate relevant issues with appropriate advance notice and adequate information given?
	• Do we meet our project commitments with regard to scope, schedule, and budget?

IT Leadership at MaxTrade

Richard Fanning surveyed his home office gloomily as he pondered the disaster before him. He'd just completed a month's worth of fact-finding on the state of IT at his newest client, MaxTrade, and he was beginning to realize just how deep the company's IT problems were. As an IT turnaround specialist, Richard was often asked to take on difficult CIO positions on a temporary basis, and he was used to facing management challenges, but MaxTrade (if he took the job, and he wasn't sure yet if he would) would be the toughest of his career. "How could this have happened?" he asked himself. "Money certainly isn't the issue." The company was spending lots . . . but on what? There was no IT plan. Backup and recovery planning was minimal. System outages were increasing. The internal auditors' reports were highly critical of the rapidly escalating operational risks.

MaxTrade is a brokerage firm set up to make extensive use of IT. It was founded by a career entrepreneur who provided the initial inspiration but is no longer involved in daily operations. CEO Bruce Robinson, who holds the next-largest share, developed the company and oversaw its impressive growth. The firm now has six divisions: besides research and analysis, institutional trading, and investment banking, it has other business units that are responsible for different types of trading accounts. Online trading allows clients to make their own trades; discount trading fills buy and sell orders but offers no investment advice; wealth management provides full service. Clients may also view their accounts online without making any trades.

The company is highly profitable; the bottom line is the first consideration in every decision. As Robinson explained to Richard in their first interview, "The one thing that people in this industry are clear about is that they're all in business to make money." And short-term thinking is the order of the day. "In this business long-term planning is where we're going to go for lunch," remarked one business executive

Richard interviewed during his fact-finding. In the volatile and dynamic world in which Max-Trade operates, priorities are constantly changing and whole business units have to be able to turn on a dime to take advantage of new opportunities. Staff make real-time decisions that could make or cost the firm millions of dollars. The risks are extremely high. A solid IT infrastructure, available 100 percent of the time, is essential.

At first, MaxTrade's IT was handled by a CTO, but it had clearly outgrown his capabilities. The initial technology requirements were straightforward: get an online brokerage off the ground by bringing the required technologies together to provide an online trading platform. As the company grew, however, it became evident to the CEO that he was the wrong person to develop the IT department beyond its infant state. Many poor decisions were made, resulting in the waste of hundreds of thousands of dollars in unutilized software licenses, server capacity, and development. Sour relationships with vendors resulted in frequent switching and an integration nightmare.

"Over the last two years, no one was happy—not the business unit heads, not the users, not the CTO," Robinson told Richard. "Finally, he resigned and for the past three months, we've been looking for someone to take the job of CIO. But we're in such a mess, it's been a tough sell. What I need is to have you get us on track again within the next twelve months. You'll have my support, of course, and you'll report to me, but you'll need to get the business unit heads on board as well. They have a lot of independence here at MaxTrade because of the money they make for us. You've got to convince them they can make more money your way than the way things are today."

Richard considered the company's current situation. It was no wonder they couldn't find anyone to take the job, he thought. At present, the politics involved in determining what IT worked on were so sensitive that no one in IT dared to say no to any new project. As a result, IT had 932 projects on the books that the users *thought* were all being worked on, even though the company had only 152 IT people to do development. Morale was at rock bottom. Turnover was approaching 50 percent annually.

The senior management at MaxTrade clearly felt as though they were standing on a "burning platform" with regard to IT. They were looking to Richard to turn things around, but the question was, did he want the job? Surveying the scope of the problem, the answer was clearly no. The situation was dire, and it was going to be next to impossible to get the whole thing working properly. And yet . . . he could see how much they needed a solution. He had spent hours talking to people in all parts of the company, and he *knew* he could make a difference not only to the organization's future, but to the lives of many of its staff. And despite the ghastly experiences he knew were yet to be discovered, he also knew that he'd always be sorry if he let such a challenge go by. He picked up the phone to call Robinson. "I'll do it," he told him. "But let's get started before I recover my sanity and change my mind."

The necessary first steps were clear, and Richard's first month as temporary CIO was as brutal as he had expected. He began by doing a thorough assessment of the current technology situation at the company. At the same time, he spent long hours in all parts of the firm, getting to know both the business and the people involved. He logged many twelve- to fourteen-hour days, speaking with users, sitting with them and learning what they did, going on sales calls, and finding out firsthand the issues they faced on the job. Socializing was part of this work too, to build up the trust that would be the foundation for the difficult job ahead. "This is something I always do when I start at a new company," he explained to Robinson. "Many IT people don't do this, but there is no substitute for spending the time to get to know the business well."

Eight weeks into his time with MaxTrade, he at least had the basis of an action plan in mind, but it would take all his leadership skills to pull it off. He believed that the company was not going to be able to use IT effectively in an increasingly competitive marketplace or even keep up with simple business requests unless a number of key changes were made—especially how IT work was done and how decisions about it were made. "These are tough people. Not all of them are going to be receptive to my ideas," he said to himself. "I'm going to have to put my job on the line to get them to do it differently."

Never one to pull punches, Richard also had to deliver some tough messages to senior management about systems development. Not only did he need their support for some fairly drastic actions, but he had to get them thinking differently about their own business if he were going to make any headway in delivering new functionality. It was a hard reality that not all 932 projects could be worked on. Somehow the resources available would have to be made to match the work to be done.

The tough talk would have to continue within IT to ensure that it could deliver on these projects. What was needed soon was a culture of customer service to the users of what IT provided. "The immediate challenge here," he explained to Robinson, "is to build a team capable of providing innovative solutions on a timely basis and to start treating the business units as customers. We have to convince everyone that we all work together and IT is committed to building a partnership with them."

"It's going to take a lot to make IT credible enough for that to happen," Robinson answered, "but, as I said before, you can count on my support."

"OK," Richard said, "this is what the action plan is going to look like . . ." ∎

DISCUSSION QUESTIONS

The CEO Robinson tells Richard, "What I need is to have you get us on track again within the next twelve months."

1. What does it mean to be "on track"?

2. What are the next steps?

3. Is one year achievable? Why or why not?

MINI CASE

Investing in TUFS

"Why do I keep this around?" Martin Drysdale wondered. "It infuriates me every time I see all that satisfaction over something that is now the bane of my existence."

He looked gloomily at the offending photo, which showed the project team happily "clinking" pop cans and coffee cups in a toast: "Here's to TUFS!" The Technical Underwriting Financial System (TUFS) was the largest single investment in IT ever made by Northern Insurance, and it was going to transform Northern by streamlining the underwriting processes and providing strategic e-business capabilities. The TUFS team had brought the project in on time and on budget, so the party was a thank-you for all of the team's dedicated, hard work. But it was two years ago when the camera captured the happy moment for posterity, and Martin, CIO for Northern, had celebrated with the rest.

"Yeah, right," Martin grimaced as he turned from the photo to the e-mail message on his computer screen, summoning him to a meeting with his boss that morning to discuss TUFS. The system had turned into a nightmare in its first few months of operation. Now his job was on the line. What was supposed to have brought efficiency to the underwriting process and new opportunities for top-line growth had become a major corporate money pit. TUFS was still eating up the vast majority of Northern's IT budget and resources to fix the underwriting errors that kept appearing, and resistance to the system had grown from sniping and grumbling into calls for Martin's head. "No wonder we're not saving any money, though, with senior underwriting managers still insisting on receiving some of their old reports, even though TUFS lets them look up the same information online anytime they want," Martin fumed. The meeting with the CFO was to discuss TUFS and the company's "very significant investment in this system." Feeling like a condemned prisoner on his way to the gallows, Martin grabbed his suit jacket, straightened his tie, and headed up to the seventh floor executive suite.

An hour later Martin was feeling very well grilled as he was confronted with a long list of the problems with TUFS. The CFO, Melissa Freeman, had done her homework. Before her was a binder full of TUFS documentation, stretching back almost three years from when the project had been first identified. "According to my calculations, Northern has spent almost $4 million on this system, if you include all of the resources dedicated to fixing the problems identified *after* implementation," she noted. "And I have yet to see any cost savings in the underwriting department. Why?"

"It's true that there have been some unanticipated changes to the system that have cost us, but the underwriters have never bought into the system," Martin conceded. "They insist on following their old procedures and then using the system at the last possible moment as a 'double-check.' What can we do if they won't use the system the way it was designed?"

"Could there *possibly* be a reason why they don't like the system?" Freeman asked. "It seems to me from looking at these change reports that the system hasn't been meeting our basic underwriting needs."

Martin acknowledged that there had been some problems. "But my guys are technicians, not underwriters. They didn't get much participation from the underwriters in the first place. The underwriting department wouldn't take the time to bring my people up to speed on what they needed and why. As well, we were facing a very tight deadline, which meant that we had to defer some of the functionality we had originally intended to include. That was senior management's decision, and everyone was informed about it when it was made." He added that they were now asking for a TUFS training program and a help desk to handle questions that underwriters might face while using the system!

"A help desk and training program weren't in our original plan," Martin reminded Freeman. "These 'extras' are eating away at the system's benefits." According to the business case prepared by the users, TUFS was supposed to pay for itself over its first two years of operations from savings realized from the underwriting process. The system's problems certainly accounted for some of the extra costs, but the users hadn't made any of the process changes that would help those savings be realized. "They think we can just plug in the system and cost savings will appear like magic. And other parts of the system are going to take time to deliver benefits."

The "other parts" he was referring to were the e-business capabilities that TUFS provided. "If you will recall, this system was approved in the days when we *had* to have e-business or we were going to be dinosaurs. In retrospect, we could have cut back on this functionality more easily and left some of the underwriting functionality in, but who knew?"

"Well, as you know, our financial resources are very limited at present." Freeman leaned forward. "I've been asked to make some recommendations to the executive committee about whether or not we should put more money into this system. TUFS has been our number one priority for two years now, and there are quite a few people saying that enough is enough—that we need to make some major changes around here."

Martin took a deep breath, waiting for the ax to fall. Freeman continued, "What I need to know now from you is this:

- What went wrong with our TUFS investment, and what can we do to prevent these problems in the future?
- What do we need to do to realize the benefits that were projected for TUFS?
- How can we measure these benefits?
- How can we best decide how to apportion our IT budget between TUFS and these other projects?"

As he slowly exhaled and felt his pulse resume, Martin nodded. "I've got some ideas. Can I get them to you in writing by the end of the week?" ■

DISCUSSION QUESTIONS

1. What went wrong with the TUFS investment, and what can be done to prevent these problems in the future?

2. What does Northern need to do to realize the benefits that were projected for TUFS?
3. How can they measure these benefits?

IT Planning at ModMeters

Brian Smith, CIO of ModMeters, groaned inwardly as he listened to CEO John Johnson wrapping up his remarks. "So our executive team thinks there are real business opportunities for us in developing these two new strategic thrusts. But before I go to the board for final approval next month, I need to know that our IT, marketing, and sales plans will support us all the way," Johnson concluded.

Brian mentally calculated the impact these new initiatives would have on his organization. He had heard rumors from his boss, the COO, that something big was coming down. He had even been asked his opinion about whether these strategies were technically doable, *theoretically*. But *both* at once? Resources—people, time, and money—were tight, as usual. ModMeters was making a reasonable profit, but the CFO, Stan Abrams, had always kept the lid screwed down tightly on IT spending. Brian had to fight for every dime. How he was going to find the wherewithal to support not one but *two* new strategic initiatives, he didn't know.

The other VPs at this strategy presentation were smiling. Taking ModMeters global from a North American operation seemed to be a logical next step for the company. Its products, metering components of all types, were highly specialized and in great demand by such diverse customers as utility companies, manufacturers, and a host of other industries. Originally founded as Modern Meters, the firm had grown steadily as demand for its metering expertise and components had grown over the past century or so. Today ModMeters was the largest producer of metering components in the world with a full range of both mechanical and, now, digital products. Expanding into meter assembly with plants in Asia and Eastern Europe was a good plan, thought Brian, but he wasn't exactly sure how he was going to get the infrastructure in place to support it. "Many of these countries simply don't have the telecommunications and equipment we are going to need, and

the training and new systems we have to put in place are going to be substantial," he said.

But it was the second strategic thrust that was going to give him nightmares, he predicted. How on earth did they expect him to put direct-to-customer sales in place so they could sell "green" electric meters to individual users? His attention was jerked back to the present by a flashy new logo on an easel that the CEO had just unveiled.

"In keeping with our updated strategy, may I present our new name—MM!" Johnson announced portentously.

"Oh, this is just great," thought Brian. "Now I have to go into every single application and every single document this company produces and change our name!"

Because of its age and scientific orientation, ModMeters (as he still preferred to call it) had been in the IT business a long time. Starting back in the early 1960s, the company had gradually automated almost every aspect of its business from finance and accounting to supply-chain management. About the only thing it didn't have was a fancy Web site for consumers, although even *that* was about to change. Today ModMeters had systems reflecting just about every era of computers from punch cards to PCs. Unfortunately, the company never seemed to have the resources to invest in reengineering its existing systems. It just layered more systems on top of the others. A diagram of all the interactions among systems looked like a plate of spaghetti. There was *no way* they were going to be able to support two new strategic thrusts with their current budget levels, he thought as he applauded the new design along with the others. "Next week's IT budget meeting is going to be a doozy!"

Sure enough, the following week found them all, except for the CEO, back in the same meeting room, ready to do battle. Holding his fire, Brian waited until each of the VPs had presented their essential IT initiatives. In addition to what needed to be done to support the new business strategies, each division had a full laundry list of essentials for maintaining the *current* business of the firm. Even Abrams had got into the act this year because of new legislation that gave the firm's outside auditors immense scope to peer into the inner workings of every financial and governance process the organization had.

After listening carefully to each speaker in turn, Brian stood up. "As many of you know, we have always been cautious about how we spend our IT budget. We have been given a budget that is equal to 2 percent of revenues, which seriously limits what we in IT have been able to do for the company. Every year we spend a lot of time paring our project list down to bare bones, and every year we make do with a patchwork of infrastructure investments. We are now at the point where 80 percent of our budget in IT is fixed. Here's how we spend our money." Brian clicked on a PowerPoint presentation showing a multicolored pie chart.

"This large chunk in blue is just about half our budget," he stated. "This is simply the cost of keeping the lights on—running our systems and replacing a bare minimum of equipment. The red chunk is about 30 percent of the pie. This is the stuff we *have* to do—fixing errors, dealing with changes mandated by government and our own industry, and providing essential services like the help desk. How we divide up the remainder of the pie is what this meeting is all about."

Brian clicked to a second slide showing a second pie chart. "As you know, we have typically divided up the remaining IT budget proportionately, according to who has the biggest overall operating budget. This large pink chunk is you, Fred." Brian gestured at Fred Tompkins, head of manufacturing and the most powerful executive in the room. It was his division that made the firm's profit. The pink chunk easily took up more than half of the pie. Tompkins smiled. Brian went on, pointing out the slice that each part of the firm had been allotted in the previous year. "Finally, we come to Harriet and Brenda," he said with a smile. Harriet Simpson and Brenda Barnes were the VPs of human resources and marketing, respectively. Their tiny slivers were barely visible—just a few percent of the total budget.

"This approach to divvying up our IT budget may have served us well over the years,"—Brian didn't think it had, but he wasn't going to fight past battles—"however, we all heard what John said last week, and this approach to budgeting doesn't give us *any* room to develop our new strategies *or* cover our new infrastructure or staffing needs. While we might get a little more money to obtain some new applications and buy some more computers,"—Abrams nodded slightly—"it won't get us where we need to go in the future."

A third graph went up on the screen, showing the next five years. "If we don't do something *now* to address our IT challenges, within five years our entire IT budget will be eaten up by just operations and maintenance. In the past we have paid minimal attention to our infrastructure or our information and technology architecture or in reengineering our existing systems and processes." A diagram of the "spaghetti" flashed on. "This is what you're asking me to manage in a cost-effective manner. It isn't pretty. We need a better plan for making our systems more robust and flexible. If we are going to be moving in new directions with this firm, the foundation just isn't there. Stan, you *should* be worried that we won't be able to give our auditors what they ask for. But you should also be worried about our risk exposure if one of these systems fails and about how we are going to integrate two new business ventures into this mess."

Tompkins looked up from his papers. It was clear he wasn't pleased with where this presentation was headed. "Well, I, for one, *need* everything I've asked for on my list," he stated flatly. "You can't expect me to be the cash cow of the organization and not enable me to make the money we need to invest elsewhere."

Brian was conciliatory. "I'm not saying that you don't, Fred. I'm just saying that we've been given a new strategic direction from the top and that some things are going to have to change to enable IT to support the whole enterprise better. For example, until now, we have always prioritized divisional IT projects on the basis of ROI. How should we prioritize these new strategic initiatives? Furthermore, these new ventures will require a *lot* of additional infrastructure, so we need to figure out a way to afford this. And right now our systems don't 'talk' to the ones running in other divisions because they don't use the same terminology. But in the future, if we're going to have systems that won't cost increasing amounts of our budget, we are going to have to simplify and integrate them better.

Tompkins clearly hadn't considered the enterprise's needs at all. He scowled but said nothing. Brian continued, "We are being asked to do some new things in the company. Obviously, John hopes there's going to be a payback, but it may take a while. New strategies don't always bear fruit right away." Now looking at Abrams, he said pointedly, "There's more to IT value than short-term profit. Part of our business strategy is to *make* new markets for our company. That requires investment, not only in equipment and product but also in the underlying processes and information we need to manage and monitor that investment."

Harriet Simpson spoke for the first time. "It's like when we hire someone new in R & D. We hire for quality because we want their ideas and innovation, not just a warm body. I think we need to better understand how we are going to translate our five key corporate objectives into IT projects. Yes, we need to make a profit, but Stan needs to satisfy regulators and Brenda's going to be on the hot seat when we start marketing to individuals. And we haven't even spoken about Ted's needs." As the VP of R & D, Ted Kwok was tasked with keeping one or more steps ahead of the competition. New types of products and customer needs would mean expansion in his area as well.

Abrams cleared his throat. "*All* of you are right. As I see it, we are going to have to keep the cash flowing from Fred's area while we expand. But Brian's got a point. We may be being penny-wise and pound-foolish if we don't think things through more carefully. We've put a lot of effort into developing this new strategy, and there *will* be some extra money for IT but not enough to do that plus everything all of you want. We need to retrench and regroup *and* move forward at the same time."

There was silence in the room. Abrams had an annoying way of stating the obvious without really helping to move the ball forward. Brian spoke again. "The way I see it, we have to understand two things before we can really make a new budget. First, we need to figure out how each of the IT projects we've got on the table contributes to one of our key corporate objectives. Second, we need to figure out a way to determine the *value* of each to ModMeters so that we can prioritize it. Then I need to incorporate a reasonable amount of IT regeneration so that we can continue to do new projects at all."

Everyone was nodding now. Brian breathed a small sigh of relief. That was step one accomplished. But step two was going to be harder. "We have a month to get back to the board with our assurances that the IT plan can incorporate the new strategies and what we're going to need in terms of extra funds to do this. As I said earlier, this is *not* just a matter of throwing money at the problem. What we need is a *process* for IT planning and budgeting that will serve us well over the next few years. This process will need to accomplish a number of things:

- It will need to take an *enterprise* perspective on IT. We're all in these new strategies together.
- It will have to incorporate all types of IT initiatives—our new strategies, the needs of Fred and others for the new IT to operate and improve our existing business, Stan's new auditing needs, and our operations and maintenance needs.
- In addition, we *must* find some way of allocating some of the budget to fixing the mess we have in IT right now.
- It must provide a better way to connect new IT work with our corporate objectives.
- It must help us prioritize projects with different types of value.
- Finally, it must ensure we have the business *and* IT resources in place to deliver that value."

Looking at each of his colleagues in turn, he asked, "Now how are we going to do this?" ∎

DISCUSSION QUESTION

Develop an IT planning process for ModMeters to accomplish the demands as set out above.

Chapter 5

IT in the New World of Corporate Governance Reforms[1]

Just when it seemed that IT could breathe a little easier after the craziness of the e-business "bubble" and Y2K, along comes the Sarbanes-Oxley Act (SOX). Designed to protect stockholders, employees, and consumers from inaccurate or misleading financial reports, SOX became law in the United States in July 2002. It makes CEOs and CFOs explicitly responsible for establishing, evaluating, and monitoring the effectiveness of internal controls over financial reporting and disclosure. Any company trading in the United States is subject to these rules. (Subsequently, many other jurisdictions have prepared and are enacting similar legislation.) Along with new privacy laws enacted in the European Union, Canada, and many U.S. states, specific industry controls (e.g., governing pharmaceuticals, certain manufacturing, chemicals, etc.) and new, strict security measures to guard against terrorism, hacking, and illegal Internet activities, *all* organizations are increasingly subject to a growing number of legal acts, regulations, and ethical expectations that weren't even on corporate radar screens a few years ago.

In the past, IT has been only marginally affected by regulatory matters. Most organizations designed their record-keeping systems as they wished, and smart programmers enabled key inputs, such as tax rates, to be easily modified. Today, however, IT is in the middle of the whirlwind of corporate governance reforms. New standards for internal controls are affecting almost every aspect of IT work—from who is able to work on what to IT processes to how work is approved. These, in turn, have significant implications on how IT is managed and IT costs and productivity. For example, many IT organizations have been so involved in developing and implementing SOX procedures that very little has actually been accomplished for the *business* itself.

---

[1]Smith, H. A., and J. D. McKeen, "IT in the New World of Corporate Governance Reforms," *Communications of the Association of Information Systems* 17, article 32 (May 2006): 714–27 (reproduced by permission of the Association of Information Systems).

This chapter explores how new compliance frameworks and governance reforms, mandated by governments and/or industry groups, are changing IT work. It is not designed to provide a detailed look at IT controls or how to achieve them, although it will direct readers to where they can find this information. Instead, it is intended to be a general introduction to the changing expectations of IT and how these are affecting IT work, structure, and governance. The first section looks at the growing impact regulatory issues are having in IT, and the second examines the costs, challenges, benefits, and opportunities of managing IT under a microscope. Section three outlines the key areas within IT that are affected and the types of issues that need to be addressed by managers. The final section describes some recommended practices to assist IT managers in implementing necessary controls.

IT AND REGULATORY LEGISLATION

Many industries and organizations have long lived in a regulated or self-regulated world. For banks, insurance companies, pharmaceutical makers, hospitals, and manufacturers (to name just a few), adhering to government legislation is simply a way of life. "Ninety percent of what we do is dictated by some law," stated a manager in a pharmaceutical firm. "They tell us what we can or cannot do and where we are free to choose but must let regulators know." Increasing layers of regulation have been applied by governments over time, and organizations have gradually adapted to them. So why does it now seem that new control, privacy, and security legislation is such a challenge for IT?

There are a number of reasons the current crop of laws is more difficult for IT to adjust to. First, in the past, systems were developed after (or at the same time as) regulations affecting a business. Furthermore, these regulations affected smaller if not isolated areas of work. Today's organizations already have significant amounts of automation. Recent legislation not only affects many different systems, but also how they work together. Thus, it has a broader impact on work than previously—even beyond the organization itself. Second, organizations are not only more dependent on automated information and processes, but through networking, are also increasingly vulnerable to security threats. Interruptions, therefore, have a much larger ripple effect than in the past. Third, systems are increasingly global in nature and are affected by the laws of many different countries. Companies doing business with the European Union, for example, must respect strict EU privacy standards even if their systems operate in the United States. Canadian and EU companies doing business in the United States must adhere to the Sarbanes-Oxley Act. In short, new legislation affects more systems and business practices than previously, and this makes it difficult and expensive for IT to respond appropriately.

At the same time, legislators and other regulatory bodies are increasingly aware of the impact electronic information and systems can have on organizations and the public. IT now has a huge effect on business practices (e.g., online business, offshore call centers). Systems provide the bulk of financial reporting data, can easily transport sensitive personal information across organizational and national boundaries, and produce inaccurate or invalid information that could mislead (either unwittingly or on purpose) auditors, tax officials, inspectors, and the public. As a result of several recent corporate scandals, there is a perceived need for improved controls over systems—how they operate and the information they produce (IT Governance Institute 2000). "There's definitely a new attitude when we deal with regulatory agencies," said a manager. "In the past there was more trust of the information we provided. Now it's 'show me how you got this.'"

SOX and privacy laws are considered the most generically onerous reforms affecting IT at present. But IT also faces other new, industry-specific legislation covering such varied issues as impact on the environment, access to persons with disabilities, capital management, and homeland security. However, the single most challenging regulation is Section 404 of the Sarbanes-Oxley Act, which mandates an annual evaluation of internal controls and procedures for financial reporting. It requires the CEO and CFO to personally certify these controls and external auditors to independently attest to their effectiveness (Damianides 2005).

In addition, SOX requires the following:

- Controls must be suitably designed to achieve control objectives using established criteria.
- Control objectives and related controls need to be appropriately documented.

The act strongly recommends that companies follow a framework for internal controls known as COSO (Committee of Sponsoring Organizations of the Treadway Commission), developed in 1985. To assist IT in implementing these controls, in 1998 the IT Governance Institute developed its own Control Objectives for Information and related Technology (COBIT). Since COBIT is an open standard and is widely used, it is the primary IT control framework companies are using to provide the "reasonable assurances" required by SOX (see Appendix A for an overview of these controls). In addition, there is a number of other, more focused control models for IT, such as the Information Technology Control Guidelines (from the Canadian Institute of Chartered Accountants) and the Security Handbook (from the National Institute of Standards and Technology, in the United States) to which companies are turning for specific guidance.

While frameworks provide a basic skeleton on which to build controls, the amount of control that is appropriate depends on the size and complexity of the organization involved (Fredericks and Tegethoff 2005). At present, it is the job of a company's external auditors to determine if its controls are "reasonable." Unfortunately, in many cases, accounting firms' interpretation of internal controls is extremely strict, and auditors are performing massive reviews not tailored to a company's size or risks (Solomon and Gullapalli 2005). This is leading to an increasing number of complaints from companies (Powell 2005; Stewart 2005). It is also driving IT managers crazy and forcing them to focus on "a minutiae of operational details" embedded in both their companies' information handling systems *and* in their own internal IT processes.

THE IMPACT OF REGULATION ON IT

There is no question that complying with the many new regulations imposed on organizations has led to significant IT costs. A recent survey of large U.S. companies found that they spent more than $5.5 billion in 2004 alone meeting SOX requirements and that $1 billion of that was in IT (Surn 2004). The same study found that many firms had underestimated the costs involved and a majority of those surveyed planned to increase their compliance budgets in the future. One CEO of an insurance company estimates that just addressing SOX will cost his firm $30 million a year (Stewart 2005). Another study estimates large companies are spending about $35 million a year on SOX compliance, while the impact on smaller firms is proportionately greater (Powell 2005).

In the end, implementations of *all* regulations, frameworks, and guidelines tend to land at least partially in IT's court. "Different regulations affect our business units differently, but they *all* impact IT," said one manager. "While the business has different teams for each set of regulations, everyone in IT is affected." As regulations become more numerous and complex, some organizations are finding that *only* IT-based controls are effective in ensuring compliance.

Because of the way it is being interpreted and implemented, SOX legislation is having the largest impact on IT at present. However, the IT management issues associated with this act are applicable to many other regulations. Two categories of impact in IT are identified:

1. *Costs and challenges.* Compliance clearly involves huge costs for IT. However, these involve much more than just money. New regulations generally mean that "IT takes an enormous productivity hit. . . . It is a huge distraction and an enormous drain" (Koch 2004). With SOX, for example, "All work on enhancements to systems had to be stopped for two months while we were documenting our existing controls," according to a manager. The increased rigor required also adds to new project costs and lengthens their development schedules. "The business case payback is changing with SOX," said another manager. "Small projects are no longer cost effective, and manual processes are sometimes more attractive than automated ones."

Regulation affects everyone from the CIO to the most junior IT staffer. This is particularly true when it comes to the dreaded "separation of responsibilities" in SOX, which requires the person purchasing equipment to be different from the person receiving it and the person programming a change to be different from the person testing it. CIOs must personally attest to the effectiveness of IT's internal controls and quality of information produced by systems. They must also ensure their function is able to provide the right information to both internal and external auditors and to their CEO and CFO. There are steep learning curves for every member of the organization (Leon 2005). One focus group participant stated, "An IT person has to understand the whole gamut of regulations. The learning curve tends to be all-consuming and takes a long time to build into the mindset of staff." In this organization (a highly regulated one), typically two weeks a year are devoted to training each staff member in compliance issues.

Because of SOX's emphasis on documentation, the skills required of IT staff are also changing. "Written communication skills are becoming more important," explained a manager. This can be problematic because English is often not the first language of many technical staff and editing is not a skill that has been valued in IT. "Documentation is the bane of our existence!" complained a participant. Keeping documentation up to date after it has been produced is essential as well. Many organizations have to develop document retention strategies and knowledge bases of process and system documents. "In some cases, where regulations have been built in to a legacy system, we are having major problems documenting what actually happens," said another manager. "The regulations are embedded, and the developers have disappeared long ago." When combined with stiffer requirements for testing and quality assurance, the total cost of ownership for systems has increased dramatically after implementation.

Two particularly challenging aspects of SOX and privacy legislation are the segregation of duties and restrictions on who has access to data. The first requires that a person who makes a purchase or develops a system should not be the same person who accepts the purchase or the system. The second relates to who can view and change data. Both require substantial analysis of systems, personnel, and data to identify who should be doing what.

Finally, there is a significant morale impact on IT staff. "People don't like all the shifting goals, and they don't like oversight," said a manager. Regulation has led to policies and procedures within IT that have raised the bar of what is expected of IT staff. It is important to watch out for "malicious compliance" (or work to rule), said another participant. If people simply mechanically follow processes, mistakes will be made. They must understand, and accept, *why* they are being asked to do this. At more senior levels, there is a danger that leaders will focus more on processes than on common sense (Stewart 2005). Morale issues are often enhanced by frustration when staff cannot get the answers they need from their firm or external auditors. "In many cases it's hard to find out what 'compliance' really means," said a manager. A common problem at all levels of IT is that, because auditors don't truly understand how to interpret the legislation themselves, they are not able to provide clear guidance about what should be done (Koch 2004). Often they err on the side of nitpickiness and are "overly cautious and mechanical" (Solomon and Gullapalli 2005). The result is driving up costs out of fear and causing a massive waste of resources (Powell 2005).

2. *Benefits and opportunities.* On the other side of the ledger, there are some who see that an increased focus on controls for systems and information will eventually lead to benefits for the organization. "We can take either an opportunity or a fear mindset towards regulation," said a manager. "There are many positive improvements we can make in our practices that will deliver benefits to the organization." Companies that see compliance from a purely tactical perspective will likely not see the value of increased controls. If, however, they see regulation as a chance to streamline and revamp business processes and IT governance, some believe that compliance costs will eventually decline (Koch 2004). Others even see compliance as strategic. "Companies need to redirect their focus from compliance as a necessary evil to compliance as a competitive advantage" (Damianides 2005).

The recent spate of regulations, particularly SOX, has dramatically elevated board and executive attention on IT, although not necessarily in the way IT managers have been hoping for (Damianides 2005). They have also increased the relative importance of many elements of IT, such as security, quality, data architecture, and change management, which have previously been given short shrift by businesspeople. Nevertheless, in most companies controls are still seen as overheads. Therefore, it is necessary to put a positive "spin" on them. "We emphasize that improved controls and processes will lead to improved quality, simpler audits, and easier learning curves for staff," said one manager. Another noted that audits are an opportunity to "demonstrate how good we are."

Ideally, regulation should help organizations have the proper people, policies, and overall control structures in place to create an environment that ensures confidentiality, integrity, and the availability of critical information (Fredericks and Tegethoff 2005). Properly implemented in IT, a strong internal control program in IT ensures the following benefits, some of which IT has been trying to achieve for a long time (Damianides 2005):

- Improved overall IT governance
- Enhanced understanding of IT by senior executives
- Better business decisions based on more accurate information
- Improved IT alignment with the business
- Reduced risk of system security breaches
- Reduced difficulty complying with new regulations
- More efficient and effective operations
- An integrated approach to security
- Enhanced risk management competencies

Overall, companies have mixed feelings about the benefits of new regulations on IT. Most agree that IT has "room to improve" in certain areas. "There's always a need to find better ways to do our work," stated one participant. However, while trying to look on the bright side in the long term, most IT organizations feel thoroughly overwhelmed by the new elements of IT they have to implement or upgrade and the new roles and responsibilities they have to take on to address immediate regulatory needs.

ELEMENTS OF EFFECTIVE COMPLIANCE IN IT

To better understand how IT is affected by new regulations, the main areas of IT that will have to be developed or enhanced are presented in Figure 5.1. The key impacts on each element in the figure are then discussed.

1. Enabling IT Work

These are the "basics" that IT must have in place in order to do the rest of its work.

- *Physical and virtual access.* Most organizations already have some physical and virtual access controls, but these now need to be extended to all office areas and buildings, workstations, and company data and better integrated with each other. "We do this well in some areas, but in others changes can take weeks," admitted one manager. Procedures for granting and denying access need to be streamlined to dynamically and immediately enable new staff to be added, departing staff removed, and role-based access provided (Smith and McKeen 2005a).
- *Security architecture.* Protection of systems and data is of rapidly escalating concern to organizations in our networked world. Today's hardware, software, and data are more and more vulnerable to threats both from a sophisticated army

Figure 5.1 Key IT Elements Affected by Regulation

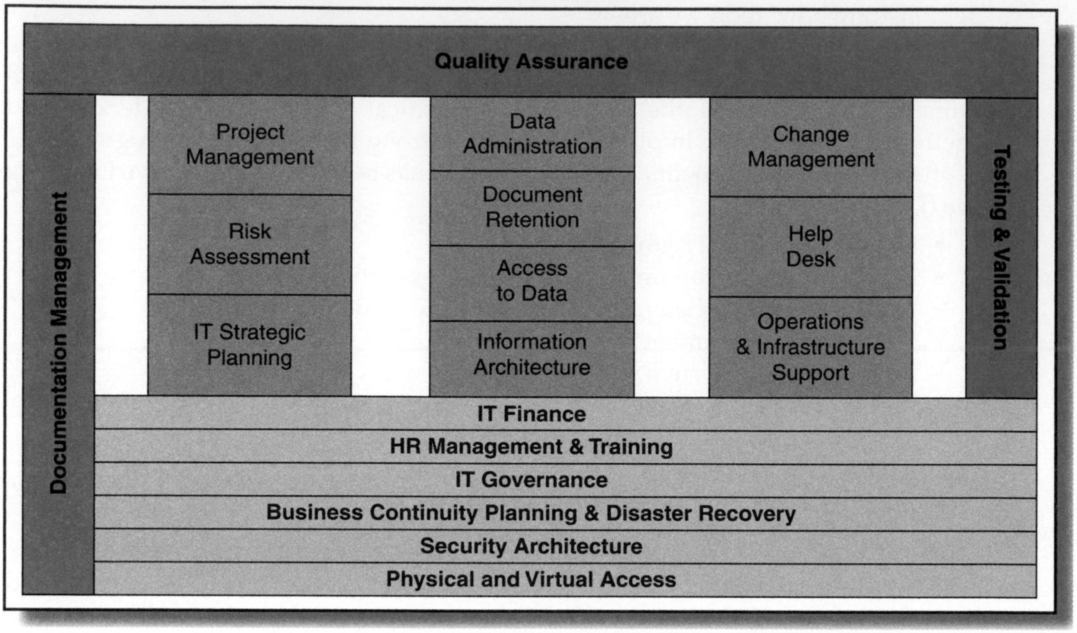

of hackers, viruses, worms, and bots and from insiders (whether malicious or inadvertent) (Smith and McKeen 2005b). To address this risk, organizations need a planned, integrated, and evolving set of practices for dealing with these threats, rather than the patchwork approach that has developed in too many companies.

- *Business continuity planning and disaster recovery.* Organizations got a wake-up call in this area by the 9/11 disaster and the 2003 blackout, and most have implemented improved plans and practices to address disasters affecting operations and data. New regulations require these plans to be tested, validated, and kept up to date as new vulnerabilities are identified.

- *IT governance.* Governance is the structure of relationships and processes that enable the enterprise to direct and control IT in order to achieve enterprise goals while balancing risk versus return (IT Governance Institute 2000). In practice, this refers to the structure, roles, procedures, and internal and external relationships that ensure that IT is well managed and can provide the necessary information to run the organization. Whereas, in the past, enterprise governance was supported by IT, today it is widely acknowledged that IT governance also has a strong influence over what the enterprise knows and is able to do (IT Governance Institute 2000). Therefore, much more attention must be paid to ensuring IT governance is effective, both internally within IT and externally in collaboration with that of the organization.

- *HR management and training.* Along with new controls and needed capabilities come new roles and competencies to be filled and developed. A significant amount of compliance awareness training must also be developed and provided to all IT staff to ensure they truly understand the nature and importance of their responsibilities in this area.

- **IT finance.**   IT is a large and growing part of the enterprise's budget. Many SOX regulations around segregation of duties, risk assessment, and quality affect how IT budgets are spent. IT managers must put processes in place to ensure that IT funds are spent wisely and are properly monitored.

2. New Systems

These elements address the work that is done to develop new applications or to acquire them.

- **IT strategic planning.**   To ensure IT resources are effectively deployed, all new development must be mapped against business strategies (Damianides 2005). While IT organizations have been trying to do this for several years, there are still many organizations where this is not being done or being done badly, often because of the lack of a clearly articulated business strategy (Smith, McKeen, and Singh 2007).
- **Risk assessment.**   This is a major area where IT capabilities need improvement. Practices and procedures need to be put in place not only to identify the risks that need to be understood and mitigated in each IT project, but also to manage these on an ongoing basis throughout a project's life cycle.
- **Project management.**   Most IT organizations already recognize this as a key skill, but many do not have the procedures to properly monitor projects or to ensure that controls applying to new projects are effectively addressed. Attention also needs to be paid to adding appropriate control documentation in each phase of a project's development.

3. Information

These elements address all data and information produced and/or stored by IT. However, because much of it comes from and is used by the business, this is a huge area of overlap with business controls.

- **Information architecture.**   Organizations have only just begun to address the huge amounts of data and information that exist in a wide variety of forms today. The number of paper documents, data, reports, Web pages, and digital assets has literally grown exponentially in recent years, and very little has yet been done to control or organize it (Smith and McKeen 2003). Until companies know what information they have, how it is produced, who has access to it, and how it is used, it is extremely difficult to control information access—a key requirement of much privacy legislation. "This is a huge culture shift for organizations," explained a manager. "We have to develop data ownership awareness and recognition of the data owner's responsibilities." It is also a substantial analysis job.
- **Access to data.**   This is another area where most companies are experiencing problems. Because few have a complete information architecture and limited experience with information management, they are only just beginning to grapple with the issues involved in determining who in their organizations has and should have access to which data.

- *Document retention.* New regulations and recent lawsuits are leading organizations to comprehensively address which documents and electronic information (e.g., e-mail) are kept, where they are stored, and for what period of time. Different industries have different requirements in this area, but document retention is one area that needs to be better understood and more effectively, comprehensively, and consistently managed. For example, a regulatory requirement to produce *all* records (both paper and electronic) within days (or even hours) is leading to the conclusion that retention practices alone are not enough and that there is a need for entirely new retrieval systems. Furthermore, regulations in many jurisdictions (e.g., British Columbia, Ireland) now require that data be stored within geographic borders, adding further complexity to this challenging issue.
- *Data administration.* All organizations need to create or collect, organize, analyze, maintain, and archive information so it can be accessed and used when needed. This involves addressing such issues as accuracy, timelines and quality, ongoing stewardship, taxonomies and metadata, and dynamic access management (Smith and McKeen 2003).

4. Daily Operations

These are the elements that run existing hardware, software, and networks and ensure ongoing operations, as well as those that make needed changes and deal with problems as they occur.

- *Operations and infrastructure support.* Work has been done in this area already by IT professionals, but some are better at ensuring high service levels and low costs than others. Operations staff need training in their regulatory responsibilities just as much as other IT staff. Often companies need to look more closely at how they identify and allocate costs in this area, what metrics are collected and reported, how third-party services are managed, and how problems and incidents are addressed at the root cause.
- *Help desk.* Help desks are the front line of business support. As such, they are often the first to identify problems and risks with systems, operations, and information. At one company, help desk staff must take twenty modules of training about the regulations applying to their work and how they are expected to respond to a wide variety of circumstances. Help desk training and documentation for each new system is also an essential control process and should be considered part of every new initiative.
- *Change management.* Controlling how enhancements are made and implemented to existing systems has become extremely important to prevent major system disruptions. Processes to ensure the proper testing and validation of changes and integration with other operational systems create much extra work but can also save significant headaches. Segregation of duties is especially important to ensure that all control procedures have been properly followed.

5. Controlling IT Work

These are elements that ensure that all work done in IT is properly completed, meets all control standards, and can be demonstrated to do so with "reasonable assurance."

- *Testing and validation.* This is one of the most important areas of control. It is also one that is growing exponentially in cost, complexity, and impact on the organization. Ensuring that all IT outputs—systems, information, hardware, software, and networks—are working as expected, meet established requirements, and will not disrupt other parts of the business is becoming fundamentally important to IT. Many organizations have now created a standard test environment and data sets to ensure this. As well, it is no longer possible for users to shirk their responsibilities in this area. Acceptance testing *must* be completed by properly trained and qualified users who sign off on the accuracy of the results.
- *Documentation management.* As noted earlier, documentation of *everything* is rapidly becoming a standard for IT. Processes that were once "understood" must now be written down and maintained as they evolve. Project documents and sign-offs must be retained and catalogued, and different versions must be accessible by auditors. As a result, some IT organizations are creating new roles for librarians and document administrators.
- *Quality assurance.* Finally, many companies also have an IT quality assurance group (sometimes external to IT) that ensures compliance with all controls and corporate standards.

GOOD PRACTICES IN ENABLING IT COMPLIANCE

There are really no such things as "best" practices as yet in how IT copes with regulation. Like everything else in IT, as managers learn what works and what doesn't, practices will evolve. Expectations on IT will also change as auditors learn from their own experiences and legislation is amended or reinterpreted. However, we can still learn a great deal from those organizations (particularly in the banking and pharmaceutical industries) that have made significant progress in this area. Focus group members suggested five sets of practices will be helpful:

1. *Organize for compliance.* Compliance cannot be something that is "tacked on" to an existing IT structure. While different organizations will approach it differently, compliance takes dedicated responsibility from a core group. Because it is an ongoing process, IT managers should recognize that after an initial "remediation phase," there will still be a considerable amount of work to do to reduce the ongoing costs of compliance, ensure procedures are followed, and of course, deal with new regulations. At the most senior level, many companies have SOX (or other) steering committees on which the CIO sits (Koch 2004). CIOs also need to educate their boards of directors and executive committees about the changes and costs and opportunities of compliance (Damianides 2005). To assist them in these matters and provide a consistent approach, many companies now have directors of compliance within IT.

Unfortunately, it has often been difficult for IT staff to get answers to compliance questions from either their own internal audit staff or their external auditors. Dedicated internal compliance staff can develop expertise that can be leveraged across all parts of IT. IT managers may also need to add other staff functions related to controlling

IT work (e.g., quality assurance, creating and maintaining a standard test environment, documentation management). Greater attention to security and information may also require the creation of dedicated staff groups with specialized expertise in these areas. Finally, there was strong consensus that, while many IT development and support staff can be decentralized, IT compliance functions should be centralized.

2. *Use standards and frameworks.* There are several reasons to use these. First, there is no point trying to reinvent the wheel when there are good, generally accepted frameworks available. Already organizations are converging around a number of key standards, such as COSO and CobiT, and are mapping their existing control procedures against them (Fredericks and Tegethoff 2005). This mapping can help identify gaps in current control procedures and a set of accepted practices against which to benchmark. Second, they provide critical success factors, tools, and key performance indicators that offer auditors "reasonable assurance" that controls are effective (IT Governance Institute 2000). Third, external auditors are advising that control and compliance programs based on standards and frameworks are more likely to be deemed acceptable by regulators. Finally, they help to establish a common perspective between the external auditor and the organization, thus avoiding misunderstandings (Fredericks and Tegethoff 2005).

3. *Emphasize training and awareness.* Training is essential to ensure that all staff understand their responsibilities in complying with regulations. Compliance is everyone's job. Training fosters a common sense of purpose, enables everyone to make better decisions, and helps staff understand the implications of IT work for the organization as a whole. Employees who truly understand what controls are trying to achieve can sense the right ways to comply without going about it mechanistically. "People who are aware and informed will be proactive and will be predisposed to ensure compliance every day in many small ways," stated one manager. Training should be geared to roles as well as creating general awareness. One highly regulated organization has specific training programs for system and process owners, development, and help desk staff. "It's extremely important that people understand *why* we have the controls we do," stated the focus group member involved. "Becoming a compliant organization is a huge culture change, and it takes a long time to develop." Furthermore, because regulations, standards, and strategies for addressing compliance are still in a constant state of flux, managers recommended developing a comprehensive general visibility and communications strategy around these matters.

4. *Ensure appropriate business resources.* Business staff have an important role to play in IT compliance. From ensuring that business strategy is properly communicated so IT strategy can support it, to taking ownership for systems and processes and being responsible for their outcomes and results, to knowledgeably signing off on key system development documents and test results, business staff must be actively involved in enabling IT staff to comply with regulations affecting their company. While in the past, IT staff have often "helped" in these areas (i.e., largely done it for them), today's controls require knowledgeable and qualified users who must be accountable for their own systems, information, and decisions. While this increases overhead in the business areas, it is the only way that assurances about the effectiveness and efficiency of systems and the accuracy of information can be given.

5. **Caveat emptor** *regarding compliance technology.* The shortcomings of most IT organizations tend to revolve around gaps in policies, standards, and documentation

(Fredericks and Tegethoff 2005). Thus, most of the challenges facing IT around compliance can*not* be solved by adding more technology. Compliance tools can help but only after detailed analysis to understand what control elements are lacking and what is required (Leon 2005). There is no shortage of tools on the market to help organizations become SOX compliant. These can be very helpful in some key areas, such as in tracking, documenting, and retaining evidence. In addition, a central repository for project documentation plays a crucial role—as a living document as enhancements and changes are made. Interestingly, while excellent tools are available for development work in achieving compliance, they are currently lacking for enhancement work. Finally, tools that document work and information flows and connections among systems are also helpful.

The focus group also foresaw the need to assist the business with the automation of some of its compliance processes to save the time and expense of controls. However, they are proceeding cautiously in this area at present as it is still unclear how control standards will evolve.

CONCLUSION

There is no question that new laws and regulations governing organizations, their finances, and their information are having a huge impact on IT. As enterprises become increasingly dependent on systems and electronic information, they become more vulnerable and government legislation becomes necessary to protect the public. Unfortunately, the regulation is coming fast and furiously, and the pace is increasing. As a result, in many organizations a significant amount of IT time and resources are being spent on the "overhead" of compliance. Almost every area of IT is affected, and IT managers are struggling to implement new controls and document existing ones while still ensuring business as usual and trying to develop the new systems their companies need. As with other "firsts" affecting IT, after an initial period of turbulence and uncertainty, managers are slowly getting the situation under control with a combination of standards and frameworks, common sense, hard work, and the judicious application of technology. But when the dust settles, it is highly unlikely that the fast and freewheeling world of IT of the past few decades will remain. The world is requiring IT to become thoroughly professional about what it does. The IT of the future will, therefore, of necessity be increasingly controlled, standardized, and bureaucratized. It remains to be seen whether or not management will be able to use this "new and improved" IT for competitive advantage.

REFERENCES

Damianides, M. "Sarbanes-Oxley and IT Governance: New Guidance on IT Control and Compliance." *Information Systems Management* 22, no. 1 (Winter 2005): 77.

Fredericks, P., and E. Tegethoff. "Compliance Hindsight: What Organizations Have Learned from Early Compliance Approaches." *CIO* (April 6, 2005).

IT Governance Institute. *COBIT Executive Summary*, 3rd ed. (July 2000).

Koch, C. "The Sarbox Conspiracy." *CIO* (July 1, 2004).

Leon, M. "Hard-won Lessons from the Compliance Front." *InfoWorld* 27, no. 14 (April 4, 2005): 42.

Powell, S. "Seeking a Cure for Sarbox." *Barron's* 85, no. 18 (May 2, 2005): 41.

Smith, H. A., and J. D. McKeen. "Enterprise Content Management," *Communications of the Association of Information Systems* 11, article 33 (June 2003): 647–59.

———. "Information Delivery: IT's Evolving Role." *Communications of the Association of Information Systems* 15, article 11 (February 2005a): 197–210.

———. "Strategic Information Risk Management." *The CIO Brief* 11, no. 1 (2005b).

Smith, H. A., J. D. McKeen, and S. Singh. "Developing IT Strategy for Business Value." *Journal of Information Technology Management* XVIII, no. 1 (June 2007): 49–58.

Solomon, D., and D. Gullapalli. "Moving the Market: Auditors Get Sarbanes-Oxley Rebuke." *Wall Street Journal*, May 17, 2005.

Stewart, S. "Manulife Chief Lashes out at 'Onerous Governance.'" *Globe and Mail*, May 6, 2005.

Surn, J. "The Rising Cost of Compliance." *CIO* (August 15, 2004).

Recommended COBIT *Controls*
(IT Governance Institute 2000)

- Plan and organize (IT environment)
- IT strategic planning
- Information architecture
- Determine technological direction
- IT organization and relationships
- Manage the IT investment
- Communication of management aims and direction
- Management of human resources
- Compliance with external requirements
- Assessment of risks
- Manage projects
- Manage quality
- Acquire and implement (program development and program change)
- Identify automated solutions
- Acquire or develop application software
- Acquire technology infrastructure
- Manage changes
- Deliver and support (computer operations and access to programs and data)
- Define and manage service levels
- Manage third-party services
- Manage performance and capacity
- Ensure continuous service
- Ensure systems security
- Identify and allocate costs
- Educate and train users
- Assist and advise customers
- Manage the configuration
- Manage problems and incidents
- Manage data
- Manage facilities
- Manage operations
- Monitor and evaluate (IT environment)
- Monitoring
- Adequacy of internal controls
- Independent assurance
- Internal audit

Creating and Evolving
a Technology Roadmap[1]

There is an adage that says, "If you don't know where you are going, any road will take you there." It applies rather well to technology roadmaps. In the past, companies have followed a number of different technology paths that have not always led to the "promised land" despite conscientious effort. There are many reasons for this. First, the target evolves, which means that development of a technology roadmap should be an ongoing process. To continue the analogy, we are forever "traveling" but never "arriving." Second, technology has many different masters. Vendors, trade associations, standards-setting boards, alliance and/or trade partners, merger/acquisition initiatives, growth, strategic directional change, new technological development, and economic shifts (e.g., price performance, adoption patterns, and obsolescence) are all continuously influencing where companies want to go with technology. Third, unexpected roadblocks occur, for example, the company that produces the application platform that runs your business just declared bankruptcy. If building and evolving a technology roadmap were easy, it would be done well.

Why do we need a technology roadmap? IT managers believe that without the guidance of a roadmap, their companies run the risk of making suboptimal decisions—technology choices that make sense today but position the company poorly for the future. There is also a strong sense that the exercise of developing a technology roadmap is valuable even if the actual roadmap that is developed is subject to change. Another adage applies: "Plans are nothing; planning is everything." It is through the articulation of a technology roadmap that you learn what you did well, where you failed, and how to improve the process. Finally, a technology roadmap limits the range of technology options and reduces the decision-making effort compared to facing one-off

---

[1]McKeen, J. D., and H. A. Smith, "Creating and Evolving a Technology Roadmap," *Communication of the Association of Information Systems* 20, article 21 (September 2006): 451–63 (reproduced by permission of the Association for Information Systems).

decisions repeatedly over time. Because a roadmap has cast the evolution of technology on a certain path, it means that an organization can simply accept this decision and not revisit it repeatedly. Thus, a technology roadmap reduces the organization's cognitive workload.

This chapter begins with a general discussion of technology roadmaps and presents a model to explain various input factors. It then describes each of the components of a technology roadmap and offers advice derived from the shared experiences of the focus group's managers.

WHAT IS A TECHNOLOGY ROADMAP?

It is important to develop an understanding of what a technology roadmap actually is. To do so, we can build on the analogy of a travel map. A travel map is a guide that tells you where you are now by positioning you within the greater environs and highlights existing options to get you where you want to go. In offering directions, it can suggest travel times, routes, and scenic alternatives, but that's about as far as it goes. A technology roadmap differs. Unlike a travel map, it is difficult to purchase a "map" for the simple reason that organizations all have uniquely different starting points, different goals, and therefore, different destinations. Travel maps accommodate travel regardless of destination or purpose. Technology roadmaps must also entertain external factors such as industry trends, the competitive landscape, and vendor strategies and offerings. Finally, alternative technology options are not self-evident and must be identified through research and exploration (and sometimes experimentation). Thus, each option bears a different cost and time structure. As an analogy, the travel map provides an excellent starting point, but when creating a technology roadmap, more is needed. The first step is to develop a common understanding of what exactly is meant by the term *technology roadmap*.

In this focus group, every member used a different definition of the term. Upon analysis, we reached consensus on aspects of the definition. It was clear that the main purpose of a technology roadmap is to establish the technology direction for the organization. It has two objectives. The first is to articulate how technology will support the enterprise's overall vision, strategy, and objectives. This was evident in the definition used at one company:

> *Our technology roadmap is the collective vision of the opportunities for technology to serve the business.*

The second goal is to frame and constrain technology solutions to provide coherence and integration among those solutions across the enterprise and to define target architectures to implementers. These dual objectives simply recognize the need for IT to forge a relationship between IT and the business while, at the same time, serving the unique internal needs of IT. After some discussion, the group agreed on the following definition:

> *A technology roadmap is a mechanism for the identification, justification, planned evolution, and orchestration of technologies to enhance business performance.*

THE BENEFITS OF A TECHNOLOGY ROADMAP

The fact that every participating organization had a technology roadmap suggests that there are perceived benefits in building and evolving one. These fit into two categories—external and internal—reflecting the dual purpose of the technology roadmap as described previously.

External Benefits *(Effectiveness)*

External benefits relate to aligning IT with the business, result in IT *effectiveness,* and include the following:

- *Achieving business goals.* A technology roadmap compares the business plan with the current technological environment to identify gaps. To the extent that the technology roadmap effectively addresses these gaps, business goals should be supported by technology.
- *Reducing complexity.* The technology environment is highly complex due to the degree of interaction among systems. The adoption of a technology roadmap typically reduces the number and variety of technological choices, thereby simplifying things. Just getting to single versions of applications, such as one e-mail program, greatly reduces complexity.
- *Enhancing interoperability of business functionality across lines of business (LOBs).* Identifying the technology that supports different LOBs is the first step toward integration. The degree of integration and interoperability is first and foremost a business decision. The technology should be designed to support this vision.
- *Increasing flexibility.* This begs the question of whether differentiation or integration enables flexibility. With respect to technology, the argument is usually won by commonalities.
- *Increasing speed of implementation.* Common standards, methodologies, and technology platforms relieve the learning burden and, thereby, increase the time to market with new systems.
- *Preserving investments in new and existing systems.* Mapping technologies on an evolutionary trajectory means that IT investments are based on long-term considerations.
- *Responding to market changes.* Having an up-to-date technology roadmap means that IT can respond accurately and appropriately to market changes. Organizations without the benefit of a technology roadmap are forced to build decisions "from the ground up" as opposed to building from an established framework.
- *Focusing investment dollars.* Having a technology roadmap means that investments in IT can be much more focused. Fewer dollars, better targeted produce enhanced results.
- *Responding to new legislation.* Compliance with new legislation (e.g., the Sarbanes-Oxley Act, privacy, environmental programs) is greatly simplified with a rationalized technology roadmap.

- *Reducing difficulties associated with deployment of new technologies.* New technologies require learning and change. Therefore, fewer technologies, common platforms, and similar approaches effectively relieve this burden.

Internal Benefits *(Efficiency)*

Internal benefits attribute to IT directly and result in IT *efficiency,* including the following:

- *Providing a common design point.* This facilitates the end-to-end integration of reusable components and applications.
- *Building a consistent and cohesive technology base.* Without the proliferation of haphazard technology, one can create a critical mass of skills dedicated to select technologies.
- *Ability to move forward in planned phases.* With technologies mapped onto a life cycle, there is an orderly evolution for each technology, which creates synergies.
- *Consolidating global solutions.* For global companies, the local in-country technologies are synched to the global technology roadmap, which introduces even greater consistency across business processes, reducing overall IT expenditure.
- *Lowering the cost of development and maintenance.* Because technology roadmaps provide an inventory of technology, it makes it possible to increase the reusability of system components, leverage commodity components available in the marketplace, standardize techniques across multiple applications, and prevent the "disintegration" and proliferation of execution, development, and operations architectures.

It is interesting to note that no companies in the group were able to demonstrate the *financial* impacts attributable to their adoption of a technology roadmap. Perhaps more surprising was the fact that they had not been asked by senior management to produce such a benefit statement. The initial development of a technology roadmap is typically an initiative of the IT department. This suggests that IT departments understand the benefits of a technology roadmap and appear not to question the value of committing resources to this activity. Perhaps the internal benefits of building a technology roadmap—which are significant, judging from the above list—justify the exercise all by themselves. These benefits appear to be more tangible and immediate than external benefits.

ELEMENTS OF THE TECHNOLOGY ROADMAP

The process of developing a technology roadmap is depicted in Figure 6.1. It hinges on a gap analysis to assess the extent to which the current state of technology supports the current and forecasted needs of the business. From this are derived the organization's future technology requirements, which, coupled with a migration strategy, constitute the core of a technology roadmap. Participants identified seven

Figure 6.1 The Process of Developing a Technology Roadmap

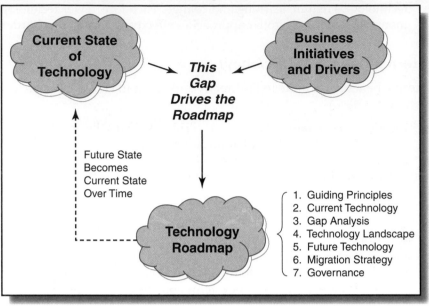

important activities in developing and maintaining a technology roadmap. These are described below and are interspersed with strategies suggested by the group, based on their experiences. At the outset, it is important to dispel the notion that the development of a technology roadmap is a "once every five years" undertaking. Instead, there was strong consensus that a technology roadmap should constitute a working instrument to be updated and revised annually. Otherwise it becomes inflexible, perhaps dated, and as a result, unresponsive to the business.

1. *Guiding principles.* When launching a technology roadmap, it is important to establish a set of principles that will guide its development and enhancement. First and foremost, this is a statement about the role and purpose of technology within the business that should clearly convey aspirations and purpose. It outlines how technology will support the business, stipulating the envisioned role for technology to play. This should be a statement about the *type* of technology support to be delivered to the business with a sense of performance. For example, contrast the following two statements: "We will provide technology that is proven, reliable, and cost effective" versus "We will provide leading-edge technology."

In addition to establishing the role and purpose for the technology roadmap, it is important to outline its goals. One company's goal for its technology roadmap was "to increase the speed of developing, deploying, and productively executing future business models." It then outlined three strategies to accomplish this:

   a. Decouple the business processes from the underlying IT applications
   b. Decouple business applications from the infrastructure
   c. Establish a new collaboration environment that supports the rapid introduction and productive use of the new business processes

This signaled to the organization that IT was adopting a service-oriented architecture (SOA). Because SOA was not well understood by the business, the technology roadmap spoke to the desire to identify components of the business model, which could be designed as reusable software services; adopt integrated and standardized processes for optimizing cost; accelerate integrated data/information architecture to enable horizontal integration across the enterprise; and provide a stable, secure, and ubiquitous workspace for employees to be more effective in their roles and efficient in their jobs by delivering information, applications, and people to easily collaborate within the context of business processes. This established the mandate of the technology roadmap, its purpose and goals, using language appropriate for the organizational context.

With the purpose and goals established, guiding principles can then be articulated to explain other key factors and decisions that would impact technology and, therefore, have a bearing on the technology roadmap. The following statements are examples of key principles used by focus group members:

- *Establish investment boundaries.* "We will invest in technology at a rate necessary to sustain our business growth."
- *Outline the role of technology for the organization.* "We will adopt a 'fast follower' strategy, aggressively adopting proven, architecturally compliant technologies."
- *Outline the role of technology within the industry.* "Technology is a core business competency."
- *Reinforce the role of standards.* "All components will adhere to open industry standards."
- *Specify the role of support.* "We will assist employees with technology problems that occur via call centers, desktop support, self-help, and/or service-level agreements."
- *Specify the impact on resident IT skills.* "We will draw technology expertise from our existing large skill base."
- *Outline development preference.* "We will buy first, build second."
- *Establish expectations.* "Service levels and availability are outlined for all production systems."
- *Adherence to standards.* "We will be security and privacy compliant."
- *Specify timeframe.* "The 'future' in our technology roadmap has a three- to five-year horizon."

2. *Current technology.* This is basically an inventory. It should outline what technologies you currently have and describe their status (e.g., standard, unsupported, discontinued). The first task is to develop a classification scheme to assist in managing the inventory. For each type of technology domain (e.g., operating systems; hardware, desktops, servers, and storage; telecommunications and networks; applications; and databases), members recommended recording the following minimum information: business process area, platform, vendor, level of support, dependencies (products, applications), critical versus noncritical, and life cycle.

The next step is to assign a technology custodian/owner so someone within the firm is responsible for each technology domain. At one company, these individuals are referred to as technology "domain architects." Typical duties of such individuals include acquiring the technology, maintaining the relationship with the vendor, updating and enhancing the technology, facilitating in-house training for those working with the technology, accreditation regarding the technology, recording all applications of the technology, maintaining documentation (e.g., licensing; financing; and establishing service levels, guarantees, and warranties), and retiring the technology when appropriate. This can be a major responsibility as some individuals will have more than one domain assigned to them.

One of the key tools in managing the technology inventory is a framework to classify technologies. One such tool, the Application System Asset Management (ASAM) Decision Chart (Mangurian 1985), assesses the business importance (i.e., the application's overall value to the business), functional support (i.e., how well the system meets the business requirements), and technical support (i.e., the system's efficiency and effectiveness). This particular tool has been used successfully over a number of years by one firm. On an annual basis, all application systems are evaluated against these three criteria, leading to one of the following actions: maintain, renovate, replace, augment, or eliminate.

Another company uses a two-by-two matrix that evaluates applications on the basis of their criticality to the business (i.e., whether or not they support business processes deemed critical to the business units) and their strategic importance (i.e., those providing global functions that will not be replaced over the next two years). Placement within this matrix (i.e., maintenance classification) dictates service levels: strategic/critical applications receive "gold" service; critical/nonstrategic applications receive "silver" service; strategic/noncritical applications receive "bronze" service; and nonstrategic/noncritical applications receive "blue" maintenance. Yet another company uses the "WISE" chart to evaluate technologies on the basis of their strategic value and longevity, yielding four life cycle stages: watch, invest, support, and eliminate (McKeen and Smith 2003).

The focus group agreed that the specific classification scheme matters less than the fact that a company has a scheme to manage its technology inventory. The technology inventory also provides input to other processes such as risk management, team development, and skills planning.

3. *Gap analysis.*   With a technology inventory in place, organizations can then perform a gap analysis between the technology that is currently available and that which is required. The first step is to identify the required technology. This ties the technology roadmap directly to the business and is perhaps the most crucial step in developing an effective plan. One manager made this point rather emphatically by saying, "Get this wrong, and the roadmap is junk." Others suggested that simply asking business leaders for their future requirements will not work for a number of reasons. First, business leaders do not think in terms of requirements; they think in terms of growth, customers, sales, markets, costs, suppliers, and shareholders. It takes a lot of work and skill to translate this view of the business into technology requirements. Second, the roadmap has to be ahead of the business; that is, it must reflect the fact that because business changes faster than technology, you have to build technology in anticipation of business change and growth. A technology roadmap cannot afford to be reactive; it must be proactive regardless of whether your technology vision is "quick second" or "late adopter." Third, business is driven by innovation and differentiation, while IT benefits from standards, common

features, and universality. This will always put IT at odds with the business. According to one participant, it boils down to this question: "When is a line of business so different that common systems don't make sense?" What criteria do you apply to test this?

Eliciting business drivers and building a composite picture of the technology required to support the business vision is more of an art than a science. It requires close cooperation between IT and the business. This cooperation happens at many levels within the organization and should be an ongoing activity. The annual IT planning cycle articulates the applications to be introduced over the next year, but attempting to derive a technology roadmap from this activity is a case of "too little, too late." IT has to be working with the business closely enough to be well ahead of the annual planning cycle. At one company, their domain architects are being reoriented to align them more closely with the business units to create a better early-warning system for application needs driven by growth and changes to the business model. Its manager stated the following:

> The enterprise has a vision, and each line of business has a vision, and the job of the domain architects is to put all these visions on the table to expose gaps. To do this, architects need to be 75 percent business and 25 percent technology. Today they are the reverse.

At another company, business analysts work together with enterprise architects to "get a fix on future business directions." While we tend to think of architects and technical experts as playing the key roles, the focus group pointed out that the best vantage point for performing a gap analysis between the existing technology and emerging business drivers is the CIO office, due to the fact that the CIO sits at the same table as other senior executives to set the strategy for the business. They pointed out that having the CIO at these sessions provides a significant advantage in terms of forecasting the future for technology within the company.

With a "line of sight" to the business strategy coupled with an accurate technology inventory, all the tools to perform a gap analysis are in place. The outcome of the gap analysis is an articulation of the technology required to support the business's vision and strategy. Unfortunately, a technology roadmap cannot be simply created from this analysis because it must also be governed by trends in the external environment.

4. *Technology landscape.* The group was unanimous in its recommendation that firms must invest in research and development (R & D) continuously if they are to keep abreast of technology. The size of this investment, however, differs depending on how critical IT is to a firm. The roadmap should articulate how large this investment will be, how it will be enacted, who is responsible, and what guidelines are in place to assist this initiative. Setting these structures in place is the easy part; knowing when enough is enough is more difficult.

In the past much of a company's technology was dictated by its choice of vendor; if asked what its technology roadmap was, a firm could simply reply by naming a single vendor. Today's lock-in by vendors is much reduced, particularly with the widespread adoption of open standards, interoperability among various platforms, and Web services. Interestingly, this has probably resulted in the need for downstream firms to bear a greater portion of the R & D burden where, in the past, they could leverage the vendor's R & D to a greater extent. Focus group members shared a number of different approaches to R & D, but all shared a common challenge—capital funding.

At some companies R & D flies "below the radar" as "skunkworks." Here the IT department uses its own money that it has squirreled away over time, treating R & D similar to a cost of doing business. In others R & D is financed by a technology investment fund (i.e., a tax to the business levied as a percentage of technology usage). This fund is governed by a committee composed of senior managers who guide the investment in R & D. In another firm IT maintenance is reduced by 10 to 15 percent per year, and the dollars are reallocated to strategic IT investments, much of which are funneled to a "technology adoption program" described as a "sandbox where new technologies are tried, improved, tested, scaled, and assessed for business value." These latter approaches are preferable because they don't attempt to hide R & D. In fact, they make R & D transparent to the organization. Business leaders understand the need for reinvestment in the physical plant; IT is no different.

5. *Future technology.*   This should contain a description of the technologies to be adopted in the future. These future technology roadmaps should not be simple lists. They should also include the *logic* that was used in the decision to follow a certain path. If, for instance, your technology roadmap depicts a preferred vendor strategy, equally if not more important is the reasoning that was used in selecting this strategy. Making this explicit within the roadmap permits others to challenge the logic without challenging the actual decision. This is essential particularly if you wish to obtain constructive input from business managers when creating your technology roadmap.

As important as the logic behind the roadmap are the assumptions built into the roadmap. IT professionals are frequently guilty of assuming that it is obvious to others why a certain strategy has been adopted. Hence, there is value in making all assumptions explicit. As with the need to present the logic of the roadmap, it is also vital to expose all embedded assumptions. These assumptions may reflect trends in the competitive marketplace (e.g., vendor A will continue to dominate with its software offerings), the general environment (e.g., open standards adoption will accelerate), specific technologies (e.g., thin client architecture's time has arrived), or general trends (e.g., new development will move toward SOA). This exposure provides the basis for meaningful conversation to help clarify the roadmap's dependence on widely accepted (but perhaps not articulated) assumptions.

The group felt that describing the technology was fairly straightforward, using major technology domains such as hardware, software, applications, and networks. The difficulty often is with regard to the granularity of future technology. The question is this: How do you decide the level of detail in future technology platforms? According to one manager, "If your roadmap is severely impacted by business change, your roadmap is probably too tactical." The opposite, creating a technology roadmap that is too high level, is equally inadequate. The goal is to find the "sweet spot" between the two extremes, which is "more art than science," he said.

6. *Migration strategy.*   A technology roadmap should also outline a migration strategy to get you from today's technology platforms to tomorrow's. At first glance, the implementation of a technology roadmap appears similar to other major IT initiatives. The focus group, however, was quick to point out the differences. Of these, the primary one is that a technology roadmap is not a self-contained project; it affects *every* project as technologies are embedded within the entire spectrum of applications, many of which cross lines of business, geography, and generations. By positioning each technology domain on a life cycle (e.g., watch, invest, support, eliminate), two dominant migration strategies emerge: "gradual" versus "big bang."

The gradual strategy focuses on the application (i.e., as new applications are implemented or reworked, their technology is updated to fall in line with the new technology directions). The big bang strategy emphasizes the technology (i.e., all instances of a given technology are updated across all applications). The choice is not an either-or situation nor is it a "technology only" decision. Rather the choice is (or should be) dictated by the business. There are few situations where the big bang approach is absolutely necessary simply because there are always means of staging the conversion over time, applications, business lines, and/or platforms. As one participant noted, "Even large architectural builds/deployments are typically done within a program across several phases." Sometimes, though, the big bang is a business necessity due to the need to reap advantages in a reduced timeframe.

A major challenge facing the migration strategy is the need to assign priorities to the various technology components that need to be changed. One organization uses the following criteria to assess the criticality of migration in order to assign order of execution:

- Technology elements that are inflexible
- Elements that do not meet the strategic direction
- Components that are expensive to maintain
- Components that do not meet nonfunctional requirements (e.g., scalability, extensibility)
- Architectural designs built to reflect obsolete business strategies (e.g., segmentation silos, line-of-business silos)

Once priorities are assigned, timelines can be established for the migration of various technologies.

A migration strategy should explicitly recognize a number of dominant trends within technology such as the movement toward service-oriented applications and the deconstruction of applications into layers (e.g., presentation, business process, and data). While such trends provide useful high-level guidance, they need to be augmented by more tactical guidelines (see Appendix). Of particular interest here is the need for a migration strategy to explicitly plan for the migration of *people* skills in alignment with the future technology demands.

7. *Governance.* Every organization should have an established process in place to articulate who is responsible for creating the technology roadmap, how and on what basis, by whom it is updated and enhanced, and finally who approves the technology roadmap. Most organizations in the group felt that the technology roadmap was legitimately the responsibility of the enterprise architecture function, which is responsible for mapping out the architectural platforms to support the various lines of business. The majority of companies recognized the need for two distinct levels of architecture governance within their organizations:

- *Strategic.* Individuals and groups at this level (typically, senior executives from IT and the business) set the overall architecture direction and strategy and ensure alignment with business objectives. They set standards and approve deviations from these standards. In addition, they monitor the overall attainment of the goals as articulated within the technology roadmap.

- *Tactical.* Members of this tactical group tend to be from the IT ranks, including architects, analysts, and managers. They typically work across lines of business as well as within lines of business with responsibility for the execution of the strategy (as opposed to its development). A key role is the provision of architecture consulting services to project teams.

At one company the key personnel of the tactical group are domain architects who have responsibility for broad categories of technology (e.g., server platforms); subdomain architects who have responsibility for technologies within a larger domain (e.g., desktops); and product stewards who have responsibility for specific products (e.g., Microsoft Windows XP). Accountability cascaded down this hierarchy with domain architects responsible for setting strategy, understanding the marketplace, and controlling proliferation of technology and product stewards responsible for new releases and versions of technologies as well as troubleshooting. At this organization, ultimate accountability rested with the executive architecture review board—a committee composed of senior business and IT architects—who ratify the technology roadmap and make final decisions regarding proposed deviations to the roadmap. If a need arises for an "off-profile" (that is, "noncompliant") technology, it must be brought before the architecture review board for an "opinion." According to the manager, this is a very effective mechanism because "most people don't want their project elevated to the executive architectural review board!"

A major part of governance is enforcement. Effective enforcement requires IT to develop a new breed of "corporate" architect who is business focused and businesscentric. According to one member, "Techcentric architects tend to be seen as police officers . . . there to enforce the law." It is better to have a businesscentric architect who can entertain business solutions that violate the preferred technology direction in light of increased technology risk (i.e., the risk of doing it) and business risk (i.e., the risk of not doing it) and arrive at a decision that best suits the business. The difference in approach is one of accommodation, as opposed to denial and prevention.

At one company the IT group did not want to ever have to "tell a business unit that they could not buy a specific package." The trade-off was to let the business specify the application's requirements and to let IT choose the product. Another firm tackled this problem by charging the business for the additional costs of a noncompliant application, such as extra in-house skills, application integration, conversions, and interfacing software. The overriding goal in all these firms was to achieve optimal decisions for the business, not rigid adherence to a technology roadmap.

A repository can be an aid to tracking decisions as well as a means of listing assigned responsibilities. At one company this "architecture library" lists all technology domains (e.g., hardware, applications, etc.) and all products within each domain. Product metadata includes the following:

- Status (i.e., emerging, contained, mainstream, declining, retirement, obsolete)
- Proposed replacement product
- Name of product steward, subdomain architect, and architect

- Business impact analysis
- Interdependencies
- Total cost of ownership

Knowing that a specific product is "declining," who the product steward is, the name of the replacement product, and the business impact analysis demonstrating exactly where and how this product affects business processes is extremely valuable information to the organization. Such a resource requires a significant amount of work to build but, once built, greatly reduces the complexity of maintaining and evolving a technology roadmap.

FINAL RECOMMENDATIONS

As part of the meeting, focus group members were asked the following question: If you were a "roadmap consultant," what advice would you offer to management?" When their suggestions were combined and analyzed, the collective wisdom reduced to the following four recommendations. Interestingly, this advice would arguably apply to many, if not most, IT initiatives.

1. *Be bold and innovative when planning the roadmap.*
   - What you have done should not be the gauge by which you determine what you should do.
   - Innovation is key; start with a blank piece of paper.
   - Invent your future. Inspire others to help you build it.
2. *Align technology with the business.*
   - Determine what role technology will play in satisfying the business vision.
   - Focus on using technology to solve business problems and deliver business value.
   - Know when it is appropriate to choose leeding-edge technology over being a late adopter/quick second.
   - Ensure that the roadmap is flexible, extensible, and attainable to change with the business.
   - Ensure that the organizational structure supports the delivery of a technology roadmap.
3. *Secure support for the roadmap.*
   - Ensure that the funding model supports a technology roadmap.
   - A migration strategy and roadmap requires an executive sponsor, ownership, and accountability. Ensure that strategic decisions are made at the right level.
   - Stay the course!
4. *Don't forget the people.*
   - Every technology change requires changes in people's skills.
   - Map new technologies to required skill acquisition.
   - Take steps to ensure that IT personnel understand the technology roadmap and its logic, ramifications, and time frame.
5. *Control, measure, and communicate progress.*
   - Measure progress along the way; use leading indicators.

- A successful roadmap must be measurable and updated at appropriate checkpoints.
- Communication of the roadmap is essential to success.
- Establish a governance process to manage technology and vendor choices.

CONCLUSION

The purpose of a technology roadmap is to guide the development of technology in an organization. But as pointed out in this chapter, it serves a much greater purpose for a business. It communicates the role that technology will play in advancing business goals. It outlines the explicit assumptions on which the roadmap is based and describes how these assumptions directly affect the rate and order of attainment of goals. It suggests the impact of future technology on the set of required in-house skills for the IT department. And it provides a vehicle for explaining the logic of technology-related decisions to business managers who otherwise interpret such decisions as overly rigid and unproductive. As such, a technology roadmap should be viewed as an important opportunity for IT to engage the business in meaningful and productive dialogue focused on furthering business goals. To limit this activity to simply forecasting technology is to miss a significant opportunity.

REFERENCES

Mangurian, G. E. "Alternative to Replacing Obsolete Systems." Cambridge, MA: Index Systems Inc., 1985.

McKeen, J. D., and H. A. Smith. *Making IT Happen.* Chichester, England: Wiley, 2003.

Appendix

Principles to Guide a Migration Strategy

One focus organization adopted the following four key principles to guide its migration strategy:

1. Migrate from productcentric to processcentric applications architecture using a service-based architecture that is grouped into layers such as presentation, business process, and data.
   * Maintain a sourcing strategy to develop strategic systems with competitive advantage in-house. Nonstrategic systems will be sourced through packages and services as available.
   * Maintain a technology skills base for critical technologies.
   * Utilize strategic partnerships to bring in leading-edge technology skills to accelerate implementation while, at the same time, transferring knowledge to your staff to permit in-house support and future development.
2. Deploy modular or component-based applications to minimize test and utility life cycle costs.
   * Adhere to a component-based and layered architecture with standardized, generic interfaces.
   * Ensure conformance of application development initiatives to the logical architecture specifications in order to engineer quality into the applications.
   * Build flexibility into the application components by allowing end users to establish and change business rules.

3. Utilize components based on industry standards as the building blocks of architecture services.
   * Adhere to (or adopt) industry-accepted standards and methodology to promote ease of integration.
   * Minimize the complexity of application interfaces by adopting flexible data interface standards, for example, extensible markup language (XML).
   * Adhere to corporate technology and application development standards in order to improve the efficiency, effectiveness, and timeliness of application development initiatives.
4. Insulate applications from being affected by changes in other applications through middleware.
   * Enterprise application integration (EAI) middleware services will be used to integrate application services across and within business domains.
   * Application interfaces will be well defined and documented in a metadata repository that includes interface methods, purpose, and terms of usage.
   * EAI services will include both application interface services and work flow integration services both within the department and in the extended enterprise.
   * Increase the degree of information and work flow integration across customer- and vendor-facing processes.

7

The IT Budgeting Process

Don't ever try to contact an IT manager in September because you won't get very far. September is budget month for most companies, and *that* means that most managers are hunkered down over a spreadsheet or in all-day meetings trying to "make the numbers work." "Budgeting is a very negative process at our firm," one IT manager told us. "And it takes way too long." Asking many IT managers about budgeting elicits much caustic comment. Apparently, there are significant difficulties with IT budgeting leading to widespread disenchantment among IT leaders who feel much of the work involved is both artificial and overly time consuming.

Others agree. While there has been little research done on IT budgeting per se (Hu and Quan 2006; Kobelsky et al. 2006), there appears to be broad, general consensus that the budgeting processes of many corporations are broken and need to be fixed (Buytendijk 2004; Hope and Fraser 2003; Jensen 2001). There are many problems. First, budgeting takes too long and consumes too much managerial time. One study found that budgeting is a protracted process taking at least four months and consuming about 30 percent of management's time (Hope and Fraser 2003). Second, most budgeting processes are no longer effective or efficient. They have become disconnected from business objectives, slow, and expensive (Buytendijk 2004). Third, rigid adherence to these annual plans has been found to stifle innovation and discourage frontline staff from taking responsibility for performance (Hope and Fraser 2003; Norton 2006). And fourth, while many researchers have studied how organizations choose between strategic investment opportunities, studies show that, all too often, the budgeting process undercuts management's strategic intentions, causing significant frustration among managers at all levels (Norton 2006; Steele and Albright 2004).

Finally, the annual planning cycle can cast spending plans "in concrete" at a time when the business needs to be flexible and agile. This is particularly true in IT. "Over time . . . IT budgeting processes become institutionalized. As a result, IT investments become less about creating competitive advantages for firms [and] more about following organizational routine and creating legitimacy for management as well as organizations" (Hu and Quan 2006). Now that senior business leaders have at last recognized the strategic importance of IT (Smith, McKeen, and Singh 2007) and IT has become many firms' largest capital expenditure (Koch 2006), a hard look at how IT budgets are created and spent is clearly called for.

This chapter first looks at key concepts in IT budgeting to establish what they mean for IT managers and how they can differ among IT organizations. Then it explores why budgets are an important part of the management process. Next the chapter examines the elements of the IT budget cycle. Finally, it identifies some recommended practices for improving IT budgeting.

KEY CONCEPTS IN IT BUDGETING

Before looking at how budgeting is actually practiced in IT organizations, it is important to understand what a budget *is* and *why* an effective IT budgeting process is so important, both within IT and for the enterprise as a whole. Current organizational budgeting practices emerged in the 1920s as a tool for managing costs and cash flows. Present-day annual fixed plans and budgets were established in the 1970s to drive performance improvements (Hope and Fraser 2003). Since then most organizations have adhered rigidly to the ideals of this process, in spite of much evidence of their negative influence on innovation and flexibility (Hope and Fraser 2003). These problems are clearly illustrated by the impact this larger corporate fiscal management process has on IT budgeting and the problems IT managers experience in trying to make their budget processes work effectively. The concepts and practices of the corporate fiscal world bear little similarity to how IT actually works. As a result, there are clear discontinuities between these two worlds.

These gaps are especially apparent in the differences between the fiscal view of IT and the functional one. **Fiscal IT budgets** (i.e., those prepared for the CFO) are broken down into two major categories: *capital expenditures* and *operating expenses*, although what expenditures go into each is highly variable across firms. In accounting, capital budgets are utilized to spread large expenses (e.g., buying a building) over several years, while operating expenses cover the annual cost of running the business. The distinction between these two concepts gets very fuzzy, however, when it comes to IT.

Generally speaking, all IT organizations want to capitalize as much of their spending as possible because it makes their annual costs look smaller. However, CIOs are limited in what types of IT expenditure they can capitalize by both organizational and tax policies. It is the CFO who, through corporate financial strategy, establishes what may be capitalized, and this, in turn, determines what IT can capitalize in its fiscal budget and what it must consider operating expense. As a result, some firms capitalize project development, infrastructure, consulting fees, and full-time staff, while others capitalize only major technology purchases.

How capital budgets are determined and the degree to which they are scrutinized also varies widely. Some firms allocate and prioritize IT capital expenses out of a corporate "pot"; others manage IT capital separately. Typically, capital expenses appear to be more carefully scrutinized than operating expenses, but not always. It is surprising to learn how different types of expenses are handled by different firms and the wide degree of latitude allowed for IT costs under generally accepted accounting principles. In fact, there are few accepted accounting principles when it comes to IT spending (Koch 2006). As a result, researchers should use caution in relying on measures of the amount of capital spent on IT in firms or industries.

It is within this rather fuzzy fiscal context that the structure and purpose of **functional IT budgets** (i.e., those used by IT managers as spending plans) must be understood because these accounting concepts do not usually correspond exactly with how IT managers and researchers view IT work and how they plan and budget for it. In contrast to how fiscal IT budgets are designed, IT managers plan their spending using two somewhat different categories: *operations costs* and *strategic investments*:

- *Operations costs.* This category consists of what it costs to "keep the lights on" in IT. These are the expenses involved in running IT like a utility. Operations involves the cost of maintenance, computing and peripheral functions (e.g., storage, network), and support, regardless of how it is delivered (i.e., in-house or outsourced). This category can, therefore, include both operating and capital costs. Between 50 and 90 percent of a firm's IT budget (average 76 percent) is spent in this area, so the spending involved is significant (Gruman 2006). In most firms there is continual pressure on the CIO to reduce operations costs year after year (Smith and McKeen 2006).
- *Strategic investment.* The balance of the IT budget consists of the "new" spending; that is, on initiatives and technology designed to deliver new business value and achieve the enterprise's strategic objectives. Because of the interactive nature of IT and business strategy these days, this part of the IT budget can include a number of different types of spending, such as business improvement initiatives to streamline processes and cut costs, business-enabling initiatives to extend or transform how a company does business, business opportunity projects to test the viability of new concepts or technologies and scale them up, and sometimes infrastructure (Smith, McKeen, and Singh 2007). Because spending in this area can include many different kinds of expense (e.g., full-time and contract staff, software and hardware), some parts of the strategic investment budget may be considered capital expenses while others are classified as operating.

Another fuzzy fiscal budgeting concept is *cost allocation*—the process of allocating the cost of the services IT provides to others' budgets. The cost of IT can be viewed as a corporate expense, a business unit expense, or a combination of both, and the way in which IT costs are allocated can have a significant impact on what is spent in IT. For example, a majority of companies allocate their operating expenses to their business units' operating budgets—usually using a formula based on factors such as the size of the business unit and its previous year's spending. Similarly, strategic expenses are typically allocated on the basis of which business unit will benefit from the investment. In today's IT environment, these approaches are not always effective for a number of reasons.

While many strategic IT investments involve the participation of more than one business unit, budgeting systems still tend to be designed around the structure of the organization (Norton 2006). This leads to considerable artificiality in allocating development resources to projects, which in turn can lead to dysfunctional behavior, such as lobbying, games, nonsupportive cross-functional work, and the inability to successfully implement strategy (Buytendijk 2004; Norton 2006). "We don't fund corporate projects very well," admitted one manager whose company allocates all costs to individual business units.

Allocations can also lead to operational inefficiencies. "The different allocation models tend to lead to 'gaming' between our business units," said another participant. "Our business unit managers have no control over their percentage of operating costs," explained a third. "This is very frustrating for them and tends to be a real problem for some of our smaller units." Because of these allocations, some business units may not be willing to share in the cost of new hardware, software, or processes that would lead to reduced enterprise costs in the longer term. This is one of the primary reasons so many IT organizations end up supporting several different applications all doing the same thing. Furthermore, sometimes, when senior managers get disgruntled with their IT expenses, this method of allocating operations costs can lead to their cutting their IT operational spending in ways that have little to do with running a cost-effective IT organization. For example, one company cut back on its budget for hardware and software upgrades, which meant that a significant percentage of IT staff then had to be redeployed to testing, modifying, and maintaining new systems so they would run on the old machines. While IT managers have done some work educating their CEOs and CFOs about what constitutes effective cost cutting (e.g., appropriate outsourcing, adjusting service levels), the fact remains that most business executives still do not understand or appreciate the factors that contribute to the overall cost of IT. As a result, allocations can lead to a great deal of angst for IT managers at budget time as they try to justify each expense while business managers try to "nickel and dime" each expense category (Koch 2006).

As a result of all this fuzziness, modern IT budgeting practices do little to give business leaders confidence that IT spending is both effective and efficient (Gruman 2006). And the challenges IT managers face in making IT spending fit into contemporary corporate budgeting practices are significant.

THE IMPORTANCE OF BUDGETS

Ideally, budgets are a key component of corporate performance management. "If done well, a budget is the operational translation of an enterprise's strategy into costs and planned revenue" (Buytendijk 2004). Budgets are also a subset of good governance processes in that they enable management to understand and communicate what is being spent and where. Ideally, therefore, a budget is more than a math exercise; it is "a blueprint for fiscally sound IT and business success" (Overby 2004). Effective IT budgeting is important for many reasons, but two of the most important are as follows:

1. **Fiscal discipline.** As overall IT spending has risen, senior business leaders are paying much closer attention to what IT costs and how its budgets are spent. In many organizations there is still a great deal of skepticism that IT budgets are used wisely, so reducing spending, or at least the operations portion of the budget, is

now considered a key way for a CIO to build trust with the executive team (Gruman 2006). Demonstrating an understanding and appreciation of the realities of business finance has become a significant part of IT leadership (Goldberg 2004), and the ability to create and monitor a budget is, therefore, "table stakes" for a CIO (Overby 2004).

It is clear that senior executives are using the budgeting process to enforce tougher rules on how IT dollars are spent. Some organizations have centralized IT budgeting in an effort to better understand what is being spent; others are making the link between reducing operations spending and increasing investment in IT a reason for introducing new operations disciplines (e.g., limiting maintenance, establishing appropriate support levels). Still others have established tighter requirements for business cases and monitoring returns on investment. Organizations also use their IT budgets to manage and limit demand. "Our IT budget is capped by our CEO," stated one manager. "And it's always less than the demand." Using budgets in this way, while likely effective for the enterprise, can cause problems for CIOs in that they must in turn enforce spending disciplines on business unit leaders.

Finally, budgets and performance against budgets are a key way of holding IT management accountable for what it spends, both internally to the leadership of the organization and externally to shareholders and regulatory bodies. Improperly used, budgets can distort reality and encourage inappropriate behavior (Hope and Fraser 2003; Jensen 2001). However, used responsibly, they can be "a basis for clear understanding between organizational levels and can help executives maintain control over divisions and the business" (Hope and Fraser 2003). Research is beginning to show that there is a positive relationship between good IT budgeting practices (i.e., using IT budgets to manage demand, make investment decisions, and govern IT) and overall company performance (Kobelsky et al. 2006; Overby 2004).

2. *Strategy implementation.*   Budgets are also the means to implement IT strategy, linking the long-term goals of the organization and their short-term execution through the allocation of resources to activities. Unfortunately, research shows that the majority of organizations do not link their strategies to their budgets, which is why so many have difficulty making strategic changes (Norton 2006). This is particularly true in IT. As one manager complained, "No one knows what we're doing in the future. Therefore, our goals change regularly and at random." Another noted, "The lines of business pay little attention to IT resources when they're establishing their strategic plans. They just expect IT to make it happen."

Budgets can affect IT strategy implementation in a number of ways. First, *where* IT dollars are spent determines the impact IT can have on corporate performance. Clearly, if 80 percent of IT expenditures are going to operations and maintenance, IT can have less strategic impact than if this percentage is lower. Second, *how* discretionary IT dollars are spent is important. For example, some companies decide to invest in infrastructure, while others do not; some will choose to "bet the company" on a single large IT initiative, while others will choose more focused projects. In short, the outcome of how a company chooses among investment opportunities is reflected in its budgets (Steele and Albright 2004).

Third, the budgeting process itself reflects and reinforces the ability of strategic decision making to have an impact. Norton (2006) states that because budget processes are inherently biased toward the short term, operational needs will systematically preempt strategic ones. In IT the common practice of routinely allocating a fixed percentage of the IT strategic budget to individual business units makes it almost impossible to easily reallocate resources to higher-priority projects at the enterprise level or in other business units. In addition, siloed budgeting processes make it difficult to manage the cross-business costs of strategic IT decisions.

Overall, budgets are a critical element of most managerial decisions and processes and are used to accomplish a number of different purposes in IT: compliance, fiscal accountability, cost reduction, business unit and enterprise strategy implementation, internal customer service, delivering business value, and operational excellence, to name just a few. This, in a nutshell, is the reason IT budgeting is such a complex and challenging process.

THE IT PLANNING AND BUDGET PROCESS

Given that IT budgets are used in so many different ways and serve so many stakeholders, it is no wonder that the whole process of IT budgeting is "painful," "artificial," and in need of some serious improvement. Figure 7.1 illustrates a generic and simplified IT planning and budgeting process. This section outlines the steps involved in putting together an IT budget utilizing some of the key concepts presented above.

Figure 7.1 A Generic IT Planning and Budgeting Process

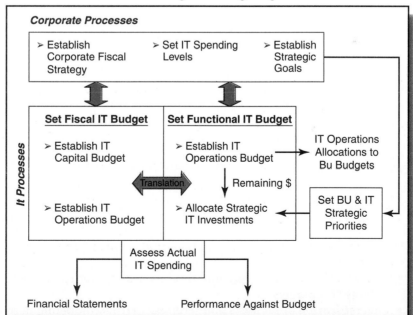

1. *Corporate processes.* These three activities set the corporate context within which IT plans and budgets are created.

- *Establish corporate fiscal policy.* This process is usually so far removed from the annual budget cycle that IT leaders may not even be aware of its influence or the wide number of options in the choices that are made (particularly around capitalization). Corporate fiscal policies are not created with IT spending in mind but, as noted above, can significantly impact how a fiscal IT budget is created and the levels of scrutiny under which certain kinds of expenses are placed. A more direct way that corporate fiscal policies affect IT is in company expectations around the return on investment for IT projects. Most companies now have an explicit expected return rate for all new projects that is closely monitored.

- *Establish strategic goals.* Conversely, IT budgeting *is* directly and continuously affected by many corporate strategic goals. The process of establishing IT and business unit strategies occurs within the context of these overall goals. In some organizations there is tight integration between enterprise, business unit, and IT strategic planning; in others these are more loosely coupled, informal, and iterative. However, what is truly rare is a provision for enterprise funding for enterprise IT initiatives. Thus, corporate strategic goals are typically broken down into business unit budgets. As one manager explained, "First our executives decide our profits and then the business units decide how to achieve them and then IT develops a plan with the business unit . . . We still don't do many corporate projects."

- *Set IT spending levels.* Establishing how much to spend on IT is the area that has been most closely studied by researchers. This is a complex process, influenced by many external and internal factors. *Externally,* firms look to others in their industry to determine the level of their spending (Hu and Quan 2006). In particular, companies frequently use benchmarks with similar firms to identify a percentage of revenue to spend on IT (Koch 2006). Unfortunately, this approach can be dangerous for a number of reasons. First, it can be a strong driver in inhibiting competitive advantage and leading to greater similarities among firms in an industry (Hu and Quan 2006). Second, this metric tells management nothing about how well its money is being spent (Koch 2006). Third, it does not address IT's ability to use IT strategically (Kobelsky et al. 2006).

    A second and increasingly strong external driver of IT spending is the regulatory environment within which a firm operates. Legislation, standards, and professional practices are all beginning to affect what IT can and cannot do and how its work is done (Smith and McKeen 2006). These, in turn, affect how much is spent on IT and where it is spent (Hu and Quan 2006). Other external factors that have been shown to affect how much money is spent on IT include the following:

    - *Number of competitors.* More concentration in an industry reduces the amount spent.
    - *Uncertainty.* More uncertainty in a business's external environment leads to larger IT budgets.
    - *Diversification of products and services.* Firms competing in more markets will tend to spend more on IT (Kobelsky et al. 2006).

Internal factors affecting the size of the IT budget include the following:

- *Affordability.*   A firm's overall performance and cash flow will influence how much discretion it has to spend on IT.
- *Growth.*   Growing firms tend to invest more in IT than mature firms.
- *Previous year's spending.*   Firm spending on IT is unlikely to deviate significantly year to year (Hu and Quan 2006; Kobelsky et al. 2006).

2. *IT processes.*   These are multilevel and complex and frequently occur in parallel with each other.

- *Set functional IT budget.*   This budget documents spending as it relates to how IT organizations *work*; that is, what is to be spent on IT operations and how much is available to be spent on strategic investments. As noted above, the operations budget is relatively fixed and contains the lion's share of the dollars. In spite of this, there are a number of machinations that IT managers must go through annually to justify this expenditure. Most IT organizations are still seen as cost centers, so obtaining budget approvals is often a delicate, ongoing exercise of relationship building and education to prevent inappropriate cost cutting (Koch 2006). Once the overall IT operations budget has been established, there is still the challenge of allocating it to the individual business units, which, given the complexity of today's shared technical environment, is often a fixed or negotiated percentage of the total. Business units can resent these allocations over which they have no control, and at best, they are viewed as a "necessary evil." In organizations where the IT operations budget is centralized, IT managers have a better opportunity to reduce expenses year by year by introducing standards, streamlining hardware and software, and sharing services. However, in many companies, operations budgets are decentralized into the business units and aggregated up into the overall IT budget. This approach makes it considerably more difficult for IT managers to implement effective cost-reduction measures. However, even in those firms that are highly effective and efficient, the relentless pressure from executives to do more with less makes this part of the annual budgeting process a highly stressful activity.

  Allocating the funds remaining to strategic investments is a completely separate process in which potential new IT projects are prioritized and their costs justified. Companies have many different ways of doing this, and most appear to be in a transition phase between methods of prioritization. Traditionally, IT organizations have been designed to parallel the organization structure, and new development funds have been allocated to business units on the basis of some rule of thumb. For example, each business unit might be allotted a certain number of IT staff and dollars to spend on new development (based on percentage of overall revenue) that would remain relatively stable over time. More recently, however, with greater integration of technology, systems, and data, there has been recognition of the cross-business costs of new development and of the need for more enterprise spending to address these. Increasingly, therefore, organizations are moving to prioritize some or all new development at the enterprise level, thereby removing fixed allocations of new development resources from the business units.

However it is determined, the strategic portion of the functional IT budget also involves staffing the initiatives. This introduces yet another level of complexity in that, even if the dollars are available, appropriate IT resources must also be available to be assigned to particular projects to address the organization's cost-cutting requirements. Thus, undertaking a new project not only involves cost justification and prioritization, but it also requires the availability of the right mix of skills and types of staff. While some firms use fixed percentages of full-time, contract, and offshore staff in their projects, most use a mix of employees and contract staff in their development projects in order to keep overhead costs low. As a result, creating new IT development budgets often involves a complementary exercise in staff planning.

- *Set the fiscal IT budget.* A second, parallel stream of IT budgeting involves establishing the *fiscal* IT budget, which the CFO uses to implement the company's fiscal strategy and provide financial reports to shareholders and regulatory and tax authorities. This is seen largely as a "translation" exercise by IT managers where the functional IT budget is reconstituted into the operating and capital spending buckets. Nevertheless, it represents an additional "hoop" through which IT managers must jump before their budgets can be approved. In some companies capital funding is difficult to obtain and must be justified against an additional set of financial criteria. Some organizations require IT capital expenditures be prioritized against all other corporate capital expenses (e.g., buildings, trucks), which can be a very challenging exercise. In other firms CFOs are more concerned about increasing operating expenses. In either case this is an area where many IT managers set themselves up for failure by failing to "speak the language of finance" (Girard 2004). Because most IT managers think of their work in terms of operations and strategic investments, they fail to understand some of the larger drivers of fiscal strategy such as investor value and earnings per share. To get more "traction" for their budgets, it is, therefore, important for IT leaders to better translate what IT can do for the company into monetary terms (Girard 2004). To this end, many companies have begun working more closely with their internal finance staff and are seeing greater acceptance of their budgets as a result.

Assess Actual IT Spending

At the other end of the budgeting process is the need to assess actual IT spending and performance. A new focus on financial accountability has meant that results are more rigorously tracked than in the past. In many companies finance staff now monitor business cases for all new IT projects, thus relieving IT of having to prove the business returns on what is delivered. Often the challenge of finding the right resources for a project or unexpected delays means that the entire available development budget may not be spent within a given fiscal year. "We typically tend to spend about 85 percent of our available development budget because of delays or resourcing problems," said one manager. Hitting budget targets *exactly* in the strategic investment budget is, therefore, a challenge, and current IT budgeting practices typically do not allow for much flexibility. On the one hand, they can create a "use it or lose it" mentality; if money is not spent in the fiscal year, it will disappear. "This leads to some creative accruals and aggressive forecasting," said the focus group. On the other hand, IT managers who want to ensure there is *enough* money for key expenditures create "placeholders" (i.e., approximations of what they think a project will cost) and "coffee cans" (i.e., unofficial slush funds) in their budgets. The artificial timing of the budget process, combined with the difficulties of planning and estimation and reporting complexity, all mean that accurate reporting of what is spent can get distorted.

IT BUDGETING PRACTICES THAT DELIVER VALUE

Although there is general agreement that current budgeting practices are flawed, there are still no widely accepted alternatives. Within IT itself, companies seem to be experimenting with ways to "tweak" budgeting to make it both easier and more effective. The following five practices have proven to be useful in this regard:

1. *Appoint an IT finance specialist.* Many companies now have a finance expert working in IT or on staff with the CFO working *with* IT. "Getting help with finance has really made the job of budgeting easier," said one manager. "Having a good partnership with finance helps us to leverage their expertise," said another. Financial specialists can help IT managers to understand their costs and drivers in new ways. Within operations, they can assist with cost and value analysis of services and infrastructure (Gruman 2006) and also manage the "translation" process between the functional IT budget and the fiscal IT budget. "Finance helps us to understand depreciation and gives us a deeper understanding of our cost components," a focus group member noted. Finance specialists are also being used to build and monitor business cases for new projects, often acting as brokers between IT and the business units. "They've really helped us to better articulate business value. Now they're in charge of ensuring that the business gets the benefits they say they will, not IT." The improving relationship between finance and IT is making it easier to gain acceptance of IT budgets. "Having dedicated IT finance people is great since this is not what IT managers want to do," said a participant.

2. *Use budgeting tools and methodologies.* About one-half of the members of the focus group felt they had effective budgeting tools for such things as asset tracking, rolling up and breaking down budgets into different levels of granularity, and reporting. "We have a good, integrated suite of tools," said a manager, "and they really help." Because budgets serve so many different stakeholders, tools and methodologies can help "slice and dice" the numbers many ways, dynamically enabling changes in one area to be reflected in all other areas. Those who did not have good or well-integrated tools found that there were gaps in their budgeting processes that were hard to fill. "Our poor tools lead to disconnects all over the place," claimed an IT manager. Good links to the IT planning process are also needed. Ideally, tools should tie budgets directly to corporate strategic planning, resource strategies, and performance metrics, enabling a further translation among the company's accounting categories and hierarchy and its strategic themes and targets (Norton 2006).

3. *Separate operations from innovation.* While most IT managers mentally separate these two IT activities, in practical terms maintenance and support are often mixed up with new project development. This happens especially when IT organizations are aligned with and funded by the business units. Once IT funds and resources are allotted to a particular business unit, rather than to a strategic deliverable, it is very difficult to reduce these allocations. There appears to be growing agreement that operations (including maintenance) must be fully financially separated from new development in order to ensure that the costs of the first are fully scrutinized and kept under control while focus is kept on increasing the proportion of resources devoted to new project development (Dragoon 2005; Girard 2004; Gruman 2006; Norton 2006). Repeatedly, focus group managers told stories of how their current budget processes discourage accuracy. "There are many disincentives built into our budgeting processes to keep operational costs down," said one manager. Separating operations from innovation in budgets provides a level of visibility in IT spending that has traditionally been absent and that helps business unit leaders better understand the true costs of delivering both new systems and ongoing services.

4. *Adopt enterprise funding models.* While it is still rare to find organizations that provide corporate funding for enterprisewide strategic IT initiatives, there is broad recognition that this is needed (Norton 2006). The conflict between the need for truly integrated initiatives and traditional siloed budgets frequently stymies innovation, frustrates behavior designed for the common good, and discourages accountability for results (Hope and Fraser 2003; Norton 2006; Steele and Albright 2004). It is, therefore, expected that more organizations will adopt enterprise funding models for at least some IT initiatives over the next few years. Similarly, decentralized budgeting for core IT services is declining due to the cost-savings opportunities available from sharing these. While costs will likely continue to be charged back to the differing business units, the current best practice is for IT operation budgets to be developed at an enterprise level.

5. *Adopt rolling budget cycles.* IT plans and budgets need attention more frequently than once a year. While not used by many companies, utilizing an eighteen-month rolling plan that is reviewed and updated quarterly appears to be a more effective way of budgeting, especially for new project development (Hope and Fraser 2003; Smith, McKeen, and Singh 2007). "It is very difficult to plan new projects a year in advance," said one manager. "Often we are asked for our 'best estimates' in our budgets. The problem is that, once they're in the budget, they are then viewed as reality." The artificial timing of budgets and the difficulty of estimating the costs of new projects are key sources of frustration for IT managers. Rolling budget cycles, when combined with integrated budgeting tools, should better address this problem while still providing the financial snapshots needed by the enterprise on an annual basis.

CONCLUSION

Although IT budget processes have been largely ignored by researchers, they are a critical lynchpin between many different organizational stakeholders: finance and IT; business units and IT; corporate strategy and IT; and different internal IT groups. Not surprisingly, therefore, IT budgeting is much more complex and difficult to navigate than it appears. This chapter has outlined some of the challenges faced by IT managers trying to juggle the realities of dealing with both IT operations and strategic investments while meeting the differing needs of their budget stakeholders. Surprisingly, there are very few guidelines for IT managers in this area. Each organization appears to have quite different corporate financial policies, which, in turn, drive different IT budgeting practices. Nevertheless, IT managers do face many common challenges in budgeting. Although other IT practices have benefited from focused management attention in recent years (e.g., prioritization, operations rationalization), budgeting has not as yet been targeted in this way. However, as business and IT leaders begin to recognize the key role that budgets play in implementing strategy and controlling costs, it is hoped they will make a serious effort to address the budgeting issues faced by IT.

REFERENCES

Buytendijk, F. "New Way to Budget Enhances Corporate Performance Measurement." Gartner Inc., January 28, 2004, Resource ID #423484.

Dragoon, A. "Journey to the IT Promised Land." *CIO Magazine* (April 1, 2005).

Girard, K. "What CIOs Need to Know about Money." *CIO Magazine* Special Money Issue (September 22, 2004).

Goldberg, M. "The Final Frontier for CIOs." *CIO Magazine* Special Money Issue (September 22, 2004).

Gruman, G. "Trimming for Dollars." *CIO Magazine* (July 1, 2006).

Hope, J., and R. Fraser. "Who Needs Budgets?" *Harvard Business Review* 81, no. 2 (February 2003): 2–8.

Hu, Q., and J. Quan. "The Institutionalization of IT Budgeting: Empirical Evidence from the Financial Sector." *Information Resources Management Journal* 19, no. 1 (Jan.–Mar. 2006): 84–97.

Jensen, M. "Corporate Budgeting Is Broken—Let's Fix It." *Harvard Business Review* 79, no. 11 (November 2001): 95–101

Kobelsky, K., V. Richardson, R. Smith, and R. Zmud. "Determinants and Consequences of Firm Information Technology Budgets." Draft paper provided by the authors, May 2006.

Koch, C. "The Metrics Trap . . . and How to Avoid It." *CIO Magazine* (April 1, 2006).

Norton, D. "Linking Strategy and Planning to Budgets." *Balanced Scorecard Report*. Harvard Business School Publishing (May–June 2006).

Overby, S. "Tips from the Budget Masters." *CIO Magazine* Special Money Issue (September 22, 2004).

Smith, H. A., and J. D. McKeen. "IT in 2010," *MIS Quarterly Executive* 5, no. 3 (September 2006): 125–36.

Smith, H. A., J. D. McKeen, and S. Singh. "Developing IT Strategy for Business Value." *Journal of Information Technology Management* XVIII, no. 1 (June 2007): 49–58.

Steele, R., and C. Albright. "Games Managers Play at Budget Time." *MIT Sloan Management Review* 45, no. 3 (Spring 2004): 81–84.

Chapter 8

Information Management: The Nexus of Business and IT[1]

More than ever before, we are living in an information age. Yet until very recently, "information" and its sibling, "knowledge," were given very little attention in IT organizations. Data ruled. And information proliferated quietly in various corners of the business—file cabinets, PCs, databases, microfiche, e-mail, and libraries. Then along came the Internet, and the business began to understand the power and the potential of information. For the past few years, they have been clamoring for IT to deliver more and better information to them (Smith and McKeen 2005c). As a result, information delivery has become an important part of IT's job.

Now that the business recognizes the value of improved information, IT is facing huge challenges in getting it to them:

> Not only does effective information delivery require IT to implement new technologies, it also means that IT must develop new internal nontechnical and analytic capabilities. Information delivery makes IT work much more visible in the organization. Developing standard data models, integrating information into work processes, and forcing (encouraging) business managers to put the customer/employee/supplier first in their decision making involves IT practitioners in organizational and political conflicts that most would likely prefer to avoid. Unfortunately, the days of hiding in the "glass house" are now completely over and IT managers are front and center of an information revolution that will completely transform how organizations operate. (Smith and McKeen 2005a)

This points out a truth that is only just beginning to sink in to the organization's collective consciousness. That is, while information *delivery* may be the responsibility

---

[1]Smith, H. A., and J. D. McKeen, "Information Management: The Nexus of Business and IT," *Communications of the Association of Information Systems* 19, article 3 (January 2007): 34–46 (reproduced by permission of the Association of Information Systems).

of IT, information *management* (IM) requires a true partnership between IT and the business. While IT is *involved* with almost every aspect of IM, information is the heart and soul of the business, and its management cannot be delegated or abdicated to IT. Thus, IM represents the true nexus of the business and IT. Because of this, IM has all the hallmarks of an emerging discipline—the offspring of a committed, long-term relationship between the business and IT. It requires new skills and competencies, new frames of reference, and new processes. As is often the case, IT workers are further advanced in their understanding of this new discipline, but many business leaders are also recognizing their responsibilities in this field. In some organizations, notably government, IM is now a separate organizational entity, distinct from IT.

This chapter explores the nature and dimensions of IM and its implications for IT, looking at IM from the enterprise point of view. Whereas information delivery can be viewed from a purely IT perspective, information management addresses the business *and* IT issues and challenges in managing information effectively. The first section examines the scope and nature of IM and how it is being conceptualized in organizations. The next presents a framework for the comprehensive management of information. Then the key issues currently facing organizations in implementing an effective IM program are addressed. Finally, it presents some recommendations for getting started in IM.

INFORMATION MANAGEMENT: HOW DOES IT FIT?

Information management is an idea whose time has come. There are a number of reasons for this. One focus group member explained it in this way:

> In today's business environment, it is a given that we must know who our customer is and ensure our organization's information enables us to make the right business decisions. As well, emerging regulations are starting to shape the IM requirements of all companies. These include privacy and security safeguards on customer information, long-term storage of historical records, and stronger auditability. We are now being held legally accountable for our information.

Thus, IM has three distinct but related drivers: (1) compliance, (2) operational effectiveness and efficiency, and (3) strategy.

Information, as we are now recognizing, is a key organizational resource, along with human and financial capital. Captured and used in the right way, many believe it is a new form of capital, known as *structural capital* (Stewart 1999). However, unlike human and financial capital, information is not finite. It cannot be used up nor can it walk out the door. Furthermore, information capabilities—that is, the ability to capture, organize, use, and maintain information—have been shown to contribute to IT effectiveness, individual effectiveness, and overall business performance (Kettinger and Marchand 2005; Marchand, Kettinger, and Rollins 2000). Therefore, many companies now believe that creating useful structural capital is a strategic priority (Davenport and Prusak 1998; Kettinger and Marchand 2005).

Unlike information technology, which provides the technology, tools, and processes with which to *manipulate data,* or knowledge management (KM), which focuses on how

Figure 8.1 IM Is Fundamental to Organizational Success—Both IT Effectiveness and Individual Performance

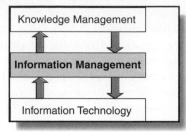

best to leverage the know-how and *intangible experience* of the organization's human capital, IM provides the mechanisms for managing enterprise information itself. IM represents the "meat" in the data-information-knowledge continuum and provides a foundation that can be used by both IT and KM to create business value (see Figure 8.1).

As noted above, organizations today are beset with demands for more and better information and more controls over it. IM is the means to get above the fray and clarify how the enterprise will manage information as an integrated resource. In theory, it covers all forms of information needed and produced by the business, both structured and unstructured, including the following:

- Customer information
- Financial information
- Operational information
- Product information
- HR information
- Performance information
- Documents
- E-mail and instant messages
- Images and multimedia materials
- Business intelligence
- Relationship information (e.g., suppliers, partners)

In practice, some of these forms will be more thoroughly managed than others, depending on the organization involved.

The "IM function" is also responsible for the complete information life cycle: acquisition or creation, organization, navigation, access, security, administration, storage, and retention. Because IM falls into the gray area between the business and IT and is not yet a separate organizational entity, many organizations are finding it is essential to develop an enterprisewide framework that clarifies the policies, principles, roles, responsibilities and accountabilities, and practices for IM in both groups.

A FRAMEWORK FOR IM

Because much information use crosses traditional functional boundaries, organizations must take an enterprise perspective on IM for it to be effective. A framework for implementing IM involves several stages that move from general principles to specific applications. While these are presented as distinct activities, in practice, they will likely evolve iteratively as the organization and its management learn by doing. For example, one company developed and implemented its privacy policy first then recognized the need for an information security policy. As this was being implemented, it created a more generic IM policy that incorporated the other two in its principles.

Stage One: Develop an IM Policy

A policy outlines the terms of reference for making decisions about information. It provides the basis for corporate directives and for developing the processes, standards, and guidelines needed to manage information assets well throughout the enterprise. Because information is a corporate asset, an IM policy needs to be established at a very senior management level and approved by the board of directors. This policy should provide guidance for more detailed directives on accountabilities, quality, security, privacy, risk tolerances, and prioritization of effort.

Because of the number of business functions affected by information, a draft policy should be developed by a multidisciplinary team. At minimum, IT, the privacy office, legal, HR, corporate audit, and key lines of business should be involved. "We had lots of support for this from our audit people," said one manager. "They recognize that an IM policy will help improve the traceability of information and its transformations, and this makes their jobs easier." Another recommended reviewing the draft policy with many executives and ensuring that all business partners are identified. "Ideally, the policy should also link to existing IM processes such as security classifications)," stated another. "It's less threatening if people are familiar with what it implies, and this also helps to identify gaps in practices that need to be addressed."

Stage Two: Articulate Operational Components

These describe what needs to be in place in order to put the corporate IM policy into practice across the organization (see Figure 8.2). In turn, each component will have several "elements." These could vary according to what different organizations deem

Figure 8.2 Operational Components of an IM Framework

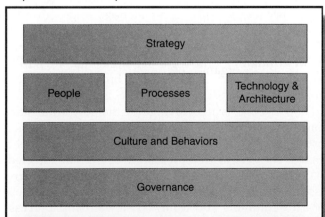

important. For example, the strategy component at one company has six elements: (1) interacting with the external environment, (2) strategic planning, (3) information life cycle, (4) general planning, (5) program integration, and (6) performance monitoring (for a description of the elements identified by this firm, see Appendix). Together, the operational components act as a context to describe current IM practices in the organization and reference existing best practices in each area. "This is a living document, and you should expect it to be continually refined," noted a focus group member.

The IM framework's operational components and individual elements act as a discussion document to position IM in the business and to illustrate its breadth and scope. "There's a danger of IM being perceived as a 'technology thing,'" stated a manager. At present, it is mostly IT groups that are spearheading the IM effort, but they recognize that it shouldn't necessarily be located in IT permanently. "Ideally, we need a corporate information office that cuts across lines of business and corporate groups, just like IT," said another manager.

Stage Three: Establish Information Stewardship

There are many roles and responsibilities associated with IM that need to be clearly articulated. These are especially important to clarify because of the boundary-spanning nature of information. Both political and practical issues arise when certain questions are asked: Who is responsible for the quality of our customer data? Whose version of name and address do we use? Who must sign off on the accuracy of our financial information? Ideally, most organizations would like to have a single version of each of their key information subjects (e.g., customer, product, employees) that all lines of business and systems would use. This would enable proper protections and controls to be put in place. And this is clearly a long-term IM goal for most. However, legacy environments, political realities, and tight budgets mean that the reality is somewhat less perfect with duplicate versions of the same information and several variants being used by parts of the business.

Information stewards are businesspeople. They should be responsible for determining the meaning of information "chunks" (e.g., customer name and address) and their business rules and contextual use. They should be responsible for the accuracy, timeliness, consistency, validity, completeness, and redundancy of information. Stewards also determine who may access information according to privacy and security policies and provide guidance for the retention and deletion of information in accordance with regulatory and legal requirements. In addition, they make the information's characteristics available to a broad audience through the organization's metadata.

Stewardship, like IM, is an evolving role that few understand fully. Ideally, there should be one steward for each information subject, but this is nowhere near the reality in most organizations. One organization has established a working group for each of its major subjects, with representatives from all affected stakeholder groups as well as IT. Their goals are to reduce duplicate records, correct information, simplify processes, and close "back doors." In the longer term, these groups hope to develop standard definitions and a formal stewardship process and ultimately use these to retool IT's data infrastructure.

"We are struggling with this concept," admitted a manager. "This is not a simple task, and no one in our business wants to take accountability as yet." Stewardship also takes time, and many business units are not yet prepared to allocate resources to it. "At present, we are hitching our wagons to other projects and hoping to make some progress in this way," said another manager. "Every area is taking some steps, but they're all at different levels of maturity. This can be frustrating because progress is so slow." All agreed that the role of information steward needs to be better defined and incorporated into organizational and HR models. New performance metrics also need to be established to monitor progress against these goals in ways that link IM activities to key business objectives.

Standards require . . .

- a unique name and definition.
- data elements, examples, and character length (e.g., name prefix).
- relationship rules.
- implementation requirements.
- spacing and order.

Stage Four: Build Information Standards

Standards help ensure that quality, accuracy, and control goals can be met. When all parts of an organization follow the same standards, it is relatively easy to simplify the processes and technology that use a piece of information, said the focus group. Conversely, different information sets standards used by different business groups will inhibit effective IM. While *setting* information standards can be challenging, it's even harder to actually *implement* them, participants noted. This is partly due to the large number of legacy applications in most organizations and also because it is difficult to get funding for this work.

Not all information needs to be standardized, however, only that which is used by more than one business unit. When information *is* used more broadly, a standard needs to be established. This is where a metadata repository is useful. This repository stores information definitions; standards for use and change; and provides cross-references for all models, processes, and programs using a particular piece of information. A metadata repository can be jointly used by the business, when beginning a new project, and IT, when developing or modifying applications. It can be invaluable to both groups (and to the enterprise) in helping them to understand how their work will affect others, thus preventing potential problems.

Typically, cross-functional working groups composed of business and IT staff establish standards. "Metadata is really where the rubber meets the road," said one manager. "It can be a very powerful tool to prevent the duplication of data in the organization." However, it is a huge undertaking and takes time to show value. "You need strong IT executive support for this," he said. "It is not something that those outside of IT initially understand." The focus group recommended starting with what exists currently (e.g., a data warehouse) then growing from there. One firm initially established a procedure that any changes to production systems had to update the metadata repository first. "We weren't prepared for the demand this created," stated the manager involved. "It's much better to incorporate this step in front-end analysis than at the end of development."

Finally, education and awareness play an essential role at this stage. "We always underestimate the importance of awareness," said a participant. "We must make sure that no project starts in the organization that doesn't use standards. The only way to do this is to keep this issue continually in front of our business executives." The other group members agreed. "Standards are the cornerstone of IM," said one. "If they are followed, they will ensure we don't add further layers of complexity and new steps."

ISSUES IN IM

As with anything new, those involved with IM in their organizations face a host of challenges and opportunities as they try to implement more effective processes and practices around information. Some of these can be mixed blessings in that they are both drivers of IM and complications (e.g., legislation). Others are simply new ways of looking at information and new perspectives on the way organizations work. Still others are genuinely new problems that must be addressed. When combined with the fact that IM "belongs" exclusively to neither IT nor the business, these add up to a huge organizational headache, especially for IT. "Sometimes the businesspeople are not ready for the disciplines associated with IM," said one manager. "If they're not ready, we move on to an area that is." Another said, "Sometimes it's more trouble than it's worth to involve the business, and we just do the work ourselves."

Culture and Behavior

In the longer term, however, the focus group agreed that IM is something that all parts of the organization will have to better understand and participate in. One of the most comprehensive challenges is changing the culture and behavior surrounding information. Marchand, Kettinger, and Rollins (2000) suggest that there are six interdependent beliefs and behaviors that are needed by all staff to support a positive "information orientation." These have been strongly correlated to organizational performance when they are present with strong IT and IM practices:

1. *Integrity.* Integrity "defines both the boundaries beyond which people in an organization should not go in using information and the 'space' in which people can trust their colleagues to do with information what they would do themselves" (Marchand, Kettinger, and Rollins 2000). Where integrity exists, people will have confidence that information will not be used inappropriately.
2. *Formality.* This is the ability to trust formal sources of information (as opposed to informal ones). Formality enables an organization to provide accurate and consistent information about the business and establish formal processes and information flows that can be used to improve performance and provide services to customers.

3. *Control.* Once formal information is trusted, it can be used to develop integrated performance criteria and measures for all levels of the company. In time, these will enable monitoring and performance improvement at the individual and work unit levels and can be linked to compensation and rewards.

4. *Transparency.* This describes a level of trust among members of an organization that enables them to speak about errors or failures "in an open and constructive manner without fear of unfair repercussions" (Marchand, Kettinger, and Rollins 2000). Transparency is necessary to identify and respond effectively to problems and for learning to take place.

5. *Sharing.* At this level, both sensitive and nonsensitive information is freely exchanged among individuals and across functional boundaries. Information exchanges are both initiated by employees and formally promoted through programs and forums.[2]

6. *Proactiveness.* Ultimately, every member of an organization should be alert to picking up new information about business conditions and open to testing new concepts.

Information Risk Management

The increasing breadth and scope of IT, combined with greater use of outsourcing, has made information more vulnerable to both internal and external fraud and raised the level of risk associated with it. Management must, therefore, take proactive measures to determine an appropriate risk/return tradeoff for information security. There are costs associated with information security mechanisms, and the business must be educated about them. In some cases these mechanisms are "table stakes"; that is, they must be taken if the company wants to "be in the game." Other risks in information security include internal and external interdependencies, implications for corporate governance, and impact on the value proposition. Risk exposures can also change over time and with outsourcing.

The focus group agreed that security is essential in the new world of IM. Today most organizations have basic information protection, for example, virus scanners, firewalls, and virtual private networks. Many are also working on the next level of security, which includes real-time response, intrusion detection and monitoring, and vulnerability analysis. Soon, however, information security will need to include role-based identity and access management. An effective information-security strategy includes several components:

- An information protection center, which does data classification and vulnerability analysis and issues alerts
- Risk management
- Identity management, including access management, digital rights management, and encryption technology
- Education and awareness
- Establishment of priorities, standards, and resource requirements
- Compliance reviews and audits

---

[2]New privacy laws in many countries inhibit the sharing of personal information for purposes other than that for which it was collected. Customer information can, therefore, be shared only with consent.

Many of the decisions involved must be made by the lines of business, not IT, as only they can determine access rules for content and the other controls that will facilitate identity and access management.

Information Value

At present, the economics of information have not yet been established in most organizations. It is, therefore, often hard to make the case for IM investments not only because the benefits are difficult to quantify, but also because of the large number of variables involved. A value proposition for IM should address its strategic, tactical, and operational value and how it will lower risk and develop new capabilities. Furthermore, an effort should be made to quantify the value of the organization's existing information assets and to recognize their importance to its products and services.

"Value" is a highly subjective assessment. Thus, different companies and even different executives will define it differently. Today businesses define *value* broadly and loosely, not simply as a financial concept (Ginzberg 2001). However, because there is no single, agreed-on measure of information value, misunderstandings about its definition can easily arise. Therefore, it is essential that everyone involved in IM activities agree on what value they are trying to deliver and how they will recognize it. Furthermore, value has a time dimension. It takes time for an IM investment to pay off and become apparent. This also must be recognized by all concerned.

Privacy

Concern for the privacy of personal information has been raised to new levels, thanks to legislation being enacted around the world. All companies need enterprisewide privacy policies that address the highest privacy standards required in their working environments. For example, if they operate globally, policies and practices should satisfy all legislation worldwide. Privacy clearly should be part of any long-term IM initiatives, but it also affects what an organization is doing *currently.* As such, it is both an IM issue and an initiative in its own right. Both existing processes and staff behavior will be affected by privacy considerations. "Privacy is about respect for personal information and fair and ethical information practices. Training should start with all new employees and then be extended to all employees," said a manager. Many countries now require organizations to have a chief privacy officer. If so, this person should be a key stakeholder in ensuring that the organization's IM practices around data quality and accuracy, retention, information stewardship, and security are also in keeping with all privacy standards and legislation.

As with other IM initiatives, it is important that senior management understand and support the changes needed to improve privacy practices over time. "Good practices take time to surface," said a manager. "It takes time and resources to ensure all our frontline staff and our information collection and management processes are compliant." Accountabilities should be clearly defined as well. Ideally, IM policy and stewards set the standards in this area with privacy specialists and operational staff (in both IT and the business) responsible for implementing them. With the increase in outsourcing, particularly to offshore companies, all contracts and subcontracting arrangements must be reviewed for compliance in this area. "Our company is still liable for privacy breaches if they occur in one of our vendor firms," noted a group member.

Knowledge Management

Although many organizations have been soured on knowledge management because of its "soft and fuzzy" nature (Smith and McKeen 2004), the fact remains that IM provides a solid foundation that will enable the organization to do more with what it knows (see Figure 8.1). Even firms that do not have a separate KM function recognize that better IM will help them build valuable structural capital. There are many levels at which this can be done. At the most elementary, data warehouses can be built and the information in them can be analyzed for trends and patterns. One company is working on identifying its "single points of knowledge" (i.e., those staff members who have specialized knowledge in an important area) and trying to capture this knowledge in a formal way (e.g., in business processes or metadata). Many firms are making customer information management a priority so they can use this information to both serve their customers better and to learn more about them.[3] This clearly cannot be done unless information is integrated across processes and accessible in a usable format (Davenport and Prusak 1998; Smith and McKeen 2005b). Finally, information can be aggregated and synthesized to create new and useful knowledge. For example, Wal-Mart takes transaction-level information from its sales process and aggregates and analyzes it to make it useful both to the sales process and to other areas of the business. It identifies trends and opportunities based on this analysis and enables information to be viewed in different ways, leading to new insights.

The Knowing-Doing Gap

While most organizations assume that better information will lead to better actions and decisions, research shows that this is not always (or even often) the case. All too often companies do not utilize the information they have. One problem is that we really understand very little about how organizations and groups actually use information in their work (Pfeffer and Sutton 2000). Some organizations do not make clear links between desired actions and the acquisition and packaging of specific information. While this may seem like common sense, the focus group agreed that the complex connections between these two are not always well understood. Effective technology, strong IM practices, and appropriate behaviors and values are *all* necessary to ensure the information-action connection is made (Smith, McKeen, and Singh 2006).

---

[3]Customer information is particularly sensitive and may be analyzed only with a customer's consent in many countries. The need to monitor consents adds a further layer of complexity to this already challenging activity.

While IM is not IT, the fact remains that IT is largely driving this work in organizations these days. Whether this will be the case in the longer term remains to be seen. Most members would like to see the situation reversed, with the business driving the effort to establish appropriate IM policies, procedures, stewardship, and standards and IT supporting IM with software, data custodianship, security and access controls, information applications and administration, and integrated systems. In the shorter term, however, IT is working hard to get IM the attention it deserves in the business.

Focus group participants had several recommendations for others wishing to get started in IM:

- *Start with what you have.* "Doing IM is like trying to solve world hunger," said one manager. "It just gets bigger and bigger the longer you look at it." Even just listing all of the information types and locations in the organization can be a daunting task, and the job will probably never be fully complete. The group, therefore, recommended doing an inventory of what practices, processes, standards, groups, and repositories already exist in the organization and trying to grow IM from there. It is most important to get the key information needed to achieve business objectives under control first. For many companies, this may be customer information; for others, it may be product or financial information. "It's really important to prioritize in IM," said a manager. "We need to focus on the right information that's going to have the biggest return." It may help to try to quantify the value of company information in some way. While there is no accepted accounting method for doing so as yet, some firms are adapting the value assessment methodologies used for other assets. "When you really look at the value of information, it's worth a staggering amount of money. This really gets senior management attention and support," noted a focus group member.

  While a top-down approach is ideal, it may not always be practical. "It took us over a year to get an information policy in place," said a participant. "In the meantime, there are significant savings that can be realized by taking a bottom-up approach and cleaning up some of the worst problems." Harnessing existing compliance efforts around privacy, security, and the Sarbanes-Oxley Act is also effective. At minimum, these will affect information architecture, access to data, document retention, and data administration for financial and personal information (Smith and McKeen 2006). "We can take either an opportunity or a fear mindset towards regulation," said a manager. Companies that see compliance from a purely tactical perspective will likely not see the value of increased controls. If, however, they see regulation as a chance to streamline and revamp business processes and the information they use, their compliance investments will likely pay off. Those interested in IM can also take advantage of the dramatically elevated attention levels of the board and executives to compliance matters.

- *Ensure cross-functional coordination among all stakeholders.* While business involvement in IT initiatives is always desirable, it is impossible to do IM without this. "No IM effort should go ahead without fully identifying all areas that are affected," stated one manager. Typically, legal, audit, and the privacy office will have a keen interest in this area. Equally typically, many of the business units affected will not. For operational groups, IM is often seen as bureaucratic overhead and extra cost. This is why education and communication about IM is essential. "You have to allow time for these groups to get on board with this concept and come around to the necessity of taking the time to do IM right," said a participant. He noted that this effort has to be repeated at each level of the organization. "Senior management may be supportive, but members of the working groups may not really understand what we're trying to accomplish."

- *Get the incentives right.* Even with IM "socialization" (i.e., education and communication), politics is likely to become a major hurdle to the success of any IM efforts. Both giving up control and taking accountability for key pieces of information can be hard for many business managers. Therefore, it is important to ensure there are incentives in place that will motivate collaboration. Metrics are an important way to make progress (or the lack of it) highly visible in the organization. One firm developed a team scorecard for its customer information working group that reported two key measures to executives: the percentage of remaining duplicate records and the percentage of "perfect" customer records. Each of these was broken down into a number of leading indicators that helped focus the group's behavior on the overall effort rather than on individual territories. Another firm linked its process and information simplification efforts to budgets. The savings generated from eliminating duplicate or redundant information (and its associated storage and processing) were returned to the business units involved to be reinvested as they saw fit. This proved to be a huge motivator of enterprise-oriented behavior.

- *Establish and model sound information values.* Because ultimately, frontline workers, who make many decisions about information and procedures, cannot cover all eventualities, all staff need to understand the fundamental reasons for key company information policies and directives. Corporate values around information guide how staff should behave even when their managers aren't around. And they provide a basis for sound decision making about information (Stewart 2004). Others have noted that senior IT leadership should primarily be about forming and modeling values, not managing tasks, and this is especially true for IM, said the focus group. Values are particularly important, they noted, now that staff are more mobile and virtual and, thus, more empowered. If such values are effectively articulated and modeled by leaders, they will drive the development of the appropriate culture and behaviors around information.

CONCLUSION

Information management is gaining increasing attention in both IT and the business. Driven by new compliance and privacy legislation, the increasing vulnerability of corporate information, and the desire for greater integration of systems, IM is beginning to look like an emerging discipline in its own right. However, the challenges facing organizations in implementing effective IM practices are many and daunting. Not least is the need to try to conceptualize the scope and complexity of work to be done. Tackling IM is likely to be a long-term task. IT managers have a huge communications job ahead in trying to educate business leaders in their responsibilities in information stewardship, developing sound IM practices, and inculcating the culture and behaviors needed to achieve the desired results. Developing a plan for tackling the large and ever-increasing amount of information involved is only the first step. The more difficult one will be involving every member of the organization—from the board to frontline workers—in seeing that it is carried out effectively. While IT can lead this effort initially and provide substantial support for IM, ultimately, its success or failure will be due to how well the business does its part.

REFERENCES

Davenport, T., and L. Prusak. *Working Knowledge: How Organizations Manage What They Know.* Boston: Harvard Business School Press, 1998.

Ginzberg, M. "Achieving Business Value through Information Technology: The Nature of High Business Value IT Organizations." Report commissioned by the Society for Information Management Advanced Practices Council (November 2001).

Kettinger, W., and D. Marchand. "Driving Value from IT: Investigating Senior Executives' Perspectives." Report commissioned by the Society for Information Management, Advanced Practices Council (May 2005).

Marchand, D., W. Kettinger, and J. Rollins. "Information Orientation: People, Technology and the Bottom Line." *MIT Sloan Management Review* Summer (2000).

Pfeffer, J., and R. Sutton. *The Knowing-Doing Gap.* Boston: Harvard Business School Press, 2000.

Smith, H. A., and J. D. McKeen. "Marketing KM to the Business." *Communications of the Association of Information Systems* 14, article 23 (November 2004): 513–25.

———. "Information Delivery: IT's Evolving Role," *Communications of the Association of Information Systems* 15, article 11 (February 2005a): 197–210.

———. "A Framework for KM Evaluation." *Communications of the Association of Information Systems* 16, article 9 (May 2005b): 233–46.

———. "Customer Knowledge Management: Adding Value for Our Customers." *Communications of the Association of Information Systems* 16, article 36 (November 2005c): 744–55.

———. "IT in the New World of Corporate Governance Reforms." *Communications of the Association of Information Systems* 17, article 32 (May 2006): 714–27.

Smith, H. A., J. D. McKeen, and S. Singh. "Making Knowledge Work: Five Principles for Action-oriented Knowledge Management." *Knowledge Management Research and Practice* 4, no. 2 (2006): 116–24.

Stewart, T. *Intellectual Capital: The New Wealth of Organizations.* New York: Doubleday, 1999.

———. "Leading Change When Business Is Good: An Interview with Samuel J. Palmisano." *Harvard Business Review* 82, no. 12 (December 2004).

Elements of IM Operations

A. Strategy

- External environment
- Strategic planning
- Information life cycle
- Planning
- Program integration
- Performance monitoring

B. People

- Roles and responsibilities
- Training and support
- Subject-matter experts
- Relationship management

C. Processes

- Project management
- Change management
- Risk management
- Business continuity
- Information life cycle:
  - Collect, create, and capture
  - Use and dissemination
  - Maintenance, protection, and preservation
  - Retention and disposition

D. Technology and Architecture

- IM tools
- Technology integration
- Information life cycle: organization
- Data standards

E. Culture and Behaviors

- Leadership
- IM awareness
- Incentives
- IM competencies
- Communities of interest

F. Governance

- Principles, policies, and standards
- Compliance
- IM program evaluation
- Quality of information
- Security of information
- Privacy of information

Chapter 9

IT in 2010[1]

D on't blink or you just might miss it. IT is in a "sweet spot." *CIO Magazine*'s "State of the CIO 2006" survey of 550 CIOs found that their "strategic role is growing, demand for IT staff is rebounding and [that their] status and profile within the organization is on the rise," (Prewitt and Cosgrove Ware 2006). Fifty-five percent predict an increase in IT headcount over the next year. Seventy-six percent sit on their organizations' management committees. Other research reports that IT represents more than 50 percent of most organizations' current capital expenditures (Nolan and McFarlan 2005). IT has now achieved much of what it has been trying to accomplish over the past twenty years: strategic leadership, business attention to IT's potential, joint accountability for delivering IT value, recognition of the importance of process and cultural changes to leverage IT, extremely reliable operations, and more. That's the good news.

The bad news is the same as ever: the death of IT is coming. As we noted five years ago, "predicting the demise of IT seems to be a theme" stretching back at least to the mid-1980s (McKeen and Smith 2003). Most recently, Nicholas Carr's book *Does IT Matter?* (2004) has taken up the cause, suggesting that IT is rapidly in the process of becoming part of the business infrastructure and, therefore, more like a utility than a source of strategic and competitive advantage. Similarly, the growth of global outsourcing has led many to suggest that IT departments will begin to shrink in the near future (Gohring 2006; Holmes 2006) and that the role of CIO will disappear.

There is no question that IT organizations are changing, but are they evolving toward extinction? Or to something else? To explore this question, we challenged our regular focus group of senior IT managers to predict the future IT organization. Participants were asked to assess how technology and organizational trends will affect IT in a number of critical areas, including IT's mission, function, self-image, governance, internal controls, staffing, systems development, hardware and software

---

[1]Smith, H. A., and J. D. McKeen, "IT in 2010," *MIS Quarterly Executive* 5, no. 3 (September 2006): 125–36 (reproduced by permission of *MIS Quarterly Executive*).

management, and use in the workplace. Particular focus was placed on IT's development over the past five years and in the five years to come. We have found that using a five-year time frame is an effective period over which to anticipate meaningful change. Both it and the focus group approach have proven in the past to be a remarkably accurate method of predicting the future.

This chapter presents our findings. It begins with an overview of how the IT function has evolved over time and the environment in which IT is presently operating. Then, using our framework, each aspect of IT's changing roles and responsibilities in each area of the framework is explored.

THE CURRENT (AND CHANGING) WORLD OF IT

Change is a constant for IT and has been for the past fifteen years. Internally, there are continual pressures on IT to do more, better, faster, cheaper. It seems that just as IT gets a handle on one part if its work, another challenging area pops up. The IT organization of today has become much more complex, sophisticated, and heterogeneous than that of the past. IT boasts many more competencies, much more professionalism, and greater alignment with the business than ever before. However, as we and others have noted before, it is being pulled in two opposite but equally important directions (Carr 2004; Fazio Maruca 2000; McKeen and Smith 1996a).

The first is toward utility computing. In 1996 we wrote, "[If IT does not change], it will eventually become simply a provisioner of computing power to the rest of the organization . . . much like any other utility today." More recently, Nicholas Carr (2004) states that IT is being transformed into a commodity product that will become an infrastructural technology shared by many companies, much like electricity. While IT cannot be taken for granted, he suggests it does not contribute to a company's competitive advantage, as has been assumed by business leaders and academics for the past two decades. He notes that connectivity and collaboration—two trends we have seen take off in the past five years—promote the rapid proliferation of standard technologies, and this, in turn, drives prices down. He concludes his book by noting the importance of making complementary investments in process and organizational innovations, as well as technology, to achieve productivity improvements.

The second and opposite trend is toward the strategic use of IT. While there is much debate about whether or not the technology *itself* generates a competitive advantage for a company, even Carr (2004) admits that the IT function can bring a number of strengths to the table when designing and implementing effective business strategy. These include the following:

- IT innovations in specialized areas where competitors will have difficulty copying
- Excellence in design of processes and activities and how they use technology
- Use of information and talent to achieve advantage
- Use of technology in consumer products and in emerging markets
- Superior ability to execute strategy
- The ability to rapidly realize benefits from advances in infrastructure

- Use of IT to "buttress" strategy
- Possibly, design and implementation of architecture

Interestingly, he also notes that IT can be used to *destroy* another company's competitive advantage—a negative spin on strategy.

Much of Carr's assessment of the future of IT is widely accepted. IT managers know and *have always known* that simply throwing technology at a business problem is unlikely to deliver business results. They have championed collaboration with the use of standards and standardized common processes in business for many years. More than a decade ago, we cited the need for improved business vision around strategy development and processes, greater attention to nontechnical organizational activities when implementing new technologies, and improved understanding and awareness of the business and its needs (McKeen and Smith 1996). In many cases today's IT organizations are *still* trying to get business to work with them to achieve these goals.

At the same time, there is broad recognition among IT managers that connectivity and collaboration is dramatically changing how organizations function. Thomas Friedman documents how the converging trends of outsourcing, connectivity, and investment in IT all "suddenly came together around 2000 . . . [to create] a platform where intellectual work, intellectual capital, could be delivered from anywhere" (2006, 7). In addition, the interoperability provided by the Web has been a huge force driving the development of open standards, which, in turn, is driving prices down and facilitating the development of new business models. These trends are enabling organizations to "do things they had never dreamed possible before or . . . forc[ing them] to do things they had never dreamed necessary before" (2006, 426).

Outsourcing is now a way of life for the majority of firms, and most have at least considered global outsourcing. These firms have recognized the dual—and sometimes conflicting—demands for lower costs and greater strategic value from IT. They are actively pursuing both at the same time, simultaneously driving for greater simplification, standards, and commoditization *and* leading business transformation and innovation initiatives. Few companies expect IT to be the same five years from now. They all accept change as a fact for their organizations and for IT functions in particular.

IT has the privilege and the challenge of sitting at the intersection of two powerful and rapidly changing forces: technical innovation and globalization. Thus, probably more than any other organizational group, it faces more dramatic changes in its roles and responsibilities. Table 9.1 outlines how these have grown and how their emphasis has shifted over time. However, it is interesting to note that a trend that we observed both five and ten years ago is still apparent. This is the "add on" nature of IT's work, where new responsibilities are added but none are ever taken away. This characteristic explains why IT is becoming increasingly complex to manage.

In the past five years, three significant new functions have been added to IT's plate in response to the unanticipated 9/11 disaster, the Enron and Worldcom scandals, and the increasing vulnerability of organizations through their greater connectivity. Business continuity management, security architecture and management, and ensuring compliance with a growing list of worldwide laws and regulations are, today, eating up large chunks of IT's attention and budgets (Smith and McKeen 2005b; Smith and McKeen 2006). While proportionately less time is being paid to

TABLE 9.1 IT's Growing List of Responsibilities, 1990–2005

RESPONSIBILITIES 1990	RESPONSIBILITIES 1995	RESPONSIBILITIES 2000	RESPONSIBILITIES 2005
Systems development	Systems development	Systems development	Systems development & assembly
Operations management	Operations management	Operations management	Operations reliability
Vendor relationships	Vendor relationships	External relationship management	External relationship management
IT administration & budgets	IT administration & budgets	IT administration & budgets	IT finance & accountability
	Data management	Knowledge management	Information & content management
	End user computing	Infrastructure management	Business platform management
	Education & training	Change management	Business transformation
	Managing emerging technologies	Environmental scanning	Innovation
	Corporate architecture	Corporate architecture	Enterprise architecture
	Strategic systems	Strategic leadership	Enterprise leadership
	Systems planning	Systems planning	Portfolio management
		Network management	24/7 communications management
		E-commerce	Pervasive business computing
		Business integration (CRM, ERP, etc.)	Business process architecture, including external integration
		Resource management	Strategic sourcing/staffing
		Risk management	Risk management
			Business continuity management
			Security architecture & management
			Compliance (privacy, SOX)

such things as ensuring reliable operations and networks and business platform management—partly due to outsourcing and partly due to improving tools, technologies, and standards—the fact remains that IT is still responsible for these activities. And woe betide any IT manager whose system crashes these days! It often makes headlines because it affects not only the business, but also customers.

As they looked ahead to 2010, the focus group predicted that the IT function would continue to change, gradually morphing into an enterprisewide entity responsible for ensuring the organization's investments in technology and processes are effectively leveraged and that the business has the right processes and technologies in place to identify and respond to new business opportunities. The following sections explore their vision for the future of IT in more detail.

Our discussion of what IT will look like in 2010 uses a ten-part framework to examine different facets of IT. While different IT managers put different emphases on the relative importance of these various elements in the future, their collective wisdom provides both a fascinating addition to our longitudinal view of IT's corporate evolution and a pragmatic vision of where IT is going in the future. Table 9.2 provides an overview of their predictions and illustrates many of the key changes that IT has undergone and that will be taking place in the future. The discussion that follows contrasts the state of IT in 2005 (as a point of reference) with predictions for 2010.

IT Mission

By 2000, most organizations had developed a significant amount of internal and external connectivity and were well aware of the potential of the Web for transforming business. It is fair to say that IT was at the "end of the beginning" of its evolution in the organization (Freidman 2006). Companies were looking both outward to customers, external alliances, and collaborative initiatives, and inward to their processes, business models, and operations. There was wide recognition within IT and from senior business management that IT could be used to do things differently. This transformative nature of IT was seen as both an opportunity to save money through streamlining and/or outsourcing traditional business activities and as a threat that new, more nimble competitors would swoop in with a new IT-enabled approach to the business, destroying stable markets and undermining current business models. The year 2000 marked the zenith of the dot.com "hype-cycle." Then the bubble burst, followed shortly after by 9/11 and the Enron scandal, and companies returned to

TABLE 9.2 IT Continues to Evolve

	1996	2000	2005	2010
IT Mission	Technology management	Corporate change	Business transformation	Intelligent business
IT Function	System automation	Corporate reengineering	Strategy mobilization	Strategy collaboration
IT Management	Reactive	Proactive	Anticipatory	Architectural
IT Self-image	Service provider	Facilitator	Catalyst	Leader
Governance	Balkan states	Federated republic	Federated network	Horizontal integration
Internal Controls	Metrics	Impact	Value	Enterprise value
Staffing	Specialists	Skilled generalists	Business technologists	Business technology conductors
Systems Development	Structured	Evolutionary	Assembled	Orchestrated
Hardware/Software Management	Planned	Confused	Minefield	Standardized
In the Workplace	Office automation	Automated office	Boundaryless office	Flexible office

what they knew best. IT budgets were reined in, and the focus turned to cost cutting. Disillusionment with IT set in.

These setbacks to IT's trajectory were widely acknowledged. "We also lost some credibility with the Y2K issue," said one manager. "The fact that nothing happened made our executives look more closely at IT budgets." Nevertheless, as of 2005, a substantial driver for IT was business transformation, as predicted. The tone of this transformation was more subdued, and the costs and benefits are more carefully scrutinized, but the business finally "got it." "They now recognize that IT is completely ingrained in how our business works," said a participant. "The business is now more intelligent about IT and more willing to work *with* us to determine what needs to be done." Some organizations had given their IT organizations a specific transformation mandate; others couched transformation in terms of "transitioning to a process structure, as opposed to a functional structure," as one focus group member put it. In addition, there is now a much broader recognition that transformation cannot be driven by IT alone, but that it must occur in conjunction with changes to culture and business practices.

It is likely that in some ways IT would be farther down the road toward business transformation if the extraordinary intervening events mentioned above had not occurred. However, there is also general recognition that these have helped refocus IT and business leaders on more pragmatic and achievable goals and less on "pie in the sky" initiatives. Transformation efforts are ongoing in most organizations and will likely continue. However, in the future, there will also be a new emphasis on the use of *information*, rather than technology, in these initiatives. The ability to deliver valuable, "just in time" information to the business is on the agenda of most firms these days, although there are still significant barriers to achieving this goal (Smith and McKeen 2005a). IT organizations are now being asked to develop dashboards, workflows, and data mining. "We want to facilitate a real-time view of the business," said one participant. On the flip side of this issue, they are also undertaking significant initiatives to protect corporate information and manage access to it (Smith and McKeen 2005b).

Others agree with this assessment. There has been an "artificial separation between systems and their content. . . . The value of any technology is indivisible from the data it stores, calculates, and transports. . . . Payoff . . . is achieved by putting critical information in the hands of employees, customers, and suppliers" (Varon 2006). "Dashboards and guided workflows help users understand how to act on information and how to incorporate it into their daily activities" (Levinson 2006b). "Information . . . is often the basis for competitive advantage" (Carr 2004). Friedman (2006) identifies "informing" as one of the ten forces currently changing the world business environment. In the late 1990s, many companies jumped on this bandwagon by establishing knowledge management functions only to see most of them die prematurely on the vine, largely because the integrated information that was needed to underpin their efforts just wasn't there.

The future IT organization will pick up these pieces but marry them with technology, integrated systems, and business process transformation to create a business that is more knowledgeable about itself and intelligent in its decision making. However, the "effortless link between information and processes doesn't happen by magic" (Levinson 2006b) and, as a result, IT functions will soon be tasked with providing their organizations with the information architectures and tools necessary to achieve process transformation. This mission will gain additional energy from the need to rationalize the diverse types of information currently floating around organizations in order to comply with governmental privacy and reporting regulations. At present, most firms have achieved compliance only with significant effort and cost. As these costs are recognized, organizations will require better management of information both to save money and to better monitor their business environments to take advantage of new opportunities.

IT Function

In 2000 we wrote, "Over the next five years, the IT function will increasingly come to be valued for its unique perspective on both the corporation and technology and its ability to use this perspective to facilitate strategy development and mobilize strategy" (McKeen and Smith 2003). Focus group managers agreed that this prediction has indeed been realized, although with a few caveats. "We're having better discussions with the business," said one participant. "Our executives now understand more about the business value of IT." Another remarked, "We are working side by side, developing strategy." Participants noted that while IT in and of itself does not automatically deliver competitive advantage, it is part and parcel of almost all business strategies. "Our executives are telling us, 'Don't give me a blank slate; let's dialogue.'" However, there is still lingering distrust among many about the value of IT, and executives are more wary of giving IT the *carte blanche* of the past. Thus, even though IT is recognized as essential to the business's survival, today's IT managers still face some credibility problems around the strategic use of IT.

However, IT is increasingly recognized for its ability to convert strategy into action. "We are a catalyst for strategy mobilization and business simplification," explained one manager. The increasing interconnectedness of the business and IT means that the lines between business and IT strategies and their implementation are blurring. Strategy is coming to be recognized not just for *what* it is, but for *how well* it is implemented. Everyone has access to the same hardware and software. The difference is how an organization uses and applies it—pulling the right pieces together to achieve a desirable result on an as-needed basis.

IT's involvement in strategy will continue over the next five years but in an increasingly integrated fashion. "In the past business and IT have led parallel lives; now we have to work more closely together," said one manager. "The wall has to be removed," said another. All agreed that business strategy is becoming more fluid, and IT simply must share in its development. "We must be in constant communication and negotiation about strategy," they agreed. In short, strategy development and execution for both the business and IT are becoming a more collaborative effort to deliver enterprise value. "Today we are mobilizing IT to support business strategy; tomorrow we will be mobilizing the business through leveraging IT," said a participant.

IT Management

Five years ago the focus group stated that because of rapidly changing business and technical environments, IT managers would be expected to anticipate coming trends and propose business strategies to take advantage of them. They suggested that IT organizations would have to improve their environmental scanning capabilities so they can get and stay ahead of the curve. To create technology that is more adaptable and responsive to business's rapidly changing needs, they predicted that in 2005, IT managers would need to become more knowledgeable about the business and develop improved partnerships across the organization.

Strategy *anticipation* is still a dream of IT managers, and most now agree that the events of the past five years demonstrate that it is impossible to truly do this well. As a result, they have changed approaches in this area, aiming to make it easier for IT to be more flexible in its ability to respond to business needs. Thus, increasing attention is being paid to architectural issues on the premise that, if done correctly and at the right level, architecture is more durable and less subject to change than specific business strategies (Weill and Ross 2004). Then only the *implementation* of the strategy needs to change as new technologies and business initiatives are introduced. Today most organizations have technical architects to create technology blueprints to guide them through the plethora of technical options available.

The goal of architecture of any type is to facilitate flexibility and change. Understanding how its different pieces fit together and ensuring they are all interoperable and based on standards gives organizations plug-and-play capability. While architectural work has been under way with hardware and software for several years, the same principles are now being applied to a much wider range of business operations. IT's analytic competencies, particularly if combined with greater business knowledge, will increasingly help a business understand its information and processes then to design them so they can be more easily adapted. Knowledge of business is a prerequisite to being able to effectively plan an organization. Over the next five years, developing architectures will be a key method of gaining business knowledge within IT. In turn, architectures will then become the foundation on which IT can assist the business to design and implement strategy in a much more organic fashion than in the past.

Thus, in the future many more types of architecture will be introduced to the organization, and much of this effort will be driven by IT, although always in conjunction with its business partners. First, as IT becomes more componentized so it can be more effectively managed and outsourced (where appropriate), internal IT systems and processes will become increasingly architected. Organizations will be able to buy modules of functionality instead of massive applications and slices of computing time instead of massive computers. IT managers will, therefore, need to better understand their own processes and how they are broken down in order to take advantage of these opportunities. Second, IT's mandate to deliver on its mission to the business will lead organizations to develop information and process architectures that integrate with technical architectures. Many will even develop an enterprisewide architecture within which the IT, technology, information, and process architectures would be integrated.

IT Self-image

How IT views itself internally is key to how it performs. As Table 9.2 makes clear, over time IT's self-image has changed to reflect its increasingly active role in the business.

As a result, IT is no longer the humble service provider of the mid-1990s. In 2005 the majority of CIOs hobnob with other CXOs and business executives, make strategic systems decisions, participate in business strategy planning, and sit on their corporate executive committees (Prewitt and Cosgrove Ware 2006). IT innovation for business value now ranks as a top IT challenge. In Chapter 2 we noted that IT will come to see itself as a catalyst in delivering new forms of value to the business. "As a catalyst, IT can start things happening in organizations which would never have occurred without it; it can stimulate new ideas and start people thinking about possibilities."

IT's role in business innovation is much on the mind of today's IT managers. "IT is very vulnerable to commoditization; we are, therefore, always on the hunt for innovation," said one participant. "This is a key focus for us," said another. "In the past we have been inhibited by our lack of business knowledge. Today this is gradually changing." As this trend continues, IT will take on more leadership responsibilities within the organization and this will become its dominant self-image in 2010.

"We see a real growth in the need for leadership in IT," said one manager. Others agreed that it is time for IT to stand up and be counted. "We are going to be seen as policy makers and thought leaders," said a participant. "While we will continue to provide technology and information services, our value will come from our combined leadership of the enterprise with the business." IT has always had a perspective different from other parts of the business. Over the next five years, this perspective will not only be more appreciated by the organization, it will also become a fundamental part of IT's responsibility. As one manager stated, "The business units are good at designing and implementing specialized strategies; our role will be to ensure that these individual efforts benefit the whole enterprise." Another predicted, "I believe that we will become more entrepreneurial in the future, taking the initiative to provide leadership in business transformation and innovation."

Governance

For the past two decades at least, the debate has raged over the most appropriate structure and governance of IT. Typically, governance has vacillated between the centralized and decentralized models, and most organizations have experienced variations of both types of structures in response to how the current executive viewed IT and its benefits. The concept of internal standards for IT was introduced in the late 1990s, and by 2000, most organizations recognized the importance of having centralized internal IT standards around security, communications, and data, if nothing else. In 2000 the focus group predicted that by 2005, standards and controls would be established from outside the firm to enable intraorganizational collaboration. This has indeed proven to be the case, largely driven through the widespread use of the Internet. The focus group also predicted that concerns for security and privacy would hasten legislation by both government and self-regulation in these areas. "While internal standards and controls will still have a place, they will be relatively diminished by the greater need to establish an open network."

The biggest surprise has been the speed with which these standards have been established and adopted. Whereas five years ago, they were still up for debate, today there is no question from either the business or IT that open standards are the way to go. Everyone is simply fed up with the challenges of making nonstandard hardware/software/applications and data interact with each other, and there is widespread recognition of the value of enterprise and interenterprise integration.

Thomas Friedman (2006) identifies ten factors that have contributed to a "flattened," globalized world that is fundamentally changing how organizations operate. Nine of these are based on the ability to interoperate: (1) connectivity, (2) outsourcing, (3) offshoring, (4) supply chaining, (5) insourcing, (6) uploading, (7) informing, (8) standardized workflow software, and (9) the growing array of computing devices. Thus, increasing integration—across the firm, between a firm and its partners and suppliers, and with its customers and other stakeholder groups—will be the dominant driver of IT governance structures in the future. Friedman notes that once a standard takes hold, it enables people and organizations to focus on the *quality* of what they are doing as opposed to *how* they are doing it. This is the direction in which IT work is moving. Over the next five years, open standards for hardware, software, data, and some applications will enable greater and greater degrees of horizontal integration—both within the organization and, as appropriate, outside the organization. Liberated from much of the need to establish and enforce these standards, the IT function will be free to design the proprietary processes, products, information, and applications that will truly lead to greater competitive advantage. Centralization or decentralization of these activities will then be determined by the level (i.e., business unit or enterprise) at which these should take place.

However, ever-greater integration, especially outside the firm, increases its vulnerability. It is no secret that organizations and consumers are more and more vulnerable to cyberattacks from numerous sources. Current laws, policing, and security measures have not kept up with their growing sophistication, and many fear that, like a chain of dominoes, entire business networks could one day be severely compromised. Consumers and governments are raising legitimate questions about how such networks should be regulated and controlled. Countries are enacting legislation to address these concerns that will have long-term impacts on how IT is managed. By 2005, many IT organizations were struggling under the weight of the requirements of the Sarbanes-Oxley Act (and other similar acts in other countries) and a host of different privacy protection requirements (Smith and McKeen 2006). The focus group believes this situation will only get worse over the next five years as new legislation comes on board. The security and access management needed to deal with changing business models will barely keep up and will represent a major nightmare for most IT managers. In short, IT governance in the future will also become increasingly dictated by external legislation and regulation that will both prescribe and proscribe important aspects of governance.

Internal Controls

In 2000 our focus group predicted the measure used to determine the success of IT by 2005 would be based on business value. "The major internal yardstick in IT's future will be the value it delivers. . . . While value will frequently be defined as new value, companies will also begin to realize that the ability to leverage existing people, technologies, and information more effectively also delivers value" (McKeen and Smith 2003). We also suggested that delivering value would come to be seen as a team effort that cannot be delivered without the skills of both the business and IT.

Finally, we anticipated that "capabilities, culture, and management themselves would increasingly come under the microscope to determine how they contribute to value" (McKeen and Smith 2003).

In 2005 both the focus group and the practitioner press agreed that business value is now the key measure of IT's success. IT has "evolved . . . to being a key part of the whole value proposition" (Varon 2006). "The true test of [IT's] stewardship . . . is whether [the business] is getting the full value it should" (Schrage 2006). "More CIOs are getting involved in business process improvement initiatives" (Levinson 2006a). Focus group members noted the following:

- "It's about *how* we apply technology and includes both the top line *and* cost."
- "We now have shared accountability with the business for delivering value; we don't just throw technology over the fence like we did in the past."
- "We are adopting joint governance structures for delivering business value."

In the future, value will continue to be the most important means of measuring IT success, but this concept will become more refined than it is at present. Value will include a variety of concepts: bottom line cost savings, appropriate use of resources (including outsourcing), better management of fixed and variable costs, ability to harvest benefits as well as delivering technology, and innovation. As well, IT's ability to see across the enterprise will increasingly become a further source of value as processes become more important to the business. "We must deliver more than cost cutting, but this is important as well, to free up resources for more valuable work," said one member. "We must be *valuable* to the enterprise, not simply deliver value," said another. To this end, IT functions will be involved in business transformation and innovation initiatives on a much larger scale than in the past, while working diligently to bring cost and process disciplines to the everyday business of IT. They will formalize practices, develop business and leadership competencies, and audit to ensure that planned benefits are actually delivered. The end result will be that, by 2010, IT will deliver significantly more enterprise value than ever before. "We will play a horizontal role so that the business units don't hurt each other and themselves," one participant stated.

Staffing

In many ways staffing has been *the* story of IT in the past five years, as companies wrestled with where in-house IT staff truly added value and where generic IT services could be more cost-efficiently provided by outsourcers. In 2000 the focus group suggested that, by 2005, companies would place greater emphasis on business *and* technical competencies and that "soft" skills (e.g., relationship management, portfolio management, and strategic thinking) would become more valued in IT organizations. The focus group also predicted that the majority of IT staff would need to become business technologists to complement a small number of highly skilled technical specialists.

There is no question that the value of business technologists is "moving higher up the food chain" in IT organizations, according to the focus group. These are not business analysts, they stressed, but a higher order of expert who has a strong knowledge of business and intuitively understands how to use collaborative technology, mobilize strategy, simplify business, and provide leadership around technology. This trend will continue over the next five years, according to the experts, with 60 percent of IT staff becoming customer facing by 2010 (Overby 2006).

However, by 2010, IT staff will also begin to act as leaders in a number of areas, including portfolio management, business controls, information management and privacy, risk management, strategic sourcing and alliances, business process transformation, and corporate governance architecture. Increasingly, therefore, in-house staff will need a wider variety of business and leadership skills as well as the ability to learn about and understand new technologies. Thus, it is likely that permanent IT staff in organizations will become more highly skilled—both personally and professionally—and more versatile in how they use these skills than ever before (Overby 2006; Prewitt and Cosgrove Ware 2006). As multiskilled business technologists, IT staff will increasingly become the conductors of enterprise initiatives involving many different skilled players and responsible for ensuring that everyone plays in harmony and to maximum effect.

Systems Development

For many years, it has been clear that the structured, life-cycle approach to systems development is too rigid for business needs. In 2000 we noted that systems work was in the process of changing gradually but radically to a more eclectic and modular approach that included packaged software, custom software, legacy software, and end-user tools. We suggested the development teams in 2005 would be likely to include equal numbers of business and technical staff and have a larger component of contractors. We also felt pressures for newer and even more flexible forms of systems development would escalate as the business environment continued to change dramatically. Therefore, by 2005, the focus group predicted that functionality would be delivered in generic components that could simply be assembled to deliver new systems.

By 2005, however, most organizations were still a long way from true system assembly. Much systems development was "package integration" rather than the true assembly of "systems services" we had predicted. However, by 2010, the trend to assembly will continue with traditional systems development becoming an increasingly smaller part of the IT organization's role. Although there will still be demand for systems functionality, intelligent architecture and standards will create a platform for doing business that will eliminate much of the need to "reinvent the wheel" that was characteristic of systems development in the past. As proprietary software gives way to truly open systems standards, assembly will become an increasingly larger part of the systems development process.

Once service components are available, however, higher-order systems skills, rather than programming, will become more and more important in the overall development process. IT staff will work with the business to envision what needs to be done; cost it out; understand the benefits and the risks involved; identify the services needed to provide the functionality; articulate the workflow and process changes involved; select appropriate technology platforms; and integrate, test, install, audit, and leverage what needs to be done. Development teams will also become increasing complex in order to manage staff working virtually from many locations, often from several different companies (e.g., vendors, partners, contractors). Such interorganizational projects will increase the need for (and change the demands of) project managers. As a result, project management, which is already an important IT competency, will gain in importance as the need for these skills will increase dramatically.

With so many people and elements involved in delivering the systems functionality of the future, systems development will become more than assembly. It will become the orchestration of all of the elements within IT and the business, as well as with external partners, needed to deliver an initiative as required. Project teams of the future will also need to jump through many regulatory, architectural, business, financial, HR, security, and risk management hoops that will have little to do with the traditional design and coding of the past but that will need to be "orchestrated" to deliver a coherent, viable business service.

Hardware/Software Management

One of the good news stories of the past five years has been in the field of hardware and software management. Whereas in the past, individual IT functions had to cope with a veritable minefield of proprietary hardware and software, the advent of the Internet has driven the growth of standards in both these areas. International standards mean that traditional hardware and software purchase decisions have become much less risky for individual companies, and cheaper. While today's hardware is almost all "plug-and-play," there are still some significant problems with proprietary software. However, the trend toward open software and standards is driving vendors to be increasingly standardized, and this is leading to much greater simplification in companies.

Greater connectivity outside the organization means that standards are being taken over by industry groups, rather than being set by individual companies. Most firms plan to adopt standards as soon as they are established, and the trend to greater standardization of the computing platform will continue over the next five years. The biggest challenges for IT managers in this area are coming from the huge numbers of new peripheral devices and applications that are flooding into the market on a daily basis. Evaluating these, determining whether or not they are "ready for prime time" and if they will add value, will become an important job. In the future the biggest need in this field will be to have a process for identifying, evaluating, and integrating new hardware and software appropriately.

In the Workplace

Offices are changing, although more slowly than we anticipated. By 2005, we predicted that offices would be increasingly open to the outside world and increasingly work would be conducted in cyberspace prompted by global sourcing, mobile computing, and home-based work. While this trend is evident, most companies moved cautiously, taking their time to test what innovations in work were truly valuable. One of the reasons for the slow pace of change has been the need to adapt HR and managerial practices (always slow) to new forms of work. Furthermore, IT security and infrastructure practices have also lagged behind the vision and have not been robust enough to truly enable a flexible virtual business platform. Finally, early experiments have shown that new tools for collaboration and communication are needed to enable true teamwork and a true virtual desktop. Over the past five years, many of these practices and tools have been put in place—at least in a rudimentary fashion—making the development of a true virtual office a possibility over the next five years.

The move to virtual work is being driven by cost economics. It is simply more cost effective to move some work to parts of the world with lower pay scales. Similarly, it costs less to enable mobile or home-based workers than to provide them with office space. Over the next five years, cost will continue to drive changes in the workplace, as will the fact that we now have the connectivity and standards to make virtual work easier to accomplish. Offices will not go away by 2010, but will continue to become more open and flexible as platforms and practices evolve. We are unlikely to see a revolution in this area but will see ongoing and visible evolution toward the goal of virtual work. Like the advent of e-business, virtual work is unlikely to eliminate the bricks and mortar of the traditional office building. Instead, it will add enhanced possibilities for work that will complement each other, enabling greater flexibilities for both organizations and their staff.

CONCLUSION

This chapter has examined how the IT function is evolving in organizations. Unlike those who predict the death of IT, we suggest that IT will simply change, becoming commoditized in some areas and adding true enterprise value in others. IT managers accept and expect this evolution to occur; in fact, they have learned over time that nothing stays the same. Many of the changes occurring now in organizations (e.g., standards, sourcing, virtual work) were originally pioneered and driven by IT—first as experiments then as ways of doing business.

IT managers have often been visionaries for their organizations, and as a result, they are now being recognized as leaders of business transformation. The next five years will see continuing emphasis on cost effectiveness in all parts of IT but will also bring many of the opportunities to truly make a difference that IT managers have been pushing for over the past fifteen years. It remains to be seen if IT can truly step up to the next level and provide real leadership to the business. This will be IT's next frontier.

REFERENCES

Carr, N. *Does IT Matter?* Boston: Harvard Business School Press, 2004.

Fazio Maruca, R. "Are CIOs Obsolete?" *Harvard Business Review* March–April (2000).

Friedman, T. *The World Is Flat.* New York: Farrar, Strauss, and Giroux, 2006.

Gohring, N. "IT Departments, They Are a Changin'." *CIO Magazine* (January 1, 2006).

Holmes, A. "The Changing CIO Role: The Dual Demands of Strategy and Execution." *CIO Magazine* (January 1, 2006).

Levinson, M. "Wanted: Business Process Experts." *CIO Magazine* (March 1, 2006a).

———. "Business Intelligence: Not Just for Bosses Anymore." *CIO Magazine* (January 15, 2006b).

McKeen, J. D., and H. A. Smith. "The Future of IS: Looking Ahead to the Year 2000." *IT Management Forum* 5, no. 1 (1996a).

——. *Management Challenges in IS: Successful Strategies and Appropriate Action.* New York: John Wiley & Sons, Ltd., 1996b.

——. *Making IT Happen: Critical Issues in Managing Information Technology.* New York: John Wiley & Sons, 2003.

Nolan, R., and F. W. McFarlan. "Information Technology and the Board of Directors." *Harvard Business Review* October (2005).

Overby, S. "The New IT Department: The Top Three Positions You Need." *CIO Magazine* (January 1, 2006).

Prewitt, E., and L. Cosgrove Ware. "The State of the CIO '06." www.cio.com/state (accessed May 25, 2006).

Schrage, M. "The Value Inside." *CIO Magazine* (April 15, 2006).

Smith, H. A., and J. D. McKeen. "Information Delivery: IT's Evolving Role." *Communications of the Association for Information Services* 15, no. 11 (February 2005a): 197–210.

——. "Strategic Information Risk Management." *The CIO Brief* 11, no. 1 (2005b).

——. "IT in the New World of Corporate Governance Reforms." *Communications of the Association of Information Systems* 17, article 32 (May 2006): 714–27.

Varon, E. "A Brief History of IT Value." *CIO* (February 15, 2006).

Weill, P., and J. W. Ross. *IT Governance: How Top Performers Manage IT Decision Rights for Superior Results.* Boston: Harvard Business School Press, 2004.

MINI CASE

Building Shared Services at RR Communications

Vince Patton had been waiting years for this day. He pulled the papers together in front of him and scanned the small conference room. "You're fired," he said to the four divisional CIOs sitting at the table. They looked nervously at him, grinning weakly. Vince wasn't known to make practical jokes, but this had been a pretty good meeting, at least relative to some they'd had over the past five years. "You're kidding," said Matt Dawes, one of the more outspoken members of the divisional CIO team. "Nope," said Vince. "I've got the boss's OK on this. We don't need any of you anymore. I'm creating one enterprise IT organization, and there's no room for any of you. The HR people are waiting outside." With that, he picked up his papers and headed to the door, leaving the four of them in shock.

"That felt *good*," he admitted as he strode back to his office. A big man, not known to tolerate fools gladly (or corporate politics), he was not a cruel one. But those guys had been thorns in his side ever since he had taken the new executive VP of IT job at the faltering RR Communications five years ago. The company's stock had been in the dumpster, and with the dramatically increased competition in the telecommunications industry as a result of deregulation, his friends and family had all thought he was nuts. But Ross Roman, RR's eccentric but brilliant founder, had made him an offer he couldn't refuse. "We need you to transform IT so that we can introduce new products more quickly," he'd said. "You'll have my full backing for whatever you want to do."

Typically for an entrepreneur, Roman had sketched the vision swiftly, leaving someone else to actually implement it. "We've *got* to have a more flexible and responsive IT organization. Every time I want to do something, they tell me 'the systems won't allow it.' I'm tired of having customers complaining about getting multiple bills for each of our products. It's not acceptable that RR can't create *one simple little bill* for each

customer." Roman punctuated his remarks by stabbing with his finger at a file full of letters to the president, which he insisted on reading personally each week. "You've got a reputation as a 'can do' kind of guy; I checked. Don't bother me with details; just get the job done."

Vince knew he *was* a good, proactive IT leader, but he hadn't been prepared for the mess he inherited . . . or the politics. There was no central IT, just separate divisional units for the four key lines of business—Internet, mobile, landline, and cable TV service—each doing their own thing. Every business unit had bought its own hardware and software, so introducing the common systems that would be needed to accomplish Roman's vision would be hugely difficult; that is, assuming they *wanted* them, which they didn't. There were multiple sales systems, databases, and customer service centers, all of which led to customer and business frustration. The company was in trouble not only with its customers, but also with the telecommunications regulators and with its software vendors, who each wanted information about the company's activities, which they were legally entitled to have but which the company couldn't provide.

Where should he start to untangle this mess? Clearly, it wasn't going to be possible to provide bundled billing, responsiveness, unified customer care, and rapid time to market all at once, let alone keep up with the new products and services that were flooding into the telecommunications arena. And he hadn't exactly been welcomed with open arms by the divisional CIOs (DIOs), who were suspicious of him in the extreme. "Getting IT to operate as a single enterprise unit, regardless of the product involved, is going to be tough," he admitted to himself. "This corporate culture is not going to take easily to centralized direction."

And so it was. The DIOs had fought him tooth and nail, resisting any form of integration of their systems. So had the business unit leaders, themselves presidents, who were rewarded on the basis of the performance of their divisions and, therefore, didn't give a hoot about "the enterprise" or about anything other than their quarterly results. To them, centralized IT meant increased bureaucracy and much less freedom to pick up the phone and call their buddy Matt or Larry or Helen or Dave and get that person to drop everything to deal with their latest money-making initiative. The fact that every time they did this, it cost the enterprise more and more didn't concern them—they didn't care that costs racked up: testing to make sure changes didn't affect anything else that was operational; creation of duplicate data and files, which often perpetuated bad data; and loss of integrated information with which to run the enterprise. And those didn't even cover the fact that the company needed an army of "data cleansers" to prepare the reports needed for the government to meet its regulatory and Sarbanes-Oxley requirements—wasn't *their* concern. Everyone believed his or her needs were unique.

Unfortunately, while he had Roman's backing *in theory*, in practice Vince's position was a bit unusual because he himself didn't have an enterprise IT organization as yet and the DIOs' first allegiance was clearly to their division presidents, despite having a "dotted line" reporting relationship to Vince. The result was that he had to choose his battles very, very carefully in order to lay the foundation for the future. First up was redesigning the company's internal computer infrastructure to use one set of standard technologies. Simplification and standardization involved a radical reduction of the number of suppliers and centralized procurement. The politics were fierce and painful with the various suppliers the company was using, simultaneously courting the DIOs and business unit leaders while trying to sell Vince on the merits of *their* brand of technology for the whole company. Matt Dawes had done everything he could to undermine this vision, making sure that the users caused the maximum fuss right up to Roman's office.

Finally, they'd had a showdown with Roman. "As far as I'm concerned, moving to standardized hardware and software is nondiscussable," Vince stated bluntly. "We can't even *begin* to tackle the issues facing this company without it. And furthermore, we are in serious noncompliance with our software licensing agreements. We can't even tell them how many users we have!" This was a potentially serious legal issue that had to be dealt with. "I promised our suppliers that we would get this problem under control within eighteen months, and they've agreed to give us time to improve. We won't have this opportunity again."

Roman nodded, effectively shutting down the argument. "I don't really understand how more standardization is going to *improve* our business flexibility," he'd growled, "but if you say so, let's do it!" From that point on, Vince had moved steadily to consolidate his position, centralizing the purchasing budget; creating an enterprise architecture; establishing a standardized desktop and infrastructure; and putting tools, metrics, and policies in place to manage them and ensure the plan was respected by the divisions.

Dawes and Larry Hughes, another DIO, had tried to sabotage him on this matter yet again by adopting another manufacturer's customer relationship management system (and yet another database), hoping that it could be up and running before Vince noticed. But Vince had moved swiftly to pull the plug on that one by refusing the project access to company hardware and giving the divisional structure yet another black mark.

That episode had highlighted the need for a steering committee, one with teeth to make sure that no other rogue projects got implemented with "back door funding." But the company's entrepreneurial culture wasn't ready for it, so again, foundational work had to be done. "I'd have had a riot on my hands if I'd tried to do this in my first few years here," Vince reflected as he walked back to his office, stopping to chat with some of the other executives on his way. Vince now knew everyone and was widely respected at this level because he understood their concerns and interests. Mainly, these were financial—delivering more IT for less cost. But as Vince moved around the organization, he stressed that IT decisions were first and foremost *business* decisions. He spoke to them in business terms. "The company wants one consistent brand for its organization so it can cross-sell services. So why do we need different customer service organizations or back-end systems?" he would ask them. One by one he had brought the "C"-level executives around to at least *thinking* about the need for an enterprise IT organization.

Vince had also taken advantage of his weekly meetings with Roman to demonstrate the critical linkage between IT and Roman's vision for the enterprise. Vince's motto was "IT must be very visible in this organization." When he felt the political climate was right, he called all the "Cs" to a meeting. With Roman in the room for psychological support, he made his pitch. "We need to make all major IT decisions *together* as a business," he said. "If we met monthly, we could determine what projects we need to launch in order to support the business and then allocate resources and budgets accordingly."

Phil Cooper, President of Internet Services, spoke up, "But what about our *specific* projects? Won't they get lost when they're all mixed up with everyone else's? How do *we* get funding for what we need to do?"

Vince had a ready answer. "With a steering committee, we will do what's best for the organization *as a whole*, not for one division at the expense of the others. The first thing we're going to do is undertake a visioning exercise for what you all want our business to look like in three years, and *then* we'll build the systems and IT infrastructure to support that vision."

Talking the language of business had been the right approach because no one wanted to get bogged down in techno-jargon. And this meeting had effectively turned the tide from a divisional focus to an enterprise one—at least as far as establishing a steering committee went. Slowly, Vince had built up his enterprise IT organization, putting senior IT managers, reporting to *him*, into each of the business divisions. "Your job is to participate in *all* business decisions, not just IT ones," he stated. "There is *nothing* that happens in this company that doesn't affect IT." He and his staff had also "walked the talk" over the past two years, working with the business to identify opportunities for short-term improvements that really mattered a lot to the divisions. These types of quick wins demonstrated that he and his organization really cared about the business and made IT's value much more visible. He also stressed accountability.

"Centralized units are *always* seen to be overhead by the business," he explained to his staff. "That's why we must be accountable for everything we spend and our costs must be transparent. We also need to give the business some choices in what they spend. While I won't compromise on legal, safety, or health issues, we need to let them know where they can save money if they want. For example, while they can't choose not to back up their files, they *can* choose the amount of time it will take them to recover them."

But the problem of the DIOs had remained. Used to being kings of their own kingdoms, everything they did appeared to be in direct opposition to Vince's vision. And it was apparent that while Roman was preaching "one company," IT itself was not unified. Things had come to a head last year when he'd started looking at outsourcing. Again they had resisted, seeing the move as one designed to take yet more power away from them. He'd offered Helen a position as sourcing director, but she'd turned it down, seeing it as a demotion rather than a lateral move. The more they stonewalled him, the more determined he became to deal with them once and for all. "They're undermining my credibility with the business and with our suppliers," he'd complained to himself. "There's still so much more to do, and this divisional structure isn't working for us." That's when he'd realized he had to act or RR wouldn't be able to move ahead on its next project—a single customer service center shared by the four divisions instead of the multiple divisional and regional ones they had now.

So he'd called a meeting, ostensibly to sort out what would be outsourced and what wouldn't. Then he'd dropped the bombshell. "They'll get a good package," he reassured himself. "And they'll be happier somewhere else than always fighting with me." The new IT organization charts, creating a central IT function, had been drawn up and the memo appointing his management team had been signed. Vince sighed. That had been a piece of cake compared to what he was going to be facing now. Was he ready for the next round in the "IT wars"? He was going to have to go head-to-head with the business, and it wouldn't be pretty. Roman had supported him in getting the IT house in order, but would he be there for the next step?

Vince looked gloomily at the reports the DIOs had prepared for their final meeting. They documented a complete data mess—even within the divisions. The next goal was to implement the single customer service center for all divisions, so a customer could call one place and get service for all RR products. This would be a major step forward in enabling the company to implement new products and services. If he could pull it off, for the first time, all of the company's support systems would talk to each other and share data.

"We can't have shared services without common data, and we can't have good business intelligence either," he muttered. *Everything* he needed to do next relied on this, but the business saw it differently when he'd last tried to broach the subject with them. "This is *our* data, and these are *our* customers," they'd said. "Don't mess with them." And he hadn't . . . but that was then. Now it was essential to get their information in order. But what would he have to do to convince them and to make it happen? ∎

DISCUSSION QUESTIONS

1. List the advantages of a single customer service center for RR Communications.
2. Devise an implementation strategy that would guarantee the support of the divisional presidents for the shared customer service center.
3. Is it possible to achieve an enterprise vision with a decentralized IT function?
4. What business and IT problems can be caused by lack of common information and an enterprise IM strategy?
5. What governance mechanisms need to be put in place to ensure common customer data and a shared customer service center? What metrics might be useful?

MINI CASE

Creating a Process-Driven Organization at AgCredit

Kate Longair knelt on the floor of the CEO's office as she unrolled the twenty-foot-long diagram of all of the processes and systems in the company and how they interconnected. Dressed in "Saturday casual" jeans, white shirt, and boots, she looked more like a suburban soccer mom than a high-powered, up-and-coming banking executive. But Saturday was the only day she could get a couple of uninterrupted hours with her boss, Jim Finney. "I never thought business transformation would be such physical work," she joked as the two of them struggled to move the furniture in order to spread out the huge document and pin it down so it wouldn't roll back up again.

This was the culmination of three months of nonstop work for Kate and her team, and she knew it would be a key decision point for AgCredit. Would Finney get it? He wasn't a technical person, and while he had agreed to be the corporate sponsor of her Enterprise Integration Program (EIP), there was a chance he'd be overwhelmed with the detail on this chart and simply abdicate responsibility to his chief of operations. That would be the kiss of death for EIP. While the COO, Steve Stewart, was a great guy, only the CEO would have the clout to push through the radical changes she was proposing for the company.

She began her spiel by reminding Finney why she was here. "Three months ago you asked me to fix AgCredit's 'systems problems,'" the remnants of her Scottish upbringing breaking through her Midwestern accent every now and then. Briefly, she took him back through her mandate. AgCredit, the MidWest Agriculture Credit and Loan Company—a midsized financial institution focusing on agribusiness—had grown significantly in the past few years and was holding its own against other, much larger banks because of its extensive customer knowledge. But Finney had recognized that its people and processes were taxed to the hilt. "We can't keep throwing people at our problems," he'd said to his executive team at the time. "We've got to get some better technology in here to support them."

That comment had opened a can of worms. "IT's a mess," complained Stewart. "Nothing works well and nothing talks to anything else. Whenever I ask them to do anything, they tell me it's going to cost a million bucks. I vote we outsource the whole thing." Paul Manley, the SVP of e-business, agreed. "Our IT is completely broken. I wouldn't ask any of them to solve our business problems. *I* could do a better job!" The others chimed in with their war stories of project delays, bad information, customer complaints, and IT staff who didn't know which end of the business was up. The upshot of the meeting was that while all of the business executives wanted much better systems integration, not one of them had any idea where to start or the time and skills to do the job. So Kate had been given the mandate to form a team and figure out the best approach to achieving systems integration.

"We began by interviewing each of the executive team about their business strategy and the barriers they saw in achieving it," she explained to Finney. "The first thing we noticed was that, while everyone knew what he wanted to do and how it would add value to the company, no one understood how *their* business strategy would fit with everyone else's to deliver *enterprise* value. The second thing we realized was that we didn't understand our *business* processes and how they worked together. And if we didn't understand these, it was going to be impossible to get the right systems in place to support them." IT had been saying this for quite a while, she reflected silently, but it simply didn't have the credibility with the business to be believed.

"That's when we realized we had to understand our key strategic drivers and how our current business processes worked to enable them." These processes had never been written down before, so most of the previous months had been spent trying to understand and document them in workshops with key business subject matter experts. At the same time, some members of her team had documented AgCredit's systems and what they did. The result was the twenty-foot chart at their feet. The top part showed all the current business processes, and the bottom part showed all the systems that supported these business processes. When the north-south linkages between systems and processes were added to the chart, the problems became readily apparent.

Using a laser pointer, Kate walked Finney through just how many systems frontline staff had to access for a simple business process, such as renewing a loan. All of these connections made the diagram look like a plate of spaghetti. "What a mess!" he commented when the presentation was finished. "We've got to do something to fix this. What do you recommend?"

"Well . . ." she began hesitantly. "This is a bit radical, but I'd like to stop all new systems development for at least six weeks until we get a better handle on what our desired future *business* processes will look like. We've got about $40 million worth of projects on the books, but until we know where we're going as an enterprise, it's hard to tell what's worthwhile and what isn't." Because each of the four business divisions had their own pet projects, the only person who could make this call was Finney. "Let's do it," he said. "We've got to get this situation under control if we're going to be able to compete the way I want us to." Finney was referring to AgCredit's key strategic drivers, which included continuous growth, expanded customer relationships, the ability to spend more time with the customer, the ability to cross-sell between business divisions, and the ability to provide a consistent customer experience across all delivery channels.

With Finney's unconditional support, Kate was able to avoid much of the political fallout of the system development halt. "I wouldn't have survived without it," she commented to a colleague over lunch a few weeks later. "If he'd thrown me to the wolves, we'd have been toast. Everyone would have sat on the fence and

waited for me to fail. At least this way, they *have* to work on this with me." Over the next few weeks, Kate and her team developed a high-level vision of AgCredit's future business processes that fully supported Finney's enterprise strategy and led to the creation of a roadmap for transforming how the business operated, but the IT portion of the chart remained a problem.

It was clear to Finney that he needed a CIO who could work with and support the EIP team with technology, someone who had the complete trust of the business and who was a highly effective executive capable of driving both a business *and* an IT transformation agenda forward. No sooner was the need articulated than the answer walked by his office. "Paul, have you got a minute?" Finney called. As Manley entered the office, stepping carefully around the chart still spread across the floor, Finney dropped his bombshell. "You've often said you could do a better job of running IT if we gave you the chance. Now you can put your money where your mouth is!" This was said as a joke, not a challenge. If anyone was up to the job, it was Manley. "Wow!" said Manley. "I guess you're desperate." It was a gutsy move because Manley had little formal technical expertise, although he had masterminded AgCredit e-business initiatives for the past three years. Both Finney and Manley knew it. This move would be watched very carefully, and both of their personal reputations were on the line. But Manley relished the challenge and accepted the offer without hesitation, wasting no time diving into the confusion and disarray.

The first problem Manley faced was buying some time to figure out what needed to be done in IT, so after consultation with Kate and Finney, the stoppage on all systems development was extended for a further forty-five days. This was not a popular decision, but it underscored the importance of making some changes in IT and also getting some agreement on the new key business processes and the transformational roadmap—which was proving to be a challenge—before spending any more money on IT solutions. "At least," he said wryly to Kate, "working on their priorities will distract the business away from what I'm going to be doing in IT."

His first survey of his new "empire" was discouraging. IT was in a significant state of disarray.

There were no IT governance and architecture. IT was organized in silos to mirror AgCredit's divisional structure, and each business unit owned and governed its own IT projects. This resulted in business unit leaders making IT decisions based on their current needs and essentially "mortgaging the future" because they wouldn't fund the foundational work needed to operate IT at an enterprise level. Furthermore, because IT was considered a necessary evil, the company had outsourced chunks of IT, sometimes for the wrong reasons. As a result, his IT staff felt highly disengaged from the company, scoring 30 percent versus the overall company engagement score of 69 percent. Many staff were unclear of their roles or were performing roles for which they were unqualified. There was a significant lack of technical skills in certain areas, and the organization was also missing senior IT managers who could be "thought leaders." Finally, there were many unfilled vacancies because the company couldn't find qualified staff for what they were willing to pay.

A key problem was the applicationcentric approach the organization took to its work. Businesspeople would come to IT and say "I need a new system." Most businesspeople had been trained by IT to think in terms of existing systems. And IT staff were always injecting "IT reality" into business thinking, telling them they couldn't do something because "the system wouldn't allow it." This had led to a complete data mess, among other things. AgCredit had four major systems, each with its own database, and special interfaces had been built to enable them to communicate with each other. As a result, the company now had a Tower of Babel where the same information appeared in different formats, which were difficult to reconcile. This was a significant challenge when creating accurate reports for banking and other government regulators.

Now he had the high-tech guru he'd hired in his office telling him that going to a service-oriented architecture (SOA) was going to solve all his problems! Dirk Schader's eyes gleamed as he laid out the benefits of this latest technological panacea. "If we adopt SOA principles in IT, everything will be deconstructed into separate 'services.' We'd have foundational services, such as forms management and identity management; internal services, which would decompose applications into small pieces of functionality, such as loan servicing or changing customer address; and finally, we could *buy* external services, like credit rating. I think this is just what AgCredit needs!"

Manley struggled to get his thoughts together about this. Theoretically, the case for SOA was compelling, but would it really work? Schader was a highly reputable consultant, and services *would* match with processes quite well, but was the company ready for this? Was IT? Was the technology ready for prime time? "I think you've got something here," he said cautiously, "but I want to think this through carefully. First, we have to make sure it's the right technical approach and not just another high-tech fad."

Schader interrupted. "I don't think there's any other way, to be frank. You need to integrate different technologies and platforms without completely replacing them, right?" Manley nodded. "So SOA is technology neutral. What it really is, is an approach and principles for technology design *and* it supports Web services, which is a language that works across all technologies."

"We've traditionally bought and customized software packages and integrated them at the back end," stated Manley, showing off his newly acquired technical knowledge. "How would SOA be different, and would our existing packages work with SOA?"

"Good questions," answered Schader. "Almost all vendors *say* they can handle SOA, but many of them can't. We're going to have to be very careful about who we choose to buy components from. Some of these guys *say* their stuff is based on open standards, but when you get into the guts of it, you find it's got some proprietary code built in. SOA is tough to do—no question—but given all the good business process work you've done *and* the fact that you are going to completely redesign and restructure IT, I think you've got a shot at making it a success."

"I agree," said Manley, "but we're going to have to *prove* it to the executive team *and* we're going to need some basic foundational work on our data. Before we even start this SOA stuff, we have to get a handle on that. Can you work with

Kate to put a plan together for creating a single set of customer information that would work with each of our systems temporarily? Maybe if the two of you 'bang a few heads' in the business and now that we've got Finney's support, we can finally make some progress in this area. Then you could get started on creating a single customer information file. If we can get this far when no one else has been able to, I bet they'll trust us to try out SOA with a small business process."

Schader nodded. "Sure thing, and I'd like to get Samantha Secord involved with this. She's got some really good business analytical skills, which I think could be developed. She's been stuck coding, and it's not really her thing."

Manley groaned at the reminder that his staffing was a mess. "Go for it," he agreed. "I'll work something out with HR." While SOA and customer information were great ideas for the future, his bigger problems were going to be getting at the nuts and bolts of IT transformation. He now understood the function's current problems, but without a new IT organization structure and governance, agreement from the business, and supportive corporate processes, nothing was going to get fixed permanently and they'd have no hope of supporting Kate's business transformation. "We've got to develop our capabilities, and the business has to see we can do what we say we'll do," he muttered to no one in particular. "And we've got to do it quickly." He turned to his PC and began to sketch out a plan.

Two days later Manley called a meeting of all his managers to explain the need for the new IT organization structure. "Our first critical success factor is not going to be whether we can develop new systems or use new technologies, although those are important. It's about how to position IT to be successful in a processcentric organization. I'm going to need all your help to do this properly. We've got to work in partnership with the business, but we've also got to recognize the strengths we bring to the table. This won't happen overnight. Here's what I have in mind . . ." ■

DISCUSSION QUESTIONS

1. Propose an organizational structure for the IT department that you feel would support the transformation of AgCredit into a processcentric organization.
2. Outline a project selection process for AgCredit to ensure alignment with the enterprise business vision.
3. How should Manley "make the case" for SOA to ensure that the executive team at AgCredit buys in?
4. What new internal IT capabilities will have to be developed in order to create an IT department to support AgCredit's future business architecture?
5. What aspects of IT governance do you think would be important in supporting this transformation?

Chapter 10

Strategic Experimentation with IT[1]

The role of IT is changing. According to Smith and McKeen (2006), it is bifurcating into separate roles: commodity service and competitive differentiation. Seemingly schizophrenic, these dual perspectives simply reflect the fact that organizations need to balance their bottom-line focus with their top-line focus; that is, take the costs out of the business while growing revenues through IT-enhanced products and services. Although IT is experienced at reducing internal costs, a top-line focus is new and different. It requires a customercentric orientation. Developing systems for employees is not the same as for real customers who lack allegiance, skill, and/or patience. A top-line focus also requires experimentation with new products and services that are predominantly technology enabled. Such experimentation (e.g., trying new offerings) is well established in most organizations, but it is new terrain for the IT function. It means new collaborations (e.g., marketing, business development, research and development), and it entails new skills/roles (e.g., forecasting, marketing timing). The upshot is to put IT "front and center." With services Web enabled and products downloadable, most of what customers know and think about an organization is now based on its Internet presence. As an anonymous CEO quipped to a group of IT executives, "Welcome to the world of consumer behavior."

This chapter explores how IT is being used for strategic IT experiments (e.g., where IT is being used to drive a new business venture), as opposed to "experiments with new IT" (e.g., where promising new technologies are examined). It is clear that strategic IT experimentation cannot be examined in isolation. In most firms, strategic experimentation occurs within a larger organizational framework of innovation—an organization's need to reinvent its products and services and occasionally itself—and, as a result, is best understood within this context. Therefore, in the next section

---

[1]McKeen, J. D., and H. A. Smith, "Strategic Experimentation with IT," *Communications of the Association of Information Systems* 19, article 8 (January 2007): 132–41 (reproduced by permission of the Association of Information Systems).

we describe the nature of innovation and the role of strategic experimentation. Following this, we present a typical innovation life cycle and show where experimentation fits within this model. In the final section of the chapter, we offer advice for managing strategic IT experiments.

INNOVATION AND STRATEGIC EXPERIMENTATION

The need to innovate is well established as necessary for long-term organizational survival (Christensen and Raynor 2003; Hamel and Välikangas 2003). According to Christensen (1997), there are two types: sustaining and disruptive. *Sustaining* innovation improves an existing product or enhances an existing service for an existing customer. In contrast, *disruptive* innovation targets noncustomers and delivers a product or service that fundamentally differs from the current product portfolio. Sustaining innovation leaves organizations in their comfort zone of established markets, known customers, and realizable business models. Disruptive technologies enjoy none of these benefits. To be successful for the initiating organization, the disruptive innovation must meet two basic requirements: it must create value as perceived by customers, and it must enact mechanisms to appropriate or capture a fair share of this new value (Henderson et al. 2003). For other organizations and particularly dominant players, disruptive innovation can be devastating. Christensen (1997) refers to this as "the innovator's dilemma." For an excellent discussion of disruptive technologies and a review of six leading theories of innovation, see Denning (2005).

Innovation comes about through organizational change, and here, too, we see two dominant forms: *continuous change* versus *punctuated equilibrium*. Brown and Eisenhardt (1997) describe continuous change as "frequent, relentless, and perhaps endemic to the firm," while the punctuated equilibrium model of change "assumes that long periods of small, incremental change are interrupted by brief periods of discontinuous, radical change." In this latter case, change is primarily seen as "rare, risky, and episodic." While it is tempting to equate sustaining innovation with continuous change and disruptive innovation with punctuated equilibrium, it is not so simple. In fact, Brown and Eisenhardt (1997) as well as Meyer (1997) cite examples where firms have successfully reinvented themselves through continuous change as opposed to abrupt, punctuated change. In fact, these authors suggest that "in firms undergoing continuous change, innovation is intimately related to broader organization change."

Innovation frequently involves experimentation (Govindarajan and Trimble 2004). Experimentation invokes the notion of testing or trying something new. Learning is paramount; whether the experiment succeeds or fails is secondary to what is learned during the conduct of the experiment. Experiments also conjure up a sense of the unknown, trying something that no one has actually tried before. The juxtaposition of the word *strategic* with *experiment* introduces direction, purpose, importance, and future criticality for the organization. Strategic experiments are not happenstance. Although distinctions are sometimes fuzzy, many authors differentiate strategic experiments from process and product innovations that tend to be narrower and more focused on existing offerings. Nicholls-Nixon, Cooper, and Woo (2000) define *strategic experimentation* as:

> . . . a series of trial-and-error changes pursued along various dimensions of strategy, over a relatively short period of time, in an effort to identify and establish a viable basis for competing. (496)

Govindarajan and Trimble (2004) further highlight the inherent risky nature of strategic experiments, which they characterize as:

> . . . a multiyear bet within a poorly defined industry that has no clear formula for making a profit. Potential customers are mere possibilities. Value propositions are guesses. And activities that lead to profitable outcomes are unclear. (67)

As such, strategic experiments represent a rather unique management challenge. According to Govindarajan and Trimble (2005), strategic experiments constitute the "highest-risk, highest-return category of innovation and require a unique managerial approach." Where the goal is learning, results are vastly different from those normally monitored and measured within organizations. Even expectations take on altered meaning—sometimes heretical—where failure is tolerated and perhaps even expected. There is also a strong element of "trying to manage the unmanageable." Strategic experiments benefit from none of the controls easily imposed in a laboratory setting; for instance, control groups may not be available; results may be ambiguous; it may not be possible to shield experiments from outside influences; experiments may not be repeatable and/or verifiable. Furthermore, attempts to manage these experiments may destroy them. Management is a delicate balance where:

> . . . successful multiple-product innovation blends limited structure around responsibilities and priorities with extensive communication and design freedom to create improvisation within current projects. This combination is neither so structured that change cannot occur nor so unstructured that chaos ensues. (Brown and Eisenhardt 1997)

Of interest for our purposes is the fact that IT often plays a key role in innovation and change. In fact, many recent innovative products (e.g., Blackberries, iPods) and services (e.g., eBay, VoIP) are clearly enabled by information technology. One pundit suggests that innovation and transformation are becoming the new *I* and *T* in IT (Slofstra 2006). The term *strategic IT experimentation* focuses on the subset of strategic experiments that are based on information technology similar to the above examples. Interestingly, very little attention has been paid to strategic IT experimentation. Henderson and others (2003) introduce the concept of "platforms" (e.g., technology platforms, capability platforms, and business platforms) as enabling conditions offered by IT to support innovation. Sambamurthy, Bharadwaj, and Grover (2003) suggest a role for IT as a "digital options generator." Both of these studies look at IT from the standpoint of its role as a facilitator and/or enabler of innovation and agility. In this chapter we examine the management issues and challenges involved with actually conducting strategic IT experimentation. In order to do so, we first describe the innovation life cycle as the context for strategic IT experimentation.

STRATEGIC EXPERIMENTATION WITHIN THE INNOVATION PROCESS

Organizations typically do not assign responsibility for strategic experiments to individual departments. In fact, few organizations even use the term *strategic experiment*. Instead, organizations commit resources (space, funds, and people), build infrastructure, articulate procedures, and provide incentives all in an effort to instill a culture of innovation. We refer to this collection of activities as the *innovation process*. Strategic IT experiments exist within such a process and must be understood in this context. Two examples of how companies incorporate strategic experimentation into their innovation processes are as follows:

- **BP** challenged its lines of business to use IT as a source of innovation. Because the rate of change is so much faster with IT as compared to other forms of technology, BP realized that its traditional approaches for assessing and adopting new technology wouldn't work. As a result, the company created an abbreviated innovation process. New ideas/opportunities (arising from employees, suppliers, universities, partners, and/or venture capitalists) must now pass three filters: (1) relevance, (2) technical readiness, and (3) economical viability. Once passed, a line of business must then be willing to sponsor an experimental pilot. If this is successful, the idea/opportunity becomes part of an "upscale pilot," which greatly expands its range and reach. Success here leads to adoption by a line of business. The whole process, from idea to adoption, happens within a year.

  In this process strategic IT experimentation begins with business sponsorship of the experimental pilot and continues into the upscale pilot (as various features of the innovation are tried). Often experiments involve BP's partners. In essence, BP "provides the business milieu within which its technology partners can hold large-scale, real-life experiments" (Smith 2006).

- **Telco** has a somewhat different innovation process centered on the fact that all its products and services involve technology. It consists of four stages:

  1. *Idea.*   Ideas are generated through informal processes (e.g., brainstorming sessions or competition activity) as well as formal processes (e.g., market research or industry trend analysis), and the sources of ideas are varied (e.g., vendors, peers, product and marketing, customers, laboratories). Ideas must meet certain requirements in order to pass to the next stage, including specific and targeted objectives that address "pain points" or core business offerings, technical measurement, and identification of business sponsors and champions. On an annual basis, about forty to fifty ideas are approved for the next stage.
  2. *Proof of concept.*   At this stage, teams are assigned to specific ideas in order to conduct the proof of concept. Testing is done within a formal or informal laboratory setting using typical controlled experimentation. The process is very agile and adaptive, and the original idea can morph substantially. The team is highly focused and intentionally kept small. The entire proof-of-concept stage occurs over one to four weeks. Of the forty to fifty original ideas, only five to ten make it successfully through this stage. Requirements for passage to the next stage include addressing issues of

intellectual property protection as well as providing a service description for the new idea.

3. *Trial or pilot stage.* This stage is described by the firm as "contained production exposure" as the idea is exposed to the market in a limited and measured way. A market segment is defined, and certain customers (who may be employees) are offered the chance to experiment with the product or service. Measurements are taken to reveal the marketing/branding issues, the financial "price points," and the operational impacts. The trial/pilot occurs within a window of four to twelve weeks, but occasionally it is extended. In addition to favorable results (i.e., marketing, financial, and operational), requirements for the next stage include complete product designs and business and system requirements. Many ideas are killed at this stage.

4. *Transition stage.* This stage is the "go to market" stage, and the idea now enters the full system development life cycle to ensure that the product or service is "industrial strength." Many shortcuts (i.e., "duct tape" solutions), which served well enough for the pilot, must now be engineered to meet production standards. It is interesting to note that IT has some unique opportunities and dangers when transitioning from an experiment to a full-fledged offering. Our Telco manager suggested that "you can sometimes go too fast from concept to the one you actually drive."

In both these innovation processes, strategic experimentation begins *after* an idea has been vetted and deemed relevant and *before* it is transitioned into a full component of the business—whether product, service, new technology, or new process. Thus, strategic IT experimentation begins at the proof-of-concept stage (corresponding with BP's experimental pilot) and continues through the trial/pilot stage (corresponding with BP's upscale pilot). A feedback loop may be involved at the trial or pilot stage (see Figure 10.1).

Figure 10.1 Strategic Experimentation Is Part of the Innovation Process

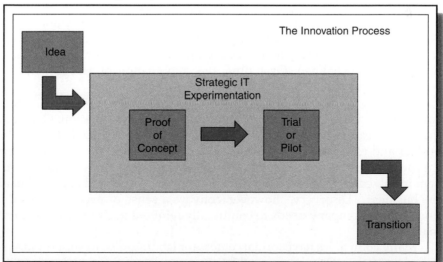

STRATEGIES FOR SUCCESSFUL IT EXPERIMENTATION

There are three necessary conditions for strategic IT experimentation to be successful: (1) motivation, (2) support, and (3) direction. As one manager stated, "Without motivation, little will happen; without support, little can happen; and without direction, anything can happen." The focus group's recommendations to others seeking to improve strategic IT experimentation include the following:

1. *Motivate: Establish rewards for strategic IT experimentation.* Although many individuals are naturally drawn to experimentation, the demands of everyday work often drive this interest and inclination into remission. Furthermore, experimentation is risky, and not all people are willing to stick their necks out. As a result, experimentation and innovation do not flourish without intervention. According to focus group members, the way to create an innovation-enabled organization is twofold: provide incentives and rewards to support experimentation and risk taking and make it everyone's job. Good ideas are good ideas, and experience shows that they are as apt to originate at the customer interface as they are within the laboratory or the executive ranks.

Taking this a step further, one company has made innovation a component of everyone's annual performance measurement. In addition, it also offers five specific types of formal rewards for innovation ranging from patentable ideas to emerging business opportunities. Not all rewards need be formal. One firm uses a system of frequent informal rewards (e.g., books, tickets, cards, recognition days, and executive citations) to recognize innovative IT ideas and encourage and reward strategic experimentation with IT. Another company discovered that the best reward for IT personnel is simply the opportunity to work and play with new technology! In this company enterprising IT personnel win the right to experiment with new technology without the need for champions or sponsors. According to the manager involved, this activity is funded by "skunkworks" and "beg and grovel."

2. *Support: Create infrastructure to support experimentation.* Offering rewards for experimentation sends employees the signal that experimentation and innovation are encouraged and will be recognized. This provides the motivation for individuals to experiment, but organizations need to provide support for such experimentation if they want it to happen. Over time, the combination of recognition and support builds a culture of innovation.

However, notwithstanding this, many firms believe it is also necessary to build some infrastructure around IT innovation and experimentation. One company, for instance, created the position of "chief scientist" and provided that office with a budget and resources. This was the organization's "way to signal to everyone that the lifeblood of the organization is discovery . . . not just innovation," said the manager involved. At this company, "innovation is a given" and expected in all parts of the business. "Discovery," however, conveys a sense of urgency as well as the notion that the company needs to continually reinvent itself in order to survive in the marketplace.

Many companies have formal centers (or laboratories) to support innovation and experimentation. Depending on the firm, the roles of these centers vary from "new product introduction" to "new technology introduction" to "business venturing" to "incubation centers." Where IT is considered a key business driver, they usually focus almost exclusively on strategic IT experimentation. The critical aspect of their creation is the provision of support and infrastructure to enable idea review and experimentation. Most centers are formally entrenched within the organization with ongoing funding, permanent staffing, and well-developed procedures and processes to encourage, guide, and support innovation. According to one manager, the key element is "to link sponsorship to innovation," reflecting the fact that "good ideas don't make it on their own."

While companies in the group reached consensus on the mandate for innovation centers, they disagreed about their governance. Two distinct strategies surfaced:

- *Insulate.* This strategy creates innovation centers as places where "all lines of business can come together to address common problems." According to proponents, the key benefit of this approach is the ability to foster synergies across the business in the belief that innovation is best "nurtured away from the mainstream business."
- *Incubate.* Those following this strategy place their innovation centers within specific lines of business (LOBs). Proponents suggested that forcing innovation to be housed within a single LOB leads to IT experimentation focused on "real" problems and opportunities and committed local ownership.

The innovation infrastructure that was common to virtually all organizations in the group was the maintenance of an intranet for launching ideas. These sites are considered to be effective for soliciting, vetting, and sharing ideas and/or opportunities. According to one manager, their chief value is that "anyone can input and everyone gets access" to build on ideas. In firms with innovation centers, intranets are effective "feeder" systems. In organizations lacking the formal support of an innovation center, ideas identified on the intranet require a sponsor to marshal support in order to turn them into realizable products and/or services.

A common form of financial support is the establishment of internal venture funds. In about half of the participating organizations, funding mechanisms had been set up to support IT experimentation. Typically, such funds are made available on a competitive basis with an oversight committee in place to award resources and to monitor progress and completion.

3. *Direct: Manage innovation strategically.* One manager pointed out that "experimentation never fails as long as there has been learning." Strictly speaking, the focus group agreed *but* felt that "any such learning would have to be strategically important for the organization" for it to be considered successful. According to the group, learning for the sake of learning was "an activity enjoyed by academics"—much to our chagrin! They suggested that providing motivation and support for individuals to experiment freely would be a recipe for disaster. Organizations must provide *direction* for these activities. Strategic IT experimentation does not occur by happenstance. Some participant suggestions for directing IT experimentation in order to ensure that it was strategically relevant include the following:

a. *Link experimentation and innovation to customer value.* A simple yet effective way to accomplish this is to focus on emerging pain points. At one company all new ideas had to articulate the specific customer pain point (CPP) that would be addressed. This requirement, in and of itself, produced results. As the manager involved related, "The identification and surfacing of CPPs stimulated considerable and sometimes heated discussion. Many people were surprised to learn of CPPs, and many potential solutions emerged. It was a case of 'if only I had known.'" Unfortunately, failure to articulate business value to the customer is a common phenomenon.

b. *Link experimentation to core business processes.* The opposite approach focuses IT experimentation internally on core business functions. One participant, whose organization is "currently reluctant to experiment in the market," focuses all its experiments on core business activities. "Our belief is that IT experimentation is strategic only if it produces significant efficiencies for internal operations in a way that can be captured on the bottom line," she said.

c. *Use venture funds to guide strategic initiatives.* While establishing venture funding for IT experimentation is a form of support (see above), the governance of such funds can be instrumental in achieving strategic alignment. Venture funds are typically given for initiatives that do the following:

- Make greater use of innovation resources
- Focus on new business models
- Explore new/disruptive technologies
- Focus on penetrating new markets
- Leverage cross-organizational capabilities
- Streamline decision making
- Focus on opportunities that can scale

FROM EXPERIMENTATION TO INNOVATION: LESSONS LEARNED

Focus group members shared examples of both successful and unsuccessful IT experiments. Of the three dramatic failures mentioned, all involved not the experiment itself, but the transition from successful experiment to broader practice or to the marketplace. Since the goal of a successful experiment is to ultimately become an innovation from which the business derives value, navigating the transition from experiment to innovation is especially important. While three is a small sample upon which to draw conclusions, these failures had several elements that were common. From these experiences, the group reached consensus about how to approach this critical transition point:

- *Focus on achievable targets.* Strategic IT experiments should be manageable and targeted but, at the same time, built so they can scale up easily. According to one manager, "It is far easier to ramp up a proven venture than to plan, build, and deliver a winner." At one company an experiment involved a "proof of concept" for a new technology involving six sites. Management then rapidly decided to expand the experiment to three hundred sites! This action literally ended experimentation, and the task immediately became one of a large-scale implementation.

- *Don't rush to market.*   Positive results from an experiment should be viewed as justification for further experimentation, not as a "license to launch." At one company, a decision to go to market based on very favorable results from a strategic IT experiment quickly ran into difficulty. The customers involved in the experiment turned out to be unrepresentative of the overall customer base, and the uptake in the market plummeted as the rollout broadened its base.
- *Be careful with "cool" technology.*   Because IT experimentation deals with technology, it is sometimes easy to be misled by cool technology. The buying public may not understand what the technology does (e.g., it's an Internet pen), may have no need for the things that the technology does (e.g., it tracks unvisited sites), and/or may not find the technology appealing (e.g., it's a mouse with arms and hands). On the other hand, this same technology may become the item that every teenager on the planet must have! Therefore, exercise caution.
- *Learn by design.*   The goal of an experiment is to learn. The group provided several examples of experiments where nothing was learned. In these cases insufficient controls were designed into the experiment to enable the organization to ascertain after the fact what had happened. Was failure due to product features or due to functioning? A lack of effective marketing? The price point? Thus, the first step in a strategic IT experiment should be to identify the critical questions that need to be answered then design these into the experiment.

CONCLUSION

Stressing top-line growth brings IT into the mainstream of product and service innovation, which, in turn, means that the IT function must become more customercentric, assimilate new skills, and work collaboratively with the business development arm of the organization. It also leads a company into the realm of strategic IT experimentation. This reflects the ubiquitous nature of information technology and represents a new and exciting role for IT. This chapter has outlined some of the issues and challenges IT managers are experiencing as they begin to move into the uncharted waters of innovation. At present, in most organizations, strategic experimentation is merely a collection of activities and procedures for testing out new ideas. As managers become more experienced in this area, however, it can be expected that many of the practices outlined above will become better understood and IT will be able to use strategic experimentation more effectively to successfully spin good ideas into innovation gold.

REFERENCES

Brown, S. L., and K. M. Eisenhardt. "The Art of Continuous Change: Linking Complexity Theory and Time-paced Evolution in Relentlessly Shifting Organizations." *Administrative Science Quarterly* 42, no. 1 (March 1997): 1–34.

Christensen, C. *The Innovator's Dilemma: When New Technologies Cause Great Firms to Fail.* Boston: Harvard Business School Press, 1997.

Christensen, C., and M. Raynor. *The Innovator's Solution: Creating and Sustaining Successful Growth.* Boston: Harvard Business School Press, 2003.

Denning, S. "Why the Best and Brightest Approaches Don't Solve the Innovation Dilemma." *Strategy & Leadership* 33, no. 1 (2005): 4–11.

Govindarajan, V., and C. Trimble. "Strategic Innovation and the Science of Learning." *Sloan Management Review* 45, no. 2 (2004): 66–75.

———. "Building Breakthrough Businesses within Established Organizations." *Harvard Business Review* May (2005): 59–68.

Hamel, G., and L. Välikangas. "The Quest for Resilience." *Harvard Business Review* September (2003).

Henderson, J. C, N. Kulatilaka, N. Venkatraman, and J. Freedman. "Riding the Wave of Emerging Technologies: Opportunities and Challenges for the CIO." Working paper, Boston University, School of Management, 2003.

Meyer, M. H. "Revitalize Your Product Lines through Continuous Platform Renewal." *Research Technology Management* 40, no. 2 (March/April 1997): 17–28.

Nicholls-Nixon, C. L., A. C. Cooper, and C. Y. Woo. "Strategic Experimentation: Understanding Change and Performance in New Ventures." *Journal of Business Venturing* 15 (2000): 493–521.

Sambamurthy, V., A. Bharadwaj, and V. Grover. "Shaping Agility through Digital Options: Reconceptualizing the Role of Information Technology in Contemporary Firms." *MIS Quarterly* 27, no. 2 (June 2003): 237–63.

Slofstra, M. "CEOs Who Get It." *Edge* 5, no. 2 (May/June 2006): 4.

Smith, H. A. Notes from a private presentation the Society for Information Management's Advanced Practices Council, Chicago, 2006.

Smith, H. A., and J. D. McKeen. "IT in 2010." *MIS Quarterly Executive* 5, no. 3 (September 2006): 125–36.

Chapter 11

Enhancing the Customer Experience with Technology

Historically, IT developers designed systems for *internal* customers as opposed to *external* customers. This was challenge enough as they wrestled with "usability engineering" in order to create user-friendly interfaces, decision-impelling formats, logical layouts, adherence to common usage function keys, multiple-application password logins, hot keys, and common look-feel screens. Now that world looks like a cake walk. You can provide training for internal customers and help desk staff. Moreover, these individuals work for the same organization that you do, and when push comes to shove, they can be made to comply with a system. Not so with external customers who are apt to disappear if frustrated or confused.

For financial institutions, the first major customer exposure to technology was likely the automated teller machine (ATM). This exposure not only provided a technical contact point for customers (a "touch point"), but also introduced customer self-service. The Web was soon to follow. As soon as Web interfaces could be linked to legacy applications, self-service ramped up quickly. Customers are now offered such services as online flight check-ins, biometric identification (e.g., the United States' automated border-crossing system, INSPASS), Web/phone/kiosk transactions, smart cards to access government services, mobile/wireless ordering, e-payments, and artificial intelligence for anticipatory customer service. Want to track your courier delivery package in real time? Perform a banking transaction? Order a sweater? Enter the retail world of 24/7, "always on" technology. If enhancing the customer experience is the question, it seems technology is the answer.

In this chapter we explore the various practices leading organizations are using to enhance the customer experience with technology. First, we examine the notion of an "experience economy." We then review the concept of "flow," the nature of customer interactions, and the role of technology in such interactions. The chapter then presents a number of proven strategies to enhance customer experiences with technology, based on the collective insight of the focus group managers.

THE EXPERIENCE ECONOMY

According to Pine and Gilmore (1999), we are currently in the throes of a new economy (or evolving a new economic dimension)—the "experience" economy.

> Experiences are a fourth economic offering, as distinct from services as services are from goods, but one that has until now gone largely unrecognized. Experiences have always been around, but consumers, businesses, and economists lumped them into the service sector along with such uneventful activities as dry cleaning, auto repair, wholesale distribution, and telephone access. When a person buys a service, he purchases a set of intangible activities carried out on his behalf. But when he buys an experience, he pays to spend time enjoying a series of memorable events that a company stages—as in a theatrical play—to engage him in a personal way. (Pine and Gilmore 1999, 2)

The authors claim that the nature of economic value follows a natural progression from commodities to goods to services then to experiences. They use coffee to illustrate this evolution. The coffee bean is a *commodity* widely traded on the futures market. When roasted and packaged, it becomes a *good* distributed through various retail channels (e.g., grocery stores). Once brewed, it becomes a *service* widely available at cafés, restaurants, bars, and deli counters. When served "in a five-star restaurant or espresso bar, where the ordering, creation, and consumption of the cup embodies a heightened ambience or sense of theater," it becomes a distinctive *experience.* Interestingly, the price one is willing to pay for the coffee as a commodity, good, service, and finally experience increases by orders of magnitude with progression along this evolutionary path. This fact has not gone unnoticed by many leading-edge companies who now create experiences within which to envelop their customers.

Pine and Gilmore (1999) offer the following definitions:

- *Commodities:* materials that are extracted typically by slaughtering, mining, or harvesting. Processing and/or refining may be necessary, as is bulk storage, before being transported to market. Commodities are fungible and pricing is typically established on the basis of costs and availability.
- *Goods:* items such as cars, baseballs, and clothing that are created using commodities (e.g., cotton, steel) and marketed to largely anonymous customers. Price is based on costs but also differentiation (e.g., designer clothes).
- *Services:* intangible activities customized to the individual request of known clients. These services are provided using goods (e.g., a lawn caretaker will use a lawn mower).
- *Experiences:* events that engage individuals in a personal way. Providers intentionally use services as the stage and goods as props to create a memorable happening for the client ("guest").

Experiences differ in many respects; however, two dimensions are paramount according to Pine and Gilmore (1999). The first is the level of *participation,* and the second is the type of *relationship.* Passive participation is listening to music; active participation is driving a race car. On the relationship dimension, absorption occurs when the experience enters your mind (e.g., watching TV) while immersion occurs when you enter the experience (e.g., virtual reality). The richest experiences encompass aspects of all four realms—passive absorption, active absorption, passive immersion, and active immersion (Pine and Gilmore 1999). The challenge, then, is to design experiences that meld elements of absorption and immersion and active and passive participation within the experience to create a "sweet spot." When achieved, the customer is fully engaged in the experience that has been staged.

It is not clear whether marketing *caters to* a need for experiences or, in fact, *creates* these needs. Truth probably lies in the middle. Nevertheless, with opportunities for increased economic value through the staging of experiences, there is ample incentive for organizations to examine the experiences they are currently offering their customers. When the offering is a commodity, good, or service, the interaction with the customer tends to be somewhat transactional. Even with express goals, including delighting the customer, creating customer loyalty, and customer retention, in many instances the focus of the interaction with the customer is primarily on the sale. The danger here is to ignore the opportunity to engage the customer in a much more meaningful and emotionally rich and satisfying experience.

THE CONCEPT OF "FLOW"

According to Novak, Hoffman, and Yung (2000), the word *flow* is used to describe a state of mind sometimes experienced by people who are deeply involved in some activity. One example of flow is the case where a professional athlete is playing exceptionally well and achieves a state of mind where nothing else matters but the game; he or she is completely and totally immersed in it. The experience is not exclusive to athletics; many people report this state of mind when playing games, engaging in hobbies, or working.

Early work to define and measure this phenomenon focused on workplace applications such as voice mail and e-mail (Webster, Trevino, and Ryan 1993) as well as on the Web (Steuer 1992). Novak, Hoffman, and Yung (2000) had this to say about it:

> *Customers who achieve flow on the Web and perceive the online experience to be compelling are so acutely involved in the act of online navigation that thoughts and perceptions not relevant to navigation are screened out, and the consumer focuses entirely on the interaction. Concentration on the navigation experience is so intense that there is little attention left to consider anything else, and consequently other events occurring in the consumer's surrounding physical environment lose significance. Self-consciousness disappears, the consumer's sense of time becomes distorted, and the state of mind arising as a result of achieving flow on the Web is extremely gratifying.*

Due to their navigation activity, someone in the state of flow would tend to be actively participating and fully immersed/absorbed in the experience. It is also possible for someone in a state of flow to be less active navigating (perhaps led through a navigation path as part of the experience). What is most interesting is the realization that organizations are able to create such a level of engagement during online shopping episodes; that is, a state of flow is not only possible, but attainable. According to Novak, Hoffman, and Yung (2000), the Internet is best thought of not as a simulation of the "real world," but as an alternative real yet computer-mediated environment in which the online customer experience becomes paramount.

CUSTOMER EXPERIENCES

Many terms have been coined to describe how companies and customers interact in the online world: *moments of truth, points of presence, touch points, contact points,* and/or *service encounters.* Smith and Wheeler (2002) use the term *branded customer experience.* All convey common notions about the nature of customer interactions with organizations. Specifically customer encounters tend to be the following:

- Sporadic—as opposed to continuous
- Subject to recency effects—recent interactions affect impressions more than past interactions
- Customer initiated—organizations might wish to initiate more such encounters in order to exercise control over the nature and context of the interaction, but the majority remain customer initiated
- Triggered by express needs—a new car, birthday gift, or a complaint
- Opportunities for dialogue—every encounter provides an opportunity for the organization to nurture the relationship with the customer (whether prospective or existing)
- Significant events—in many cases these interactions are "make or break" situations where the sale/customer is won or lost

Care must be exercised in differentiating two very dissimilar classes of service encounter. If it is *transactional*, customers are primarily interested in completing a transaction correctly, efficiently, accurately, and as quickly as possible. Decreasing the time required to complete the transaction—sometimes referred to as a *time rebate*—and providing assurance that the transaction is indeed completed successfully are the key attributes of transactional encounters.

Service encounters may also be *relational*. Relational encounters (such as chatting online, browsing, or choosing a vacation B&B) often require the development of trust, mutual understanding, and shared goals in order for both parties to reach a level of comfort with each other. With such encounters, the role of technology is to help create experiences conducive to engendering these relational elements. Such experiences may, in fact, elongate the encounter in hopes of giving greater satisfaction to the customer. Reducing the time is not likely to be in the best interests of either the customer or the firm. Strategies for dealing with both types of customer encounter are presented at the end of this chapter.

The importance of these encounters is widely recognized. Unfortunately, customer interactions are not universally well managed. At any cocktail party with only modest encouragement, individuals will share personal stories of disastrous interactions with organizations. The prevalence of these customer anecdotes provides ample and compelling evidence of our inability to provide satisfactory, let alone rewarding, experiences for our customers. This dilemma is exacerbated by the existence of a significant trend toward self-service. If customers are willing to conduct the transaction themselves, companies will offer them greatly increased flexibility in terms of "when and where," but the interaction must be a positive one if customer satisfaction is to be enhanced.

SELF-SERVICE TECHNOLOGIES

The interface through which customers experience organizations is largely facilitated and/or mediated by technology. Because of this, much of what customers know (and, therefore, think) about organizations is conditioned by technology. Whether a Web site, an automatic banking machine (ABM), a self-service point-of-sale (POS) terminal, an interactive voice response (IVR) system, or a kiosk, the mediation role played by technology is critical. It is through this interaction that the customer forms impressions of the organization. Furthermore, the customer learns how the organization views him or her as a customer and determines the value that is placed on the relationship. In short, in many customer interactions these days, the face of the organization is technological. Therefore, it is important to understand the customer experience with self-service technologies.

According to Meuter and others (2000), there are four types of self-service interfaces (ranked from greatest to least flexibility): telephone/IVR (due to the ubiquity of telephones); online/Internet (any browser, any time, anywhere); interactive kiosks (location specific, access limited); and finally, video/DVD (due to acceptance and availability). It should be noted that many of these interfaces may be combined. For example, it is becoming common to offer online/Internet customers the opportunity to connect to a telephone/IVR system or to a video clip. Interactive kiosks may provide an Internet browser. Second, many services are offered via multiple interfaces. Package tracking, for instance, may be available online or through an IVR system or indeed by means of a kiosk. This overlapping of services over different interfaces is done consciously to maximize possible service channels to accommodate different needs and/or preferences of customers. These key interfaces are described briefly below. In addition, some emerging technologies that promise to enhance these interfaces are introduced.

1. *Telephone/IVR.* Interactive voice response systems route incoming customer calls to service representatives or to information sources based on the nature of the customers' needs. The system presents the caller with menu-based options following a hierarchical logic structure leading to successive levels of detail. When the system determines exactly what the customer's needs are, the customer is connected to an appropriate service representative who knows (or should know) who the caller is and has (or should have) the caller's information at hand. Customers are typically given the option of skipping the IVR system to speak directly with a service representative if they so choose. This exit also accommodates customers without touch-tone phones.

2. *Online/Internet.*   Undoubtedly the ultimate in self-service flexibility, Web sites allow you to browse, shop, buy, sell, ship, locate information, track orders, communicate, make payments, plus a thousand other activities at any time and at any place as long as you have a connection to the Internet through a browser. A medium, once text-based and monochromatic, is now enlivened with color, animation, and sound. In combination, virtually limitless options in terms of form and function are now available. As the portal product market matures (Phifer 2001), the ability to create customer experiences is unbounded.

3. *Interactive kiosks.*   These kiosks are typically located within malls and other areas where customer traffic is high. They may provide information regarding maps/directions, a listing of retail outlets, restaurant options, and places/things of interest. Kiosks may also provide transactions such as vehicle licensing, movie tickets, and airline boarding passes.

   One of the more promising technologies to support interactive kiosks is radio frequency identification technology.[1] One of many possible uses for this technology allows a customer to simply leave the store with merchandise whose embedded e-tags tell the store what they are and, hence, what the customer just bought. RFID tags are also used for "pay at the pump" service by providing customers with e-tags that communicate with the gas pump kiosk to automatically bill the customer's fuel account.

4. *Video/DVD.*   Due to their lack of "connectness," this type of interface is unable to offer transactions and self-service. It is, however, widely used for self-help encounters and, as has been pointed out earlier, often combined with other interfaces to enrich the capabilities of the customer interaction. Video/DVD technologies have the advantage of wide customer availability and acceptance, far surpassing that of either Internet or kiosk interfaces. In addition, the advantages of full-motion video are obvious to anyone who has experienced the alternatives.

THE ROLE OF TECHNOLOGY

Because of its pervasiveness, it is clear that technology plays a key role in how a customer "experiences" a company. Research, examining the nature of customer service through technological interfaces, has found that customers using various self-service technologies give the following reasons for *satisfaction* (Meuter et al. 2000):

1. *"Better than the alternative."*   For these individuals (68 percent), satisfaction is driven by the improvement or additional benefits provided by using the self-service technology. Specific reasons included "saved time" (30 percent),

---

[1]RFID involves embedding tiny computer chips (called electronic tags or "e-tags") in products. These e-tags are capable of broadcasting product identification information to nearby e-tag readers. This enables products to be detected merely by proximity, thus eliminating the line-of-sight requirements of barcode readers.

"easy to use" (16 percent), "when I want" (8 percent), "saved money" (6 percent), "where I want" (5 percent), and "avoid service personnel" (3 percent).

2. *"Did its job."* For this group of respondents (21 percent), satisfaction results from the mere fascination with the capabilities of various self-service technologies and the fact that they actually work!

3. *"Solved intensified need."* Typically these individuals (11 percent) are faced with an urgent situation that could be remedied by the availability of some sort of self-service option.

If little else, these results demonstrate the importance of convenience (when, where, availability, and ease of use) as well as cost (money, time) for self-service customers. As an alternative form of service, one might speculate that satisfaction with self-service may be due to the avoidance of existing (and less than adequate) interpersonal service!

When asked what caused *dissatisfaction,* a different picture emerged based on the following reasons:

1. *"Technology failure."* The single greatest cause of dissatisfaction (43 percent) is either outright technical failure (e.g., ATM was out of order) or cases where the technology fails to work properly (or as intended).

2. *"Poor design."* This group (36 percent) encountered problems with the design of the service experience. The reasons for their dissatisfaction could be further broken down into the following categories:
   a. "Technology design problem" (17 percent) (e.g., not obvious how to log off)
   b. "Service design problem" (19 percent) (e.g., would not accept separate "bill to" and "deliver to" addresses)

3. *"Process failure."* In these incidents (17 percent), the technological interface functions properly, but there is a breakdown subsequent to the customer-technology interaction (e.g., a product was correctly ordered but never delivered).

4. *"Customer-driven failure."* These customers (4 percent) acknowledge that the failure of the self-service technology occurred, at least in part, because of their own actions (e.g., forgetting a PIN).

The key source of dissatisfaction with self-service technologies is performance. Whether due to technology, design, process, or customer, the inability to complete an intended transaction is a major source of dissatisfaction. This highlights the relationship between satisfiers and dissatisfiers in the context of self-service technologies. Stated simply, they appear to be flip sides of the same coin. The removal of a dissatisfier (resulting in the successful completion of the transaction) simultaneously creates a satisfier ("did its job" or "better than the alternative" or perhaps even "solved an intensified need"). This also highlights the difference between interpersonal encounters and self-service encounters. With interpersonal encounters, a customer may have an unpleasant experience with the provider, but the service is still provided (Meuter et al. 2000). No such ambiguity exists with self-service technologies where failure is more objective and obvious. Furthermore, failure may go undetected, leaving the organization without option for recovery.

Technology Strategies for Enhancing the Customer Experience

If customer interactions are viewed within a larger context of serving customers by creating engaging experiences, then we will have to reexamine how we manage the technological interface. Below we offer a number of strategies suggested by members of the focus group based on their combined experiences.

1. Eliminate Dissatisfiers as Top Priority

The primary source of dissatisfaction when using self-service technology is the simple failure to perform (i.e., the customer tried to "self-serve" but was unsuccessful), as noted above. This failure is due to one of four causes: (1) the technology, (2) its design, (3) the underlying business process, or (4) the customer. The first three causes, which collectively account for 96 percent of all failures, are the responsibility of the organization.[2] This fact suggests that correcting these problems should be given top priority. The good news is that the elimination of the sources of dissatisfaction is entirely under the control of the organization.

The elimination of each of the top three causes of failure should be made a distinct management focus and should be addressed in different ways:

Technological failure.   There is no escaping the fact that technology sometimes fails outright. It follows, then, that correct defense is detection, not avoidance. By building in redundancy and the ability to self-monitor, most technology systems can provide virtually continuous service.[3] When failure happens, it is detected, redundant systems take over, and repair/replacement procedures are enacted without loss of service or customer awareness. This level of redundancy, however, is very expensive. As a result, the decision to minimize the possibility of technological failure must be balanced against the full costs of outage (i.e., loss of business, loss of customer goodwill, etc.). Participants recommended that scenario planning procedures can be used effectively here to ensure that the risks/costs of technological failure are understood and that appropriate protective procedures are enacted.

Design failure.   Due to poor design, a customer can be unsure how (or unwilling) to proceed, and the encounter fails as completely as if it were due to technical failure. The effect, however, may be more devastating than technical failure because the customer frustration may exceed that of a service being temporarily out of service. The solution is good design, and good design flows from discipline. Group members suggested that organizations should adopt the following policies and

---

[2]This 96 percent may be overstated due to the incorrect attribution of customer-initiated failure.

[3]Meuter and others (2000) claim that "this is similar in many respects to what firms such as Caterpillar and Xerox already do in anticipating equipment breakdowns through remote monitoring systems."

practices to assure uniform and consistent high-quality interfaces for all customer interactions and reduce the chances of design failure:

- Establish rules/guidelines for the design of technical interfaces.
- Force all technical interfaces to follow established design procedures.
- Create metrics for design (e.g., response time).
- Force compliance testing for all such interfaces before they proceed to production.
- Require training for all interface designers (and perhaps the creation of a center of excellence).

Process failure.   A self-service encounter typically initiates a service fulfillment process, which typically consists of a series of internal activities. Each of these, unfortunately, introduces a possible point of failure as information is "handed off" from system to system and person to person. Like the proverbial chain that is only as strong as its weakest link, these internal processes may be less automated than the interface.[4] The solution is to track each transaction from beginning to end to ensure that the process is well engineered. Address the weak points first. One manager suggested using critical incidents to investigate malfunctions. When a customer queries an order that took four days to deliver instead of two, take the time to trace this order through the system to discover where and how it got sidetracked. Often slick interfaces simply front legacy systems bound together by duct tape. Such a system invites process failure.

2. Differentiate Transactional and Relational Encounters

Because transactional encounters are primarily focused on the achievement of a specific transaction (e.g., paying a bill, booking a flight), navigation should be direct and convenient; the transaction easy, straightforward, and understandable; and confirmation of the completeness and accuracy of the completed transaction should be automatic. The design of transactional encounters is well developed (usually referred to as web/information architecture and usability) but still remains a mix of art and science, thus permitting creative license. Usability has a lot to do with navigation and navigational expectations. Furthermore, usability experts bring strong methodologies for testing Web sites (e.g., Information Architecture Summit 2003).

One manager shared his organization's five key questions *a customer should never have to ask:*

1. Did I do it right?
2. Is this system waiting for me, or am I waiting for it?
3. What do I do next?
4. Am I done?
5. Did it work?

---

[4]One focus group member described an online transaction that was printed offline and transferred manually to a separate business function where the information was reentered.

Like transactional encounters, relational encounters are purposeful and goal oriented. They differ in that they are focused on a *task* as opposed to the accomplishment of a specific transaction. From an organization's point of view, relational encounters are more apt to occur by happenstance than by design. For instance, a customer may encounter an organization while searching for hotels, comparing mortgage rates, or finding the nearest supplier of a certain product or service. That is, the customer is not likely to have a particular organization in mind when the search begins. This has definite ramifications for the design of Web sites.

Organizations, not being prescient, have no means of knowing the purpose for a customer's visit to their Web sites on arrival. This is typically ascertained by providing options on the introductory Web page (e.g., customer sign-in, new member, take a tour, view our products, search). Once the purpose of the visit is identified, the interaction can proceed more deliberately. Once ascertained, the intention is to satisfy the customer's need for information to assist him or her through the stages of visitor to prospective customer to actual customer.

At a minimum, firms must accommodate both transactional and relational encounters and must design their Web sites for the broadest range of potential customers.

3. Design Interfaces for Usability, Navigation, and Experience

Interfaces, particularly Web sites, must be designed with three goals in mind. The first is *usability* (i.e., providing sufficient information to satisfy the customer's needs and to provide appropriate confirmatory feedback); the second is *navigation* (i.e., to enable the customer to know where he or she is, how to get back, and how to proceed); and the third goal is to create an enhanced customer *experience*. Most organizations focus on the first two of these design goals and ignore the third. With all three goals, design should proceed from the customer's perspective and work backward.

The topics of usability and navigation are well studied. The design and creation of customer experiences, however, are less well developed. Novak, Hoffman, and Yung (2000, 39) offer the following advice to encourage a state of "flow":

> *Website design must provide for enough challenge to arouse the consumer, but not so much that she becomes frustrated navigating through the site and logs off. Unexpectedly, greater challenge corresponds to greater focused attention online. This means that engaging consumers online will arise in part from providing them with excitement. Conversely, if the site does not provide enough challenges for action, potential customers will quickly become bored and log off.*

Pine and Gilmore (1999) further refine this notion by suggesting that, to achieve an engaging experience, one must design the technological interface to meld elements of absorption and immersion as well as active and passive participation. It is undoubtedly true that the means to accomplish such "experiential states" are currently more art than science; however, the incentives to enhance the customer experience are as many and varied as the benefits in doing so.

4. Correct the Obvious Problems with Your IVR Systems

IVR systems appear to be a necessary evil. For the majority of customers, it is difficult to see how an IVR system works to their benefit. Navigating through an "IVR tree" (e.g., select "1" for existing customer or "2" for new customer . . . please enter your sixteen-digit customer account . . . if this is correct, press "1" . . . select "1" if you wish to pay a bill . . . etc.) is rarely preferable to telling a live person that you have a question concerning your latest bill. To be told that "your business is important to us" following the message about how all service representatives are currently busy does not improve the situation. And don't even mention the elevator music! Where is the invitation to press "1" if you would like to eliminate the music?

Obviously, IVR systems save money. What other reason explains why organizations continue foisting them on their paying customers? Given the fact that customers are predisposed to dislike the IVR experience, the first step is to eliminate the obvious annoyances and glitches so the system works smoothly and efficiently. The strategy is to create an IVR "experience" that, if not enjoyable, is at least not irritating. Some simple suggestions offered by the focus group follow:

- Use caller-identification software. This technology simply identifies the caller and displays either the telephone number or the name (according to the telephone company records). Telephone companies routinely offer this capability ("caller ID") as an extra billable service. By developing information systems that can read the caller ID, companies are able to grab the information from an incoming call and scan their customer databases for a match. If found, the entire customer's record appears on the screen of the person receiving the call. In some instances, this information appears before the phone actually rings! This technology is widely used in call centers to serve clients much more effectively and satisfactorily. The dilemma is how to deploy this technology to enhance the customer experience.
- Pass all information completely through the IVR session. When the service representative arrives, it should be unnecessary to ask you for your account code, which you painstakingly typed in (and verified) two steps earlier. The service representative should have this information at hand.
- Don't inform the customer that the session may be recorded to ensure its quality if you do not inform the customer how to request that it *not* be recorded.
- Provide information as to how long the wait is likely to be. Customers can then use this information to decide whether or not to remain on the line.
- Provide sufficient capacity to queue all callers. One manager shared the following experience. After calling the 1-800 number repeatedly for about fifteen minutes, he finally got through. He then answered eight questions, working his way through the IVR tree. At this point, he was told that he was being transferred to the appropriate customer representative. He was also told the following: "While being transferred, you will hear a click followed by a pause, which is normal, so please stay on the line. If you hear a busy signal, please hang up and dial again." As you might have expected, he heard the click . . . followed by the pause . . . followed by the busy signal! And this repeated four times in a

row. The fifth time he dialed the 1-800 number, he refused to answer any questions and was transferred to a service representative (the system assumed that he was calling from a rotary phone). The person transferred him to the appropriate representative, whereupon he received the same busy signal and was again defeated! Fortunately this organization did not include the "your business is important to us" message on their IVR because your business obviously isn't important to them![5]

5. Enhance Your IVR Systems with Technology

If caller identification can be used, an organization can use technology to gain sufficient information by matching this ID with its customer database to enable a customer to skip the first couple of levels within the IVR tree (e.g., preferred language, account code, etc.) simply by verifying who the caller is. (Note the caller may not be calling from his or her home phone.)

The hierarchical logic of IVR trees makes perfect sense *from the organization's perspective*. It can make little sense to customers. Wading through IVR levels of interaction simply to make a credit card payment seems overly taxing. One organization within the group, recognizing these difficulties with standard IVR systems, invested in a natural language front-end for its IVR system. This allowed a customer to simply state the reason for the call. The system was intelligent enough to understand the language the customer was using and respond in the same language. If the person said, "I have a question about my last bill," the system would simply transfer that person to a representative who handled billing. Based on limited experience with this product (because of its recency), this organization has already discovered that its system is capable of leapfrogging over multiple levels of the IVR tree with a high degree of accuracy. While arguably not as satisfactory as speaking to a real person, this system is definitely a vast improvement over the standard IVR system.

6. Create Opportunities for "Memorable Satisfying Experiences"

Research has shown that the three drivers of memorable satisfying experiences are (1) excellent service recovery, (2) customization/flexibility, and (3) spontaneous delight (Bitner, Booms, and Tetreault 1990). Technology has a role to play with each of these.

Excellent Service Recovery

Even if all possible precautions are taken, service encounters fail on occasion. *Service recovery* is the ability of a firm to rectify such failed encounters. Self-service encounters pose special problems for service recovery, not the least of which is the customer's inability to notify the firm of a service breakdown (as with a technology failure) and, hence, the firm's unawareness of the breakdown at the time of occurrence. The

---

[5]The worst IVR example shared by a participant involved a government agency that informed callers that they must be eighteen years of age or older because if they chose to proceed, they would be charged $3.00 per minute. This charge would appear on their phone bills!

seriousness of service breakdown is underlined by the fact that, when it occurs, all options available to the customer result in a loss to the providing firm.[6] When confronted with a technology failure (or a design failure), the transaction is thwarted. In contrast, a process failure leaves the customer *thinking* that the transaction has been completed correctly, which causes significant complications when the failure becomes apparent.

Service breakdown, if detected, provides an opportunity for the firm to "turn a negative into a positive." This is due to the realization that dissatisfiers are simply the flip side of satisfiers, *at least for self-service interactions*. Successful recovery in the wake of a service delivery failure is satisfying to customers, whereas a failure to recover is highly dissatisfying (Tax and Brown 1998). The key is detection. The focus group offered the following suggestions:[7]

a. Offer pop-up windows to guide/prompt/advise customers when a time lag is noticed during an online interaction/transaction.
b. Provide feedback as to the completeness of the transaction, the next steps, and when final delivery (if not instantaneous) will occur.
c. Provide the means of recourse should a failure occur (in advance of the failure). For example, "Should you not receive confirmation of this transaction within five seconds, hit the back button and . . .").
d. Reward customer patience with an offer such as "This transaction is taking longer than normal, so we are sending you a coupon."
e. Many online systems capture customer information as the customer interaction progresses. With the proviso that all confidential information is treated appropriately and in accordance with privacy regulations (and sensitivities), it may be possible to detect an aborted attempt by a customer to conduct a transaction. If detected, it may also be possible to contact that customer immediately (if the failure is due to design) or at a later time (if the failure is due to technology). This provides an opportunity for the providing firm to redress its failure to comply with the customer's needs.

Customization/Flexibility

When customers express their satisfaction with self-service due to its "availability when and where I need it," they are reflecting the fact that customization and flexibility are important determinants of satisfaction. This has been observed for interpersonal interactions but has dramatic impact on technological interfaces. One of the main benefits of technology is its virtually unlimited ability to be tailored to suit individual customers. For example, Amazon.com allows customers to search for books how they want, to get the type of information they desire, and even choose how they pay (Meuter et al. 2000). This represents the "my-page.com" phenomenon. Firms

---

[6]According to Meuter and others (2000), in the face of technology failure, the customer may (1) be driven to switch service providers (resulting in a lost customer), (2) revert to the interpersonal service delivery alternative (at increased cost to the firm), or (3) decide not to use the service or to use it at a later date (which either eliminates potential revenue or delays it).

[7]It is assumed that the previous strategies of improving the reliability of the technology, its design, and the internal support processes have been exhausted first.

should aggressively explore possibilities for technological customization and flexibility during customer interactions.

Spontaneous Delight

Spontaneous delight occurs when a firm provides a customer with an unexpected and pleasing experience. Saving time and money alone appears to offer such rewards. Fortunately, it is possible to go far beyond this as technology allows an endless array of opportunities to create such experiences. Based on information culled from customer databases, organizations could send recognition rewards to valued customers. Alternatively, they could apprise customers of new services and offerings tailored to meet their individual profiles. One of the more intriguing ideas is to package resident knowledge within an expert system and offer it to customers to assist them with business problems. One company offered its commercial clients a diagnostic tool to troubleshoot its networking operations. Clients participated actively with the system and became quite absorbed by the clever visuals used to model the network. In terms of the "realms of experience," an "educational" experience was created. In many cases firms have a lot more knowledge than is captured within their products and services. This knowledge can often be embedded within an expert system to create a valuable customer experience. Rather than just giving the knowledge away (or trying to package it as an additional billable service), organizations should think more creatively about the possibilities to engage their customers using technology.

CONCLUSION

We conclude where we started—with a realization that technology is increasingly the face of the firm. As such, IT professionals need to design systems with the firm's customers in mind. Furthermore, design is more than just navigation and usability. As members of the experience economy, customers are looking for experiences that engage them effectively. Firms that offer truly memorable and satisfying experiences to their customers will be rewarded in the marketplace. In essence, it is a "brave new role" for IT professionals.

REFERENCES

Bitner, M., B. Booms, and M. Tetreault. "The Service Encounter: Diagnosing Favorable and Unfavorable Incidents." *Journal of Marketing* 54, January (1990): 71–84.

Information Architecture Summit. Portland, Oregon, March 21–23, 2003. http://www.asist-events.org/IASummit2003/ (accessed February 2003).

Meuter, M., A. Ostrom, R. Roundtree, and M. Bitner. "Self-service Technologies: Understanding Customer Satisfaction with Technology-based Service Encounters." *Journal of Marketing* 64, July (2000): 50–64.

Novak, T., D. Hoffman, and Y. Yung. "Measuring the Customer Experience in Online Environments: A Structural Modeling Approach."

Marketing Science 19, no. 1, (Winter 2000): 22–42.

Phifer, G. "Portals in 2002: A Year of Major Change." Research Note SPA-15-0306. Gartner Inc. (December 12, 2001).

Pine II, B. J., and J. H. Gilmore. "The Experience Economy." Boston: Harvard Business School Press, 1999.

Smith, S., and J. Wheeler. "Managing the Customer Experience: Turning Customers into Advocates." Harlow, England: Financial Times Prentice-Hall, 2002.

Steuer, J. "Defining Virtual Reality: Dimensions Determining Telepresence." *Journal of Communications* 42, Autumn (1992): 73–93.

Tax, S. S., and Stephen W. Brown. "Recovering and Learning from Service Failure." *Sloan Management Review* 40, no. 1 (1998): 75–88.

Webster, J., L. Trevino, and L. Ryan. "The Dimensionality and Correlates of Flow in Human Computer Interactions." *Computing and Human Behavior* 9, no. 4 (1993): 411–26.

Chapter 12

Information Delivery:
IT's Evolving Role[1]

It wasn't so long ago that IT was called "data processing" (DP) and information delivery consisted of printing out massive computer listings full of transaction data. If DP was particularly enlightened, business got summary reports, which might or might not contain useful information. The advent of online systems made data marginally easier to use, but it was still mostly data; that is, facts with very little context or analysis applied to them. While "usability" was talked about, this aspect of information delivery was largely ignored. As a result, it was not unusual to find customer service representatives switching between ten or more different "screens" (each representing a different organizational data silo) to get the information they needed to do their job. But with the advent of Web technologies, organizations realized that while they could force their employees to wend their way through an enterprise's Byzantine organization structure and bits and bytes of data, customers were not going to do this. Data had to be made meaningful, provide an integrated picture of their interactions and generally be significantly easier to interpret and understand. In other words, data had to become information and it had to be delivered in ways customers could use.

While information delivery channels and practices were evolving, so, too, were organizations' needs for information. Many firms now realize that rather than simply processing transactions, they can "mine" what they collect to uncover new insights, often leading to substantial savings and/or revenue growth opportunities. Until recently, however, investments in information analysis and decision support languished as companies undertook higher-priority projects with more direct and immediate impact on their bottom lines. Today the success of how some companies use information for competitive advantage and operational effectiveness (e.g., Wal-Mart,

---

[1]Smith, H. A., and J. D. McKeen, "Information Delivery: IT's Evolving Role," *Communications of the Association of Information Systems* 15, article 11 (February 2005): 197–210 (reproduced by permission of the Association for Information Systems).

Dell) is causing business leaders to look more carefully at how well their firms are leveraging information.

Web technology has dramatically changed the ease with which information can be integrated and delivered on an ad hoc basis. Today it is both technically and financially feasible to deliver literally millions of pages of text to desktops as needed. As well, the technologies available to manage different types of information are improving rapidly and converging. Traditionally, different software has been used to manage documents, records, and other information assets (Kaplan 2002). Now the lines of demarcation between them are blurring. Software, while still imperfect, is opening the door to a host of new possibilities for information management and delivery. All of these factors are placing new pressures on IT to focus more thoughtfully on the *information* component of its function.

This chapter first surveys the expanding world of information and technology and why information delivery has become so important so rapidly. Then it discusses the value proposition of information in organizations. Next it describes the important components of an effective information delivery function in IT. Finally, it looks at how information delivery will likely evolve over the next five to ten years and what this will mean for IT and organizations.

INFORMATION AND IT: WHY NOW?

In the late 1990s, information management and delivery was barely on the radar screens of most IT managers (McKeen and Smith 2003). Today it is consuming a considerable amount of IT effort and has blossomed into a number of multifaceted, high-value IT activities. While IT organizations have had some data management functions for many years, these have been largely limited to database design and administration. As one participant claimed, "We've been talking around the subject of information for a long time, but it hasn't really been critically important until recently."

There are a number of reasons for this new attention to information. First, there is no doubt that organizations are overwhelmed by all sorts of information. The number of documents, reports, Web pages, data items, and digital assets has literally grown exponentially in recent years. "Our ability to store and communicate information has far outpaced our ability to search, retrieve, and present it" (Varian and Lyman 2000). Research shows that the average knowledge worker now spends about a quarter of his or her day looking for information either internally or externally (Kontzer 2003).

Second, companies have begun to realize that information and how it is used has considerable value. Almost all organizations believe they could be doing more with the information they already have (Davenport et al. 2001). This is coupled with a new understanding of how value is derived from IT. While traditionally organizations have expected to deliver value from their information systems alone (often through greater efficiencies in transaction processing), new research shows that improved information stemming from good information management practices *in combination with* excellent systems, is a stronger driver of financial performance (Marchand, Kettinger, and Rollins 2000). Participants noted that today information is being used in their organizations for much more than transactional decisions. "We are using all sorts of information in new ways," said one. "We are trying to understand the data drivers of our business and use it to manage our processes more effectively. We are also using data analysis to uncover strategic new business opportunities." Another noted, "In the past we sent reports to executives who would consider the information they contained and issue directives to their staff. Now we are sending information directly to frontline staff so they can take action immediately."

In addition to recognizing the value of transactional, operational, and strategic information, companies are also coming to realize that embedding information in their workflows can be extremely valuable. A firm's ability to extract and leverage explicit knowledge from its employees by formalizing it in systems and procedures directly contributes to its structural capital (Smith, McKeen, and Jenkin 2006). Some companies (e.g., Skandia) have already realized significant benefits from standardizing their information as structural capital and distributing it appropriately (Kettinger, Paddack, and Marchand 2003).

Third, new laws governing what can and cannot be done with information are also leading to greater awareness in IT about what information is collected and how it is used and protected. Addressing privacy concerns, for example, requires developing more sophisticated methods of user identification and authorization, permission management, controls over information flows, and greater attention to accuracy and analysis of where and how individual items of information can be used (Smith and McKeen 2003). No longer can huge customer records be sent from system to system, for example, simply because some data elements are needed. Companies risk not only contravening the law, but also embarrassment in the marketplace. Financial accountability legislation (e.g., Sarbanes-Oxley) is also driving greater attention to the integrity of information at every step in its collection. Requiring senior officers to *guarantee* the accuracy of the firm's financial statements is changing many of their previously *laissez-faire* attitudes toward information.

Finally, information possibilities are rapidly expanding. New technologies are creating different types of information, opening up innovative channels of information delivery, and providing new ways of organizing and accessing information. Just a few years ago, e-mail, instant messaging, and the Internet simply didn't exist. Today they are both major sources of new information *and* new delivery channels. Navigation tools, wireless technology, and vastly improved storage media (to name just a few) are driving new information applications that were not possible in the recent past. As the pace of new technology innovation ramps up, information delivery challenges and possibilities are, therefore, also escalating. In short, today IT is finding that information delivery is a key element of almost every aspect of its work and has become a fundamental part of its ability to derive value from technology.

DELIVERING VALUE THROUGH INFORMATION

There are several new areas in which information delivery is playing a critical role in delivering value in organizations:

- *More effective business operations.* Although information has long been used to run organizations, in the past it was largely paper and transaction based. Today executives have access to online "dashboards" that combine a wide variety of transaction, process, and supply-chain metrics to give them a much broader and more detailed picture of their operations. Typically, dashboards are designed differently for different needs (e.g., sales, logistics), functions (e.g., HR, accounting), and/or processes (e.g., inventory management) and for different spans of control. They usually include "drill down" capabilities, highlight problem areas, and integrate information from several systems. Other types of operational information that are available to organizations include predictive analysis (e.g., trends, timelines), benchmarks (both internal and external), quality measures (e.g., defects, stock-outs), and "scorecard" information (e.g., financial, internal business, customer, and learning and growth). What's also new is that these types of information are being given to frontline staff so they can better manage their own areas of responsibility, identify and avoid exceptions, and take action before problems arise. Operational information is often integrated with guidelines that direct courses of action so staff will better understand how to use it effectively.

- *E-business.* This new channel is having considerable impact on how organizations present information about their products and services to customers. In the past, customers would often get conflicting information depending on which "door" they entered (i.e., which part of the business they contacted). E-business has forced organizations to confront their own internal inconsistencies, identify information gaps and inaccuracies, and deal with inadequacies in their offerings, which are much more apparent when presented in this medium. IT and senior executives often have to take a hard line with line-of-business leaders who tend to have a function-specific perspective on information. As one manager noted, "Taking the customer's point of view in e-business development cuts across our established lines of business and organizational distinctions. Often there are political issues about information ownership, organization, and presentation. These must be nipped in the bud and everyone forced to put the customer's needs first."

The Web has also become a significant driver of interactions among companies, enabling them to transact business in new ways, manage their roles in different supply chains, and offer new services to business clients that didn't previously exist. In both the B2C and B2B spheres, e-business is largely about how information is integrated and presented to improve products and services. However, it is also changing the competitive landscape by making it considerably easier to comparison shop online. In the past, companies were able to be competitive by offering complex combinations of products and services, which discouraged one-to-one comparisons. Today whole new businesses have grown up to facilitate comparison shopping. These firms are placing themselves as intermediaries between a company and its customers (e.g., online travel, insurance quotes). Thus, companies that continue to use information to obfuscate their services, rather than inform their customers, could easily find themselves disintermediated and at a strategic disadvantage.

- *Internal self-service.* New information channels are driving significant internal change as well. The Web is being used to simplify employee access to human resources materials and procedures, streamline procurement, manage approvals, provide information on benefits and entitlements, and maintain telephone numbers, to name just a few types of information that are now routinely accessible online. Microsoft makes more than 2.2 million documents available to its staff, and two-thirds of its employees visit its internal site at least twice a day (Gilchrist 2001; Williams 2001). U.S. Air Force staff can now access more than eighteen thousand types of forms online. As with e-business, however, internal self-service is driving a complete reanalysis of what information is collected and how it is presented, navigated, and used. "Portals and online self-service make administrative problem areas more visible. They also force managers to simplify policies and procedures," said one manager. Phase 2 of the U.S. Air Force self-service initiative, for example, will try to reduce the number of forms in the organization from eighteen thousand to seven thousand (Bednarz 2003).

• *Unstructured information delivery.* Increasingly organizations want to be able to access *all* their information online, including that which has traditionally been retained as paper documents. New software, navigation, and storage technologies are leading to the convergence of the records management, library management, and electronic document management functions in organizations (Kaplan 2002). In the past IT has had very little to do with unstructured information. Now it is being required to develop taxonomies, navigation, and access methods for it and even to integrate structured and unstructured information into work processes delivered to the desktop.

Another major area of unstructured information delivery in which IT is involved is e-mail and instant messaging. These technologies have captured the organizational imagination so rapidly that policies and best practices in this area are still catching up. Jurisprudence has recognized that these interchanges are corporate records. In response, organizations are developing procedures for managing these more effectively. The barrage of messages from outside corporate boundaries in combination with personal use of corporate e-mail and the vulnerability of corporate information to external hackers are giving IT managers severe migraines. Archiving e-mail, filtering spam, coping with viruses that tag along with messages, building sophisticated firewalls, and creating business cases for messaging technologies are all new IT activities that have sprung up to better manage these new forms of wanted and unwanted information.

Finally, IT is also investigating collaborative technologies that help capture and leverage the work of teams and groups. Providing the means whereby knowledge workers can share information about what they are doing, capture best practices, brainstorm, track key decisions, and document a project's history are just some of the ways these technologies are being effectively used. Often IT workers themselves are the first users of these technologies, bearing the brunt of the learning involved before they are rolled out to the rest of the organization.

• *Business intelligence.* This is a function that is currently well developed in some organizations and not in others. However, it is growing rapidly in importance in organizations due to increased competition and the speed with which organizations must respond to competitive threats. Business intelligence includes both internal intelligence gathering, often known as data mining, and external intelligence gathering about trends, competitors, and industries. IT organizations are, at minimum, expected to design an effective internal information environment (aka a data warehouse) developed from their business information systems, within which users of a variety of skill levels can operate. Typically this requires an understanding of the context in which information will be used, modeling how data will be represented and providing appropriate tools for different types of users. End users can access this information in a variety of ways from ad hoc queries to generating predesigned reports. More sophisticated organizations have full-time data analysts on staff whose jobs can range from answering questions for users to exploring the data to uncover new opportunities (Brohman and Boudreau 2004).

A key IT concern in the design and management of internal data warehouses is the speed with which inquiries can be answered. It is not unusual for a user to build an inquiry that will bring a modern computer system to its knees. Therefore, protecting operational systems and optimizing routine queries is of paramount importance. Many IT organizations design parallel universes in which data warehouses can operate without affecting the production environment.

External business intelligence gathering is a relatively new field. For some companies, this simply means providing access to news wires and online "clipping services." Other organizations, however, are designing sophisticated criteria that can be used to "crawl" the Web and organize information about competitors' products and services. In companies where product innovation is an important function, access to external research services is important. Many IT organizations now have librarians whose job is to assist users to find external information electronically. However, the future ideal will be to integrate external information more seamlessly into work processes and present it to users when needed.

• *Behavior change.* Organizations already recognize that people pay more attention to what is measured. As a result, they have become increasingly more sophisticated about designing the metrics and scorecards they use to monitor both individual and corporate performance (see Kaplan and Norton 1996). It is less well recognized that information can both drive and inhibit certain behaviors in individuals. One participant explained, "More and more, our job is less about technology and more about behavior change. How we present information plays a big part in driving the behaviors the organization is looking for."

Promoting information-positive behavior means ensuring that the information that is available is trustworthy and of high quality and that information about the business is widely available to all levels of employees to help shape their behavior.

> People can sense information effectively only when they understand a company's business performance and how they personally can help to improve performance. . . . This common sense of purpose fosters an environment in which people begin to look beyond their own jobs and become concerned about the information needs of others. Sensing is enhanced and information valuation assessments become more precise. (Marchand, Kettinger, and Rollins 2000)

Some companies have begun to use greater information transparency to modify and guide staff behavior with extremely positive results (Smith, McKeen, and Street 2004), but organizations have just scratched the surface of what is possible in leveraging the complex linkages between information and behavior. In general, information transparency highlights both strengths and weaknesses, successes and failures. Highlighting key information helps staff to focus their efforts in areas that are of concern to management. For example, publishing infection statistics by ward in a hospital can change staff hand-washing habits. Similarly, stressing overall "file completion" information can help customer service staff solve holistic customer problems, rather than processing the individual transactions involved, and thus, provide more effective customer service.

EFFECTIVE INFORMATION DELIVERY

The explosion of new information delivery opportunities in organizations has left IT departments scrambling to organize themselves appropriately and develop new skills, roles, practices, and strategies. Even more than with systems development, effective information delivery involves careful attention to the social and behavioral dimensions of how work is done. "Politics is a huge dimension of information delivery," said a participant. "Defining data means establishing one version of the truth and one owner. As we move to standardized definitions, single master files for corporate data items, and common presentation, we get into major battles. In the past we have had ten systems for ten nuances of information. Everyone built their own thing." Another said, "Information integration is very difficult to achieve on a large scale. This problem becomes even more difficult and important in global enterprises and with strategic alliances."

New Information Skills

Better information delivery means clarifying and making visible the knowledge frameworks and mental models that have been applied to create both data and information (Li and Kettinger 2004). Business and IT practitioners must recognize the existence of these frameworks and make appropriate judgments about how they affect the information that is delivered. While IT staff have been doing this for years when designing reports and screen layouts, the organization's increasing reliance on structured information for decision making means that it is critical to consciously make appropriate decisions about how information is designed and presented. IT staff, therefore, not only need new skills in thinking about information, they also need better training in analyzing how it will be accessed and used. Furthermore, with more integrated data, it is now essential that business rules be applied to who gets to see what information. "Our systems serve a number of different types of users," said an IT manager at a major pharmaceutical firm. "It is essential that we know who they are. Salespeople, doctors, pharmacists, hospitals, regulatory agencies, and patients all have different information needs and rights. We cannot afford to put the information into the wrong hands." Finally, as pointed out above, navigation and usability have long been afterthoughts of systems analysis and design. Today this must be an integral part of every IT deliverable.

New Information Skills within IT

- Political judgment
- Information analysis
- Workflow analysis
- Information access
- Business rules for information use
- Usability
- Information navigation

New Information Roles

IT has a number of new or enhanced roles for managing the logistics of information delivery as well. IT's information responsibilities now include the following:

- Data custodianship
- Storage
- Integration
- Presentation
- Security
- Administration
- Personalization and multilingual presentations
- Document indexing and searching
- Unstructured content management and workflow
- Team and collaboration software
- Network and server infrastructure for information hosting/staging.

In addition, IT often hosts several key information management functions, such as library and information services, records and information management (e.g., archiving, regulatory compliance), information solutions delivery (including portal design), and data architecture and modeling.

Business responsibilities for information include ownership, quality, and currency. However, even here IT must sometimes establish and enforce the procedures and policies within which business will exercise these responsibilities. For example, some organizations have a formal system of information "expiry dates" for non-system-generated information, and reminders are sent to owners to ensure that it is reviewed and updated appropriately.

New Information Practices

Effective information delivery involves developing practices to manage different forms of information over their life cycles (see Figure 12.1). For each type of information, strategies, processes, and business rules must be established to address each of the four life cycle stages.

Figure 12.1 The Information Management Life Cycle

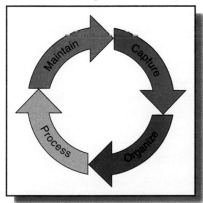

1. *Capture.* This includes all activities involved in identifying (i.e., analyzing and integrating) information for possible use. Typically, gaps appear at the borders between silos of information and when trying to connect structured and unstructured information. Capture may also involve digitizing information that is currently in paper format (e.g., documents). At present few organizations formally capture external business intelligence information such as economic, social, and political changes; competitive innovations; and potential problems with partners and suppliers. In the future, however, such information will be captured from an increasingly wide range of sources from both outside and inside the organization (Marchand, Kettinger, and Rollins 2000). Furthermore, users will increasingly demand real-time or near-real-time information, and this will require further refinement of information-capture practices.

2. *Organize.* Organizing information involves indexing, classifying, and linking sources together. At the highest level, this involves creating a taxonomy; that is, a systematic categorization by keyword or term (Corcoran 2002). This provides an organizing framework for information that facilitates ease of access. A second layer of organization involves creating metadata; that is, information about content and location. Metadata provides a roadmap to information, much as a card catalog points to the location and information about a book (Lee, Kim, and Kim 2001). Metadata is especially important for workflow design, the overall management of information, and information exchange among enterprises or different software applications. A third layer of organization is provided by processes that identify information ownership and ensure that it meets the necessary corporate, legal, and linguistic standards. These processes also manage activities such as authorship, versioning, and access. A final component of organization involves information presentation. Many organizations have developed a common look and feel for their materials, such as Web or portal pages, to enable ease of navigation and interoperability among platforms.

3. *Process.* As noted above, organizations have only begun to leverage the value of their information. New information-delivery technologies and channels as well as the recognition of the business value of information are driving the development of new organizational capabilities based on information and technology. IT plays a significant role in the analysis of information and its capture in the form of structural capital. However, organizations also need businesspeople with deeper analytic skills who can combine their knowledge of business with knowledge of data. Statistical modeling and analytic skills will also be increasingly needed to identify opportunities and make sense of huge amounts of data.

4. *Maintain.* Different types of information must be maintained differently. For unstructured content, such as documents and Web pages, maintenance involves keeping information up to date. All information needs to be regularly assessed as to how well it is meeting the business's needs. Finally, principles and standards must be established for information retention and preservation and for its disposal.

New Information Strategies

A final element of effective information delivery involves strategy. All organizations have a generic vision of delivering the right information to the right person at the right time. However, achieving this goal involves careful consideration of what an organization wants to accomplish with information and how it proposes to derive business value from it. Interestingly, many organizations are currently placing their highest priority on using information for internal management and administration. Employee self-service cuts out much administrative overhead in human resources management, procurement, and accounting. "There are huge savings to be gained by delivering better information on our operational processes and using information to better manage workflows and approvals," said a participant.

Some firms are also developing "microstrategies" for particular areas of the business or types of user. These small-scale initiatives often involve giving users subsets of data containing the specific information they need and appropriate analysis tools. One company has developed an information-access architecture that provides different types of tools to users depending on their abilities to use them to "mine" data. Basic users are given canned inquiries with drill-down capabilities and the ability to export information into an Excel spreadsheet. More skilled users are given basic analytic tools and access to metadata, while expert users are given professional analytic tools.

Information Delivery Best Practices

- Approach information delivery as an iterative development project. No one gets it right the first time.
- Separate data from function to create greater flexibility.
- Buy data models and enhance them. This will save many person-years of effort.
- Use middleware to translate data from one system to another. This is especially important for companies using several different packaged systems, each of which contains its own embedded data model.

- Evolve toward a real-time customer information file. While these files are notoriously difficult to build all at once, having a single source of customer information makes managing customer privacy much easier and also enables new integrated product and service offerings.
- Design information delivery from the end user (whether external customer, employee, or supplier) backward. This substantially reduces internal in-fighting and focuses attention on what is really important.

At the other end of the strategy scale are companies such as CEMEX, Dell, and Wal-Mart that have made information a strategic priority. Each of these companies has an enterprisewide strategy for using information. Wal-Mart's sophisticated operational architecture collects information on all its transactions. It shares this information with its suppliers in near real time so they are better able to control production and distribution. It also uses a data warehouse to extract trend data, which is combined with real-time transaction information to develop a high degree of local awareness. Each manager is able to identify opportunities and take appropriate action (Cebrowski and Garstka 1998). CEMEX uses information to control every aspect of its cement production and delivery logistics worldwide. Dell shares production and product specification information with its partners to create a seamless supply chain that is owned by Dell, even though the company has limited contact with the actual products it sells (Kettinger and Marchand 2004).

THE FUTURE OF INFORMATION DELIVERY

Organizations have begun to discover the power of information, but they have barely scratched the surface of what will be possible over the next decade. Already there are new technologies awaiting widespread implementation that will have as big an impact on information delivery as the Internet has had in the past decade. They will not only change what is possible to do with information, but they will also change how we view the world of information delivery and how organizations and individuals behave with respect to information. Some of the most important future directions for information delivery include the following:

- *An Internet for physical information.* Wireless communications, radio frequency identification (RFID) product tags, and cheap "mote" computers will soon enable organizations and industries to track individual physical objects and what happens to them (e.g., cans of beans, car parts) as they move through the supply chain. Already, Wal-Mart is conducting large-scale trials of this technology with two hundred of its major suppliers. Within a few years, RFID will replace the Universal Product Code (Langton 2004). And this is just the beginning. As these technologies become more sophisticated, organizations will be able to track and remotely monitor the status of everything from the freshness of lettuce between the field and the store to the location of hospital supplies. While this technology is almost ready for prime time, most organizations are nowhere near ready to cope with making sense of such a large influx of information. This will be one of the biggest challenges of the coming decade (Smith and Konsynski 2003).

- *Networkcentric operations.* The growth of standardized communication protocols, network devices, and high-speed data access will soon make it possible to collect, create, distribute, and exploit information across an extremely heterogeneous global computing environment in the near future. Value will be derived from the content, quality, and timeliness of the information moving across the network. Three critical elements must be in place to achieve this goal:

  1. *Sensor grids.* These should be coupled with fast and powerful networks to move raw data. Small sensory devices and computers will be connected to other machines to evaluate and filter a wide variety of information, highlighting areas and anomalies to which the organization should pay attention.

  2. *High-quality information.* Along with sophisticated modeling and simulation capabilities and display technology, this will provide dramatically better awareness of the marketplace. This will enable more targeted strategies, support more focused logistics, and provide full-dimensional understanding of the business environment at a variety of locations and levels.

3. *Value-added command and control processes.* Superior information will make the loop of control shorter, effectively taking decision rights away from competitors and providing rapid feedback to frontline workers.

These new capabilities will be developed to achieve information advantage (i.e., to know more) and execution advantage (i.e., to produce less friction between parts) over competitors.

- *Self-synchronizing systems.* Traditionally, leaders have worked from the top down to achieve synchronization of effort. When decisions are made in this way, each iteration of the "observe-orient-decide-act" (OODA) loop takes time to complete with the front line passing information up the hierarchy until enough is accumulated to make a decision, which is then passed back down the organizational levels to the front line to take action. In contrast, we know that complex processes organize best from the bottom up (e.g., markets, the Internet, and evolutionary processes). They are efficient and can allocate resources without high overheads. Such self-synchronization eliminates the lags in the OODA loop and accelerates responsiveness.

  In the future, information in organizations will be used to promote self-synchronization to enable a well-informed workforce to organize and coordinate complex activities from the bottom up without management involvement. Systems themselves will be designed to self-monitor and self-correct in a similar way. This will dramatically change the role of management and how organizations operate. Leaders will set the "rules of engagement" but be much less involved in the day-to-day running of their organizations (Smith and Konsynski 2003).

- *Feedback loops.* A central feature of self-synchronization is the creation of closed feedback loops that enable individuals and groups to adjust their behavior dynamically. Researchers are already demonstrating the power of feedback to change behavior (Zoutman et al. 2004). Feedback mechanisms built into systems will require the creation of new metrics for monitoring such individual behavioral factors as transparency, information sharing, and trust. Similarly, organizations will incorporate feedback loops into their operations, continually scanning and evaluating and adapting strategies, tactics, and operations. With the right technology and infostructure (i.e., appropriately organized and managed information), different views can be brought to bear on a situation and adjustments made on an ongoing basis.

- *Informal information management.* Finally, organizations have a significant unmined resource in the informal information kept by knowledge workers in their own personal files. Information-delivery mechanisms of the future will look for opportunities to organize and leverage this information in a variety of ways. For example, software exists today that crawls people's address books to find who in an organization knows people whom others in the organization want or need to contact. Other types of software analyze personal files to compile an expertise profile of individual employees. The field of informal information management is still in its infancy, but it is certainly one to which IT managers should pay attention because it represents a huge, untapped pool of information.

CONCLUSION

Information delivery in IT is an idea whose time has finally come. While IT practitioners and experts have been talking about it for years, it is only recently that the business has truly begun to understand the power and the potential of information. New technologies and channels now make it possible to access and deliver information easily and cheaply. As a result, information is now being used to drive many different types of value in organizations, from business intelligence to streamlined operations to lower administrative costs to new ways to reach customers. The challenges for IT are huge. Not only does effective information delivery require IT to implement new technologies, but it also means that IT must develop new internal nontechnical and analytic capabilities. Information delivery makes IT work much more visible in the organization. Developing standard data models, integrating information into work processes, and forcing (encouraging) business managers to put the customer/employee/supplier first in their decision making involve IT practitioners in organizational and political conflicts that most would likely prefer to avoid. Clearly, IT managers are front and center of an information revolution that will completely transform how organizations operate. The changes to date are just the tip of the information iceberg. In the not-so-distant future, new streams of information will be flooding into the organization, and IT managers will be expected to be ready with plans for its use. For the first time, senior business executives are ready to hear about the value of information. IT managers should take advantage of this new openness to develop the skills and capabilities they will need to prepare for the coming deluge.

REFERENCES

Bednarz, A. "Air Force Streams Electronic Paperwork." *Network World* 20, no. 2 (January 13, 2003): 17–18.

Brohman, K., and M. Boudreau. "The Dance: Getting Managers and Miners on the Floor Together." Proceedings of Administrative Sciences Association of Canada, 2004.

Cebrowski, A., and J. Garstka. "Network-centric Warfare: Its Origin and Future." *Naval Institute Proceedings* 124, no. 1 (January 1998).

Corcoran, M. "Taxonomies: Hope or Hype?" *Online* 26, no. 5 (September/October 2002): 76–78.

Davenport, T., J. Harris, D. De Long, and A. Jacobson. "Data to Knowledge to Results: Building an Analytic Capability." *California Management Review* 43, no. 2 (Winter 2001): 117–38.

Gilchrist, A. "Corporate Taxonomies: Report on a Survey of Current Practice." *Online Information Review* 25, no. 2 (2001): 94–102.

Kaplan, R., and D. Norton. *The Balanced Scorecard.* Boston: Harvard Business School Press, 1996.

Kaplan, S. "Emerging Technology." *CIO Magazine*, January 15, 2002.

Kettinger, W., and D. Marchand. "DELL Inc.: Working an Informated Opportunity Zone." Unpublished case study prepared for the Society for Information Management's Advanced Practices Council, Chicago, May 2004.

Kettinger, W., K. Paddack, and D. Marchand. "The Case of Skandia: The Evolving Nature of I/T Value." Unpublished case study prepared for the Society for Information Management's Advanced Practices Council, Chicago, January 2003.

Kontzer, T. "Search On." *Information Week* issue 923 (January 20, 2003): 30–38.

Langton, J. "Wal-Mart Tests Alternative to Bar Code." *Globe and Mail*, June 3, 2004.

Lee, H., T. Kim, and J. Kim. "A Metadata Oriented Architecture for Building Datawarehouse." *Journal of Database Management* 12, no. 4 (October–December 2001): 15–25.

Li, Y., and W. Kettinger. "A Knowledge-based Theory of Information: Clarifying the

Relationship between Data, Information, and Knowledge," Draft paper, Management Science Department, Moore School of Business, University of South Carolina, Columbia, 2004.

Marchand, D., W. Kettinger, and J. Rollins. "Information Orientation: People, Technology and the Bottom Line." *Sloan Management Review* Summer (2000).

McKeen, J., and H. Smith. *Making IT Happen.* Chichester, England: Wiley, 2003.

Smith, H., and B. Konsynski. "Developments in Practice X: Radio Frequency Identification (RFID)—An Internet for Physical Objects." *Communications of the Association of Information Systems* 12, no. 19 (September 2003).

Smith, H., and J. McKeen. "The CIO Brief on Privacy." The CIO Brief, School of Business, Queen's University, Kingston, Canada, 2003.

Smith, H. A., and J. D. McKeen, and T. A. Jenkin. "Exploring Strategies for Deploying Knowledge Management Tools and Technologies." *Journal of Information Science and Technology* 3, no. 2, October 2006.

Smith, H. A., and J. D. McKeen, and C. Street. "Linking IT to Business Metrics," *Journal of Information Science and Technology* 1, no. 1 (2004).

Varian, H., and P. Lyman. "How Much Information?" 2000. http://www2.sims.berkeley.edu/research/projects/how-much-info (accessed May 2004).

Williams, S. "The Intranet Content Management Strategy Conference." *Management Services.* 45, no. 9 (September 2001): 16–18.

Zoutman, D., D. Ford, A. Bassili, M. Lam, and K. Nakatsu. "Impacts of Feedback on Antibiotic Prescribing for Upper Respiratory Tract Infections." Presentation available from the authors, Queen's University, zoutman@cliff.path.queensu.ca (2004).

Chapter 13

Digital Dashboards[1]

The notion of a dashboard conjures up visions of a cockpit festooned by instruments producing critical, real-time information that enables a pilot, in control of immensely powerful technology, to perform superhuman feats. The business analogy is equally compelling: a manager, armed with a system to monitor the vital signs of the organization, taking appropriate actions when triggered to do so. Perhaps this vision explains the recent flurry of interest in digital dashboards in business. The question is this: Why now?

From a historical perspective, the current interest in digital dashboards appears to be the result of the confluence of four major developments:

1. *Critical success factors.* The concept of critical success factors (CSFs) is that there are a limited number of factors (perhaps four to six) that must be monitored by managers on a continuous basis in order to stay in control (Rockart 1979). By extension, information systems focused on CSFs would guarantee the provision of mission-critical information. One can think of CSFs as an early-warning system; when signals appear, managers are called to action. The CSF methodology does not (nor does it purport to) identify what action to take; it is simply a minimalist approach to information overload.

2. *Executive information systems.* Executive information systems (EISs) introduced the notion that information needs to be tailored to managers in order to be useful (Crockett 1992; Nord and Nord 1995; Paller 1987; and Sang and Chen 1997), partially in revolt against the information glut of standardized reporting. With EISs, managers could pull together information from discrete systems and "drill down" into details as needed. However, due to the expense of designing and building these systems tailored to the whims of specific executives, not to mention the ongoing maintenance required to provide near-real-time feeds

---

[1]McKeen, J. D., H. A. Smith, and S. Singh, "Digital Dashboards: Keep Your Eyes on the Road," *Communications of the Association of Information Systems* 16, article 52 (December 2005): 1013–26 (reproduced by permission of the Association of Information Systems).

from disparate systems, it is no surprise that they were made available for executives only and very few of those.

3. *Balanced scorecards.* Balanced scorecards (Kaplan and Norton 1996) articulated a comprehensive framework for corporate goals that could be cascaded down the hierarchy via subgoals as well as aggregated and rolled back up into corporate goals. It demonstrated how unit performance could be linked to high-level initiatives within a framework to recognize and balance the financial, people, customer, and learning goals of the organization.

4. *Technology.* The combination of browser-based technology (e.g., portals, intranets) and technology enabling the integration of information and data (e.g., online analytic processing, query and reporting, ad-hoc analysis, data integration, and application-development tools) facilitated the collection and dissemination of information to all members of the organization on a cost-effective basis. These developments changed EISs from *executive* information systems to *everyone's* information systems.

Taken together, these developments paved the way for digital dashboards whose promise is no less than the delivery of a robust, integrated system of accountability and performance that puts managers in the driver's seat. This chapter explores how organizations are developing and deploying these dashboards and some of the challenges and opportunities companies face in using them effectively. The next section describes the concept of a dashboard more fully, and following that, we examine how dashboards are being used in organizations. Then the chapter discusses issues associated with dashboard design and development and looks at some of their benefits. The concluding section discusses some strategies for implementing them successfully.

WHAT IS A DASHBOARD?

Although companies use many different definitions of this term, for the purposes of this chapter, we define a *digital dashboard* as an "electronic interface (typically a portal) that provides employees with timely, personalized information to enable them to monitor and analyze the performance of the organization."[2] There is an information component inherent within this definition, as well as a delivery component. While this definition has its roots in executive information systems (Lee and Chen 1997; Van den Hoven 1996), it differs in two key aspects: digital dashboards are not limited to "executives" (in fact they are not limited to even managers) and they are not necessarily "interactive." As such, digital dashboards have much broader application within organizations than EISs. Whereas earlier executive-based systems were not only "hand-tooled" exclusively for executives, they were also designed for (and based on the anticipation of) executives performing what-if analyses. In contrast, today's

---

[2]One participant defined a *dashboard* as a "method of displaying results for key operating metrics aligned to overall business strategy for decision-making purposes." Another suggested that a dashboard "is a portal that aggregates information across the value chain, turning information into knowledge and providing the user with the capabilities to make timely, relevant, and actionable decisions."

digital dashboards appear to be much more focused on the *provision* of information (i.e., access) and much less focused on supporting the *analysis* of the information provided. While this difference may appear nuanced, it represents a profound difference in terms of how the management function is supported by information technology. Members of the focus group provided many examples of digital dashboards, which presented key information in a variety of graphical forms complete with drill-down capability; however, none presented dashboards with embedded analytic models for managers to explore different scenarios under different sets of assumptions. One manager stated categorically that "the last thing we want our managers doing is sitting at their desks all day noodling over the numbers!"

Members were also clear to differentiate dashboards from reports. According to one, dashboards "offer real-time or near-real-time access to data and are automated to the point of requiring little or no manual intervention to process and summarize information." There was also a sense that reports tended to be more standardized and institutionalized within the organization, offering much less capability for customization. One manager pointed out the difference as "reports have names" while "dashboards are generic." Drawing on the cockpit metaphor, dashboards should offer *all* of the critical information required for the task at hand. Thus, reports tend to be more specific, without the expectation of being comprehensive.

Digital dashboards are also unique in terms of presentation media. Due to advances in technology, dashboards might appear on a workstation, laptop, PDA, or cell phone. One company uses a wall-mounted electronic bulletin board in its manufacturing facility to supply real-time information on performance against standard metrics and plant-level goals. This presents an interesting case. The "user" of this dashboard is every employee within the plant. Why would an organization invest in this type of dashboard? Dover (2004) suggests that such dashboard usage may be instrumental in converting an organization into a "performance-accountable" organization:

> The right technology can tell you how your business is performing at any moment. That technology produces dashboards, which can ultimately change the culture of your business by transforming it into a performance-accountable company. A company begins to become a performance-accountable organization when management commits to increasing each person's knowledge and understanding of what drives performance. (Dover 2004, 43)

How Are Dashboards Being Used?

When asked about their usage and deployment of digital dashboards, group members agreed that usage is definitely increasing, primarily focused on operational and/or financial data, and they are being used "right across the business . . . and at all levels." Furthermore, they reported a significant pent-up demand for dashboards within their organizations. According to one manager, "Today everyone wants a snapshot of their business . . . like a one-stop shop." An analysis of the various examples of dashboards revealed three different categories: (1) performance based, (2) project based, and (3) opportunity based.

The most popular category of dashboard usage is *performance based*. These dashboards display a basic mix of financial and nonfinancial results broken out by this year versus last year, actual versus target, sometimes earmarking performance against competition. Content might be product sales, cash flow, inventory management, sales growth, market trends, or repeat versus new business. Most offer drill-down capability and near-real-time if not real-time information. Standard dashboard formats are color coded "traffic signals"; that is, green indicates "OK," yellow indicates a "warning," and red indicates a "problem." Everything displayed relates to outcomes. The implicit intent of this category of dashboard is to alert employees to either an impending or an existing problem requiring action.

Another category of dashboard is *project based*. Information presented by these dashboards relates primarily to status reporting where the only comparative data is "actual to budget." These reports might reflect completion of key tasks and/or milestone events, assignment and availability of resources, modifications to plan, revision of estimates and progress tracking, and implementation forecasts. Traffic signaling can be used as well as a number of typical project charts such as Gantt charts and critical path diagrams. As with all dashboards, while the form is at the discretion of the user, the content is dictated by the overall responsibility. For example, a project leader would have a dashboard specific to his or her project; a senior project manager would have a dashboard to report on the status of all of the projects for which he or she is assigned; and the VP in charge of business systems would "see" all major new developments plus maintenance and enhancement broken out by lines of business.

While the first two categories offer the ability to monitor the business, the goal of the *opportunity-based* dashboard is to guide employees toward new opportunities for enhancing the business. For example, the sales division of a pharmaceutical company uses a dashboard to target and track the prescribing physicians' leading objections to certain drugs and provides to the sales force research to counter or answer these questions. Another dashboard broadcasts industry trends (again to the sales force dashboards) outlining how to position the company's products most effectively in this market. A third simply presents "gaps" in the firm's operations, such as interesting observations and/or trends in the marketplace that might have potential for the firm to expand. A manufacturing firm uses its dashboards as a platform to share best practices among similar operating units. On a sporadic basis, unit managers discover a lightbulb icon on their dashboard, which signals a best practice has been posted. When clicked, details are provided. According to this manager, the best part is that "it provides strong motivation to apply best practices and to create them" as recognition is granted to those who share.

It is interesting to compare published research and observed practice with regard to usage and deployment of digital dashboards. Vandenbosch (1999) suggests that there are four management information uses of executive support systems: (1) score keeping, (2) problem solving, (3) focusing organizational attention and learning, and (4) legitimizing decisions.

- *Score keeping.* Score keeping is typically a standardized process that evolves over long periods of time in an organization. It provides consistency among time periods so comparisons are easy to make.

- *Problem solving.* This consists of a sequence of steps, including recognizing the existence and nature of a problem, outlining alternative possible corrective actions, and deciding on the best action then implementing it.
- *Focusing organizational attention and learning.* This first aims to obtain agreement on what the targets of attention should be then provides a feedback loop to link attention, action, and outcome.
- *Legitimizing decisions.* Legitimizing decisions represents information-collecting activity to justify past decision making, rather than to guide future decision making.

When we examine the three types of digital dashboards and their examples, we observe that performance-based and project-based dashboards predominantly represent score keeping and problem-identification applications and offer little capability for problem solving and analysis. The opportunity-based dashboard, in contrast, works to focus organizational attention and facilitate learning and offers very little score-keeping and problem-solving activity. It could be argued that the ability to focus organizational attention and legitimize decisions is built into the design of the various dashboards; that is, the decision as to what is most important to monitor via the dashboard is a decision about where organizational attention will be focused. This fact alone underscores the importance of dashboard design and probably explains much of the effectiveness of these initiatives. Vandenbosch's study confirms this as she discovered that those EISs that focus organizational attention have the strongest relationship to organizational competitiveness.

DASHBOARD DESIGN AND DEVELOPMENT

Designing and developing dashboards is a responsibility shared between IT and the business. As one manager explained, "IT builds and implements our dashboards. Even though the tools to design the controls are simple, the logic and calculations to extract the data from the databases to feed the dashboard requires a higher level of skill." In addition to having the requisite skills for data extraction, there are other responsibilities that are expected to remain with IT such as tool management, integration, and operations support. While recognizing specific areas where IT needs to retain responsibility, participating organizations were also actively moving toward a self-service model where it made sense. One company's approach is this:

> *IT builds the prototypes for various dashboards. The complexity of the task dictates that IT is involved. Building cubes, delivery mechanisms, and data-marts is a complex task which requires some level of expertise. That said, my company is committed to deploying a self-service reporting framework to empower the enterprise. We do not view IT as a "creator" of reports or information. Rather, we view ourselves as building the "delivery vehicles" to expose the information to the end user.*

The issues with respect to dashboard design and development primarily relate to content and delivery. While content issues focus on the information that is included within the dashboard, delivery issues focus on how that information is presented. Logically, the two are separate; in practice, they are closely related. For instance, the information that you can present depends on the device the manager is using. Delivering information to a cell phone is not the same as delivering the information to a desktop. For this reason, we highlight some of the key issues regarding content and delivery in combination.

- *Balancing "hot" information and long-term baseline information.* Some users of "traffic light" (i.e., red/yellow/green) dashboards will ignore everything if their dashboard is green and attend to issues only when they "heat up" (i.e., turn yellow or red). The managers provided examples of when "green wasn't always good" and "yellow/red wasn't always bad." The design of dashboards must, therefore, be closely tied to the task, the decision maker, and the metrics used to monitor the organization.
- *Tailoring the dashboard.* Participants stated that, to be effective, dashboards must be tailored to a job, a task, and a location then personalized by the individual. To do this requires "identity management" capabilities. For example, as a salesperson, your access to information will depend on your current role (e.g., territory, product line), your current location (e.g., in the office or in the field), and your access device (e.g., PDA, cell phone, laptop) so the information can be linked to appropriate business metrics.
- *The granularity and timing of information.* How far you can drill down or whether you can see other comparable organizational units' performance relates to your entitlement as dictated by your identity. In addition, it is important to synchronize the dashboard information with a decision framework. At one company, J. D. Power is used to measure customer satisfaction, and results are provided daily to dashboards. When new campaigns are launched, care must be taken to align the customer satisfaction data temporally with other information to assess the distinct impacts of the campaign. With targets set on a monthly basis, customer satisfaction linked directly to personal evaluations, and managers receiving real-time feeds, significant angst can be caused by timing differences.
- *Personalization.* While dashboards are most effective when managers are allowed to personalize them, it is also important to set limits on how much personalization to allow. For instance, there is a need for common metrics so managers can compare themselves (and be compared) to other like units within the organization. One manager felt that dashboards need to be "personalizable but not individualistic," which perhaps best captures the balance being sought. Most companies offer the ability to select from a set of "widgets" (i.e., standardized graphical components) to be included on their dashboards as well as the ability to rearrange their dashboards perhaps to "push key information to the top." Most companies design dashboards to be as flexible as possible so users can react to (and reflect) key business imperatives as they arise.

WHAT ARE THE BENEFITS?

Digital dashboards are a recent phenomenon. As such, the dashboard literature is premature, perhaps somewhat faddish. To remedy this, we augment the dashboard literature with a review of research that pertains to digital dashboards (i.e., executive support systems, executive information systems, and decision making). The basis for the majority of this work is provided by Simon (1977), who delineated the stages of decision making and focused on the role of information in the process of decision making. Years later Rockart and DeLong (1988) proposed four ways that executive support systems can create value. From most to least valuable, they are listed here:

1. Enhancing the way executives think about the business
2. Providing executives with better planning and control capabilities
3. Leveraging executives' time
4. Educating executives about the use and potential of IT

Interestingly, we would not likely argue much with these today and certainly not with the order of their importance. Like the executive support systems of the past, the intent of today's digital dashboards is to focus employees on the right issues by anchoring their dashboards on a critical set of metrics well aligned with the corporate goals, alert decision makers to those situations needing attention, and help users to understand what is happening by observing patterns all in the aid of making everyone's time count.

Other benefits attributable to dashboards have been suggested as well. According to one author (Anonymous 2004), an energy company attributed 2 percent of its $1.3 million annual savings directly to the usage of its dashboard. The dashboard played a pivotal role within a corporate-wide initiative targeted at improving operations, increasing sales, reducing expenses, and improving repair-call efficiency. The key role was in highlighting the need for employee skills, training, measurement, and development as revealed by district performance comparisons. The benefits were attributable to an energized workforce who, perhaps for the first time, could link their contributions directly to corporate objectives. Dover (2004) claims that dashboards can actually transform an organization's culture into a "performance-accountable" company. Similar to the previous example of the energy company, he suggests that dashboards alter culture by the straightforward mechanism of "allowing individuals to see the big picture and, more importantly, understand the impact of their actions on the rest of the company . . . this, in turn, drives a culture of transparency throughout the organization because they monitor progress toward achieving corporate, department, or individual goals."

A couple of benefits cited in the literature are actually side benefits. In an article about business intelligence, Williams (2004) makes a strong argument for the need for dashboards (and all analytic reporting systems, for that matter) to operate from the same set of facts—the so-called single view of the truth. The process of creating digital dashboards provides the incentive to agree on the specific metrics to be included and on the definition and measurement of these specific metrics. To do anything less would be to undermine the value, credibility, and eventual impact of the dashboard. So while dashboards do not "produce" data definitions, they do produce the context and impetus for management attention to data quality. In a similar vein, one manager recounted how the development of a digital dashboard spurred her company to develop a methodology for aligning different functions within the business with overall corporate goals. Miller and Cioffi (2004) share a similar experience with marketing digital dashboards at Unisys.

Lee and Chen (1997) argue that a manager must engage in three types of thinking: (1) *retrospective* (i.e., thinking back in time to review and interpret past events and experiences), (2) *introspective* (i.e., reflecting and examining one's own thoughts, beliefs, and assumptions; looking into one's own mental models), and (3) *prospective* (i.e., thinking out into the future and envisioning the future state of the organizational environments). The implicit argument is that digital dashboards provide benefits to the extent that they can support all three types of management thinking. However, the focus group suggested that few *individual* dashboards support this full range of thinking but dashboards *are capable* of supporting each specific type of thinking (e.g., retrospective). To an extent, this depends on when the data presented within a dashboard is anchored; for example, in the present, past, or future state. One company anchored most of its dashboards in the future. This was a conscious decision to "get away from simply meeting targets." They wanted "all eyes to the future," and their managers focused on how best to get to this future state.

Other firms use a blend of leading versus lagging indicators to extract trends and support more prospective thinking. According to one manager, "From a retrospective view, dashboards can provide analysis of a particular time period and enable a manager to examine the effectiveness of a particular course of action. Forward-looking dashboards (when interpreted appropriately) highlight trends in data which can provide the catalyst to propel new business opportunities. Good managers and effective leaders are continually looking to identify trends in information." Another manager commented that most dashboards provide historical information based on comparative metrics. But he also explained that "these same dashboards support introspection as the rules that trigger the event state changes are really just a reference to current beliefs." He felt that dashboards are also prospective because "they provide an aggregate view of many data sources where such a view would otherwise not exist. Assuming a trend is a predictive model of future behavior, dashboards do provide prospective value."

In contrast to the claims made by the energy company above (Anonymous 2004), some believe that the most severe shortcoming of executive information systems (and dashboards, by extension) is that they help managers understand only where the organization is today and do little to help them visualize where it can be in the future (Lee and Chen 1997). The focus group was in partial agreement with this statement. All agreed that a major function of the majority of dashboards is to provide a status report but that enhanced reporting is certainly available for dashboards. According to one manager, the former is referred to as the "dashboard as speedometer" model. An enhanced dashboard would provide the ability to ascertain *appropriate* speed given the context of traffic congestion, road condition, weather, and visibility.

The general point of agreement was that participants believed that dashboards are indeed providing realizable benefits to organizations. Demonstrating these benefits in hard numbers, however, is not so easy. For instance, none of their firms had effectiveness measures for dashboards. Some had just started to solicit feedback from dashboard users. They cited the following benefits as being fully or partially attributable to dashboard development within their organizations:

1. Alignment with strategy and accountabilities
   - They focus attention on critical issues for the business.
   - They introduce clearly assigned accountability for key performance indicators. Managers now focus on those components that they directly control or influence, which drives ownership of results.

2. Enhanced decision-making support and analysis

- They provide management with better insights from data.
- Management spends more time on value-added analysis, which supports better decision making.
- Management focuses on a limited number of metrics that combine both operational and financial measures, as well as forward-looking indicators, which provide input for proactive performance management.

3. Improved integrity and timeliness of data

- Dashboards provide faster access to information, effort avoidance for information gathering and analysis. They enable an enterprise to disseminate information to any number of people very quickly and accurately.
- They are directly or indirectly responsible for the increased accuracy and consistency of the information being reported.
- Development of one database of operational and financial information drives improved integrity—"one source of truth."

4. Operational efficiencies

- Dashboards create a self-serve environment, which reduces traditional, centralized functions and the burden on other areas of the business (e.g., report writers).
- Standardization of data definitions, reports, and associated processes reduces cycle time.
- They streamline data aggregation and reporting processes, supported by standard tools and processes.
- Increases in the degree of automation drives timely reporting of results and facilitates the reallocation of resources to more value-added activities.

STRATEGIES FOR SUCCESS

Benefits "do not simply fall out of the sky and land on your head," said the group. Based on their experiences, members articulated the following strategies, which they believe would contribute to the successful deployment of digital dashboards:

1. *Make a good first impression.* The old adage that "first impressions can be lasting" applies to the introduction of dashboards. According to Dover (2004), the "power of dashboards relies significantly on the success of user adoption. It comes down to how rapidly a critical mass of users will adopt the dashboard interface to perform their daily activities." And this can depend heavily on the initial dashboard launch. One company used a pilot approach for building and introducing its dashboards. Five dashboards were assembled within six weeks from "start to launch." These rapid pilots delivered identifiable benefits by doing the following:

- Creating a lot of excitement around dashboards
- Getting rapid executive buy-in
- Providing a great source for design requirements
- Generating a lot of goodwill
- Getting the development team moving quickly

The only downside to this approach was creating unrealistic expectations in terms of how fast "industry strength" dashboards could actually be implemented.

However you introduce dashboard technology, it is important to "get it right the first time" as you seldom get a second chance surrounded by the same level of interest and excitement. It is also imperative to move ahead with a dashboard initiative fairly quickly in order to signal intent and commitment to the organization and perhaps ride the early interest created by the novelty of dashboards. In contrast with what Dover (2004) refers to as "drip feeding" the technology over a period of time, expecting usage to grow voluntarily, the focus group preferred to have the organization require dashboards as the corporate standard tool for viewing the business results.

2. *Metrics first . . . dashboards second.*   Be careful what you measure! The reason for this is that people will make every effort to perform well against established measures, and sometimes this unexpectedly produces dysfunctional behavior. In one company call center, metrics included time to respond to call, time to resolve problem, frequency of problems solved by first agent, duration of call, and frequency of call-backs. Managers soon discovered that agents would answer calls within the guaranteed minimum time then "park" the caller. After a short elapsed time, the customer who was parked was transferred to another agent without recording the agent who "parked" the call originally. Agents would simply disconnect a call as the maximum time allowed for a call approached. Within months, the company had modified its original metrics to reward agents who were able to resolve clients' requests satisfactorily even if it meant spending more time.

Dashboards are a means to an end; they are not the end. Interest in dashboards should naturally arise from a larger corporate initiative to focus the organization's attention on key issues. The ideal situation is an organization with an established balanced scorecard (see Kaplan and Norton 1996) or some similar well-articulated measurement framework in place. In these organizations dashboards can be based on a set of specific metrics that have already been established and accepted. These dictate the information to be contained within the dashboards of the managers at each of the various levels within the organizational hierarchy with assurance that lower-level dashboard results can be rolled up into corporate-level dashboards. Miller and Cioffi (2004) suggest that much of the success of the Unisys Marketing Dashboard was attributable to the methodology that was used to "provide direct connections between five key information categories: corporate goals, marketing goals, objectives, activities or tactics, and metrics." This is the type of structure upon which successful dashboards should be built.

3. *Use "decision-impelling" designs for dashboards.*   The majority of the information provided by a car's dashboard is essential for monitoring its operation. Furthermore everything is designed to be observed with a glance. Safe driving entails keeping one's eyes on the road in order to react to situations that present themselves, sometimes with very little warning. Information presentation tends to follow internationally accepted standards: it uses a limited range of colors (e.g., "yellow" for warning gauges); it uses a mix of analog, digital, and graphical displays; and information is always displayed in the same spot. Imagine if you had to search the dashboard to find the speedometer each time you glanced to check your speed!

Similar design criteria should be adopted for digital dashboards. As Einstein once said, "Make it as simple as you can but no simpler." The following guidelines were recommended and follow this principle:

- Adhere to standardized designs.
- Use common templates.
- Apply the KISS rule; that is, keep it short and simple.
- Move critical stuff to the top.
- Colorization should be uniform among dashboards (e.g., traffic lights).

One manager gave an interesting example of trying to adopt common color standards within a global company. He experienced difficulties with project managers because "red" means different things within different cultures. In Canada it means a project requires senior executive attention, while in Mexico, it means "yeah, we can fix it."

4. *Align dashboards with prevailing organizational culture.* Dashboards are not for everyone. Numerous stories were shared about the adoption (also nonadoption and misadoption) of dashboards. What each story had in common was some level of friction between "dashboard behavior" and generally accepted organizational norms and values. This led us to conclude that dashboard deployment should adhere to whatever culture is in place or risk dysfunctional behavior. It is easy to underestimate the impact of resident norms and values. A few examples will illustrate this point.

At one organization with strong business unit management, accepted practice dictates that "no information goes up the hierarchy without first being sanctioned [some used the term *laundered*] by unit management." At this organization a corporate-level dashboard was demoed to the CEO by the CIO. During this demo, the CEO drilled down on a couple of business units and observed certain results. Immediately following the demo, the CEO called the business unit head and asked some very specific questions about unit operations. The unit manager had no idea that the CEO had access to this information and was understandably taken quite by surprise. He subsequently shared his views on this subject with the CIO!

Drill-down capability is typically offered on a "need to know" basis. In the above story, the point was not that the CEO was not entitled to see this data. Rather, it was that no one was aware that the CEO had this capability. Drill-down capability makes it very easy for management to view detailed results in their raw, unsanitized form. Unless the organization is ready for this level of transparency, the focus group warned that provision of data via dashboards should be carefully vetted with those who will be impacted.

Another manager commented that senior-level executives at his organization have an aversion to viewing reports online. They sought the "comfort of having the reports in their hand, particularly when heading into a meeting." At another organization there was "some resistance by lower-level executives because dashboards were seen as a top-down requirement pushed upon the business units." At a third organization, "finance likes to control the communication of results," which are published on a monthly basis after they have been scrutinized by executives. The lesson here is that just because direct information feeds are technically possible does not mean that they should be implemented. It is easy to innocently breach well-trodden communication patterns. Accordingly, don't confuse "access, availability, and disclosure" when implementing digital dashboards.

5. *Design dashboards for action, not analysis.* In Vandenbosch's study (1999), she found that three uses of executive support systems (problem solving, focusing organizational attention and learning, and legitimizing decisions) were positively related to competitiveness but that the fourth use (score keeping) was negatively associated with competitiveness. Out of interest, we polled the focus group to find out how they use their dashboards. Focusing attention was the highest-ranking usage. All attested to the power of dashboards to "get everyone on the same page."

None of the members felt that their dashboards were focused on problem solving. Furthermore, they were adamant that dashboards *should not* be focused on problem solving. According to one manager, "designing a system to suggest (or trial) solutions to problems is a waste of resources . . . let *people* explore solutions . . . let *people* do what they are good at doing . . . use the numbers to discover trends and patterns and to help people understand what is going on . . . then let them take corrective action."

Problem solving aside, everyone agreed that dashboards need to be action oriented if they are to be effective. In fact, one company makes a conscious effort to include only "actionable" information on its dashboards, believing it is "too easy to blame the weather or blame the buyers," so it limits its dashboards to include only information that relates to decisions that can be legitimately carried out by managers. Its design rule is that "real-time availability should be balanced against ability to act." Otherwise it makes little sense. Dashboards can "create a panic if there is no solution set behind it." To alleviate this, one company tied dashboards to actions by providing "action guides" for different dashboard outcomes. At this point, dashboards almost become a workflow tool. The ultimate goal for dashboards at this company was "to align their dashboards to objectives and compensation and to align their data to processes."

CONCLUSION

There is nothing new with digital dashboards. Promises of the "big picture" based on comprehensive information have been used to justify IT projects for decades. Quite simply, digital dashboards are a data-delivery vehicle—no more, no less. However, when they are successfully implemented within a well-articulated measurement framework, they hold the promise of transforming organizations into "performance-accountable" entities. Like so many other IT-based initiatives, the key phrase is *when successfully implemented.* Inappropriate metrics, unaligned goals, nonstandard data definitions, ambiguous interpretation of results, the absence of senior management support, and/or the lack of a unifying vision for the overall initiative will doom a dashboard program to extinction. This chapter, based on the insights and hard-won experiences of senior IT managers, provides some direction toward the successful implementation of digital dashboards. The rewards of getting it right are substantial. So while nothing is new, everything is possible.

REFERENCES

Anonymous. "Dashboards Energize Employees." *Strategic Finance* 86, no. 4 (October 2004): 46.

Crockett, F. "Revitalizing Executive Information Systems." *Sloan Management Review* 33, no. 4 (Summer 1992): 39–47.

Dover, C. "How Dashboards Can Change Your Culture." *Strategic Finance* 86, no. 4 (October 2004): 42–48.

Kaplan, R., and D. Norton. *The Balanced Scorecard*. Boston: Harvard Business School Press, 1996.

Lee, S. M., and J. Q. Chen. "A Conceptual Model for Executive Support Systems." *Logistics Information Management* 10, no. 4 (1997): 154–63.

Miller, A., and J. Cioffi. "Measuring Marketing Effectiveness and Value: The Unisys Marketing Dashboard." *Journal of Advertising Research* September (2004): 237–43.

Nord, J. H., and G. D. Nord. "Why Managers Use Executive Support Systems: Selecting and Using Information Technology for Strategic Advantage." *Industrial Management & Data Systems* 95, no. 9 (1995): 24–28.

Paller, A. "Executive Information Systems: Definitions and Guidelines." *AFIPS Conference Proceedings* 56, National Computer Conference, June 15–18, Chicago, Illinois, 1987.

Rockart, J. F. "Chief Executives Define Their Own Data Needs." *Harvard Business Review* 57 (1979): 81–93.

Rockart, J. F., and D. W. DeLong. *Executive Support Systems: The Emergence of Top Management Computer Use*. Homewood, IL: Dow Jones-Irwin, 1988.

Sang, L. M., and J. Q. Chen. "A Conceptual Model for Executive Support Systems." *Logistics Information Management* 10, no. 4 (1997): 154.

Simon, H. A. *The New Science of Management Decision*. Englewood Cliffs, NJ: Prentice-Hall, 1977.

Van den Hoven, J. "Executive Support Systems & Decision Making." *Journal of Systems Management* 47, no. 2 (March/April 1996): 48–55.

Vandenbosch, B. "An Empirical Analysis of the Association between the Use of Executive Support Systems and Perceived Organizational Competitiveness." *Accounting, Organizations and Society* 24 (1999): 77–92.

Williams, S. "Delivering Strategic Business Value." *Strategic Finance* 86, no. 2 (August 2004): 40–48.

Chapter 14

Managing Electronic Communications[1]

The proliferation of communication technologies (e.g., e-mail, voice mail, mass mail, messaging, enhanced PDAs, Wi-Fi, Bluetooth) has ushered in the "always on, always connected" world of today, giving us the ability to communicate virtually instantaneously regardless of time or place. The array of available communication technologies has simultaneously eased the burden of communication, multiplied the number of communication options, increased accessibility, lowered costs, and expanded both the reach and range of targeted audiences with whom to communicate. In addition, it comes with its own lexicon ("Let's text him." "Can I IM you?" "Is this a hotspot?"). While it is interesting to speculate about the reasons for this growth—Is it simply catering to an enhanced need to communicate? Is it a reflection of an increasingly mobile workforce? Is our basic human need for connectedness behind the growth in adoption of communication technologies?—it is a fact of modern organizational life. It is also an area in which IT management has become increasingly necessary. Whereas just a few years ago, electronic communication was a relatively straightforward commodity, today there are a wide variety of issues that must be managed.

In this chapter we explore electronic communication and some of the many management issues associated with it, such as legal factors, etiquette, information security, storage management, and quality of work life and communication. In the next section, we define electronic communication and differentiate it from other forms of communication. We then discuss its management, addressing each of the above issues and outlining proven strategies for their effective management.

---

[1]McKeen, J. D., and H. A. Smith, "Electronic Communications: Strategies for Coping with the Deluge," *Communications of the Association of Information Systems* 13, article 14 (February 2004): 167–76 (reproduced by permission of the Association for Information Systems).

ELECTRONIC COMMUNICATION: DEFINITION AND TECHNOLOGIES

There is a substantial degree of variation in how managers define electronic communication (see box).

Electronic communication is . . .

- any message sent in analog or digital form in a person-to-person exchange.
- anything that is broadcast, created, sent, forwarded, replied to, transmitted, stored, held, copied, downloaded, displayed, viewed, read, or printed by any electronic communication system or service.
- something that entails the use of e-mail, phone (wireless and landlines), fax, pager, PDA, Internet, public file storage, video, or distance-learning tools to exchange information from person to person(s).
- the World Wide Web, Internet-based discussion groups, electronic bulletin board systems, electronic mail, telephone, voice mail, fax, or any type of wireless transmission.
- e-mail (and attachments), Internet Web pages and downloads, instant messaging, voice mail, video conferencing, Webinars, phone conversations, fax, and B2B (e.g., file transfers, EDI, and Web alternatives).
- any communication not handwritten or spoken face-to-face.
- IVR (interactive voice response) systems, customer contacts, call-outs (e.g., customer notifications), e-mail (internal, external to customers, B2B), and calendaring.

It was not that long ago that communications were limited to face-to-face conversations, telephone calls, and written correspondence. Now communications take place over a number of channels using a wide variety of technologies. While some of these technologies can be deployed interchangeably, they tend to differ in significant ways. For instance, they differ with respect to synchronicity in terms of time and/or location (see Figure 14.1). Synchronous communication devices, such as the telephone, permit enhanced degrees of interactivity not possible with asynchronous communication such as e-mail.

Electronic communications also differ with respect to who is sending and receiving the message; that is, some electronic communications are person-to-person, but many are increasingly person-to-system and system-to-person (see Table 14.1).

Because our study focused on its *management,* we adopted an inclusive definition of *electronic communication:* any form of electronic communication that can be recorded and retained. This includes written materials, such as handwritten notes, that can be easily scanned and recorded. Only unrecorded interpersonal conversations are excluded.

MANAGING ELECTRONIC COMMUNICATIONS: ISSUES AND STRATEGIES

One manager described his general strategy for managing electronic communications based on its purpose, content, and delivery: the **purpose** of the electronic communication and its **content** should suggest the appropriate **delivery** mechanism.

Figure 14.1   Time and Location Communication Synchronicity

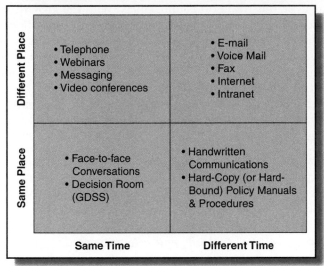

Highly confidential information should not be conveyed over unprotected communication channels. Large attachments should be placed on an intranet where individuals can be directed via e-mail. This obviates the "reply all" with massive attachments syndrome. While this provides general guidance, the group identified six specific issues in managing electronic communications and strategies for dealing with them.

Issue #1: Storage

Electronic communication storage issues relate to volume (i.e., the amount of electronic communication to be handled) and the legal requirements to retain information. The legal issues will be addressed in a later section of this chapter. Suffice it to say, as legal requirements are imposed on information to be retained, storage requirements increase.

Volume is directly related to the *number* of communication transmissions. One participant, who had been tracking them, reported that e-mail volumes in his organization are growing at more than 400 percent annually. As a result, storage requirements are growing at a commensurate rate. Others agreed that the volume of electronic communications is also increasing dramatically within their organizations. One suggested that the growth in electronic communications is partially offset by the decline in non-

TABLE 14.1   Sender-Receiver Targets

Person-to-person (P2P)	System-to-person (S2P)	Person-to-system (P2S)
• E-mail	• Mass mailings	• Surveys
• Instant messaging	• Spam	• Forms
• Telephone	• Subscriptions	• E-commerce
• Fax		

electronic communications—basically, the trade-off between filing cabinets and disk drives. However, this trade-off is unbalanced with the growth in electronic communications exceeding the decline in nonelectronic communications by substantial multiples. Volume is also related to the *size* of electronic transmissions and their *retention*. If each communication doubles in size, storage requirements double even if volume remains constant. Similarly, if an organization doubles its retention period, storage requirements double.

Addressing storage issues requires both clarifying retention requirements and setting limitations and guidelines for how and how much storage should be used. There are several ways in which this can be done.

- *Store and administer electronic communications centrally.* Storing messages on central servers ensures that electronic communications will be both protected (e.g., auto-archive facilities) and accessible via a number of different devices. Central administration ensures that standards can be uniformly adopted, applied, and enforced. Policies governing electronic communications retention should be developed centrally and communicated to (and promoted throughout) the organization.

- *Charge for storage but allow the business to set size limits.* A majority of organizations now impose limits on e-mail, such as the size of messages and the total size of individual mailboxes. These limits should be justified and set by the business with the proviso that they satisfy existing legal requirements. Currently, organizations tend to set limitations somewhat arbitrarily. The consensus of the group was that limits should be based on sound business needs as well as the ability and willingness to pay. Stated differently, if a business unit demands extra storage and is willing to pay for it, there are few arguments for not providing it.

- *Enforce limits.* Once set, limits can be applied with varying degrees of enforcement. Some organizations provide (increasingly impolite) warnings to staff whose mailboxes are full. Other mail systems are programmed to disallow new messages when a mailbox reaches capacity. Communications must also be aged. At one organization the mail system is programmed to automatically delete all mail older than ninety days unless it is flagged as "business critical," in which case it is moved to a secure server. In this organization, business-critical information is "information deemed necessary for satisfying corporate legal requirements, corporate tax requirements, or for conducting business operations." The enforcement of these limits motivates managers to remove unnecessary communications.

- *Delegate responsibility to individual managers.* Individual managers should take responsibility for deciding the "criticalness" of their communications. They must actively delete messages as they become unnecessary and ensure that information is moved to a secure server before it gets accidentally removed. Awareness of the criticality of managing personal communications must be promoted to all staff so they understand the reasoning behind the limitations. One manager suggested this:

  A retention policy is the starting point for managing electronic communications. Retention policies are different from enforcement policies; managing storage is different from managing security. While education is an effective way to help reinforce policies, culture is the best way to proceed. Managing communications must be seen by everyone as essential to the ongoing success and viability of the organization.

- *Consider all costs.*   Mailbox management activities consume critical managerial time. IT managers should consider three critical questions:
    1. How much time and effort should managers expend on this activity?
    2. How critical is this activity?
    3. Can it be accomplished by any other means?

    An internal study in one organization showed that the total cost of mailbox management is roughly four times the actual cost of storage. Thus, setting communication policies and limits too stringently and/or too rigidly might increase the time spent in compliance beyond that which was truly intended. The full costs of a storage strategy should, therefore, be considered.

Issue #2: Perceptions of Overload

Overload is reached when it is no longer possible to respond appropriately and in a timely fashion to electronic communications. Overload is a relative term as individuals may differ as to how much communication their jobs entail and how much they can tolerate. Given the increase in the volume of electronic communication, it comes as no surprise that perceptions of overload are also widespread. One participant stated that it is not uncommon for individuals within her firm to receive in excess of two hundred e-mail messages per day!

The severity of the overload problem is dependent on the nature of a particular role. It is often quite severe for senior professionals and management. One cited reason for this is the misuse of two e-mail features: "copy all" and "reply all." The group felt strongly that individuals and the firm have roles to play in tackling this problem. However, they also agreed that currently the burden falls mostly on the individual as firms have been reluctant to offer either formal or informal assistance. Thus it is common for individuals to spend considerable overtime and/or personal time dealing with electronic communications. As one manager stated, "E-mail manages us; we don't manage it!"

Strategies suggested by the focus group include the following:

- *Communicate best practices as a productivity issue.*   Individuals often feel that they are on their own in dealing with communication overload. To combat this, it was suggested that organizations treat overload as a productivity issue. If it is treated as a "rules" issue, then individuals see it as a compliance matter and behavioral changes can be prolonged. As one manager observed, individuals tend to continue doing the same things the same way. Therefore, there is a need for the organization to offer training and education. Thus, when coping with e-communication overload as a productivity issue, organizations can communicate "helpful hints and tips," "shortcuts," and "lessons learned." They can also use it as an opportunity to explain advanced features of various communication packages.

- *Deploy technology wherever possible.* While formal technological solutions to help combat overload exist, none appear to be overly effective and most offer only limited assistance. Nevertheless, they should be deployed where possible. For example, an e-mail system could automatically sort mail for individuals with respect to urgency and/or upcoming calendar events. Although it is easy to abuse the "urgent" designation, it can also be very effective when there are established expectations surrounding its use. Some more sophisticated technologies attempt to channel communications based on message attributes such as content, committee membership, and events. However, they were deemed to have limited applicability and accuracy to date.

Issue #3: Communication Responsibilities

There was general agreement in the focus group that *all electronic communications are owned by the organization.* Individuals are held personally responsible for proper usage of electronic communication. Misuse is grounds for termination. Furthermore, most firms require their employees to sign annually a code of business conduct that specifies the following:

- The appropriate usage of any form of communication
- The appropriate usage of the Internet
- Compliance with security regulations
- Respect for individual privacy

Signing a code of business conduct is typically a condition of employment due to the fact that a firm is liable for the actions of its employees. These codes stress that the organization has the right to monitor e-mail and Internet usage and that, as a result, employees should consider all messages to be public. One manager stated that anyone in his company found visiting a pornographic site, for example, would be given a warning against continuation of this practice. Personal usage, while unsanctioned, is tolerated within reason by most organizations.

Strategies for enforcing these responsibilities include the following:

- *Assign overall responsibility for communications within the organization.* There is wide variance concerning who is responsible for managing electronic communication. While IT assumes ownership for some of the technical issues (e.g., storage, archiving, encryption standards), it is often reluctant to take on the role of compliance enforcement of communication policies. If not IT, then who should assume overall responsibility? Legal? HR? There is probably no best answer other than *there should be someone charged with this responsibility.* Otherwise, communication policies, behaviors, and compliance become happenstance.

Issue #4: Etiquette

Rules of etiquette evolve with experience using a new technology. While they are developing, individuals and organizations can experience problems associated with a communication technology's inappropriate use (e.g., "flaming" e-mails, cyberbullying, or use of PDAs during meetings). E-communication etiquette is often unwritten and gradually becomes part of the generally accepted norms and values. One manager shared her firm's "unwritten but strictly adhered to" rules of etiquette as follows:

E-mail

- Include subject lines
- Use categorization
- Include signature information
- Use "out of office" notifications
- Never "blind copy"

Voice mail

- Issue standard messages containing expected turnaround time
- Change message daily
- Offer contact options (e.g., an assistant's number, a direct line, paging instructions)

Use of electronic devices in meetings

- Ground rules are established by the meeting facilitator
- Don't handle mail
- Don't talk on the phone
- If they must be left on, put phones on vibrate
- Use pagers for only critical support/contact
- OK to take minutes or to note action items

Another firm has incorporated communication etiquette in its soft-skills HR courses. Most organizations (and particularly global organizations) have significant cultural diversity among their personnel. As a result, there is ample opportunity for different communication behaviors to be misinterpreted. At this company, HR offers a number of soft-skills courses on topics such as ethnic diversity, thinking styles, and interpersonal behavior all played out within different business scenarios. These scenarios involve common business situations, such as meetings, correspondence, sales contacts, and hosting clients. These courses also provide opportunities to introduce individuals to the accepted rules of e-communication etiquette, while at the same time explaining why some behaviors might not be as "logical" to individuals of different ethnic backgrounds.

Issue #5: Security

Spam is interpreted to be "unsolicited commercial electronic mail" according to a bill before the U.S. House of Representatives (U.S. Congress 2003). Research by the Radicati Group Inc. (Rola 2003) claimed that spam constituted 45 percent of all e-mail messages and predicted that it would increase to 70 percent by 2007. One manager reported that his organization found that its weekly total of spam mail had increased from one thousand to almost twenty-four thousand over a period of only forty-two weeks! The impact of this growth is significant. A Gartner Group report advises that a "business would experience a 30 percent savings in the time employees spent managing e-mail if it rid itself of spam" (Rola 2003).

The following strategies are suggested for dealing with the security and productivity issues associated with this deluge.

- *Use antispam and antiviral technologies.* The majority of antispam technologies involve content-based filters. Some are based on the Bayesian combination of the spam probabilities of individual words (Graham 2003). There are two types of filtering errors—false positives (i.e., innocent e-mails that get mistakenly identified as spam) and false negatives (i.e., spam that gets through). Graham points out that false positives are considered much worse than false negatives, and most filtering software guards against false positives at the risk of false negatives. Implementing filtering software incurs two types of costs—degrading the performance of mail servers and the costs of the software itself (plus continuous upgrades). However, almost all organizations feel these costs are easily outweighed by the benefits to the organization in productivity gain and nuisance avoidance.

  Viruses, being contagious, pose an even nastier problem for electronic communication where the potential for damage and/or disruption is significant. Antiviral software is essential. It must be current and all devices scanned regularly. Constant vigilance is required.

- *Develop a policy regarding usage of corporate IDs for personal use.* The usage of corporate IDs for personal usage (i.e., sending personal e-mails from a corporate e-mail system) is a tricky problem. On the one side are employees saying that "I spend so much time at the office, I need to be allowed to do some personal stuff at work (online banking, telling the spouse I'll be late, etc.)." On the other side are the raft of abuses that can occur in addition to the virus and other risks noted. Furthermore, the amount of spam one receives seems to be directly related to Web usage. It would appear that the greater the number of sites visited, the greater the chances of your e-mail address being detected. In some organizations, personal usage of corporate IDs is formally disallowed; individuals adopt separate e-mail addresses for personal usage. In contrast, some organizations argue that personal e-mail access through free addresses such as Hotmail generate more viruses and problems than do corporate IDs. This conundrum aside, it is important that organizations tackle this situation and respond with a clearly articulated policy to govern personal usage of corporate IDs.

- *Actively support legislation.* Organizations must also ensure that they are not sending spam. One participant rather apologetically suggested that his organization might be considered a source of spam given their e-marketing practices! As these activities may be subject to privacy legislation, most firms are already quite proactive in assessing and implementing privacy practices in their organizations. One company routinely asks its customers for permissions (e.g., do they wish to receive confirmations via e-mail?), which are maintained in a database.

Issue #6: Communication Quality

The purpose and content of a given message should dictate the appropriate delivery channel. Communication channels differ with respect to bandwidth (i.e., media richness) as well as security. Once the delivery channel is selected, it is imperative that senders transmit the full intent and meaning of the communication in order to avoid miscommunication. Technological aids, such as emoticons (e.g., ☺, ☹, ☺), are often used to convey feelings to complement text and enrich the quality of communication. Emoticons tend to be used more frequently during instant messaging. Usage, however, implies recipients' knowledge of emoticons, which cannot always be assumed. They, therefore, suggested adopting the following practices:

- *Agree on communication rules.* One company developed and circulated "rules of the road" covering such things as date-stamping entries/pages, ensuring accuracy, showing consideration for the source/destination/usage of the information, using spell checkers, and peer reviews (not for every message but perhaps for mass mailings). Others agreed with this approach but stressed that individuals must be provided with sufficient instruction and motivation in how to use such rules. Communication norms represent cultural artifacts and, as such, are better adopted by group persuasion and example than by legislation. All participants endorsed the need for education, feeling that it is unreasonable to expect individuals to adopt proper communication behaviors if not informed.
- *Recognize cultural differences.* In global organizations language translation is often a requirement of effective communication. Due to the increased risk of misinterpretation, senders need to maximize message content when working in a cross-cultural context. Something as innocent as different phrasing can cause messages to be interpreted incorrectly. Avoiding jargon and highly cryptic messages, allowing redundancy, and editing for clarity are effective practices.

Issue #7: Legal

There are a host of legal issues surrounding electronic communications, but most relate to retention and access (i.e., archiving). It is not surprising, therefore, that most firms are struggling with how to capture, search, and store e-mail and other types of electronic messages in order to be compliant with existing legal requirements. For instance, few firms archive instant messages as yet. Some firms treat them the same as e-mail, while others believe they should be treated like a "hallway conversation." Upcoming challenges are how to archive text messages on cell phones and VoIP (i.e., voice-over-Internet protocol) phone calls. Some firms simply disallow text messages, preferring to being perceived as "dinosaurs" by not allowing people to use the communications tools they already use in everyday life.

While best practices do not exist for archiving electronic messages, at a minimum, the following strategies should be adopted:

- *Establish and enforce a retention policy for electronic communications.* Whether a firm creates a policy to "delete all e-mail after a set period of time" or to "save all messages," the key is consistent enforcement of the retention policy. If a company is not diligent in administering its policy, then it can be legally vulnerable. A compromise position is creating mailboxes with specific purposes, to which messages pertaining to a purpose can be saved. Then other e-mail can be purged. Care needs to be exercised here as, even if an official version of an e-mail is deleted, forensic specialists can often find copies in backups or on people's hard drives.

An officer within the organization needs to assume overall responsibility for managing the retention policy in order to ensure that it is up to date and adhered to by all employees. While it is necessary for this officer to rely on the organization's legal teams to help determine policy in this area, responsibility need not reside within the legal department.[2] In many companies, for example, overall responsibility resides within IT due to the dominant and ever-changing role of technology for electronic communications. Regarding adherence, most firms mandate that all employees sign a statement acknowledging the company's e-mail policy. Some make this an annual exercise. Failure to follow these policies commonly results in termination for cause.

- *Plan for future access.* A key benefit of having a communications retention policy is not incurring the cost of litigation. Nevertheless, it is hard to avoid all litigation. Therefore, having tools to narrow the focus of a legal team's search is very useful. As a result, there is a growing market for tools to manage electronic messages. Beyond tools, designing for eventual access, as opposed to just retention, can result in substantial savings in terms of resources should a future legal need arise. The realization is that, beyond legal fees, litigation can be very expensive in terms of IT resources.

In terms of future access, some companies also require documents to be classified and have expiration dates. This facilitates version control. Furthermore, given the ease with which electronic documents can be modified, determining the "real" document is very important. As a result, some companies are adopting an information model that is "contact sensitive."

CONCLUSION

As with any new technology, the introduction and rapid escalation of the usage of electronic communications has created a unique set of management issues. This chapter has explored these issues and suggested appropriate strategies for addressing them. These management strategies are still evolving rapidly, however.

Given the nature of communications and the rapid development of related technologies, communications management will continue to chase a moving target. Nevertheless, proactive steps taken now will most certainly reduce the risk of potential security breaches, inappropriate usage, and their concomitant outcomes.

REFERENCES

Graham, P. "A Plan for Spam." Paper presented at 2003 Spam Conference. Cambridge, MA, January 2003. www.paulgraham.com/spam.html.

Rola, M. "Spam Battle Hinges on Awareness: Symantec." *IT Business*, www.itbusiness.ca/print.asp?sid=52371 (accessed 2003).

U.S. Congress, Bill H.R. 2515, 108th Congress, 1st Session. www.spamlaws.com/federal/108hr2515.html (accessed June 18, 2003).

---

[2]Participants noted that policies are sometimes based on whether a company is being sued (in which case it wants to keep as little information as possible) or is suing others (in which case it wants to keep as much information as possible).

MINI CASE

Information Management at Homestyle Hotels

It had seemed like a good idea at the time, Ben Garrett thought glumly: just collect all information on the availability of each hotel room and provide it to management over the company's intranet. It would help each hotel manager adjust room rental rates according to whether or not they wanted to stimulate more reservations. Connect the information in that system to the on-line reservation system and *voila!*—a dynamic, real-time, sense-and-respond application able to automatically raise rates when demand was high and reduce them when demand declined. Now everyone was up in arms about it, and Ben, Homestyle Hotels' information services director, was uncomfortably deep in alligators.

Homestyle Hotels Inc. was formed as the result of a merger of Lifestyle Resorts and Home-Away Hotels and was now one of the larger chains in North America. When Ben joined them five years ago, they were still in the dark ages, technologically speaking. Each individual hotel operated as its own little fiefdom with its own collection of hardware and software—some state of the art and some outrageously outdated. Each hotel manager was responsible for purchasing his or her own technology, and as a result, almost every hotel had a different reservation system. Thus, it was impossible for the company to provide a consistent "look and feel" to their services, and this made branding and marketing extremely difficult. For example, some hotels knew if a customer had stayed with them before; others didn't. Furthermore, even basic information on such things as operating costs, occupancy, and profit and loss took at least a month to compile at each hotel. *Then* the central accountants took another six weeks to reconcile and adjust the numbers, so each quarterly report was almost a full quarter out of date before it arrived on the executives' desks.

"This is unacceptable," declared Fred Gains, the gruff COO who had hired him. "If we're going to compete as a national brand, we need better information to manage the chain as an enterprise."

That had been Ben's initial mandate—to rejuvenate and consolidate the firm's IT—so senior management would have better control over branding, marketing, and operations and, hence, make the chain more profitable. His top priority at the beginning had been common financial statements. "We can't move forward unless we know where we stand at present," he had told the IT steering committee. They had agreed, and had only just committed to spending money on an ERP system to replace the company's hodge-podge of financial applications. For the next three years, they had all sweated. While Ben and his IT colleagues struggled to implement the ERP and get each hotel to adapt to common processes and financial information, the business was struggling to stay afloat after the most recent economic downturn. They had done it—barely—but it had taken three years for the company to turn a profit again. Everyone felt lucky to have survived.

Last year the purse strings had finally loosened. Ben had begun to develop a true information strategy with his business partners in the resorts and hotels, and it wasn't too long before they bumped up against their first major problem. They had all been sitting in the conference room talking about the reservation system when it had dawned on Ben that everyone was talking about a different "client." The resorts worked largely with travel packagers. The bulk of their business came from tours and conferences; to them, a *client* was a tour company. The people actually occupying rooms were known as *customers*. The Home-Away people, on the other hand, dealt for the most part directly with the people who stayed in their rooms, whom they called *clients*. As a result, everyone had a different idea of what information should be gathered and how it should be used.

That problem had been resolved, but it had taken a lot of table thumping to get there. Defining the requirements was turning out to be a nightmare. Every piece of information—from customer name and address to room rates and descriptions—was in a different format or meant something slightly different to each hotel manager. Room rate, for instance, might reflect the "rack" rate, discount rate, seasonal rate, preferred rate, loyalty rate, corporate rate, or association/affiliate rate. Then there was the information that people were collecting in the so-called unused data fields. For example, certain hotel managers had adopted a series of codes to indicate whether a client was a problem or was suspected of stealing or destroying hotel property. They had put these codes in a field that had originally been designed to capture customer preferences. Other managers collected detailed information in on-line contact directories about customer preferences. Still others used an industry standard rating structure to denote common preferences (e.g., no-smoking rooms).

Now the project had deteriorated into a series of long, boring meetings about the meaning of each and every piece of information each hotel collected and trying to define it in a data dictionary. Enthusiasm for the effort had declined with each meeting, and positions were hardening. The Lifestyles people said their information needs were *different* from those of the Home-Away people and that they should have a different system altogether. "How could these people have let their data get into such a *mess*," Ben wondered for the ten thousandth time. They were spinning their wheels on this one—*still* in the requirements definition phase—and everyone (Ben included) was unsure how they were going to pull this one off. "Maybe we should just *buy* a generic industry information application and force the hotels to comply with its data definitions," he mused aloud. Picking up the phone, he called the architecture team to set up a meeting to evaluate the available options.

The following week found Ben, his information architect; the technical architect; and Marie Bonheur, the recently promoted director of the Home-Away division (and the only businessperson who had seemed remotely in touch with the reality they were facing), sitting around a conference table sharing glossy brochures extolling the latest and greatest technology. Like most other large corporations, Homestyle Hotels was inundated with vendors flogging a great assortment of IT solutions. The ERP system had forced the company to adopt technical standards, and it was the technical architect's job to weed out any nonstandard hardware and software before it came to the attention of anyone else in the organization. Information standards were quite another matter, of course. As this project had shown, Homestyle was all over the map in that respect, with the single exception of the financials.

The choice soon came down to two software applications. Each provided a data dictionary, which users were allowed to tweak. Each provided a Web-enabled interface, which could be modified to show different views of the information. Each one would interface with Homestyle's ERP. There were some differences, however. Hotels Confidential (HC) appeared to provide exceptionally good information protection for customers. This was important when customers were connecting online, although Homestyle already had a firewall and virus scanners. Clear Reservations (CR) appeared to have better content management functions. "We absolutely need to get the business involved in this decision," said Bonheur. "We need their support if we're going to get their agreement to change their business processes."

"Let's set it up," said Ben. "But let's put a little effort into this first. Let's get the vendors to use some of our data. That will make it easier for the business to see what they're getting."

The two vendors, hungry for a huge national sale, had agreed to work with a select team to provide a live test involving a single hotel. The Home-Away Chicago had been chosen because it was the one that had adopted one of the industry standards that both HC and CR supported. After a few glitches, they were able to connect with the Chicago systems, and with a little "duct tape and a few toothpicks," they had managed to populate the prototypes on the salesmen's PCs. A room had been booked for the day. Each vendor had an hour to demo its wares; after that there would be a question period, followed by discussion and, they hoped, a decision.

The HC team was already assembled when Ben, the architects, and Bonheur and her business colleagues, including Fred Gains, arrived. After brief introductions and the obligatory joke about how they hoped HC would find a "home" with Homestyle, Ray Santos got down to work, bringing up a huge version of the HC software on the movie-sized screen at the end of the room. Stressing each of its features in turn, Santos emphasized the points he had been told were his software's strengths. "With HC, complete privacy for your customers is built in. Our password protection has four levels so that different employees only see the information they *need* to do their job. Only system administrators can get at *all* the data. Security is built in. Hotel managers control and adjust room availabilities by monitoring their occupancy rates as often as they wish. They also have the ability to select and adjust key productivity metrics so they can better manage their individual costs. Individual staff members get specialized screens, depending on their role in the hotel. For example, housekeeping can see the unmade rooms and guest preferences, while reservations sees contact and credit card information. Once a week, the system collects a set of standard metrics that are made available to everyone in the executive suite."

The CR team arrived soon after Santos and his associates had been ushered out. After another stale joke about the company's name, Sandra Sawh began her presentation. She, too, focused on the CR software's strengths. "With our product lines, we can offer you cradle-to-grave information management," she stated. She then went on to demonstrate the functions it provided for data mining and for drilling down into data. "For example, every executive can see the status of every hotel on this color-coded chart every day. If the chart shows a hotel is red, he or she can click on the hotel and see its metrics, and if they still want more, they can look at the hotel's occupancy rates and compare them with previous years and months. Naturally, we offer a full Web-based interface for customers, but we believe your existing information security should be enough to protect it. As for privacy, we also offer role-based screens."

After seeing CR's team out, Ben opened the floor to discussion. Gains started, "Well, there's no question in *my* mind that we have to go with CR. That's the only way head office will get some control over the individual hotels. Right now none of us knows *what* they're doing until it's too late! I'm going to call the manager in Chicago as soon as this presentation's over; I want to know why his availability rate is so high!"

Bonheur spoke up. "Well, I must say I have to disagree with you, Fred. HC is definitely the better product for the way we work. Let's look at the facts. We have two different *types* of hotels that work in two different ways, *and* they're spread out all over North America. The hotel managers are in the best position to know their customers and to know what the information *means*. They can't have head office down their throats every time they turn around!"

Ben looked around. Half of the people in the room were nodding in agreement with Bonheur. The other half had their arms crossed and hostile expressions on their faces. No guesses which ones were going with Gains and which with Bonheur. This had *seemed* like a good idea at the time, Ben thought, but it was now clear that the controversy lay not just in *what* information was collected, but also in *who* got it and *when*. World War III was about to begin. Just then a temporary reprieve arrived in the form of the waiter with their lunch trolley. "Ladies and gentlemen, I suggest we all take a lunch break and come back at this issue in an hour. While you're doing that, I'll see if I can pull together some recommendations that will make sense for our organization." ■

DISCUSSION QUESTIONS

1. Does it make good business sense to integrate across the different lines of business represented by Lifestyle Resorts and Home-Away Hotels? What exactly would you integrate (beyond financial information) and why?

2. Outline a process for Homestyle to follow in order to decide between the two software options (i.e., HC and CR)? What selection criteria would you use? Who should make the decision?

MINI CASE

Knowledge Management at Acme Consulting

"So I guess you're our new 'knowledge czar'!" one of his colleagues teased in passing. Josh Stein, Acme Consulting's new director of knowledge management, flinched inwardly as he laughed dutifully at the joke that he'd already heard several times over the past couple of weeks. Going along with her, he replied pompously, "Yes, and I will soon be the fount of all wisdom at this firm!"

As if! For one of the world's most prestigious strategy consulting firms with more than a thousand employees, Acme was a real mess from a knowledge perspective. It had great people who worked hard—much harder than they should. It was not uncommon for consultants to work seventy to one hundred hours, or even pull all-nighters. Often they were based at client sites for weeks on end. But it seemed that everyone had forgotten that old maxim, "Work smarter, not harder."

The managing partner, Jeff Oulton, had raised the alarm about the lack of productivity and increasing burnout among junior staff. "Knowledge is our lifeblood," he had told the partners and principals a few weeks before. "We're not doing what we should to reuse what we know and to shorten the learning curves of our juniors. Our goal is to add value for our clients. They're beginning to complain that we aren't building on top of our previous work."

Josh, an Acme principal and a respected senior consultant, had been asked by Oulton to take on the job of harnessing Acme's knowledge resources more effectively. In his first two weeks of working on the task, Josh was shocked to learn just how much information wasn't being used. Because most consultants worked directly on their laptops wherever they were, almost all the information they needed—reports, requests for proposals (RFPs), technical specifications, background information on customers—was available digitally *somewhere* in the firm. It was all *supposed* to be on the intranet, but not all of it made it there.

Usage of the intranet had fallen to a rate of about thirty hits per day. Clearly, consultants did not perceive value in what they were getting from it. "I don't bother with the intranet anymore," one consultant told Josh. "I just find someone who's worked with my client before and get them to send me whatever they've got on their personal computer. From these documents, I can usually find other people who can tell me what I need to know. Trust me, it's easier and faster than that dumb intranet." Usage among junior consultants, who would benefit most from learning from the company's previous experiences, hovered around 5 percent. "I can't find anything on it when I do sign on," one complained. "My security clearance is so low, the system won't let me see most of what's there anyway." Another remarked, "I'd use it more if it were easier to get around and find things, but I have to sign on and off so many databases, it's more trouble than it's worth."

The company's intranet consisted of a dozen loosely organized Web sites, each requiring a separate login. Each site served a different purpose. As a result, most consultants were unaware of the full set of knowledge resources. Information was often misfiled on the wrong Web site. Some sites had higher security provisions than others, and it was often unclear which types of information had to go where. A recent memo on protecting client privacy meant that consultants were dumping everything into the "top security" site, which only partners could access without permission. Even within a Web site, search and navigation features were limited, meaning that you really had to know what you were looking for before you could find it. At Acme it really seemed that the most effective knowledge access was based on who you knew—a big problem for junior consultants.

Many consultants also complained about the lack of up-to-date technology for their use.

"My computer is so slow!" one moaned. "It's at least five years old. I feel like it should have a big key in the back to wind it up! Can't they get me something faster? It takes forever to download things. Besides, I'm only in the office once every week or so." As Josh knew from his own experience, consultants spent most of their time on the road, working from client sites. Because Acme's intranet could not be accessed remotely, everything had to be done during precious time in the office. Hence, the need to plan their information access discouraged consultants from using or updating the intranet site.

In his next meeting with Oulton, Josh reported, "We could be doing a lot more with the knowledge that we have, but we need a knowledge management strategy and we'll have to invest more in technology to do it properly."

Oulton winced. "The partners don't like spending money on technology unless it's absolutely necessary. And we're going to need a pretty good business case to justify it." With a grin, he added, "But I think you can probably do that."

"I agree," Josh said enthusiastically. "But that's just the beginning of what we need to do to use what we know! I've been reading some books and articles on knowledge management, and they say that we need to change how our people work and collaborate with each other.

Our 'every man for himself' culture doesn't encourage people to use and share knowledge."

"You may be right," said Oulton with a sigh, "but that airy-fairy 'culture' stuff isn't going to fly with the partners either. Technology, they'll understand. But culture? No way! What we need to give them is a concrete plan for this stuff that makes sense to them. I suggest that you focus on some very pragmatic and easy-to-implement steps that will demonstrate the business value of knowledge. If you can do that, it will be easier to implement a broader knowledge management strategy in the future. Why not focus first on what it takes to get intranet usage up?"

Back in his office, Josh flipped through the knowledge management books and articles he'd accumulated. "Where's the beef here?" he asked himself. "You'd think with all the high-powered brains behind this stuff, there would be some simple plans we could adopt." It was clear that there was a big gap between the ivory tower and the real world when it came to using knowledge and that no one was going to make his job easy for him. "I guess I'll have to do this myself," he said to no one in particular. "Let's go back to the beginning." As he worked on analyzing the knowledge problems facing the firm, a plan began to develop in his mind. Josh turned to his computer and began to outline what was needed to bring Acme into the information age. ■

DISCUSSION QUESTIONS

Oulton says to Josh that he should "focus on some very pragmatic and easy-to-implement steps that will demonstrate the business value of knowledge. If you can do that, it will be easier to implement a broader knowledge management strategy in the future. Why not focus first on what it takes to get intranet usage up?"

1. Develop a strategy for increasing intranet usage across Acme.

2. What additional elements would a "broad knowledge management strategy" require?
3. How should Josh address the cultural aspect of knowledge management?

MINI CASE

CRM at Minitrex

Georges Degas, Director of Sales at Minitrex, looked at his salesman with concern and sympathy as the man described another sales call where he had been made to look unprofessional! It was bad enough that he didn't know that the company he'd just phoned was already a Minitrex customer, but being told that he was the third caller this week from Minitrex was horrible. "I'd be better off with a Rolodex and handwritten notes than this system," he grumbled.

To keep track of customer information, salespeople use the Customer Contacts system, the brainchild of Georges's boss, Jon Bettman, VP of Marketing. Bettman's position was created eighteen months ago in an effort to centralize sales and marketing activities at Minitrex. The sales and marketing team is responsible for promoting and selling an array of products to its customers. There are two distinct product lines, each developed by a separate division (insurance and financing) that also provides after-sale customer service. The idea behind having a department dedicated to sales and marketing was to create opportunities for cross-selling and up-selling that didn't exist when salespeople were tied to just one of the company's product categories.

The insurance division, led by Harold Blumfen, Vice President of Insurance, is a major profit-maker for Minitrex. Blumfen's group is divided into industry-specific teams whose goals are to develop deep industry knowledge and design short-term insurance products to meet clients' needs. Irascible and brilliant, Blumfen believes that computers are good for billing and other accounting functions but cannot replace people for customer knowledge and support. His division uses a credit administration system (developed more than twenty years ago) to track customer billings and payments and a general management system to keep track of which products a customer has bought and what services the customer is entitled to. Both are fundamentally back-end systems. The industry

teams keep front-end customer knowledge in their own documentation and in their heads.

The mission of the financing division is to provide business sectors with financing services that are competitive with those of the big banks. As with the insurance division, its products and customer service are designed and delivered through its own industry-specific teams. However, unlike Blumfen, the VP of financing is an IT enthusiast. Mariella Hopkins joined Minitrex about four years ago after a successful banking career. Her mandate, which she has undertaken with alacrity, was to "combine big banking services with small company flexibility." To do this, her division funded the development of a management business center application, which acts as an online customer self-service system. Customers can obtain statements and financing online and often can get credit approved instantly. Customer-service representatives use the same basic system, with additional functionality, to track customer transactions and to provide customer support as needed.

The company is always promising better systems, thought Georges, but when it comes down to it, no one can agree on *what* to do. Being customercentric seems to depend on whose view of the customer is being used. Meanwhile, salespeople can't do their jobs properly. Just imagine what our customers think!

Bettman has been trying to get the company to see the importance of having timely, accurate, and integrated customer information without much success. To give his sales force a better way to keep track of sales prospects, he developed his Customer Contacts system, which schedules sales calls on a periodic basis and provides mechanisms for generating and tracking new leads; it also forms the basis on which the marketing department pays the salespeople's commissions. Real-time information on sales by product, salesperson, and region gives Bettman and his team excellent feedback on how well their centralized marketing strategies are performing. The Customer Contacts system also feeds data into the insurance and financing divisions' systems after sales are made, for purposes of invoicing and servicing the accounts.

"I'll see what I can do about this," Georges had promised his frustrated salesman, knowing that it would take a miracle to improve the situation. "I'll speak with the director of IT today and get back to you."

Georges put in a call to Denny Khan, Minitrex's long-suffering director of IT. Khan, who reported to the CFO, was outranked by Bettman, Blumfen, and Hopkins. To his surprise, Khan answered the phone right away. "I was just leaving for lunch," he explained. "What can I do for you?"

As soon as Georges began to explain what had happened that morning, Khan cut him off, "I know, I know. But the VPs would say, 'Our systems work fine for our needs, so why change them? We have a lot more urgent IT needs to spend our money on.' Blumfen doesn't want to spend a nickel on IT and doesn't want to have to work with Hopkins. Hopkins is open to collaboration, but she doesn't want to compromise her existing system, which is working well. And Bettman can't do anything without their cooperation. Furthermore, none of them will assign dedicated business staff to help us put together a business case and requirements. Their line is,

'We don't have the budgets for this. Of course, we'll answer IT's questions, but it's their job to give us the systems we need.'"

"I see the same attitude in our business activities," agreed Georges. "Our sales force often doesn't know what services the business teams are providing to the customers. I don't see how management can expect to make informed decisions when they're not sharing basic information. Isn't there some way we could at least get common customer data—even if we use it in different ways? And surely, with each unit identifying, prioritizing, and paying for IT opportunities, the duplication of support services must cost an arm and a leg."

"Sure," Khan agreed, "but each unit developed its own terminology and specialized data items over time, so these only work for *their* systems. Sharing is impossible unless everyone agrees on what information everyone needs about our customers. I'd like to see something done about this, but when I take it to the IT prioritization committee, it always seems to get bumped off the list. To the best of my knowledge, there has never been an effective business case to improve CRM. And anyway, I don't own this issue!"

"You're probably right, but I'm not sure how to go about this," said Georges. "Let me think about it and get back to you." ∎

DISCUSSION QUESTIONS

1. Explain how it is possible for someone at Minitrex to call a customer and not know (a) that this is a customer, and (b) that this is the third time this week that they had been called?

2. Outline the steps that Bettman must take in order to implement CRM at Minitrex. In your plan be sure to include people, processes, and technology.

MINI CASE

Managing Technology at Genex Fuels

"You have got yourselves into a terrible predicament," said V. R. "Sandy" Sandhuramen, his soft Indian accent belying the gravity of his words. "You are incredibly lucky you have managed to do business as well as you have, but this situation cannot be allowed to carry on." Sandy, a high-priced technology consultant, had been hired by Genex Fuel's new CIO, Nick Devlin, to review the company's technology portfolio and help him and his newly appointed IT architect, Chuck Yee, get a handle on the firm's technology needs.

Genex, a major producer of crude oil and natural gas, is the largest marketer of petroleum and petroleum products in the region. It is structured into three distinct business divisions, each comprising a number of functional segments. Until recently, IT had been decentralized into the three divisions, with their own directors of IT who reported to the divisional EVPs. Devlin, formerly the director of the corporate division, had been appointed CIO and given the specific mandate to bring in SAP as the primary technology platform for all the divisions.

"We have to start behaving like we're one business," said the CEO when he appointed Devlin. "I want a much more agile and responsive IT organization than we've had in the past. It seems to me that every time I ask IT to look into something I've heard or read about, they always come up with a thousand and one reasons why it *won't* work. We need to be able to use technology competitively, and that won't happen unless you can get ahead of the curve."

The excitement of his new mandate had lasted just about a week, until the true scope of the challenge became clear. He had asked each divisional IT director for an inventory of hardware and software currently in place and to briefly outline the work that was in their plans for the coming year. "We must have one of every piece of hardware and software ever produced," Devlin marveled as he scanned their reports. On the one hand, there was a new customer management system called COMC, which had been implemented to improve real-time information exchange between the company's 135 bulk fuel sites and Genex headquarters. On the other hand, they were still running an archaic DOS-based marketing system called MAAS to provide customer service and reports. "And they want to bring in SAP!" he groaned. "We need a plan and we need it soon."

That was when Devlin had engaged Sandy to work with Yee. "First, I want a no-holds-barred assessment of our current situation," he had said, and now they were in his office, outlining the "terrible predicament."

"The biggest problem you face at present," said Sandy, "is the fact that you have absolutely no standards and no integration, as you discovered for yourself, Nick." There was a lot of technology out there—both old and new—and it was a political hot potato. Almost every system had its group of advocates, some very senior in the company. Each EVP had invested his technology budget in the hardware and software that he felt could best support his work. The problem was that maintaining this mishmash was now costing an arm and a leg. And it was highly doubtful that the company was getting true value for its technology investment.

"We should be able to leverage our existing investments so we can invest in new technology," said Yee. "Instead, almost all our budget is taken up with holding these systems together with toothpicks and Scotch tape."

"One of the most challenging situations," Sandy went on, "is Price One."

Obsolete but absolutely essential, Price One is the fuel-pricing system that stores the pricing algorithms for all fuels marketing functions, including aviation, marine, retail, branded associates, and industrial and wholesale. While pricing is an integral part of marketing, Price One cannot communicate with COMC and is not easily adaptable to changes in the business environment. Price One perfectly reflected the business and technology that existed ten years ago, but this has now become a real drawback. To get around these limitations while continuing to use Price One, staff manually feed information from pricing requests in COMC to Price One to get approval because both systems use different terminology in coding products for different pricing methods.

Price One also lacks the ability to link information from different systems to ensure data integrity. As a result, Price One has accumulated some irrelevant data groups under pricing for products, and such corrupted data can be detected only by an experienced individual who has been dealing with that product group for decades and who would know at a glance the validity of the data. Its inability to link with other systems, such as COMC, and to pick up competitive market information in order to approve price is a critical flaw with Price One. Previous plans to rewrite this system have been resisted strenuously by management because of the expense. Now the system is on its last legs.

"And like most oil and gas companies," Sandy observed, "you have automated very few of your information assets as other types of organizations have done." Typically for the industry, Genex had grown by acquiring other, smaller firms and had inherited an enormous amount of physical data. It now has more than two million items of paper and microfilm. It has one hundred twenty thousand tapes of data. Some items date back to the 1940s and came from numerous sources. The company's seismic assets, on which it bases many of its decisions and has a replacement cost estimated at more than two billion dollars, are stored on a wide variety of media

from analog tapes, magnetic reels, and cartridges to optical discs to paper, film, and microfilm. They are spread out across five conventional physical warehouses.

This system of data management is problematic for two main reasons. First, with land sales occurring every two weeks, it is extremely difficult to make timely decisions based on all known information about a property. Clearly, the more seismic information a company can bring to bear on its decisions, the better it can decide where it wants to do further work. Second, the company's data assets, on which its future depends, are extremely vulnerable. There is no backup. When needed, the only copy of the information requested is physically transported to Genex's offices. The tapes on which the data reside deteriorate further with each reading. Furthermore, much information resides on obsolete forms of media and is getting increasingly difficult to access.

"Finally, IT is getting a lot of pressure from the executive office," reported Sandy. "These guys have seen what's going on in other companies, and they want to see Genex move into the twenty-first century. Staff at Genex cover vast territory and must work from home, from local facilities, or on the road. Not only does Genex need to provide a virtual working environment for these workers, but it also needs to consider how they can work together as a team without having physical colocation for communication."

"Well, I guess we have it all," said Devlin. "Integration problems, outdated hardware and software, inconsistent data, expensive workarounds, pressure to modernize, and substantial budget limitations." Turning to Yee and Sandy, he smiled. "Now what are we going to do about it? Where do we start?" ∎

DISCUSSION QUESTIONS

1. What evidence is the CEO using to suggest that Genex is not using technology competitively?
2. Did Devlin need to hire Sandy, a "high-priced technology consultant," to tell him that technology at Genex was a mess?
3. Devise a strategy to successfully implement enterprisewide systems (such as SAP) at Genex.

Chapter 15

Developing IT Capabilities[1]

> IT professionals are usually the best in the organization when it comes to business process re-engineering. Why is it, then, that the IT group often has some of the most "under-engineered" processes in the company? It's true. IT is great at looking at business processes in other parts of the organization but not as comfortable looking at how its own work gets done. (Gomolski 2004)

This observation has not been lost on senior IT executives. They are the first to admit that they may not have standard, verifiable, and high-performing capabilities across the IT department. Furthermore, today's competitive environment is driving these same executives to provide guaranteed levels of service at reduced costs. This can be achieved only by enhancing the way in which IT work is done. As a result, IT executives are investigating revamping their internal IT capabilities as a vehicle to reduce IT costs, gain efficiencies, and improve the quality of their service in order to reap enhanced benefits from the IT investment.

This chapter explores how companies are managing and developing their internal IT capabilities and looks at how IT capabilities are identified, how people's skills are mapped onto these capabilities, and what outcomes can be expected from a focus on capabilities. The first section offers some definitions to clarify the discussion and describes the perceived value of focusing on IT capabilities within organizations. Then it presents a five-step framework for developing and managing IT capabilities.

---

[1]McKeen J. D., H. A. Smith, and S. Singh, "A Framework for Enhancing IT Capabilities," *Communications of the Association of Information Systems* 15, article 36 (May 2005): 661–73 (reproduced by permission of the Association of Information Systems).

WHY FOCUS ON IT CAPABILITIES?

In IT, terms such as *competencies, capabilities, skills, resources, services, experiences, processes, attitudes, procedures,* and even *methods* are often used interchangeably. Therefore, it is important to clarify the terminology surrounding capability management:

- *Capability.* This is the ability to marshal resources to affect a predetermined outcome. Portfolio management, for instance, is the capability to manage a set of IT applications as a logical whole.
- *Competency.* This is the degree of proficiency in marshalling resources to affect a predetermined outcome. Thus, a capability indicates your ability to do something, whereas competency reflects how good you are at doing it.
- *Processes.* These are well-defined activities within capabilities. Portfolio management, for instance, includes the following processes: business case development, project prioritization, resource allocation, performance benchmarking, and portfolio analysis.
- *Procedures and methods.* These are "how to" or step-by-step instructions for implementing a process.

Why focus on IT capabilities? Rockart, Earl, and Ross (1996) argue that there is a direct linkage between IT capabilities and organizational value and identify eight imperatives that IT organizations must fulfill to support the organization's strategic thrusts. Ross, Beath, and Goodhue (1996) also see a direct relationship between IT capabilities and organizational value in specific IT assets that collectively guarantee long-term competitiveness for organizations. Combining these findings with their own work on IT leadership and outsourcing, Feeny and Willcocks (1998) suggest that the development of nine core IT capabilities are necessary for IT organizations to meet the three enduring challenges of uniting business and IT vision, delivering IT services, and designing an IT architecture. These IT capabilities are as follows:

1. *Leadership.* Integrating IT effort with business purpose and activities.
2. *Business systems thinking.* Envisioning the business process that technology makes possible.
3. *Relationship building.* Getting the business constructively engaged in IT issues.
4. *Architecture planning.* Creating a coherent blueprint for a technical platform that responds to current and future business needs.
5. *Making technology work.* Rapidly achieving technical progress by one means or another.
6. *Informed buying.* Developing and managing an IT sourcing strategy that meets the interests of the business.
7. *Contract facilitation.* Ensuring the success of existing contracts for IT services.
8. *Contract monitoring.* Protecting the business's contractual position, current and future.
9. *Vendor development.* Identifying the potential added value of IT service suppliers.

Other important IT capabilities include governance, business management, and skills management. While it is difficult to prove that the existence of any or all of these IT capabilities results in organizational value, there is a strong sense that enhanced IT capabilities improve the chances of successfully converting IT investments into measurable outcomes for the organization. According to Weill (1989), successful IT investments are the result of "conversion effectiveness." Hence, these core IT capabilities could collectively be considered to constitute conversion effectiveness.

A FRAMEWORK FOR DEVELOPING KEY IT CAPABILITIES

If the existence of key capabilities enables IT investments to be successfully converted to organizational value, then it logically follows that we need strategies for building these IT capabilities. Based on their experience, participants suggested that organizations should have a framework to identify, develop, and manage key IT capabilities. The framework that emerged is depicted in Figure 15.1. Each step in this framework is described in the remainder of this chapter.

Step 1: Create a Capability Management Office

The first step for organizations is the creation of a set of activities, structures, policies, and governance principles to advance the development of their IT capabilities. To accomplish this task, many firms create a "capability management office." Not only is this office the focal point for capability development and management (i.e., Steps 2 through 5), but its creation signals the importance IT senior management attaches to this activity. While most managers agreed that this was an important activity if IT

Figure 15.1   A Framework for Developing Key IT Capabilities

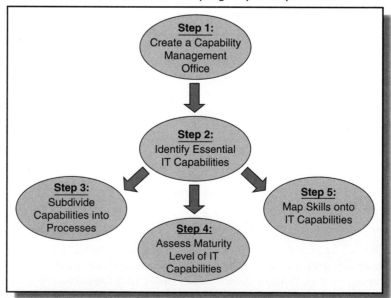

capabilities were to improve, there was significant variation among organizations in the group as to how they actually carried out this step.

One company created an entity called the "capability support group," which had the overall responsibility for the enhancement of IT capabilities. Another company formed an internal group called the "capabilities council" to investigate current practice within IT as part of a companywide ISO initiative. However the capabilities management office is configured, at a minimum it was agreed that it should administer the following activities:

- Define and assign responsibility for all capabilities.
- Develop strategies for the development of these capabilities.
- Ensure that adequate resources and funding are provided to develop them.
- Secure software support for these activities.
- Adopt a continuous capability improvement approach.
- Develop organizational training plans.
- Report the status of organizational capability performance.

It was also strongly recommended that this office, while assuming overall responsibility for the development of a capabilities management program, assign individual responsibilities to individual capabilities. According to one manager, "Making a capability someone's 'day job' is more effective at generating improvement than addressing it as a sideline or trying to grow it by committee."

Step 2: Identify Essential Capabilities Aligned with Business Goals

Each IT organization should go through the exercise of identifying its essential capabilities and linking them with business goals. However, these capabilities shouldn't be aligned too closely with current business practices. According to one manager, "Capabilities should be less functional and focus more on the outcomes that the organization needs to be able to create." This argues against simply adopting an existing list of core capabilities such as those suggested by Feeny and Willcocks (1998). Group participants felt that there was significant value in deriving one's own list . . . or at least in tailoring an existing list to suit one's particular goals. Identifying capabilities is an introspective analysis of the key activities that IT must execute effectively. It forces management to examine key business directives, not just IT challenges, and to establish priorities. This is a trip well worth taking. In some cases this exercise can bring IT much closer to the business and actually enhance alignment.

Despite the obvious linkage with the business, in practice identifying essential capabilities is largely an internal IT exercise. As a result, there is a tendency for the identification of key capabilities to result in a list that is much more *IT-speak* than *business-speak*. For instance, capabilities might be couched in terms of level of service, fail-soft mechanisms, solution delivery, and help desk provisioning. Such a list would be easily recognized by IT professionals while being somewhat obscure to their business counterparts. Participants argued that measures should be taken to ensure that the resulting essential capabilities be tied as closely as possible to the business . . . starting with the language.

Below we see two lists of capabilities. Firm B has adopted a set of capabilities that is remarkably devoid of IT terminology and, as a result, could apply to a line of business as easily as it applies to IT.

Firm A

1. Skills Regeneration
2. Enterprise Architecture
3. Shared Services Governance & Development
4. Development Methodology
5. Project Initiation and Investment Management
6. Business Process Definition & Change Management
7. Infrastructure Alignment & Crisis Control
8. Partner Management & Outsourcing

Firm B

1. People Management
2. Strategy and Planning
3. Portfolio Management
4. Resource Management
5. Solution Delivery
6. Service Management
7. Asset Management

Another company (Firm C), after identifying a set of capabilities, realized that they were not tied closely enough to the business. It feared the situation where IT could demonstrate high competence on specific capabilities while the business faltered. As a result, it revisited its capabilities, earmarking those that explicitly tied it to the business. This exercise resulted in the identification of twelve capabilities, of which five were classified as "business enablement"; the other seven were classified under the headings of "IT utility" and "business operations." The company decided to depict these capabilities as a wheel (see Figure 15.2) to reinforce their dynamic nature as well as their mutual interdependence.

It is interesting to note that Firm C identified "IT Competencies & Culture" as a capability. This is an explicit recognition that the definition and management of IT capabilities is itself a capability! Another obvious difference with Firm C is the level of detail. This begs the question of how many capabilities there should be. Within the focus group, the number of capabilities ranged from seven to twelve, which is probably a good working range. More than twelve would become too granular, while fewer would be overly generic and would risk losing focus and definition.

Step 3: Subdivide IT Capabilities into Key Processes

Once key capabilities have been identified, the next step is to subdivide them into processes. The result of this step should be a set of well-defined activities that can be measured and managed. A set of well-articulated processes enables organizations to evaluate their overall performance with respect to key capabilities. "Portfolio management," for instance, is a capability that is difficult to measure. "Business case development," however, is a well-defined component process of portfolio management,

Figure 15.2 IT Capability Wheel

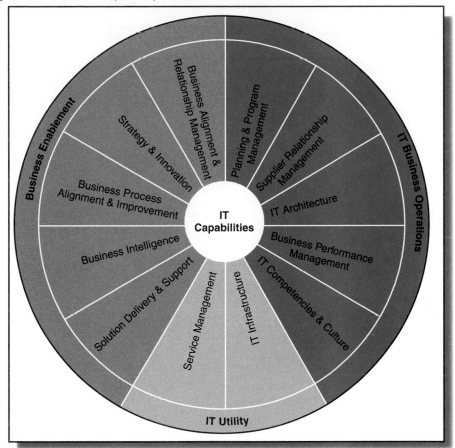

and performance on this process can be measured. Using the seven capabilities identified by Firm B above, Table 15.1 shows how these were subdivided into forty clear processes.

In the absence of accepted methodologies for subdividing capabilities into processes, managers offered some advice based on their experience. One suggested starting with the basics such as configuration/capacity management, IT asset management, procurement, or vendor management. Another suggested starting with service delivery, where there are well-identified activities such as service-level agreements, application life cycles, and quality assurance. Gomolski (2004) suggests a different approach—to focus on the "pain points" within the organization. For instance,

> . . . if your staff is still responding to end-user requests in an ad hoc fashion, you'll want to look at your request management processes. Or if you find that basic information about IT capabilities isn't getting out to your internal customers, you'll want to focus on your communications processes. Maybe IT planning is weak, or budget estimates fail to hit the mark.

TABLE 15.1 Competencies and Processes

CAPABILITIES	PROCESSESS
1 People Management	1. Recruiting and hiring
	2. Coaching and motivating
	3. Performance management and career planning
	4. Identifying and developing talent
2 Strategy and Planning	5. Account management
	6. External benchmarking
	7. Strategy development
	8. Architecture development
	9. Business process influence/enabling
	10. IT marketing
3 Portfolio Management	11. Business case development
	12. Project/service prioritization
	13. Portfolio investment determination
	14. Resource investment/allocation
	15. Performance benchmarking
	16. Portfolio analysis
4 Resource Management	17. Staffing strategy development
	18. Resource capacity management
	19. Staff sourcing
	20. Resource assignment
	21. Budget management
5 Solution Delivery	22. Project management
	23. Solution configuration
	24. Solution development and integration
	25. Architecture implementation
	26. Solution verification and validation
6 Service Management	27. Solution release
	28. Service-level management
	29. Asset availability management
	30. Asset capacity management
	31. Incident management
	32. Problem management
	33. Change management
7 Asset Management	34. Asset inventory management
	35. Asset affiliation management
	36. Asset life cycle management
	37. Security/permeability enforcement
	38. Supplier relationship management
	39. Lease/contract management
	40. Knowledge management

These approaches are inside-out approaches; that is, they focus on internal capabilities to distill component processes. There is also the outside-in approach, which takes advantage of the fact that there are external sources of well-defined IT processes already in existence. Perhaps the best-known source is the Software Engineering Institute (SEI) at Carnegie Mellon University with its capability maturity model (CMM) for software development. Other popular IT process frameworks used by some participants are the IT Infrastructure Library (ITIL) and CobiT (Control Objectives for Information and related Technology). Other available frameworks less directly tied to IT are listed here:

- *Six Sigma.* A methodology in which processes are continuously refined until their outcomes fall within an acceptable level of defects.
- *ISO.* A set of standards focused on achieving uniform business processes.

Most focus group members felt that a combination of both the inside-out and the outside-in approaches is best. They recommended starting with an external source of processes to ensure that your list is comprehensive then linking this list to your organization's key capabilities. It was suggested that adopting externally defined processes runs the risk of appearing foreign to IT staff, making it more difficult for them to develop an understanding and to foster feelings of ownership.

Step 4: Assess the Maturity Level of IT Capabilities

The reputation for developing software plagued with deficiencies has put pressure on the IT industry over the years to convert software development from an art into a science. Arguably the most successful development to date beyond the systems development life cycle and structured design has been the CMM framework. Not only is this the most widely accepted standard in North America for software development, but many companies insist on dealing with only those IT shops that can demonstrate a level of quality management prescribed by it.

Today the CMM approach has been applied to many tasks in addition to software development. The five CMM levels for software development are as follows:[2]

Level 1 (initial). Software development follows few rules. The project may go from one crisis to the next. The success of the project depends on the skills of individual developers. They may need to finish the project in a heroic effort.

Level 2 (repeatable). Software development successes are repeatable. The organization may use some basic project management to track cost and schedule. The precise implementation differs from project to project within the organization.

Level 3 (defined). Software development across the organization uses the same rules and events for project management. Crucially, the organization follows the same process even under schedule pressures, ideally because management recognizes that it is the fastest way to finish.

---

[2]www.sei.cmu.edu/pub/documents/02.reports/pdf/02tr011.pdf.

Level 4 (managed).   Using precise measurements, management can effectively control the software development effort. In particular, management
can identify ways to adjust and adapt the process to particular projects
without measurable losses of quality or deviations from specifications.

Level 5 (optimizing).   Quantitative feedback from previous projects is used to
improve project management, using the measurement skills shown in level 4.

While some organizations have adopted these CMM maturity levels, others have
created their own levels. Obviously, the definition of each maturity level must be tailored to a specific IT capability as the above definitions pertain to only software development. One company uses the following six levels:

1. *No capability.*   No observable value added
2. *Aware.*   Clear understanding of need
3. *Developing.*   Defined action plan and actively engaged
4. *Practicing.*   Demonstrating and achieving value
5. *Optimizing.*   Measuring results and investing in continual improvement
6. *Leading.*   Recognized proficiency and consistent value contribution

As long as a capability's maturity levels are well defined, the group felt that the
framework is immaterial. They agreed it is more important that the maturity levels used
be effective in assessing capabilities and driving continuous improvement. It was widely
recognized that not all processes within a capability would be at the same maturity level
at any given point in time. What does it mean for a capability if some of its component
processes are at a maturity level 2 while others are at a maturity level 3? Again, participants felt it is more important to have measurable improvement than uniformity across
and within capabilities (i.e., all component processes at the same maturity level).

It is crucial that the capability management office has a snapshot of the overall
maturity of each capability in order to focus attention correctly. At one company a
team of senior managers reviews each capability's maturity to identify high-priority
process improvement areas. They then develop a plan for the advancement of these
highlighted processes, establish a timeline, and hold individuals accountable against
delivery of these improvements. At another organization each capability is assigned
an executive owner who is tasked to meet measurable objectives regarding the maturity of his or her capability. A quarterly report outlines the capability's current state
and desired future state, timelines for deliverables, a description of overall progress
and performance, as well as a gap assessment (HR, budget, information/tools/tech-
nology, schedule, quality, sustainability, and measurement). An interesting aspect of
this report (reproduced in Table 15.2) is its usage of verbal descriptions in combination with quantitative indicators. Furthermore, each capability owner must articulate
*what will be different about the organization's performance as a result of having this future
state capability.* This unique requirement forces each capability owner to link his or
her capability directly to a distinct organizational outcome. This exercise has proven
invaluable for ensuring that any improvements in the maturity of IT capabilities
have associated business impact.

A key question for IT executives is this: What level of maturity should we target
for our capabilities? There was general consensus that IT vendors are likely forced to
"aim high," while other companies might be satisfied with midrange maturity. One
manager suggested his company felt that the gain in moving from level 2 to level 3

TABLE 15.2 IT Capability Progress and Performance Chart

IT Capability	e.g., Portfolio management		
Operational Definition	Written description of this particular capability		
Owner	Name of the individual		
Future End State Vision	Describes what will be different about IT performance as a result of having this future state capability	POD[3] 5	POA 8
		Impact	P&P
	Process 1: Description	Medium	S
End-of-Year Deliverables	Process 2: Description	High	N
	Process n: Description	Low	S
Overall Progress and Performance	What did you plan to get done this quarter, and what did get done? If there is variance, what was the source of the error?		

Gap Assessment[6]

	Process 1	Process 2	Process n	Explanation[7]
Human Resources	G	Y	G	***
Budget	Y	Y	G	***
Information/Tools/Technology	G	G	G	
Schedule	G	G	G	
Quality	G	R	Y	***
Sustainability	G	G	Y	***
Measurement	G	G	G	

[3]POD is "point of departure" (i.e., your current state) on a scale of one to ten.

[4]POA is "point of arrival" (i.e., your end state) on a scale of one to ten.

[5]P&P is "pace and performance," where "S" is satisfactory and "N" is not satisfactory.

[6]G = green, Y = yellow, and R = red.

[7]Detailed explanation required for any row that isn't "green."

on the maturity index was significant but the gain in moving higher was substantially reduced, suggesting that capability maturity levels could be subject to the "law of diminishing returns."

Step 5: Link IT Skills to IT Capabilities

The final part of the framework for IT capability development is the link between skills and capabilities. Failure to do this results in a significant disconnect between individuals and capabilities and a belief that individuals have little to do with capability maturity beyond that of following the dictates of established procedures. This is surprising in light of the fact that even a cursory glance at the processes within Table 15.1 reveals that many are very closely related to individual skills. Interestingly, only one company in the group had explicitly addressed this issue. Others, despite being well advanced in terms of identifying key processes and mapping them onto capabilities, chose indirect methods for tying individual skills to key capabilities.

Feeny and Willcocks (1998) identify three types of IT skills: (1) business, (2) technical, and (3) interpersonal. For each of their nine key capabilities, they then ranked the need for each type of skill as being high, medium, or low. An IT leadership capability, for example, requires a high level of business skills, a medium level of technical skills, and a high level of interpersonal skills. How these skills are to be developed, assessed, and linked to individuals and/or career development was not discussed.

The sole company that had addressed this issue created matrices to map individual skills (such as "conceptual thinking") against roles (such as "application architect" or "business analyst"). Different levels of these skills would be needed for particular roles; for instance, a level 3 business analyst would require greater mastery of each requisite skill than a level 2 business analyst. When roles are mapped to processes and processes are mapped to capabilities, it is possible to connect individuals to the capabilities that have been identified as being critical for the IT organization. Furthermore, these matrices make the progression between levels within roles explicit and, therefore, the focus of annual performance reviews and career advancement discussions. In this company a number of communities of practice had been established to further disseminate key skills throughout the organization (e.g., a business analyst community).

In those companies without direct links between individual skills and key IT capabilities, indirect links exist. In one firm, process improvement was made everyone's job. Anyone in the organization was encouraged to "raise a process improvement." These initiatives were maintained within a process improvement database and reviewed on a quarterly basis by a senior management team. This initiative successfully engaged individuals in terms of their awareness of the need for continuous process improvement. Another organization included organizational process skills within its internal training programs for job roles. This ensured awareness and knowledge of key processes across the IT department. The key point is that individuals must be connected (either directly or indirectly) to the process of developing IT capabilities.

CONCLUSION

The improvement of IT capabilities and processes within organizations will undoubtedly result in enhanced benefits from IT investments. Improving performance on such activities as solution delivery and asset management alone promises substantial results. When IT departments take the next step and identify those capabilities and processes that are vital to the business and develop those capabilities and processes to advanced maturity levels, the rewards promise to be dramatic. This chapter sets out a step-by-step framework that should assist IT organizations in reaching this goal.

REFERENCES

Feeney, D. F., and L. Willcocks. "Core IS Capabilities for Exploiting Information Technology." *Sloan Management Review* 39, no. 3 (1998): 9–21.

Gomolski, B. "It's Time to Re-engineer IT." *Computerworld* 38, no. 16 (April 19, 2004): 30.

Rockart, J. F., M. J. Earl, and J. W. Ross. "Eight Imperatives for the New IT Organization." *Sloan Management Review* 38 (Fall 1996): 43–55.

Ross, J. W., C. M. Beath, and D. L. Goodhue. "Develop Long-term Competitiveness through IT Assets." *Sloan Management Review* 38 (Fall 1996): 31–42.

Weill, P. "The Relationship between Investment in Information Technology and Firm Performance in the Manufacturing Sector." Unpublished PhD thesis, Stern School, NYU, 1989.

Chapter 16

IT Sourcing

Outsourcing is now a widely accepted part of doing business. In IT, companies are outsourcing everything from operations and help desks to maintenance and development. What started as a mechanism largely to lower costs has become an integral part of a much larger IT strategy. IT departments are finding that outsourcing gives them access to a wider range of skilled resources, helps them focus on their core strengths, and speeds the time to market of products and services. Lower operational costs, reduced up-front investment, and the ability to convert fixed to variable costs also make outsourcing an attractive option for some IT services.

As they have gained experience with outsourcing, IT organizations have learned to do it more effectively—to better manage the relationships, risks, benefits, and outcomes involved. As a result, interest in outsourcing is growing, although a recent study found there is still considerable reluctance to use it (Mackie 2002). Clearly, outsourcing has found a place in the IT executive's toolkit.

The danger now is complacency. Thinking that they have a handle on outsourcing, IT managers could fail to consider newer forms of outsourcing, different options, different strategies, and/or changing economies. Certainly, there are new players on the horizon and new approaches to sourcing looming that will change yet again how IT sourcing decisions are made. Some of these include strategic sourcing practices; offshore contracting; and nearshore sourcing using companies based in India, Ireland, Asia, and Eastern Europe. Better connectivity, the availability of high-quality staff, and much lower costs are changing sourcing markets and expanding sourcing possibilities for companies.

In previous research we examined outsourcing through application service providers (ASPs) and concluded the following:

> The emerging external IT services marketplace offers rich opportunities and many possibilities for IT organizations to become more cost effective . . .
> Strategic business applications development and management for mission-critical applications will [continue to] be in-house, but delivery for standard and meta-industry applications, processes and technology will be off-site. Thus . . . it is likely that external IT providers will form part of [a] future

service delivery package . . . However, as is so often the case in the IT industry, today's reality falls far short of what the industry promises. Companies wishing to take advantage now of what the external IT services marketplace can offer must evaluate [it] carefully and . . . proceed in full awareness of the risks involved. It is recommended that organizations articulate a sourcing strategy which balances internal versus external capabilities. (McKeen and Smith 2003)

This chapter first explores how sourcing strategy is evolving in organizations. Then it looks at emerging sourcing models, with particular emphasis on offshore/nearshore outsourcing. Next it discusses some new critical success factors for effective sourcing. Finally, it looks at how the role of IT itself is changing as a result.

THE EVOLUTION OF SOURCING

The concept of outsourcing IT services—that is, transferring some or all of a company's IT activities to a third party that performs them on behalf of the enterprise—has been a significant factor in IT decision making since the early 1990s (Lacity and Willcocks 2001). Globally, the outsourcing industry was estimated to be more than $1 trillion in 2000 (Kern, Lacity, and Willcocks 2002). It is growing steadily as companies explore new possible sourcing models and outsourcing companies become better at what they do and expand the range of their services. At first, sourcing decisions were driven largely by economics, with outsourcers promising to remove millions of dollars from a firm's IT budget. However, today they reflect a significant shift in business strategy from diversification to a focus on core competencies. In turn, evolving sourcing models are transforming the underlying economics of IT (Lacity and Willcocks 2001).

As our understanding of sourcing has developed, three distinct yet complementary approaches have emerged:

1. *Outsourcing for operational efficiency.* This is the most well-established approach to sourcing, dating from the early 1990s, and is still by far the most common one, according to researchers (Lacity and Willcocks 2001). Here the "utility" functions of IT (e.g., computer operations, communications, infrastructure, and help desk) are transferred to an outsourcer, often along with company staff. The objective is to save money by sharing staff and resources with other companies in areas that do not make the company distinct and that have become routinized (Carr 2003). Outsourcing companies are typically autonomous entities that use their extensive experience in these areas, economies of scale, and the discipline of a contractual relationship to reduce the overall cost to a company while generating a profit for themselves. Many organizations have found that outsourcing to businesses that specialize in these services allows them to offer the same or better service at a reduced cost. Over time, this form of sourcing has become increasingly successful as companies have learned how to negotiate and manage contracts to make outsourcing work.

2. *Outsourcing for tactical support.* In the late 1990s, companies recognized that outsourcing could be used to help free up their own IT staff to perform selected support

and development work and eliminate some of the peaks and valleys of the IT staffing cycle. "We are always under continual pressure to reduce the cost of our existing applications," stated one manager. "We spend 85 percent of our development budget on maintenance and support." Facing the dual challenges of Y2K and the dot-com bubble, and the resulting staff shortages they caused, many businesses began to use outsourcing in new ways. They offloaded their mature IT to an outsourcer who could "keep the lights on" while company staff introduced new applications. They also used outsourcers as a way to introduce new technologies quickly (e.g., e-business) through such practices as managed hosting of a Web site and using outsourced staff to transfer their experience and skills to in-house staff. With this approach to sourcing, IT managers seek to rapidly add to their capacity to deliver applications and new technology to their organizations (Lacity and Willcocks 2001). While cost is still important, the primary driver for using tactical outsourcing is to achieve flexibility and responsiveness. As tactical outsourcing has developed, contracts have become more flexible and outsourcers have come to be viewed increasingly as partners who can add other forms of value rather than simply reducing cost.

3. *Outsourcing for strategic impact.* The beginning of the new century saw a growing recognition that sourcing can be a tool for achieving an organization's strategic objectives as well as driving costs down and adding capacity. As companies have become more focused on their core competencies, new possibilities for sourcing have opened up. With greater connectivity, it is now possible to outsource whole business processes that are not considered business critical. Noncore applications (e.g., accounting) can languish in-house because they cannot justify the same business value as other projects. By outsourcing these processes, companies can get full functionality without having to develop the applications themselves. Some organizations are using outsourcing to drive organizational change. "Today we consider outsourcing at a higher level," explained a manager. "We look at sourcing holistically. While you still need to outsource routine activities, you also need to look at it from the top down. Sourcing shouldn't be an ad hoc process." Companies are seeing that outsourcing can give them access to world-class capabilities, disciplines, quality, and innovation. To this end, some have established strategic alliances with a few vendors to take advantage of what they can offer. These preferred relationships are typically broad in scope and complex in nature and are designed to deliver significant business value (Smith and McKeen 2003). "Our supplier alliances are now part of getting any project approved," said another manager. "We must present the full continuum of sourcing options in any business case." Finally, organizations are learning that "right-sourcing" (i.e., choosing the right sourcing option for a given activity) can change with time. Certain functions that have been outsourced can become business critical, while others that were deemed core can now be outsourced. One manager explained, "In our company we are constantly testing what should be outsourced. The business has to be fully engaged in the process so they understand the implications." While strategic sourcing is a trend, it is a very recent one and companies have very little experience doing it. The focus group suggested moving carefully into this area until more is known about how to accomplish it successfully. Members also cautioned that customers should watch for hidden costs at this level (e.g., the need for integration by the customer) that can be quite expensive and could kill a business case for this type of sourcing.

TABLE 16.1 Three Complementary Approaches to IT Sourcing

APPROACH	DRIVER	MODE	ACTIVITIES	RELATIONSHIP
Operational Effectiveness	Cost reduction	Utility	Infrastructure, operations, support	Fee-for-service
Tactical Support	Capacity, flexibility	Service delivery	Mature technology, new technology	Partnership
Strategic Impact	Focus, business value	Toolkit	Processes, transformation, innovation	Strategic alliance

Each of these three approaches to sourcing represents an increase in the size, scope, and impact of what is sourced. Table 16.1 summarizes these approaches. It should be stressed that one does not preclude the other. Companies tend to begin outsourcing for operational efficiency and move toward tactical and strategic approaches as they gain experience and confidence at each level.

Companies have become quite good at basic utility, fee-for-service sourcing. In fact, by far the majority of sourcing is of this type (Lacity and Willcocks 2001). All of the companies in the focus group had some sourcing initiatives to improve operational efficiency, although none had completely outsourced their services, even at this level. Overall, studies show that about 38 percent of IT functions have now been outsourced to vendors (Barthelemy 2001).

Research has also identified five factors that are critical to the success of *current* outsourcing initiatives:

1. *Use selective sourcing.* Careful selection of what to outsource and what to retain in-house is a demonstrably more effective approach than total outsourcing or total insourcing. Companies find it more controllable and satisfactory as well as considerably less risky (Chen, Tu, and Lin 2002).
2. *Have joint business-IT sponsorship.* When both the business and IT executives are involved in making outsourcing decisions, the results are far more likely to meet expectations than when either group acts alone (Lacity and Willcocks 2001).
3. *Ensure a thorough comparison with internal operations.* Too often companies don't get expected savings because they forget to include or identify the hidden costs involved in outsourcing such as extra maintenance or consulting fees when problems arise (Overby 2003b).
4. *Develop a detailed contract.* Tighter contracts with carefully thought-out flexibility, evolution, and reversibility clauses lead to more successful sourcing (Barthelemy 2001).
5. *Limit the length of the contract.* Short-term contracts (one to three years) are more likely to be successful than mid- or long-term contracts. This is because they involve less uncertainty, motivate supplier performance, help ensure a fair market price for services, and enable recovery from mistakes more quickly (Lacity and Willcocks 2001).

In spite of all that has been learned, between 14 percent and 78 percent of outsourcing functions are deemed failures (Barthelemy 2001; Overby 2003b) and repatriating functions is becoming more and more common (Overby 2003b). A major reason for this huge discrepancy in success rates is that companies are experimenting with increasingly more radical options to extend outsourcing models, thereby moving into areas of higher risk.

OFFSHORE AND NEARSHORE OUTSOURCING: EMERGING SOURCING MODELS

In addition to outsourcing larger and more complex chunks of work (e.g., innovation, business processes) and developing more complex relationships with vendors (i.e., strategic outsourcing), companies are also working with vendors at increasingly greater distances, typically in other countries. Known as *offshore outsourcing* (or simply *offshoring*), the primary driver for this sourcing model and its many variations is economic (Aron 2003; Kripalani and Engardio 2003). The increasing globalization of large companies and the need for global processes is also a factor (Chen, Tu, and Lin 2002). Vendors located in other countries, such as India, can charge a fraction of what it costs to provide the same service in the United States. Facilitated by ever-greater connectivity; ubiquitous, cheap bandwidth; and Web technologies, companies can afford to knit together people, processes, and platforms in different ways than have been possible previously (Aron 2003). Forrester Research has found that 44 percent of Fortune 1000 companies are offshoring some activities (cited in Blackwell 2003).

According to Chen, Tu, and Lin (2002), IT organizations are unclear about how offshoring fits into a company's overall sourcing strategy and are even less clear about how to make it successful. Undoubtedly, global outsourcing represents a significant shift in how organizations manage their IT activities (Elmuti and Kathawala 2000). Therefore, today's IT managers are approaching it cautiously and building on what they have learned about other forms of outsourcing. "There is certainly a lot of hype about offshore outsourcing," said one, "but we're still skeptical about its benefits. We had a bad experience ten years ago. The level of professionalism and understanding just wasn't there, so it didn't work." Nevertheless, the cost differentials and the "hype" are forcing everyone to look seriously at offshoring as part of their sourcing strategy.

Offshore Outsourcing Benefits

It is cheaper to do IT work outside the United States. Even doing work in Canada can be a reduced cost for many United States–based firms. However the big savings come from sending work to third-world countries, where salaries are 40 to 60 percent lower than in North America. Most of these countries have significant numbers of well-trained professionals and offer considerable tax breaks.[1] As a result, even with additional travel and connectivity charges, companies are expecting to save 20 to 40 percent on costs such as managing infrastructure or operating a help desk (Bhandari 2003). The differentials are so significant, the increased competition is also driving

---

[1] There are more IT engineers in Bangalore alone than there are in Silicon Valley (Kripalani and Engardio, 2003).

down the rates of traditional North American outsourcing vendors (Blackwell 2003). These vendors are also setting up centers in India so they can compete more effectively (Kripalani and Engardio 2003).

Typical activities that are being sourced offshore include help desk, personal computer repair, disaster recovery, back office processes, application maintenance, network management and operations, application and IT support, and problem resolution (Chordas 2003). These are relatively routine and straightforward utility types of functions that many companies feel very comfortable in outsourcing. Thus, in moving these functions offshore, they are limiting risk while taking advantage of the resulting cost benefits. However, many offshore outsourcers, especially in India, are also seeking to scale up the types of activities in which they are involved. Quality standards in India, for example, are often higher than in North America (Blackwell 2003). In many cases Indian companies have better software and risk management processes and have been among the first in the world to achieve the highest SEI CMM rating of five (Satyam 2003). These firms are seeking a larger presence in the high-end software development and consulting areas of the market (i.e., tactical and strategic outsourcing). Big vendors, such as Oracle, Accenture, and Microsoft, are also establishing partnerships and software development centers in India to take advantage not only of the cost savings involved, but also of the skills available (Blackwell 2003).

Offshore Outsourcing Locations

While 85 percent of offshore outsourcing work currently goes to India, several other countries are looking to increase their share of this work. China, Russia, and the Philippines are the most serious competition, although they are far behind India at present (Overby 2003a). Canada is also involved in this market because of its proximity to the United States, even though it is more expensive than other offshore vendors. Ireland, Israel, Mexico, and South Africa are also positioning themselves in this market. Forrester Research predicts that by 2015, about 3.3 million jobs will have moved offshore—70 percent to India, 20 percent to the Philippines, and 10 percent to China (cited in Chordas 2003).

While all of these countries offer reduced or substantially lower costs, they are not considered equal in other important characteristics, which should be considered before a company makes a significant outsourcing decision. These factors include language, cultural similarities, time differentials, political stability, quality, project management skills, education, and infrastructure. Table 16.2 summarizes these for the five main countries involved in offshore sourcing with the United States.

Offshore Outsourcing Risks

As Table 16.2 shows, offshoring involves considering a number of factors, such as language and political stability, which have not traditionally been part of outsourcing decision making. Comments from practicing IT managers clearly illustrate some of the risks involved.

> "We outsourced a call center to India and then brought it back. There were problems with the time to transfer calls, language, and spelling. The accents weren't bad, but there was often poor understanding on the phone."

TABLE 16.2 A Comparison of Offshore Outsourcing Nations

COUNTRY	LANGUAGE	CULTURAL SIMILARITIES	TIME DIFFERENTIAL	POLITICAL STABILITY	PROJECT MANAGEMENT SKILLS	EDUCATION	INFRASTRUCTURE
Canada	English	Many	None	Excellent	Very good	Excellent	Excellent
India	Good English	Some	Large	Good	Excellent	Excellent	Improving
China	Limited English	Few	Large	Good	Unknown	Good	Good
Philippines	Good English	Some	Large	Good	Unknown	Good	Very good
Russia	Limited English	Few	Large	Fair	Poor	Good	Unknown

(after Chordas 2003; Damsell 2003; Gallagher 2002; Overby 2003a)

"We outsourced project management and then lost all their interfaces with the users when they left. Now we have 100 percent internal project management."

"We outsourced our help desk. It was brutal. We had the mix wrong. We needed more decomposition of activities and a more granular understanding of what we were doing."

A number of additional risks must also be addressed as part of the offshore outsourcing decision-making process:

- *Hidden costs.*   These include the cost of finding a vendor, drafting the contract, and managing the effort, as well as the cost of transitioning to a new vendor if the first doesn't work out. Monitoring, bargaining, and negotiating needed changes to a contract typically add up to about 8 percent of the yearly contract amount (Barthelemy 2001). Travel and visa costs are also often substantial (Blackwell 2003). As a result, many companies are finding they are not achieving the savings they anticipated (Elmuti and Kathawala 2000).

- *Reduced control.*   While outsourcing in general reduces an organization's control over how its services are delivered, offshore sourcing can greatly increase these risks because the vendors operate in substantially different business environments. A company may, therefore, have greater liability exposure and face problems with such issues as confidentiality, security, and time schedules (Elmuti and Kathawala 2000).

- *Legal and political uncertainties.*   Working in other countries means dealing with a wide variety of unfamiliar government regulations and restrictions, legal systems that may be unable to cope with the types of disputes that may arise between companies or between companies and the government, and weak intellectual property rights (Overby 2003b). Furthermore, governments in third-world countries may be considerably less secure than in North America or Europe. India has lost work recently due to the instabilities in that part of the world following the attacks of September 11, 2001.

- *Cultural differences.* Different cultural backgrounds can cause numerous difficulties. In addition to language problems, such matters as the pace of daily life, employees' relationship to authority, attitudes to security, and adherence to socialist principles can lead to misunderstandings that can be daunting (Overby 2003b).
- *Social justice.* Practicing IT managers were also very aware of the "optics" of offshore outsourcing. "Public perceptions are important to us," stated one. Another manager noted that his company has a labor code of conduct and a risk rating for different countries that assesses their labor practices and other dimensions of risk. Government organizations in particular are especially sensitive to the issues of moving jobs out of the country. For example, a recent public outcry forced the state of Indiana to cancel a $15 million contract with a firm in India (Kripalani and Engardio 2003).

Variations in Offshore Outsourcing Models

Some of these risks and concerns are forcing vendors and companies to rethink the basic offshore outsourcing model. Some are distinguishing between offshore and nearshore sourcing. Not only are some U.S. vendors setting up sourcing centers in Canada, but some Indian firms are doing so as well. For example, Satyam Computer Services has recently opened a development center in Toronto to ensure that North American clients can "deal with a company that's always close to home, close to their unique needs" (Satyam 2003). While much work can be actually completed in India, having relationship managers and business analysis in closer proximity to their customers provides additional security and mitigates many of the risks mentioned above.

Other companies are looking at nearshore opportunities in lower-cost areas of their own countries. One Canadian firm is using nearshore sourcing to move development work to New Brunswick—a province with cheaper labor. Several Native American reservations have gone into the sourcing business as well. They argue that they can offer the same low-cost, high-value work that is done offshore but without the headaches of language barriers, remote management, or security concerns (Field 2001). These options are particularly attractive for sensitive legal and government work that should not be sent overseas.

Other firms are finding that they can get many of the benefits of offshore sourcing by working with a major vendor who will undertake to manage the offshore work and relationships. "You can have global options if you pick your vendor carefully," said one. "We triage our projects with our partner to find the best sourcing choice possible."

Sourcing today is actually a continuum of practices that can be "sliced and diced many different ways," depending on the needs of the company and the particular activity involved. Partnerships with key vendors are especially important in these situations so they can optimize the blend of internal and external staff appropriately. "You shouldn't go with a one-off project offshore," one manager explained, but rather with a carefully designed strategy that enables experimentation with different sourcing models and includes the ability to reverse a sourcing decision if it doesn't work out.

Successful Sourcing

As experience with sourcing increases, organizations are learning more about what it takes to manage sourcing successfully. However, although some critical success factors are well established (see above), as new models of sourcing emerge and as sourcing takes on a more central part of IT and organizational strategy, understanding what is involved in successful sourcing is still evolving. The focus group identified several factors that are essential in its effective management.

Sample Sourcing Criteria

What are our industry dynamics, and where are we in the food chain?	What should we be good at?
What are we good at?	Do we want to invest in this function/ activity?
What do we want to be good at?	How many vendors do we want to deal with?

Sourcing Strategy

Whether a company uses sourcing strategically or not, every organization should have an overall sourcing strategy. This helps it determine what to source, where to source, and to whom to source. Experts have suggested many different ways of determining what to source—what's core and what's not, contribution to business value, maturity of technology, activities that are routine and less knowledge intensive, and entry-level functions (Aron 2003; Barthelemy 2001; Lacity and Willcocks 2001). In practice, however, there are numerous possible approaches to "right-sourcing." What is right for one organization is not necessarily right for another. Companies should consider the following:

1. First develop an in-depth understanding of their business drivers and strategy before developing a sourcing strategy.
2. Then IT managers should develop a detailed understanding of their functions, processes, and the overall IT portfolio. Without this, it is possible that too much or too little could be outsourced, leading to significant problems.
3. Then they should apply their particular sourcing criteria to IT activities (see box) to determine which parts of IT can be successfully sourced.
4. Finally, the sourcing strategy must be continually tested and reevaluated as the industry, business strategy, and sourcing possibilities change frequently.

Risk Management/Mitigation

"War stories" abound. Every firm can cite examples of activities that had to be resourced to a different vendor, tasks that needed to be reinsourced, or contracts that were renegotiated because of problems. The fact is sourcing introduces new levels of risk to the organization. Loss of control, security and privacy problems, poor-quality work, hidden costs, lack of standards, unmet expectations, and bad publicity are just some of the problems that have been experienced. When moving into new forms of sourcing, it is important to incorporate risk management and mitigation into every aspect of sourcing.

1. Detailed planning is essential. Precise definitions of roles, responsibilities, and expectations must be developed. Specialists in outsourcing are now available to provide advice on how to select a vendor and plan the work involved. They can assist—but not replace—the IT sourcing team in understanding how to assess and engage a vendor. This is especially important when considering offshore sourcing because of the additional complexities involved.
2. Monitoring and an audit trail must be incorporated into the contract to both encourage self-correction and ensure all parties live up to their commitments.
3. All potential risks should be rated as to both the likelihood of occurrence and their impact if they do occur (Aubert et al. 2001). Appropriate steps should be explicitly taken to reduce and/or manage these risks.
4. An exit strategy must be devised. "Any well-designed sourcing strategy must retain alternatives to pull activities back in-house," explained one manager.
5. Finally, exercise caution when moving into new avenues of sourcing. The "hype" in the popular press often originating from vendors greatly inflates the benefits that can be achieved while minimizing the risks. It is recommended that you experiment with a "simple, substantial pilot" before committing the company to a significant new outsourcing initiative.

Governance

"With any sourcing initiative, governance must be super-good," said a manager. Most IT functions now recognize the importance of relationship management at all levels (i.e., the frontline, middle, and senior management) in delivering value. Nevertheless, it cannot be underestimated. "When the relationship between the client and its vendor is adversarial, the vendor will take advantage of gaps in the agreement. When there is mutual trust, vendors often work hard to deal fairly with the gaps" (Barthelemy 2001). "Layers of governance are critical to successful sourcing relationships," said one manager. Others also suggested retaining strong internal project management and ensuring that vendors also have these skills. "You can't outsource project management or the relationship with the customer," they agreed. Governance problems are exacerbated when offshore sourcing is undertaken because of the difficulties of managing relationships at a distance (Chordas 2003). This is one reason the larger offshore vendors are setting up local development centers. At minimum, an offshore outsourcer should name an internal manager who will act as the organization's champion and be responsible for quality assurance. Ideally, an outsourcing relationship should be structured to ensure shared risk so both parties are incented to make it work (Garr 2001).

Cost Structures

One of the most important elements of successful sourcing is a complete understanding of the cost structures involved. Previously, vendors have profited from their ability to squeeze value from outsourced activities because they had a better and more detailed appreciation of their costs. Furthermore, they were able to apply disciplines and service-level agreements to their work, which IT organizations were often prohibited from doing (Lacity and Willcocks 2001). Today this is changing. Companies are applying the same standards to their own work, enabling them to make more appropriate comparisons between the costs of doing an activity in-house and outsourcing it. They also have a better understanding of the true costs of outsourcing, including relationship management and contract management, which have frequently been underestimated in the past. "We need to thoroughly understand our economic model," said one participant. "Vendors have the advantage of knowing best practices and economies of scale, but they are at a disadvantage from a profit and knowledge point of view. If we can't compete in-house, we should outsource." Interestingly, many companies believe they can compare favorably in many areas with outsourcing vendors. Ongoing cost comparisons are ideal, according to researchers, because they motivate both parties to do their best and most cost-effective work (Lacity and Willcocks 2001). The reduced cost of labor is simply one element of the outsourcing value proposition. "We must learn to understand and track *every* cost involved," said an IT manager. "There are new governance costs; privacy, legal, and regulatory costs; and other hidden costs that have to be articulated and monitored." The need to better understand the total cost of ownership of each IT activity is forcing managers to become considerably more aware of the financial implications of their decisions and develop a whole new set of skills as a result.

THE CHANGING ROLE OF IT

New IT Roles and Responsibilities

- Solution delivery
- Task decomposition
- Task costing analysis
- Right-sourcing decision making

- Designing for collaboration and connectivity
- Supplier relationship management
- Contract management and monitoring
- Sourcing marketplace analysis

The growth of sourcing over the past decade has led to a number of new roles for IT managers and has changed the relative importance of key IT skills. As lower-level IT activities are outsourced, what is increasingly left behind is the high-value-added work that only knowledgeable, in-house IT practitioners can provide. "The development skills we need these days are not coding, but integration, business analysis, and project management. We need to hone these skills to do the jobs that are difficult to outsource," explained one manager. While important pieces of development can be done off-site, it is still IT's job to put all the pieces together and make technology work for the enterprise. In short, organizations need to improve their solution delivery skills, which is by no means a straightforward or simple task.

Systems thinking skills are becoming increasingly critical as well. They are fundamental to the detailed decomposition of tasks, which is the first step in better understanding both cost structures and the relative strategic importance of each task. IT organizations also need more formal processes and decision-making frameworks within which to tackle the key sourcing questions of what to outsource and how it should be done. These should include the parts of the business that will be affected by outsourcing and involve both tactical and strategic discussions with business management.

Emerging sourcing models will also need to be incorporated into the organization's technology plans as well as its business strategies. IT architectures must be designed for greater connectivity and collaboration across organizational boundaries. They should anticipate a wide variety of possible options in how the company's processes and transactions will be undertaken.

Finally, IT organizations are recognizing that they need new management skills, governance structures, and organizational processes to make outsourcing work effectively. Several companies now have a "supplier relationship management" function, at a mid to senior management level, responsible for ensuring their outsourcing arrangements are working well. Similarly, they are learning how to develop effective sourcing contracts and monitor them, both for supplier compliance and for internal satisfaction (Smith and McKeen 2003). In the future they will also need skills to better analyze the external sourcing marketplace and their industry to select the most appropriate options for their organizations.

CONCLUSION

Sourcing has become an integral part of almost all IT organizations today. Originally a straightforward mechanism for reducing operational costs, it is rapidly evolving into a strategically important means of delivering optimal IT value. At present, companies and vendors are experimenting with new models of sourcing, only some of which will be sustainable. Increasingly, it is IT's job to guide the organization in making the best sourcing decisions possible and to ensure that it is obtaining the anticipated value from its vendor relationships. This involves developing new IT skills that incorporate an understanding of technology with strong business knowledge and analytic capabilities. As a result, while sourcing is changing the nature of the work that is done internally in IT, it is unlikely that it will eliminate this function altogether or reduce its value to that of a utility, as has been suggested by some (e.g., Carr 2003). To the contrary, more and more organizations will need the systems thinking, architectural understanding, and strategic awareness embodied in a modern IT department in order to ensure that they don't end up with a hollow shell of an organization that provides limited added value.

REFERENCES

Aron, R. "Sourcing in the Right Light." *Optimize* June (2003): 26–34.

Aubert, B., M. Patry, S. Rivard, and H. A. Smith. "IT Outsourcing Risk Management at British Petroleum." Proceedings of the 34th Hawaii Conference on System Sciences, Maui, Hawaii, January 5–8, 2001.

Barthelemy, J. "The Hidden Costs of IT Outsourcing." *MIT Sloan Management Review* 42, no. 3 (Spring 2001): 60–69.

Bhandari, A. "'Near-shoring' India's IT Companies." *Toronto Star*, June 2, 2003.

Blackwell, G. "Sending It Offshore." *Edge* 2, no. 2 (February 2003).

Carr, N. "IT Doesn't Matter." *Harvard Business Review* May (2003).

Chen, Q., Q. Tu, and B. Lin. "Global IT/IS Outsourcing: Expectations, Considerations and Implications." *Advances in Competitiveness Research* 10, no. 1 (2002): 100–11.

Chordas, L. "Eyes on India." *Best's Review* 104, no. 1 (May 2003): 98–103.

Damsell, K. "Offshore Outsourcing Seen Reshaping the Tech Sector." *The Globe and Mail,* November 11, 2003.

Elmuti, D., and Y. Kathawala. "The Effects of Global Outsourcing Strategies on Participants' Attitudes and Organizational Effectiveness." *International Journal of Manpower* 21, no. 2 (2000): 112–28.

Field, T. "How to Get in and out of an Outsourcing Deal." *CIO* 15, no. 6 (December 15, 2001–January 1, 2002): 85–86.

Garr, D. "Inside Outsourcing." *Fortune: Technology Review* 143, no. 13 (Summer 2001): 85–92.

Gallagher, J. "Canada: New Outsourcing Option?" *Insurance and Technology* 27, no. 10 (September 2002): 9.

Kern, T., M. Lacity, and L. Willcocks. *Netsourcing: Renting Business Applications and Services over a Network.* Upper Saddle River, NJ: Pearson Education, 2002.

Kripalani, M., and P. Engardio. "The Rise of India." *BusinessWeek* December 8 (2003).

Lacity, M., and L. Willcocks. *Global Information Technology Outsourcing: In Search of Business Advantage.* Chichester, England: John Wiley & Sons, 2001.

Mackie, A. "Outsourcing Outlook." *Computer Dealer News* 18, no. 19 (October 18, 2002) www.itbusiness.ca (accessed February 10, 2004).

McKeen, J., and H. Smith. *Making IT Happen: Critical Issues in IT Management.* Chichester, England: John Wiley & Sons, 2003.

Overby, S. "Passages Beyond India." *CIO* 16, no. 6 (January 1, 2003a): 60–61.

———. "Bringing IT Back Home." *CIO* 16, no. 10 (March 1, 2003b): 54–56.

Satyam Computer Services Limited. Internal company document, Secunderabad, India, 2003.

Smith, H., and J. McKeen. "Strategic Sourcing at the Bank of Montreal." *The CIO Brief* 9, no. 2 (2003).

17

Delivering IT Functions: A Decision Framework[1]

In a recent article, it was pointed out how dramatically the list of IT responsibilities has grown over the past fifteen years (Smith and McKeen 2006). To the standard list of "operations management," "systems development," and "network management" have now been added responsibilities for "business transformation," "regulatory compliance," "enterprise and security architecture," "information and content management," and "business continuity management" as well as others. Never before has IT management been challenged to assume such diversity of responsibility and to deliver on so many different fronts. As a result, IT managers have begun to critically examine how they deliver their various functions to the organization.

In the past, organizations met additional demands for IT functionality by simply adding more staff. While this option remains available today, there are now several others for delivering IT functionality. Software can be purchased; customized systems can be developed by third parties; whole business processes can be outsourced; technical expertise can be contracted; data center facilities can be managed; networking solutions (e.g., data, voice) are obtainable; data storage is available on demand; and companies will manage your desktop environment as well as all of your support/maintenance functions. Faced with this smorgasbord of delivery options, organizations are experimenting as never before. As with other forms of experimentation, however, there have been failures as well as successes, and most decisions have been made on a "one-off" basis. What is still lacking is a unified decision framework to guide IT managers through this maze of delivery options.

This chapter explores how organizations are choosing to deliver IT functions. The first section defines what we mean by an IT *function* and proposes a maturity model for IT function delivery. Following this, it takes a conceptual look at IT delivery

---

[1]McKeen, J. D., and H. A. Smith, "Delivering IT Functions: A Decision Framework," *Communications of the Association of Information Systems* 19, article 35 (June 2007): 725–39 (reproduced by permission of the Association of Information Systems).

options. We then analyze actual company experiences with four different IT delivery options—(1) in-house, (2) insource, (3) outsource, and (4) partnership—in order to contrast theory with practice. The final section of the chapter presents a framework for guiding delivery decisions stemming from the shared experiences and insights of the managers in the focus group.

A MATURITY MODEL FOR IT FUNCTIONS

Smith and McKeen (2006) list the overall responsibilities for which IT is held accountable. IT functions, in contrast, represent the specific activities that are delivered by IT in the fulfillment of its responsibilities. For instance, IT is held *responsible* for delivering process automation, which it may satisfy by delivering the following IT *functions* to the organization: project management, architecture planning, business analysis, system development, quality assurance and testing, and infrastructure support. While there are myriad functions an IT department provides to its parent organization, a compendium of the key roles was created by amalgamating the lists provided by the members of the focus group (see Table 17.1).[2] This is meant to be representative, not comprehensive, to demonstrate how IT functions can form the basis of a decision framework.

Participants pointed out that not all IT functions are at the same stage of development and maturity, a fact that has ramifications for how these functions could be delivered. While some are well defined, common to most companies, and commoditylike, others are unique, nonstandardized, and not easily shared. There was general agreement, however, that a maturity model for IT function delivery has five stages: (1) unique, (2) common, (3) standardized, (4) commoditized, and (5) utility.

1. *Unique.* A unique IT function is one that provides strategic (perhaps even proprietary) advantage and benefit. These IT functions seek to differentiate the organization in the marketplace. They are commonly, but not necessarily, delivered by internal IT staff due to the strategic aspect of the function being provided. Alternately, the function may be provided either by "boutique" firms who create special-purpose applications or by firms with in-depth industry experience that cannot be matched by internal IT staff (or even the internal business managers). Examples of unique IT functions might be business analysis, application integration, or knowledge-enabling business processes. Such functions depend on familiarity with the organization's internal systems combined with an in-depth knowledge of the business.
2. *Common.* This type of IT function caters to common (i.e., universal) organizational needs. Such a function has little ability to differentiate the business, but it provides a necessary, perhaps critical, component (e.g., financial systems, HR). Providers capitalize on commonality of function and are motivated to provide

---

[2]We prefer the term *service* to *function*. We chose the term *function*, however, to avoid confusion with the current usage of *service* as in service-oriented architecture (SOA).

TABLE 17.1 List of IT Functions

IT Function	Description
Business Analysis	Liaison between IT and the business to align IT planning, match technology to business needs, and forecast future business directions
Systems Analysis	Elicits business requirements, designs process flow, outlines document management, and creates design specifications for developers
Strategy & Planning	Project prioritization, budgeting, financial planning/accountability, strategy development, policy development, and portfolio analysis
Data Management	Transactional data (e.g., invoicing, shipping), customer data (e.g., CRM), records management, knowledge management, business intelligence
Project Management	Managing the resources (e.g., money, people, time, equipment, etc.) necessary to bring a project to fruition in compliance with requirements
Architecture	Establishing the interaction of all system components (e.g., hardware, software, and networking), enterprise compliance with specifications and standards
Application Development	Designing, writing, documenting, and unit testing required code to enact specific functionality in compliance with a design specification
Quality Assurance & Testing	Testing all components of an application prior to production to ensure it is functioning correctly and meets regulatory and audit standards
Networking	Managing all networking components (e.g., hubs and routers) to handle all forms of organizational communication (e.g., data, voice, streaming video)
Operating Systems & Services	Operating systems for all hardware platforms and other devices (e.g., handhelds), upgrades, maintenance, and enhancements
Application Support	Provides enhancements, updates, and maintenance for application systems plus help and assistance for application users
Data Center Operations	Manages all operations of the production data center and data storage environment including backup, DRP, security and access, and availability
Application Software	Manages all major applications (e.g., purchased or developed) to ensure viability of functionality and upgradeability with a special emphasis on legacy systems
Hardware	Data servers, power supplies, desktops, laptops, Blackberries, telephones, and special equipment (e.g., POS, badge readers, RFID tags)

functions (e.g., CRM, quality assurance, content management) to maximize market applicability. Most print operations are now common functions, for instance. While they differ from firm to firm, they are required by most firms but are not considered to provide any competitive advantage.

3. *Standardized.* Standardized IT functions not only provide common tasks/activities, but also adhere to a set of standards developed and governed by external agencies. While multiple, perhaps competing, standards may exist, the attributes of such functions are well articulated, and as a result, these functions enjoy wide applicability due to their standardization. Providers of such functionality (e.g., billing/payment functions, check processing, forms management, facilities management, disaster recovery planning) seek opportunities beyond common functions by promoting (i.e., developing, proposing, and/or adopting) standards to enhance the interoperability of their functional offerings.

4. *Commoditized.* These functions are considered commodities similar to oil and gas. Once attributes are stipulated, functions are interchangeable and indistinguishable (i.e., any barrel of oil will suffice). Furthermore, there may be many

providers of the function. A good example is application service providers (ASPs) who deliver standard applications developed by third-party vendors to client firms without customization. Other commodity functions include network services, server farms, storage capacity, backup services, and UPS. What really distinguishes a commodity is the realization that the "risks imposed by its absence outweigh the burdens of maintaining its availability" (Marquis 2006).

5. **Utility.** A utility function is a commodity (such as electricity) delivered by a centralized and consolidated source.[3] This source typically consists of an amalgam of suppliers operating within an integrated network capable of generating sufficient resource to fulfill continuous on-demand requests. *Private* utilities operate in competition with other providers, whereas *public* utilities tend to be single providers overseen by regulatory agencies who govern supply, pricing, and size. Examples of utilities include Internet service providers (ISPs) as well as other telecommunication services (e.g., bandwidth on demand).

These stages represent an evolutionary progression (or maturation) in IT functionality. According to one manager, IT functions "migrate up the food chain." The logic is straightforward: successful, unique functions are copied by other organizations and soon become common; commonality among IT functions paves the way for standardization; standardized functions are easily and effectively transacted as commodities; and finally, commoditized functions can be provided by utilities should an attractive business model exist. The group interpreted this progression as an ongoing process; that is, individual functions would be expected to advance through the sequence of stages as they matured. Furthermore, the continual discovery of new and unique IT functions, which are required by organizations to differentiate themselves and create strategic advantage in the marketplace, would guarantee the continuation of the whole evolutionary progression as depicted below.

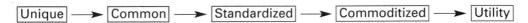

Using this maturity model, we then classified the IT functions listed in Table 17.1 according to their attained maturity stage. The results are represented in Figure 17.1. The differences among various IT functions are quite remarkable. Hardware (including servers and storage) was considered to reside at the commodity end of the maturity model due to its degree of standardization and interoperability, while business analysis remains a relatively unique IT function that differs considerably from organization to organization. Application software is more varied. As Figure 17.1 indicates, some application software is commoditylike, while other applications are highly unique to individual firms. The remaining IT functions vary similarly with respect to the maturity of their development and adoption industrywide.

---

[3]This concept has generated a significant amount of interest recently (Hagel and Brown 2001; Rappa 2004; Ross and Westerman 2004). Carr (2005), for example, speculates that not only is the utility computing model inevitable, but it will dramatically change the nature of the whole computing industry in like fashion to electrical generation of the previous century.

Figure 17.1 IT Functions Ranked by Maturity Stage

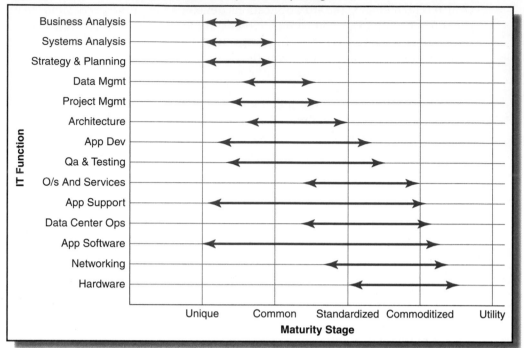

The impetus for this discussion of function maturity was an implicit assumption that mature functions would be likely candidates for external delivery, while unique functions would be likely candidates for internal delivery. According to Figure 17.1, functions such as hardware, networks, common applications, and data center operations would be natural candidates for external provisioning, while IT planning, business and systems analysis, project management, and application development would be more likely provided by internal IT staff. The group agreed that these were indeed *general* trends. What proved to be somewhat of a surprise, though, was the degree that this generalization did not appear to hold as members of the focus group repeatedly shared examples of their specific sourcing activities that ran counter to this generalization; for example, they insourced commoditized functions and outsourced unique functions. We will return to this point later.

IT DELIVERY OPTIONS: THEORY VERSUS PRACTICE

Building on classifications developed by Lacity and Willcocks (2000), there are four different delivery options for IT functions:

1. *In-house.* Permanent IT staff provide the IT function.
2. *Insource.* IT personnel are brought into the organization to supplement the existing permanent IT staff to provide the IT function.

Figure 17.2 Delivery Options for IT Functions

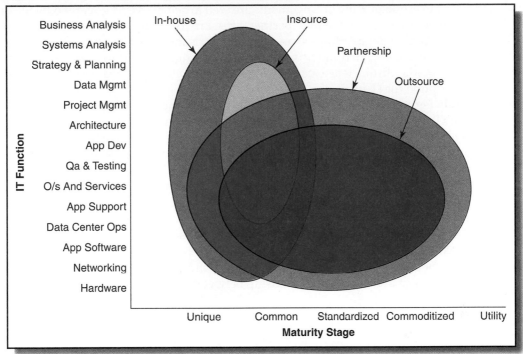

3. *Outsource.*   IT functions are provided by an external organization using its own staff and resources.
4. *Partnership.*   A partnership is formed with another organization to provide IT functions. The partnership could take the form of a joint venture or involve the creation of a separate company.

Figure 17.2 depicts the group's assessment of what the relationship between specific IT functions and delivery options *should be* and superimposes the four IT delivery options on the maturity grid. From this model it is clear that **in-house** staff should be assigned tasks that are in the unique-common maturity stages. Asking them to provide commoditylike functions would not be leveraging their unique knowledge of the business. Because of their versatility, they can provide any IT function. As a result, their area of application was seen as being on the left of Figure 17.2 from top to bottom. **Insourcing** is basically a strategy of leveraging the in-house IT staff on a temporary basis. As such, contract staff should normally be assigned to work with permanent IT staff on a subset of the full range of tasks provided internally. **Partnerships** tend to exist in the lower part of Figure 17.2 because the truly unique tasks of business/systems analysis, planning, data management, and project management tend to be limited to a single organization and its strategy. Instead, partnerships were envisioned to focus on functions such as hardware, applications, software, and networking. Such partnerships could form regardless of maturity stage, which explains the left-to-right positioning of this IT delivery option in Figure 17.2 Finally, **outsourcing** should comprise a subset of partnerships much the same as insourcing comprises a subset of in-house functions. The reason is due to differences in governance; outsourcing arrangements are well articulated and governed by SLAs (service-level agreements) while partnerships are typically governed by MOUs (memoranda of understanding). If an organization is interested in a more flexible, innovative, and open-ended initiative, it would be better advised to seek a joint venture with another firm. Hence, partnerships were seen to have broader potential as a delivery option for IT functions.

While Figure 17.2 represents the focus group's "generally accepted wisdom" regarding IT function delivery, the extent of the overlap of functions provided by the different delivery options is very pronounced. As such, Figure 17.2 provides limited guidance for managers tasked with choosing delivery options for specific IT functions. In order to gain more insight into decision behavior in practice, the group was then asked to share recent examples of IT functions they were currently delivering by each of the four delivery options. In addition, they were asked to describe the justification criteria that their firm used in making these decisions as well as the benefits they felt they had realized. These examples were subsequently analyzed and the results used to create Table 17.2.

Perhaps the most surprising result based on the examples in column 2 of Table 17.2 is the lack of evidence of a relationship between IT function and delivery option.

TABLE 17.2 Example Usage of the Four Delivery Options

DELIVERY OPTION	EXAMPLES	JUSTIFICATION	REALIZED BENEFITS
In-house	• Strategic system development • Legacy system support • New system development • Help desk/desktop support • Information/document management • Application support • Intranet development • Technology support • Business systems analysis • Project management • Security services (change control) • Business intelligence and reporting	• Need to have complete control over the intellectual property • Need it *now* • Work is strategic • Skunkworks • Internal consulting to the business	• High delivery speed • Leverage internal business and system knowledge • Ownership of intellectual property • Security of data • Protection and preservation of critical knowledge • Focus on core systems that are considered key assets
Insource	• Portal development • Specialized system (e.g., POS, CRM) development • Data warehouse development	• Need to have control over project delivery • Exposing intellectual property is not an issue	• Highly flexible (e.g., personnel, engagement, and assignments) • Best of multiple vendors can be used

TABLE 17.2 (*continued*)

DELIVERY OPTION	EXAMPLES	JUSTIFICATION	REALIZED BENEFITS
	• Database development • Intranet development • Corporate systems development • Contract staff to provide key skills • Both local contractors and offshore company on retainer	• Recurring program delivery such as ERP and CRM	• No need to expand internal IT staff • Staff easily meshed with existing teams • Semipermanent personnel if desired • Quick access to specific skill sets • Manage people as opposed to contracts • Evens out staffing "hills and valleys"
Outsource	• Infrastructure for new product • Business processes (e.g., billing, payroll) • Operations • Help desk • Field service support • Network management • Technology infrastructure (servers, storage, communications) • Web site development and hosting • Technology roll-out • New standalone project delivery	• The work is not "point of differentiation" • Company does not have the competency in-house • Deliverable is well understood, and SLAs are articulated to the satisfaction of both parties • The outsourcer is "world class"	• Speed to market for specific products/systems • Acquire instant expertise as vendors are experts (often world class) • Business risk is transferred to supplier • Outsourcer provides more "levers" for value creation (e.g., size, scope) • Lower cost than in-house
Partnership	• Common service (e.g., statement processing and payment services) • Emergency backup and support • Shared infrastructure • Special application development (e.g., critical knowledge requirement)	• Realize alignment on a benefit-sharing model • Enable collaborating partners to compete with others outside the partnership	• Future business growth and/or opportunities that arose from the partnership • Benefits were not limited to a specific product or system deliverable • Decreased learning time and shared learning costs with partners

Such a relationship, were it to exist, would provide a natural basis for a decision framework. However, not only does it not exist, but there is considerable evidence to the contrary (i.e., the observation that identical IT functions are being delivered by all four delivery options). As a case in point, various types of systems development as well as application support/maintenance functions are provided by all four delivery options. Earlier we noted the generally accepted wisdom that commodity functions are ready candidates for outsourcing, while unique functions are not, did not appear to hold up. The data in Table 17.2 further corroborates this observation. Given this, one wonders what the operative criteria for choosing delivery options are if not the type (or maturity) of the IT function.

THE "REAL" DECISION CRITERIA

In order to explore this issue, participants were asked to review a recent business case and to share the *actual* criteria that were used to select the specific IT delivery option. Column 3 in Table 17.2 illustrates the justifications used for each of the four delivery options. This paints a much clearer picture of the decision criteria being used by IT managers when selecting delivery options. Two key decision criteria, spanning the range of delivery options, are immediately evident: *flexibility* and *control*.

1. *Flexibility.* As a decision criterion, flexibility has two dimensions: response time (i.e., how quickly IT functionality can be delivered) and capability (i.e., the range of IT functionality). In-house staff rate high on both dimensions. Insourcing, as a complement to permanent IT staff, is also a highly flexible delivery option. While outsourcing can *theoretically* provide just about anything, as a delivery option it exhibits less flexibility because of the need to locate an outsourcer who can provide the specific function, negotiate a contract, and monitor progress. Finally, partnerships enjoy considerable flexibility regarding capability but much less in terms of response time.[4] Within a partnership, the goal is to create value for the members of the partnership beyond what can be created by any single organization. How this value is created is up to the partnership, and as long as the parties agree, virtually anything is possible.

2. *Control.* This decision criterion also has two dimensions: delivery (i.e., ensuring that the delivered IT function complies with requirements) and security (i.e., protecting intellectual assets). Because they rank high on both dimensions of control, in-house and insourcing options are favored in cases where the work is proprietary, strategic, "below the radar" (i.e., skunkworks), or needed immediately (see Table 17.2). Outsourcing is the preferred delivery option when the function is not considered "a point of differentiation" and the deliverable is well understood and easily governed by means of a service-level agreement. Partnerships are designed to be self-controlling by the membership, and as previously observed, the functions provided by partnerships tend to be more open ended than those provided by other options.

In Table 17.2, column 4 presents the benefits of each delivery option. For the most part, this list is closely aligned with the list of justifications found in column 3. As such, it reinforces the existence of flexibility and control as key decision criteria. But in addition, a third key factor appears—*knowledge enablement*. Mentioned only tangentially

---

[4]Response time within a partnership depends on two interdependent conditions holding: (1) a partnership must already exist, and (2) all partners must be committed to the same delivery timeline.

within the list of justifications (e.g., "competence," "internal consulting," and "world class"), it is much more evident within the list of realized benefits (e.g., "leveraging internal business and system knowledge," "preservation of critical knowledge," "quick access to specific skill sets," "decreased learning time," and "sharing the learning costs with partners"). Marquis (2006, 14) argues that "what is not easily replicable, and thus is potentially strategic, is an organization's intelligence and capability. By combining skills and resources in unique and enduring ways to grow core competencies, firms may succeed in establishing competitive advantage."

3. **Knowledge enhancement.** Behind many delivery decisions is the need to either capture knowledge or retain it. One firm cited the example of developing a new business product. While it "normally" would have been outsourced, it was intentionally developed by in-house staff augmented by key contract personnel. The reason was to enable the knowledge of this new business product to be transferred to internal IT personnel as well as to business personnel (who were also unfamiliar with this type of business offering). At another firm, the decision was made to insource key expertise "not to *do* the work, but to train internal staff *how* to do the work." The manager stated, "It would have been more logical and far cheaper to outsource the whole project." In another firm the support function for a key application was repatriated because the firm felt that it was losing an important learning opportunity that would keep staff abreast of developments in the market and develop new knowledge concerning a key line of business with growth potential. Furthermore, it is not just knowledge *development* that is the critical factor; knowledge *retention* is equally important. Whether implicitly or explicitly, knowledge enhancement appears to play a key role in most delivery decisions.

The discussion also revealed the existence of two distinct sets of decision criteria: "normal" versus "actual." Manager after manager explained their decisions with the following preface: "*Normally* we would make the decision this way, but in this case we *actually* made the decision differently." When the participants referred to the normal set, they primarily cited issues of flexibility, control, and knowledge enablement. But when they described the actual decision criteria used to select the delivery option, a fourth factor emerged—"business exigency."

4. **Business exigency.** Unforeseen business opportunities arise periodically, and firms with the ability to respond do so. Because of the urgency and importance of these business opportunities, they are not governed by the standard planning/budgeting processes and, indeed, most did not appear on the annual IT plan. Instead, a decision is made to seize the opportunity, and normal decision criteria are jettisoned in order to be responsive to the business. In these cases, whichever delivery option can produce results fastest is selected. The delivery option could be any of the four but is less likely to be a partnership unless the urgent request can be accommodated within the structure of an existing arrangement. Seen in a resource-planning context, business exigency demands constitute the "peaks" or "spikes." As one manager stated, "We have peaks and valleys, and we outsource the peaks."

It is difficult to ascertain the full effect of this last decision criterion. Certainly business exigency is a dominant factor. In an urgent situation, the fastest delivery option will take precedence. However, it is likely that the other three decision criteria play a significant role in the majority of delivery decisions regarding IT functionality. We are left to conclude that business exigency plays a more dramatic but less frequent role.

A DECISION FRAMEWORK FOR DELIVERING IT FUNCTIONS

Finally, the focus group was asked to outline a set of strategies for deciding how to deliver IT functions based on their collective experience and insights. The following step-by-step framework emerged.

1. Identify Your Core IT Functions

The identification of core functions is the first and most critical step in creating a decision framework for selecting delivery options. One manager captured this as follows:

> The days of IT being good at all things have long gone . . . Today you have to pick your spots . . . You have to decide where you need to excel to achieve competitive differentiation . . . Being OK at most things is a recipe for failure sooner or later.

It was argued that the IT organization should approach the exercise of identifying its core functions by taking a page from the business handbook; that is, decide where competitive advantage lies, buttress it with the best resources, and divest all ancillary activities. In the case of IT, "divestiture" translates into seeking external *delivery* of functions because the responsibility and accountability for all IT functions will always remain with the IT organization.

Asked what constitutes a core function, the group suggested that it would depend entirely on where and how the IT organization decides it can leverage the business most effectively. Interestingly, what was considered *core* varied dramatically across the sample of organizations represented, spreading across the entire spectrum of IT functions including legacy system enhancement, business process design, enterprise system implementation, project management, and even data center operations! The only conclusion that resonated with the entire group was that "it matters more that the IT organization has identified core functions than what those functions actually are."

The articulation of core functions has major implications. First, the selection of core functions lays the cornerstone for the decision framework for delivery options. That is because, ideally, in-house functions reflect the organization's set of core functions. The assignment of permanent IT personnel to core IT functions, by default, assigns noncore activities to the remaining three IT delivery options (as we will see in the next strategy). Second, the selection of core functions directly impacts the careers of IT personnel. For example, one manager explained that at her organization "project management, business process design, and relationship management are key skills, and we encourage development in these areas." The implications for IT staff currently fulfilling "noncore" roles can be threatening as these areas are key targets for external delivery.

TABLE 17.3 Sample Function Delivery Profile

CORE FUNCTION?	IT FUNCTION	IN-HOUSE	INSOURCE	OUTSOURCE	PARTNERSHIP
Yes	Business Analysis	✓			
	Systems Analysis		✓		
In Future	Strategy & Planning		✓	✓	
In Future	Data Management		✓		
Yes	Project Management	✓	✓		
Yes	Architecture	✓	✓		
	Application Development		✓	✓	✓
	QA & Testing		✓		
Now but not in future	Networking	✓			✓
	O/S & Services		✓		
Yes	Application Support	✓			
	Data Center Operations			✓	
	Application Software			✓	✓
	Hardware			✓	

2. Create a "Function Delivery" Profile

One participant introduced the concept of a "function delivery" profile—a device that had been deployed successfully within his organization. It is reproduced in Table 17.3 and modified to accommodate the list of IT functions found in Table 17.1. This sample profile demonstrates (1) current core functions, (2) future core functions (additions and deletions), and (3) preferred delivery options for each IT function. What is most important is that this profile is built on an internal assessment of core IT functions. The justification provided by this particular organization for its specific delivery profile follows:

- Project management, business analysis, and architecture (both system and enterprise) are primarily provided in-house but may be augmented with insourced resources as required. In-house delivery is preferred for these functions for two reasons: first, project management and business analysis are recognized strengths within the organization, and second, this gives the organization more control over project direction.
- Because it is not recognized as a core function, development is primarily outsourced or insourced depending on the scope of the project.
- Quality assurance (QA) and testing are largely insourced as these are recognized as highly specialized skills, although not core functions. As a result, an entire division of IT is dedicated to these activities. Resources within this group are primarily contractors from a variety of vendors.

- Application support is a designated core function. Given the depth of business process knowledge needed as well as the in-depth knowledge of key applications required, this function is staffed entirely by internal IT personnel.
- Networking is currently provided by in-house staff augmented by insourced staff but is in transition. A recently formed partnership will eventually make this a noncore activity, and networking will eventually by provided entirely by the partner. This delivery option allows cost sharing and accommodates future growth. The partnership does not provide competitive advantage; it just makes good business sense.
- The strategy and planning function as well as data management have been designated as future core functions. The firm is insourcing expertise from a top strategy consultancy to transition this skill to internal IT personnel. This explicitly recognizes the emerging importance of IT to the firm. Similarly, data management needs to become a key competitive strength in order to shorten product development cycles and time to market.

The sample profile depicted in Table 17.3 does not represent a "preferred" or even "typical" IT delivery strategy. Instead, it simply demonstrates how the four delivery options combine to satisfy the IT needs of a specific organization. Other organizations with a different mix of core functions (or even with the same mix for that matter) might well demonstrate a very different profile.

3. Evolve Full-time IT Personnel

Because of the alignment between core IT functions and in-house delivery, it is evident that delivery decisions should be based on leveraging an organization's full-time IT personnel. In fact, the focus group argued that this factor should be used to determine the majority of sourcing decisions. It is based on the realization that permanent IT personnel collectively represent a major investment by the organization and this investment needs to be maximized (or at least optimized). This reinforces the previous discussion of "knowledge enhancement" as one of the key decision criteria in the selection of IT delivery mechanisms. One manager said the following:

> We choose a delivery option based on how it can build strength in one of our designated core competency areas. This may involve insourcing, outsourcing, a partnership, or any combination of these [but] . . . we have never outsourced a core competency.

The sample profile in Table 17.3 suggests how the three external delivery options (i.e., insourcing, outsourcing, and partnerships) can be used to supplement permanent IT personnel. Furthermore, the group suggested that a precedence ordering should exist among the delivery options. Specifically, in-house and insourcing considerations should be resolved before outsourcing and partnerships are explored. The criteria to be used to decide between outsourcing and partnerships as delivery options should be flexibility, control, and business exigency (given that knowledge enablement is used to decide between in-house and insourcing). Insourcing, in particular, can be used strategically to bring in expertise to back-fill knowledge gaps in core IT functions, address business exigency needs, and take on new (or shed old) core functions. Furthermore, insourcing represents variable costing, so there is usually maximal flexibility, which helps to smooth out resource "peaks and valleys."

The other method suggested to evolve internal IT staff, beyond supplementing them with the three external delivery options, is to hire strategically.[5] In other words, the range of IT delivery options permits "strategic" hiring as opposed to "replacement" hiring. In the past, IT organizations felt the need to "cover all the bases" with their hiring, and as individuals departed the organization, replacements were sought. Today, however, there is no such impetus. In fact, attrition in noncore areas is considered advantageous as it permits hiring in designated strategic areas. This approach extends to permanent staff as well; that is, existing staff are strongly encouraged to develop their skills and expertise in alignment with designated core IT functions.

4. Encourage Exploration of the Whole Range of Delivery Options

Based on our sample of companies, it can be concluded that we are in the learning phase of IT function delivery. Some firms are clearly taking advantage of this opportunity and exercising their options in many different, often creative, ways. Others, perhaps more reticent, are sampling less broadly—choosing to stay within their "comfort zone"—and delivering IT functions predominantly with in-house resources. Most, however, are somewhere in the middle; that is, actively exploring different types of delivery options mostly for the first time. In all cases, exploration appears to be taking place without a strategy or guidelines; hence, decisions are taken one at a time. As a result, learning has been piecemeal—a phenomenon that may partially explain the lack of established trends in Table 17.2.

5. Combine Delivery Options Strategically

One of the key reasons for focusing on IT functions as opposed to another unit of analysis (e.g., projects, applications, or services) became clear by way of an example described by a manager. Satisfying her firm's data storage needs could involve using the provider's equipment, facilities, and staff. Or it could be the organization's hardware and staff in the provider's facilities . . . or basically any combination of the above. In each of these situations, the organization could justifiably claim that it had "outsourced" its data storage. Such a claim would be highly ambiguous. As a result, decisions need to be focused on the delivery of *specific* IT functions; that is, a micro- versus a macroview.

Adopting a microview makes it possible to entertain the use of *combinations* of delivery options for the provision of IT functions. Participants pointed out that multiple delivery options are often used within a single project. In fact, they suggested that selecting a single delivery option for a project in its entirety is fast becoming nonstandard practice. The reality is that multiple providers are necessary to meet

---

[5]While organizations continuously search for top IT talent, there appears to be a general aversion to increasing permanent staff among the focus group's companies. Reluctance to expand the IT staff naturally favors external delivery options. The consensus was that this hiring aversion is fueling the growth of delivery options such as insourcing, outsourcing, and partnerships, but the group was reluctant to use this factor to explain their IT delivery behavior. Instead, they claimed that the real driver was the existence of many alternative sourcing options, which have demonstrated the capability of providing superior results.

today's demands, particularly those of the business-exigency variety. This need for an amalgam of delivery options is easily understood with functions such as application development. Here requirements and design may be done in-house, coding may be outsourced to a third party, testing and quality assurance may be done by in-sourced experts, and implementation and rollout might be in partnership. Combining separate delivery options strategically can result in realizable benefits such as speed to market and quality of product or service. Speed to market results from parallel, synchronized development, and quality results from engaging delivery options based on demonstrated expertise and best practice.

CONCLUSION

Despite a steadily growing industry of third-party providers, IT organizations to date have ventured rather cautiously into this new area of IT function delivery. This chapter attempts to explain why this is so by examining the decision behavior and practices of a number of leading-edge organizations. From this analysis, four key decision criteria were identified: (1) flexibility, (2) control, (3) knowledge enhancement, and (4) business exigency. Today IT managers have an incredible range of available options in terms of how they choose to deliver IT functions. Clearly, the mistake is not to investigate the full range of these options. What has been lacking is greater direction and guidance in selecting IT delivery options. The concept of a maturity model for IT functions was also introduced as well as a function-delivery profile to map delivery options onto core and noncore IT functions. These elements form the basis of a decision framework to guide the selection of delivery options. Following this framework, organizations can begin to move beyond the exploration stage to develop more strategic, nuanced, and methodological approaches to IT function delivery.

REFERENCES

Carr, N. G. "The End of Corporate Computing." *MIT Sloan Management Review* Spring (2005): 67–73.

Hagel, J., and J. S. Brown. "Your Next IT Strategy." *Harvard Business Review* 79, no. 9 (October 2001): 105–13.

Lacity, M., and L. Willcocks. "An Empirical Investigation of Information Technology Sourcing Practices: Lessons from Experience." *MIS Quarterly* 22, no. 3 (2000): 363–408.

Marquis, H. A. "Finishing off IT." *MIT Sloan Management Review* 47, no. 4 (Summer 2006): 12–16.

Rappa, M. A. "The Utility Business Model and the Future of Computing Services." *IBM Systems Journal* 43, no. 1 (2004): 32–42.

Ross, J. W., and G. Westerman. "Preparing for Utility Computing: The Role of IT Architecture and Relationship Management." *MIT Sloan Management Review* 43, no. 1 (2004): 5–19.

Smith, H. A., and J. D. McKeen. "IT in 2010: The Next Frontier." *MIS Quarterly Executive* 5, no. 3 (September 2006): 125–36.

Chapter 18

Building Better IT Leaders from the Bottom Up[1]

"For IT to assume full partnership with the business, it will have to take a leadership role on many vital organizational issues. . . . This leadership role is not the exclusive prerogative of senior executives—it is the duty of all IT employees. Effective leadership has enormous benefits. To realize these benefits, leadership qualities should be explicitly recognized, reinforced, and rewarded at all levels of the IT organization. This only happens when a concerted effort is made to introduce leadership activities into the very fabric of the IT organization. Leadership is everyone's job." (McKeen and Smith 2003)

This quote, taken from a book we published several years ago, remains as true today as it was then. But a lot has happened in the interim. Chiefly, in the chaotic business conditions of late, IT leadership development got sidetracked. The dot-com boom and bust soured many companies on the top-line potential of IT and refocused most CIOs on developing strong processes to ensure that IT's bottom line was kept under control (Roberts and Mingay 2004). But the wheel has turned yet again, and there is now renewed emphasis on how IT can help the organization achieve competitive differentiation and top-line growth (IBM 2004).

The many new challenges facing IT organizations today—achieving business growth goals, enterprise transformation, coping with technical and relationship complexity, facilitating innovation and knowledge development, and managing an increasingly mobile and virtual workforce—calls for strong IT leadership. Unfortunately, few IT leadership teams are well equipped for the job (Mingay et al. 2004). Traditional hierarchical structures with command-and-control leadership are not only ineffective, they can actually become a barrier to the development of a high-performance IT

---

[1]Smith, H. A., and J. D. McKeen, "Building Better IT Leaders: From the Bottom Up," *Communications of the Association of Information Systems* 16, article 38 (December 2005): 785–96 (reproduced by permission of the Association of Information Systems).

department (Avolio and Kahai 2003). New communications technologies are enabling new ways of leading and empowering even the most junior staff in new ways. These factors are all bringing senior IT managers around to a new appreciation for the need to build strong IT leaders at all levels of their organization.

This chapter looks first at the increasing importance of leadership in IT and how leadership is changing over time. Next, it examines the qualities that make a good IT leader. Then it looks at how companies are trying to develop better IT leaders at all levels in their organizations. Finally, it outlines the value proposition for investing in IT leadership development.

THE CHANGING ROLE OF THE IT LEADER

The death of the traditional hierarchical organization structure and top-down command-and-control leader has been predicted for at least two decades (Bennis and Nanus 1985). But it's dying a slow and painful death. While much lip service is paid to the need for everyone in IT to be a leader, the fact remains that the traditional style of leadership is still very much in evidence, especially in large IT organizations.

There appear to be at least three reasons this is the case. First, until now, there has been very little pressure to change. As one manager pointed out, "We've been focusing on centralizing our IT organization in the last few years, and centralized decision making is inconsistent with the philosophy of 'everybody leads.'" Those IT managers struggling with the complexities engendered by nonstandard equipment, nonintegrated systems, and multiple databases full of overlapping but inconsistent data can be forgiven if this philosophy suggests the "Wild West" days of IT, where everyone did their own thing.

Second, the organizations within which IT operates are largely hierarchical as well. Their managers have grown up with traditional structures and chains of command. They are comfortable with them and are uncomfortable when they see parts of their organization (e.g., IT) behaving and being treated differently by their CIO (Feld and Stoddard 2004). Senior management may, therefore, pressure IT to conform to the ways of the rest of the firm. This situation has recently become exacerbated by new compliance regulations (e.g., Sarbanes-Oxley, privacy legislation) that require hierarchical accountability and severely limit flexibility. Third, many senior executives—even within IT—find it difficult to relinquish control to more junior staff because they know they still have accountability for their results. Keeping a hands-on approach to leadership, they believe, is the only way to ensure work gets done right.

However, in spite of the remarkable tenacity of the hierarchical organization, there are signs that traditional leadership modes in IT are now in retreat and there is a growing recognition that IT organizations must do a better job of inculcating leadership behaviors in all their staff (Bell and Gerrard 2004). There are some very practical reasons all IT staff are now expected to act as leaders, regardless of their official job titles:

- *Top-line focus.* CEOs are looking for top-line growth from their organizations (IBM 2004). New technologies and applications largely drive the enterprise differentiation and transformation efforts that will deliver this growth. Strong IT leadership teams are needed to take on this role in different parts of the organization and at different levels. They can do this effectively only by sharing clear goals and direction, understanding business strategy, and having the requisite "soft" skills to influence business leaders (Roberts and Mingay 2004).

- *Credibility.*   No IT leadership initiatives within business will be accepted unless IT is consistently able to deliver results. While this aspect of leadership is often called "management" and considered somewhat less important than transformational aspects of leadership, IT's credentials in the latter rest solidly on the former (McKeen and Smith 1996; Mingay et al. 2004). No business organization will accept IT leadership in other areas unless it has demonstrated the skills and competencies to consistently deliver on what it says it will do. Furthermore, distinguishing between leadership and management leads to a dysfunctional IT organization. "Managers who don't lead are boring [and] dispiriting, [while] leaders who don't manage are distant [and] disconnected" (Mintzberg 2004). We have too often forgotten that top-level leaders are developed over time from among the rank and file, and that is where they learn how to lead.

- *Impact.*   There is no question that individuals within IT have more opportunities to affect an organization, both positively and negatively, than others at similar levels in the business. The focus group felt that this fact alone makes it extremely important that IT staff have much stronger organizational perspectives, decision-making skills, entrepreneurialism, and risk-assessment capabilities at lower levels. Today, because even small decisions in IT can have a major impact on an organization, it is essential that a CIO be confident that his or her most junior staff have the judgment and skills to take appropriate actions.

- *Flexibility.*   Increasingly, IT staff and organizations are expected to be responsive to rapidly changing business needs and help the enterprise compete in a highly competitive environment. This situation requires IT staff to have not only the technical skills required to address a variety of needs, but the ability to act in the best interests of the organization wherever opportunities arise. "We are no longer order takers in IT," stated one manager. "All our staff are expected to do the right things for our firm, even when it means saying 'no' to senior business management." Similarly, doing the right things involves being proactive. These actions take significant amounts of organizational know-how to pull off—leadership skills that rank-and-file IT staff are not noted for at present.

- *Complexity.*   The responsibilities of IT have grown increasingly complex over the past two decades (Smith and McKeen 2006). Not only is IT expected to be a high-performance organization, it is also expected to offer change and innovation leadership, interact with other organizations to deliver low-cost services, chart a path through ever-growing new technology offerings, and offer content leadership (Mingay et al. 2004). The complexity of the tasks, relationships, knowledge, and the integration of these now needed in IT mean that leadership cannot rest in the hands of one person or even a team. Instead, new ways of instilling the needed skills and competencies into all IT staff must be found.

- *New technology.* E-mail, groupware, instant messaging, and the Internet are all changing how leaders work—especially in IT. Increasingly, staff are virtual or mobile and their interactions with their managers are mediated by technology. At the same time, IT staff have much greater access more quickly to the same information as their managers. New technologies change how information is acquired and disseminated, how communication takes place, and how people are influenced and decisions made. Traditional forms of control are, thus, increasingly ineffective (Avolio and Kahai 2003).

All of these factors are driving the need to push leadership skills and competencies further down in the IT organization. While traditional hierarchies will likely remain in place to define authority and accountability, *leadership* is likely to become increasingly situational—to be exercised as required by tasks and conditions (Bell and Gerrard 2004). With the demands on IT projected to be ever greater in the next decade, the need for more professional and sophisticated IT leadership is also greater than ever before (Feld and Stoddard 2004). In fact, many believe that IT leadership will determine "which [IT] organizations disappear into the back office of utility services and which ones build company-wide credibility and drive business growth and ability" (Mingay et al. 2004).

WHAT MAKES A GOOD IT LEADER?

In many ways the qualities that make a good IT leader resemble those that make any other good leader. These can be broken down into two general categories:

1. *Personal mastery.* These qualities embody the collection of behaviors that determine how an individual approaches different work and personal situations. They include a variety of "soft" skills, such as self-knowledge, awareness of individual approaches to work, and other personality traits. Most IT organizations include some form of personal mastery assessment and development as part of their management training programs. Understanding how one relates to others, how they respond to you, and how to adapt personal behaviors appropriately to different situations is a fundamental part of good leadership. One company's internal leadership document states: "Leaders must exercise self-awareness, monitor their impact on others, be receptive to feedback, and adjust to that feedback." "The higher up you get in IT, the greater the need for soft skills," claimed one member. Another noted the positive impact of this type of skills development: "It's quite evident who has been on our management development program by their behaviors." An increasingly important component of this quality for IT staff is personal integrity; that is, the willingness to do what you say you are going to do—both within IT and with external parties such as users and vendors.
2. *Leadership skill mastery.* These qualities include the general leadership skills expected of all leaders in organizations today, such as motivation, team building, collaboration, communication, risk assessment, problem solving, coaching, and mentoring. These are skills that can be both taught and modeled by current

leaders and are a necessary, but not sufficient, component of good IT leadership (McKeen and Smith 2003).

However, good IT leaders are required to have a further set of skills that could be collectively called "strategic vision" if they are going to provide the direction and deliver the impact that organizations are expecting from IT. Because this is a "soft skill," there is no firm definition of this quality, but several components that help to develop this quality at all levels in IT can be identified. These include the following:

- *Business understanding.* It should go without saying that for an IT leader to have strategic vision, he or she should have a solid understanding of the organization's current operations and future direction. This is well accepted in IT today, although few IT organizations have formal programs to develop this understanding. Most IT staff are expected to pick it up as they go along, mostly at the functional business process level. This may be adequate at junior levels, but being able to apply strategic vision to a task also involves a much broader understanding of the larger competitive environment, financial management, and marketing. "Our customers are now our end users. With our systems now reaching customers and reaching out horizontally in the organization and beyond, IT staff *all* need a broader and deeper appreciation of business than ever before," said one manager.

- *Organizational understanding.* A key expectation of strategic vision in IT is enterprise transformation (Mingay et al. 2004). This involves more than just generating insights into how technology and processes can be utilized to create new products and services or help the organization work more effectively; it also involves the effective execution of the changes involved. IT professionals have long known that technology must work in combination with people and processes to be effective. This is why they are now expected to be experts in change management (Markus and Benjamin 1997; McKeen and Smith 2003; Orlikowski and Hofman 1997). But being able to drive transformation forward involves a number of additional skills, such as political savvy (to overcome resistance and negative influences), organizational problem solving (to address conflicting stakeholder interests), effective use of governance structures (to ensure proper support for change), and governance design (to work with partners and service providers) (Bell and Gerrard 2004; Kim and Maugorgne 2003). Because IT people come from a technical background and are more analytic in their thinking, they typically do not have strong skills in this area and need to acquire them.

- *Creating a supportive working environment.* Most IT work is done in teams. Increasingly, these teams are virtual and include businesspeople, staff from vendor companies, and members from different cultures. Motivating and inspiring one's colleagues to do their best, dealing with relationship problems and conflicts, and making decisions that are consistent with the overall goals of the organization and a particular initiative are the job of every IT staff member. Since much leadership in a matrixed organization such as IT is situational, an IT professional could be a leader one day and a follower the next. Thus, that person must know how to create a work environment that is characterized by trust, empowerment, and accountability. This involves clear communication of objectives, setting the rules of engagement, developing strong relationships (sometimes virtually), and providing support to manage risks and resolve issues (Anonymous 2004; Avolio and Kahai 2003; Bell and Gerrard 2004).

- **Effective use of resources.** A good IT leader knows how to concentrate scarce resources in places where they will have the biggest payoff for the organization. This means not only making use of processes and tools to stretch out limited staff, but also understanding where resources should *not* be used (i.e., saying "no"). In the longer term, using resources wisely may mean using job assignments and budgets to enhance people's capabilities, identifying and developing emergent leaders, and using reward and recognition programs to motivate and encourage staff (Anonymous 2004). Unfortunately, IT staff have often been spread too thinly, been underappreciated, and not been given time for training. Good IT leaders value their people, run interference for them when necessary, and work to build "bench strength" in their teams and organizations.

Leadership Styles Vary According to the Degree of Involvement of Team Members

- Commanding—"Do what I tell you"
- Pacesetting—"Do as I do now"
- Visionary—"Come with me"
- Affiliate—"People come first"
- Coaching—"Try this"
- Democratic—"What do you think?"

(after Roberts and Mingay 2004)

- **Flexibility of approach.** A good IT leader knows where and how to exercise leadership. "Skill mastery must be complemented with the ability to know when and where particular behaviors/skills are required and . . . how they should be deployed" (McKeen and Smith 2003). While this is true in all parts of the organization, leadership in IT can be a rapidly shifting target for two reasons. First, IT staff are well-educated, well-informed professionals whose opinions are valuable. "Good IT leaders know when to encourage debate and also when to close it down," said a manager. Second, the business's rapid shifts of priority, the changing competitive and technical environment, and the highly politicized nature of much IT work mean that leaders must constantly adjust their style to suit a dynamic topography of issues and priorities. "There is a well-documented continuum of leadership styles . . . The most appropriate style depends on the enterprise style and the business and strategic contexts" (Roberts and Mingay 2004).

- **Ability to gain business attention.** A large component of IT leadership is focused not on the internal IT organization, but outward toward all parts of the business. One of the biggest challenges for today's IT leaders is the fact that the focus of their work is more on business value than on technology (Mahoney 2004). The ability to motivate business executives, often in more senior positions, to lead business transformation and to gain and maintain executive attention is central to establishing and maintaining IT credibility in an organization (McDonald and Bace 2004). A good IT leader knows how to position his or her contribution in tangible, business terms; how to interact with business leaders;

and how to guide and educate them about the realities of IT use. "Bringing value to the business is a very important trend in IT leadership," stated one participant.

IT leaders will need more or fewer of these qualities, depending on the scope and type of their work. Obviously, IT staff responsible for sourcing will need a different mix of these skills than those with an internal IT focus or those with a business focus. They will also be more important the higher one moves in the management hierarchy. Nevertheless, these are skills that IT organizations should endeavor to grow in all their staff from the most junior levels. Since these skills take time and practice to develop and are in increasing demand, senior IT managers should put concrete plans in place to ensure that they will be present when needed.

How to Build Better IT Leaders

Everyone agrees that fostering leadership skills throughout all levels of IT is important to IT's future effectiveness (Bell and Gerrard 2004; McKeen and Smith 2003; Mingay et al. 2004; Mintzberg 2004). However, the reality is that leadership development is very hit and miss in most IT organizations. Over the past five years, many formal leadership courses have been cut or scaled back substantially because of cost-control initiatives. When offered, most IT leadership programs limit attendance to managers. Few organizations have articulated a comprehensive program of leadership development that includes other initiatives besides training.

Leadership development in IT is not as simple as sending a few handpicked individuals on a training course. In fact, formal training may be one of the *least* effective (and most expensive) aspects of building better IT leaders (Kesner 2003). Any comprehensive leadership development program has three layers (see Figure 18.1).

Figure 18.1 Effective Leadership Development Involves More Than Training

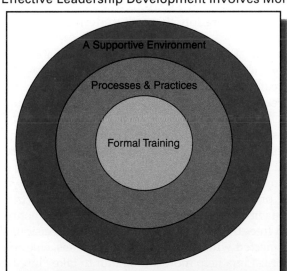

The first, most important, and probably most difficult one is an environment within which leaders at all levels can flourish. It is often suggested that leaders, like cream, will naturally rise to the top regardless of the conditions in which they work. The reality is that more and better leaders are created when organizations have a supportive process for developing them that is widely understood. What's needed is "a culture that nurtures talented managers, rather than one that leaves them to struggle through a Darwinian survival game" (Griffin 2003). There is general agreement on what constitutes this type of culture:

- *Well-articulated and instantiated values.* Values guide how staff should behave even when their managers aren't around. They provide a basis for sound decision making (Stewart 2004). "If you're going to push leadership down in the organization, you have to push values down as well," stated one manager. Others noted that senior IT leadership should primarily be about forming and modeling values, not managing tasks. Values are especially important now that staff are more mobile and virtual (Cascio and Shurygailo 2003). A strong value system is crucial to bringing together and motivating a large, diverse workforce and helping staff act in ways that support the company's brand and values. Unfortunately, while many organizations have values, they are often out of date or not modeled by management (Stewart 2004).

- *A climate of trust.* Trust that management means what it says about values and leadership development must be established early in any program. Trust is established by setting expectations and delivering results that meet or exceed those expectations. By sending clear messages to staff and exhibiting positive attitudes about staff behavior, senior IT managers will help people feel they can begin to take some risks and initiatives in their work (Cascio and Shurygailo 2003). If people feel their culture is based on fair processes and that they can draw lessons from both good and bad results, they will start to respond with the type of high performance and leadership behaviors that are expected (Kim and Maugorgne 2003). Conversely, senior managers must take steps to weed out counterproductive behaviors, such as poor collaboration, that will undermine this climate (Roberts and Mingay 2004).

- *Empowerment.* Empowerment thrives in a climate of trust, but leaders need to deliberately encourage it as well. In IT one of the most important ways to do this is to create mechanisms to support staff's making difficult decisions. One company recognized this by explicitly making "we'll support you in doing the right things" a central element in revamping its leadership promise. To make it real and visible, the company established a clear process through which junior staff can resolve potential conflicts with users when there are disagreements about what is "the right thing." Furthermore, they have established committees to help manage the risks involved in IT work, get at the root cause of recurring issues, and protect the promises made to business partners. Such processes, in conjunction with values and trust, create a management system that empowers people and frees them up to make appropriate decisions (Stewart 2004). By staying connected with staff as teachers, coaches, champions, and mentors, more senior leaders help more junior staff to take "intelligent risks" and sponsor initiative (Taurel 2000).

- *Clear and frequent communication.* As with other types of change, one cannot communicate too much about the need to create an environment to foster leadership. "In spite of all we know about communication, it's still one of our biggest leadership gaps," said a participant. Open, two-way communication is the hallmark of modern leadership. Leaders and followers are gradually learning how to effectively use the electronic nervous system that now runs through all organizations (Avolio and Kahai 2003). Use of information technology and multiple channels is now the norm, and redundancy is advisable because of the increased opportunities for miscommunication in the virtual world. Senior executives are now using IT to communicate interactively with their most junior staff (Stewart 2004). One company has established an "Ask Phil" e-mail whereby any member of IT can direct questions to the CIO. Leadership is about developing relationships with people. It engages them and helps direct them to a particular goal. Learning to leverage all conduits of communication to build and sustain an array of relationships is, therefore, central to becoming an effective IT leader (Avolio and Kahai 2003).
- *Accountability.* Acceptance of accountability is a key component of leadership. A climate where accountabilities are clear is an important aspect of a leadership development culture (Bell and Gerrard 2004). Natural leaders often first come to senior management's attention because they consistently deliver on what they promise. More recently, the concept of accountability is being extended to include expectations that IT staff will assist the business in achieving its growth goals and that IT will not create technical impediments to implementing business strategies (Mingay et al. 2004). Unfortunately, accountability has too often been lacking from IT cultures, and this has negatively affected the perceptions of IT leadership in the rest of the organization (Feld and Stoddard 2004). No member of IT should be allowed to abdicate responsibility for delivering results. However, focus group members stressed that in order to create a culture of accountability, IT leaders must also provide the processes, tools, and support to produce successful results.

The second layer of a leadership development program involves building leadership activities into IT's processes and daily work. Well-designed and documented processes for such activities as planning, budgeting, conflict resolution, service delivery, and financial reviews and approvals clearly articulate the individual elements that contribute to leadership in particular situations. They make it easier for more junior staff to carry out these activities and to learn what is expected of them (Bell and Gerrard 2004). They also establish boundaries within which staff can exercise judgment and take risks.

Human resources management practices are a key component of fostering leadership at this level as well. Many companies have begun to document the competencies that they expect staff to exhibit in each job category and level. These typically include leadership as well as technical skills. "It gets harder to do this the higher up the management hierarchy one goes," stated one manager. "At the more senior levels, leadership skills are much more individualized and are more difficult to capture, but we're working on it." Specific training and development strategies work well for each job stream at more junior levels. With more senior positions, development plans should be created for each individual.

Job assignments are one of the most important ways to develop leadership expertise. In fact, some experts suggest that 80 percent of the levers management has at its disposal in this area are related to how a company uses assignments and job postings to influence an individual's experience (Kesner 2003). Job rotations, stretch assignments, and on-the-job coaching and mentoring are all effective ways to build leadership skills. Occasionally, this may entail taking risks and not always appointing the most qualified person for a particular job (Roberts and Mingay 2004). Sometimes, this should involve moving a person out of IT into the business for an assignment. All organizations should have processes in place to identify emergent leaders and take proactive steps to design individualized strategies of coaching and assignments that will fit their unique personalities (Griffin 2003). Succession planning should be a significant part of this process as well. While recruiting leaders from outside is sometimes necessary, this is a far more risky and expensive way to address succession than growing leaders from within (Roberts and Mingay 2004).

Finally, at the core of any leadership development program is formal training. Commitment to formal leadership training in organizations has been patchy at best. Training can be internally developed or externally purchased. The fastest-growing segment of executive education is customized programs for a particular organization that are specifically tied to business drivers and values (Kesner 2003). In-house programs are best for instilling vision, purpose, values, and priorities. External training is best used for introducing new knowledge, practices, and thinking to leadership.

Because of the time and expense involved, leadership training should be used strategically rather than comprehensively. Often IT resources can be so stretched that finding time for development is the biggest challenge. One company reasserted the importance of training by promising its staff that it would spend its entire annual training budget for the first time! This organization sees training as one tool for helping individuals make their best contributions and achieving success. Interestingly, it has found that making it easier to find appropriate courses through the creation of a formal curriculum and streamlining the registration and payment processes has led to a significant uptake in employees' taking advantage of development opportunities.

INVESTING IN LEADERSHIP DEVELOPMENT: ARTICULATING THE VALUE PROPOSITION

Although leadership development is widely espoused, many organizations have reduced their budgets in recent years and formal training programs have been hard hit. One manager remarked that his staff knew senior management was serious about their development when it maintained training budgets while trimming in other areas. However, as mentioned above, training is only one facet of a good leadership development program, and doing it right will take executive time and consistent attention, in addition to the costs involved in establishing and following through on necessary communications, procedures, and planning. It is essential to articulate the value proposition for this initiative.

Experts suggest several elements of value can be achieved by implementing a leadership development program. Using a rubric established by Smith and McKeen (2003), these are discussed below:

- *What is the value?*   Because different companies and managers have different perceptions of value, it is critical that the value that is to be achieved by a leadership development program be clearly described and agreed on. Some of the value elements that organizations could achieve with leadership development include improved current and future leadership capabilities and bench strength (preventing expensive and risky hires from outside), improved innovation and alignment with business strategy, improved teamwork (both internally and cross-functionally), improved collaboration and knowledge sharing, greater clarity of purpose and appropriate decision making, reduced risk, and a higher-performing IT organization. When these value objectives are understood, it is possible to develop metrics to determine whether or not the program is successful. Having a focus and metrics for a leadership program will ensure that management pays attention to it and that it doesn't get shunted into a corner with the "soft and fuzzy stuff" (Kesner 2003).

- *Who will deliver the value?*   Because leadership development is partially HR's responsibility and partially IT's, clarifying which parts of the program should be delivered by which group is important. Similarly, much of the coaching, mentoring, and experiential components will be fulfilled by different managers within IT. It is, therefore, important for senior management to clarify roles and responsibilities for leadership development and to ensure that they are implemented consistently across the organization. Ideally, senior IT management will retain responsibility for the outer layer of the leadership program; that is, creating a supportive working environment. At one company the senior IT team created several packaged presentations for middle managers to help them articulate their "leadership promises."

- *When will value be realized?*   Leadership development should have both long- and short-term benefits. Effective training programs should result in visible behavior changes, as noted above. The initial impacts of a comprehensive leadership initiative should be visible in-house within a year and to business units and vendors within eighteen to twenty-four months (McDonald and Bace 2004). Again, metrics are an essential part of leadership programs because they demonstrate their success and effectiveness. While there is no causal link between leadership development and improved business results, there should be clear and desirable results achieved (Kesner 2003). Using a "balanced scorecard" approach to track the different types of impacts over time is recommended. This can be used to demonstrate value to IT managers themselves, who may be skeptical, and to HR and senior management. It can also be used to make modifications to the program in areas where it is not working well.

- *How will value be delivered?*   This is the question that everyone wants to ask first and that should only be addressed *after* the other questions have been answered (Smith and McKeen 2003). Once it is clear *what* IT wants to accomplish with leadership development, it will be much easier to design an effective program to deliver it.

CONCLUSION

Leadership development in IT is something that everyone agrees is increasingly important to helping companies achieve their business goals. However, all too often it is a hit-and-miss exercise, depending on management whim and budget availability. It is now clear that senior IT leaders must make leadership development a priority if IT is going to contribute to business strategy and help deliver services in an increasingly competitive environment. To do this, leadership development in IT must start with the most junior IT staff. An effective program involves more than just training. It must include the creation of a supportive work environment and the development of processes that deliver on management's promises. However, no leadership program should be implemented in a vacuum. There should be a clearly articulated proposition outlining its value to the organization and a set of metrics to monitor its effectiveness. Like technology itself, leadership development will be effective only if management takes a comprehensive approach that integrates culture, behavior, processes, *and* training to deliver real business value.

REFERENCES

Anonymous. "A Guide for Leaders." Presentation to the IT Management Forum, November 2004.

Avolio, B., and S. Kahai. "Adding the 'E' to Leadership: How It May Impact Your Leadership." *Organizational Dynamics* 31, no. 4 (January 2003): 325–38.

Bell, M., and M. Gerrard. "Organizational Chart Is Falling into Irrelevance." Research Note QA-22-2873, July 6, 2004, Gartner Group.

Bennis, W. G., and B. Nanus. *Leaders: The Strategies for Taking Charge.* New York: Harper and Row, 1985.

Cascio, W., and S. Shurygailo. "E-leadership and Virtual Teams." *Organizational Dynamics* 31, no. 4 (January 2003): 362–76.

Feld, C., and D. Stoddard. "Getting IT Right." *Harvard Business Review* 82, no. 2 (2004): 72–79.

Griffin, N. "Personalize Your Management Development." *Harvard Business Review* 81, no. 3 (March 2003).

IBM. "CEO Survey 2004: Executive Summary." IBM Consulting Services. http://w3-2.ibm.com/services/bcs/news_pubs/features/2004/0224_survey.html (accessed January 2005).

Kesner, I. "Leadership Development: Perk or Priority?" *Harvard Business Review* 81, no. 3 (May 2003).

Kim, W., and R. Maugorgne. "Tipping Point Leadership." *Harvard Business Review* 81, no. 4 (April 2003).

Mahoney, J. "Demands for Business Growth Make CIOs Reallocate Their Time." Research Note SPA-22-6613, June 29, 2004, Gartner Group.

Markus, L., and R. I. Benjamin. "The Magic Bullet Theory in IT-Enabled Transformation," *Sloan Management Review* Winter (1997): 55–68.

McDonald, M., and J. Bace. "Keys to IT Leadership: Credibility, Respect, and Consistency." Research Note TU-22-8013, June 28, 2004, Gartner Group.

McKeen, J., and H. Smith. *Management Challenges in IS: Successful Strategies and Appropriate Action.* Chichester, England: John Wiley & Sons, 1996.

———. *Making IT Happen: Critical Issues in IT Management.* Chichester, England: John Wiley & Sons, 2003.

Mingay, S., J. Mahoney, M. P. McDonald, M. Bell. "Redefining the Rules of IT Leadership." Article AV-22-9013, July 1, 2004, Gartner Group.

Mintzberg, H. "Enough Leadership." *Harvard Business Review* 82, no. 11 (November 2004).

Orlikowski, W. J., and J. D. Hofman. "An Improvisational Model for Change Management:

The Case of Groupware Technologies." *Sloan Management Review* Winter (1997): 11–21.

Roberts, J., and S. Mingay. "Building a More Effective IT Leadership Team." Research Note TU-22-5915, June 28, 2004, Gartner Group.

Smith, H. A., and J. D. McKeen. "Developing and Delivering on the IT Value Proposition." *Communications of the Association of Information Systems* 11, article 25 (April 2003): 438–50.

———. "IT in 2010." *MIS Quarterly Executive* 5, no. 3 (September 2006): 125–36.

Stewart, T. "Leading Change When Business Is Good: An Interview with Samuel J. Palmisano." *Harvard Business Review* 82, no. 12 (December 2004): 8.

Taurel, S. "On Leadership." Corporate document, Eli Lilly and Co. 2000.

Chapter 19

Developing IT Professionalism[1]

"We had visitors from overseas meeting with us. At four o'clock p.m., Jack, our senior technician, just got up and left and didn't come back. We were all left floundering. The next day, when I asked him where he'd gone, he said he'd had to catch his regular train home!"

"So many of our people are in a 'what can you do for me?' mode. They don't want to wear a pager. They are arrogant. They don't take the time to understand the impact of their work on the business. They don't seem to care."

"Some IT people simply don't understand organizational dynamics. I've seen them send blistering e-mails to people with cc's to the whole world. How can they do that?"

These anecdotes from recent conversations with IT managers suggest that IT professionalism is a growing problem for them and for their organizations. Managers are frustrated that many of their newer employees simply don't understand what it means to "be professional" in their jobs. And older staff are sometimes stuck in a comfort zone, doing a job that was acceptable fifteen years ago and not recognizing that standards of working behavior have been ratcheted up since then.

"Our colleges and universities don't teach professionalism," remarked one IT manager. Neither do companies, other managers pointed out. Instead, professionalism remains an unarticulated set of working behaviors, attitudes, and expectations. Yet IT professionalism has never been more important. The days when eccentric IT workers were hidden away in a "glass house" or ivory tower somewhere are long gone. Teamwork—with users, vendors, consultants, and business partners—is the name of the game today, and with it comes an increased dependency on and interaction with others. And professionalism is the glue that keeps teams of diverse individuals working together toward the same goal. Today IT workers are being held accountable

---

[1]Smith, H. A., and J. D. McKeen, "Developing IT Professionalism," *Communications of the Association of Information Systems* 12, article 20 (October 2003): 312–325 (reproduced by permission of the Association for Information Systems).

to this new, unwritten set of standards that governs not only their work and how they, themselves, are perceived, but also how the whole of IT is perceived by the rest of the organization and others outside it. No wonder IT managers want to polish their people up a little!

This chapter provides a composite picture of IT professionalism and how to develop it and is derived from personal interviews with IT managers and research about professionalism in several occupational groups. It first defines what is meant by *professionalism* and distinguishes it from the traditional meaning of *professional*. Next it explores the role of management in creating an environment where professionalism is either encouraged or discouraged. Then it looks at the specific ways an IT worker is expected to demonstrate professionalism and contrasts these with behaviors that are deemed to be unprofessional. Finally, it identifies several actions that managers can take to develop professionalism in their IT staff.

PROFESSIONAL VERSUS PROFESSIONALISM

While IT specialists have called themselves "professionals" for a long time, it is clear that IT work does not meet most of the traditional standards for this classification. A classic profession is characterized by a systematic body of theory; recognized professional authority; community sanctions; a regulative code of ethics; and a cul-

> Professionalism is a description you hope others will apply to you, not a set of degrees of job qualifications. (Maister 1993)

ture of norms, values, and symbols (Greenwood 1965; Caplow 1966). These characteristics are clearly met by the well-established professional groups in our society (e.g., accountants, doctors, engineers). While IT workers have a systematic body of theory, they meet none of the other criteria for an established professional group.

In contrast, *professionalism* refers to a person's attitude to, behavior on, and capabilities in the job. Many occupational groups and businesses use the term *professional* to refer to this aspect of their work, rather than to its more traditional meaning. The terminology is further confused by the fact that there is no generally accepted norm of what constitutes *professionalism*. Specific behavior or attitudes may be professional in one occupation or organization and not in another. A recent Internet search yielded literally thousands of relevant sites containing professional behavior standards for such widely diverse groups as real estate salespeople, audiologists, librarians, and party planners, as well as lawyers, doctors, and other traditional professionals. Clearly, professionalism is on people's minds.

A general list of professional behaviors in many occupational groups can read like an endorsement of motherhood. And yet these various groups have felt it is necessary to write down such expectations as the following:

- "Treat your peers with respect and consideration" (Belilos 1998).
- "Behave with integrity at all times" (Belilos 1998).
- "A professional does not make hateful or threatening statements about others" (Boushka 1998).

- "A professional does not behave in a bizarre manner" (Boushka 1998).
- "A professional shows up on time and is prepared" (Chial 1998).

On further analysis, it is clear that professionalism actually involves several different *sets* of behaviors, such as those oriented toward an employer (e.g., loyalty, identification with company values), those oriented toward clients (e.g., commitment and enthusiasm, capacity to solve problems), and those oriented toward a peer group (e.g., maintaining skills) (Scott 1967; Texas State Library 2002). In addition, professionalism also involves adherence to certain ethical standards—of an employer, the state, and one's occupational group. More recently, the term *professionalism* is also being widely used in business to refer to a broad set of job capabilities such as ability to manage commitments, the ability to deal with cultural diversity, and the ability to cope with change.

There are several different approaches that have been taken toward delineating what is meant by IT professionalism in recent years. For example, the Association of Computing Machinery (ACM) established a Code of Ethics and Professional Conduct in 1992, which outlines three main sets of imperatives (for the complete list, see Appendix):

- **General moral imperatives** (e.g., I will give proper credit for intellectual property and honor confidentiality)
- **Specific professional responsibilities** (e.g., I will acquire and maintain professional competence; I will accept and provide appropriate professional review)
- **Organizational leadership imperatives** (e.g., I will manage personnel and resources to design and build information systems that enhance the quality of working life; I will ensure that users and those who will be affected by a system have their needs clearly articulated during the assessment and design of requirements)

The University of Virginia's Department of Computer Sciences has also identified a number of areas in which IT professionalism could/should be exercised, such as censorship, hacking, fraud and dishonesty in business, netiquette, privacy, and viruses. (For a complete list, see Appendix.) Tom DeMarco describes four key characteristics of IT professionalism in *The Responsible Software Engineer* (Myers, Hall, and Pitt 1997). These are as follows:

1. *Proficient.* IT work is done with deftness, agility, and skill.
2. *Permanent.* IT professionals are permanently dedicated to IT work.
3. *Professing.* IT workers declare themselves to be part of the IT profession.
4. *Promise keeping.* IT workers make and keep promises to themselves about what they will and won't do.

While it is clearly desirable for IT workers to ascribe to all these standards, they do not fully address the areas of attitude and behavior that most IT managers want to see from their IT workers. Therefore, other writers have documented some very specific tactical behaviors that they feel constitute IT professionalism:

- A professional makes a reasonable investment in the tools of the trade, such as a PC or laptop with current technology.
- A professional makes himself available to support his work in an on-call situation with reasonable reliability and frequency.

- A professional does not overcommit his personal time in a manner that conflicts with his responsibilities.
- A professional should not criticize his employer or his employer's industry (Boushka 1998).

The problem with these types of statements is that they are too specific and fail to apply in many situations. The solution is, therefore, to identify a set of principles of professionalism that IT workers and managers can use to identify specific appropriate behaviors for their jobs and against which they can evaluate their own and others' behaviors in a wide variety of circumstances (Maister 1993).

PRINCIPLES OF PROFESSIONALISM FOR IT MANAGEMENT

Principles of Managing for Professionalism

- Corporate values and behavior can promote or discourage professionalism.
- Much professional behavior is "caught," not taught.
- Expectations of professionalism should be consistent from the top down and through all parts of the organization.
- Companies get the behavior they actually expect, not the behavior they say they want.

While professionalism in the workplace per se has not been studied by researchers, a great deal of work has been done on organizational citizenship behavior (OCB), which is a surrogate for some forms of professionalism. OCB is defined as an employee's willingness to go above and beyond the roles that he or she has been assigned (Organ 1990) and includes such behaviors as helping others, enhancing the social and psychological context that supports task performance, peacemaking, courtesy, and taking steps to avoid problems for others (Organ 1990; Podsakoff et al. 2000). Two meta-analysis studies have recently shown that such behaviors will occur if and only if employees are emotionally attached to the organization (Organ and Ryan 1995; Podsakoff et al. 2000). These findings underline the importance of an organization's leadership in establishing an environment in which people *want* to behave professionally. Thus, there are some environments in which IT professionalism will flourish and others in which it is stifled.

It is important that a positive environment for IT professionalism is created and nurtured within the organization because professionalism is not usually taught, but rather picked up by osmosis through observation and interaction with others, particularly with leaders and managers. Anecdotal evidence suggests that management is responsible for much unprofessional behavior at work. "We've turfed people out and brought in outside contractors. How can we blame them for disloyalty?" asked one manager. Another noted, "We've slashed funding for all the training in 'soft skills.' It's easy to get money for Java training but not for anything to do with emotional intelligence." One company was trying to do something about management's influence in this area. "We are working with HR to develop our senior management, from the CIO down, to change their behaviors, which will, in turn, send a message through our teams that we are changing," stated the manager.

Tips for IT Managers

- Identify your corporate values and *live them*.
- Measure and reward what you value.
- Model professionalism for your staff.

- Seek out and eliminate inconsistencies between espoused company values and actual HR and management practices.
- Provide mentoring and training (if possible) in professional attitudes and behavior.

Other parts of an organization can also drive out professionalism in IT workers. "Human resources can often create programs that discourage professionalism," stated one manager. "If you're treated as a nine-to-fiver and not given the benefits of a professional, why should you act like one?" "If people see their leaders acting without integrity, how can we expect to see it in lower-level workers?" said another. Similarly, there are too many managers who send mixed messages about the behavior they value. For example, they may *say* they want innovation and "out-of-the-box thinking," but they make it clear that mistakes and risks will not be tolerated. Tom Siebel of Siebel Systems believes that professionalism should be one of a company's core values. "Too many companies . . . have an arrogant self-image . . . I want to be absolutely certain that our values drive our behavior and not vice versa" (Fryer 2001). In other words, companies get the behavior that they model themselves.

The daily working environment can also stifle professionalism. Outside consultants are frequently perceived to be more professional than internal staff. This is often because of the "baggage" with which most IT workers have to deal. Outsiders have fewer distractions, are given better instructions about their work, have fewer demands on their time (e.g., meetings, politics), get more support, and receive less e-mail. "What has happened to our own people that we can't see professionalism in them?" asked one manager. Another answered, "They've had to endure bad management."

PRINCIPLES OF PROFESSIONALISM FOR IT WORKERS

As noted above, professionalism is actually several different sets of attitudes and behaviors that an IT worker is expected to display at all times. Five sets of behaviors can be considered indicative of IT professionalism:

1. **Comportment.** This old-fashioned word covers one's appearance and manners on the job. While *technically* neither should make a difference to one's job performance, *practically* they do. It is unfortunate but true that it is much easier to acquire the label "unprofessional" than the reverse. IT workers would be wise to be aware that perceptions of professionalism are sometimes equally as important as actual behavior

on the job. Thus, if an IT worker does not appear to fit the image of a professional, particularly if his or her appearance is at odds with that of the rest of the organization, what he or she has to say may be immediately discounted by others. A good example of this is casual dress, which is often misinterpreted by those outside IT. As Tom Siebel explains it, "Dressing in jeans and a T-shirt to greet the CEO of a major financial institution, who just got off the plane from Munich, is not acceptable" (Fryer 2001). Furthermore, "Everyone's definition of *casual* is different," stated one participant, "and it's easy to go from casual dress to casual approaches to work."

Principle 1: *An IT worker's professionalism is often judged by his or her dress and manner toward others.*

Tip: When in doubt, an IT worker should model the comportment of the *best* exemplar in the office and dress as well as one's immediate supervisor.

Similarly, manners and bearing are often perceived to be surrogates for professionalism. This explains the emphasis on treating one's colleagues and customers with courtesy and respect in many of the codes of professionalism described above. Siebel notes, "Our comportment is always professional, whether we are interacting with each other or with customers, partners, suppliers, or others" (Fryer 2001). In addition, it is not professional to take disagreements personally. "We should be able to disagree without rancor," said one manager. "IT people are particularly bad at finger-pointing when a problem arises. Defensiveness is unprofessional. It's better to just help solve the problem and get on with the job."

2. *Preparation.* No one appears more unprofessional than someone who doesn't know what he or she is doing. For an IT worker, this means having not only the technical skills to do a job, but also a good understanding of the business context in which the work is taking place. "The biggest complaint we get is that our people don't understand the business," remarked one manager. "Far too many people see technology itself as the end product, instead of as a business enabler." "Businesspeople are always asking, 'How much credence should I place in this IT person?'" explained another. Understanding the big picture is essential to doing a good job both because it helps an IT person make better decisions about the work for the organization *and* because it gives users confidence that the person working on their problem will do a good job.

Preparation is important in an IT worker's daily interactions with others as well. People are perceived as more professional if they are well organized and proactive. Good organization skills involve anticipating problems and dealing with them before they become bigger, careful planning of meetings and schedules (e.g., using an agenda), and a disciplined approach to work (e.g., a methodology, root-cause analysis). Preparation *for* work accomplishes two very important goals. First, it means that an IT professional's promises can be relied on to be met because enough homework has been done to make educated commitments. Second, it is respectful of the other people whose efforts must be integrated with those of the IT worker. Both help others to have confidence in what the IT worker says and does, and this is the very essence of professionalism.

3. *Communication.* While "a failure to communicate" can be a catch-all category when things go wrong, it remains true that good communication skills are a fundamental aspect of all professional relationships and, therefore, contribute strongly to the effectiveness of IT work. Good communication is actually made up of a number of subskills. First, IT workers need to know how to write. Misspellings, grammatical errors, and poorly organized documents are all too common in this field. They not only make the author look unprofessional, but they can also fail to get their message across because they are so difficult to read. Another common mistake is to dash off e-mails as if they were not "real" documents. However, as e-mail is increasingly taking the place of traditional office correspondence, the same care must be taken with it as with a business letter.

Beyond writing, there are a whole host of skills that must be mastered surrounding e-mail and voice communication. All IT professionals should have a routine for managing both media (e.g., updating voice mail messages daily, returning messages within twenty-four hours), even if it's just to say you'll get back to them shortly. Responsiveness is a much-desired trait in an IT professional, and living up to a reasonable standard in this area ensures that the IT worker is perceived as being in control of his or her work and able to manage commitments.

Communication concerning commitments is especially important. IT workers should document important commitments in writing and include any caveats that might change what they have promised (e.g., a schedule or a budget). Paperwork should not languish on a desk for weeks and weeks. And when situations change or problems arise, they must be willing to communicate the bad news and deal with the consequences. The following true story illustrates how an IT professional should do this:

> [When] Richard realized that the extra work was going to cost considerably more than had been planned, [he] decided . . . it was best to bring the extra costs forward to the Project Committee. "It was a brutal meeting," he remembered. "The senior guys beat us up. We had to sell like crazy." But eventually the committee agreed it was the best direction to go and gave them the money they needed to hire consultants . . . to help them do the job. (Smith 1999)

In addition, IT workers must understand how and when to communicate appropriately. Many people receive hundreds of unnecessary e-mails daily because someone hits the "Reply All" button for no good reason. Others copy large numbers of people when only one or two need to know the information. Still others, as the story at the beginning of this chapter illustrates, try to handle sensitive issues in an e-mail, rather than in person or by phone. Finally, it is unfortunate but true that most people's listening skills still need work. IT workers need to cultivate the ability to ask questions, take checkpoints in meetings, and confirm that they have indeed understood what is being said.

Principle 3: *Good communication skills are essential to building professional relationships.*

Tips: Seek advice from others who are viewed as being highly professional about how they communicate (e.g., standards of responsiveness, addressing a problem on the job).

Find out about and use resources that are available to assist with written communication (e.g., spell-checkers, editors, etc.).

Adopt communication routines and standards even if none are expected.

Document any commitments and promises, and make sure they are met.

4. *Judgment.*   IT workers often have difficult decisions to make, and it is very easy to get caught in a professionalism paradox. That is, people who are agreeable and who don't make waves are often *perceived* as being more professional than those who speak out and say "no" when they are asked to do something unreasonable. As a result, it is not uncommon to see IT people and others give lip-service commitment to a decision when they don't agree with it and don't plan to make it work. While this may buy an individual IT worker a short period of grace, it is not professional and doesn't work in the longer term. "We often wimp out, bow to pressure, and undertake something that is highly unlikely to be realized. We do this again and again" (Gack 2002). As a result, IT workers are often perceived as making bad decisions.

IT workers need to know how to make the right choices for the organization as a whole, which means being able to take a strategic view of what they are being asked to do. For example, they must know when they *must* do something, such as fixing a serious problem for the business, even if it means taking time away from another job. In short, they must know where they can add true business value. In making such difficult judgment calls, it is important for an IT worker to maintain a service orientation, while not being servile. "Inflexibility is seen as being unprofessional," one manager noted. Thus, good judgment involves being honest about the full implications of a decision, stating concerns and objections, listening to the other points of view, negotiating a direction forward that everyone can live with, and documenting what was agreed.

Good judgment also includes making sure that decisions are in keeping with the organization's ethical guidelines (e.g., privacy) and that they follow all legal and moral standards. While it is hoped that no IT worker or organization would deliberately contravene these, it is often the case that poor decisions occur simply because of ignorance. A recent furor over a company database that was outsourced to a third-party service provider, thus contravening privacy laws, is a good example. Laws and standards in computing are changing rapidly. Therefore, it is essential that IT workers maintain currency on those that affect their work and their business so they may advise others appropriately.

Principle 4: *Professionalism means making the right choices for the organization as a whole, not just a specific area.*

Tips: Make sure of all the facts before making a decision. Don't get pressured into it.

Always maintain a service orientation.

Become familiar with corporate standards and changing laws regarding computing.

Don't be inflexible; try to find a negotiated way forward that everyone can accept.

5. *Attitude.* Attitude is such an important part of professionalism that some feel that "firms should hire for attitude and train for skill" (Maister 1993). People often believe that their skills qualify them as professionals when it is actually attitude that most believe is the distinguishing feature of a true professional. Basically, professionalism is about *caring*—about doing a job to the best of one's ability and about doing the right thing for the company. People who care have a "can do" approach to their work, seek to constantly improve their skills, take reasonable risks, and take responsibility and accountability for their work. They are willing to invest their time and energy in helping others and "go the extra mile." "We are looking for passion without arrogance or cockiness," said one IT manager. "The best people are those who have an 'I can do it' attitude and who are looking for challenges, rather than those who just have particular skills. These can always be developed or supplemented," stated another. A professional is also willing to accept criticism and coaching for personal growth and works well in a team, sharing the credit and not blaming others when problems arise.

Other characteristics of a positive attitude include calmness, stability, and self-control. Professionals do not lose their temper easily, display an erratic temperament, or make highly critical remarks, especially of others or of their companies. This attitude should extend beyond daily work into the public arena as well. "People often forget that they represent our company even when they aren't at work," stated one participant. One manager from a well-known manufacturer explained how his company had set up a hotline for employees who heard about problems with the company's products while socializing outside of work. The number enabled them to do something about the problem, and this reinforced the company's image of professionalism. In smaller communities IT workers and managers may be expected to represent their companies at charitable events. Their attitude may be important in building respect for the company in their communities.

It should be pointed out that these characteristics are ideals and it is unrealistic to expect everyone to exhibit all of them in practice. "People are built in many ways and have different styles," said one manager. "We must be able to understand and accommodate them and make the blend work."

There is often a great deal of interaction between an organization's culture and individual attitudes. A stifling or highly politicized work environment, lack of appreciation and support, and poor communication about organization or team goals can destroy or dampen an IT worker's positive attitude. One manager noted that many "underperforming" staff simply need better support and education to work more effectively, and providing these can lead to dramatic differences in both attitude and productivity.

> **Principle 5:** *Professionalism means a positive attitude toward work, other people, and one's employer.*
>
> **Tips:** Seek opportunities for personal growth—courses, coaching, or new experiences.
>
> Save highly critical remarks for private communication.
>
> Recognize that you, your department and your employer will be judged by your attitude and demeanor.

DEVELOPING PROFESSIONALISM: ADVICE TO IT MANAGERS

While some people appear to have been born with professional skills, it is widely agreed that professionalism can be developed in all IT workers. The following list provides a good start to the promotion of professionalism.

- *Get consensus on the meaning of professionalism.* Because it is a "soft" skill, professionalism means different things in different organizations. A team meeting to identify the key elements of professionalism in a particular company can help clarify expectations and develop group values around these behaviors.
- *Articulate values.* It is pointless to preach one set of values and reward others. Ideally, corporate values should be consistently upheld throughout the company. However, where they are not, try to articulate where they differ and help IT workers to make effective judgments (e.g., How much will risk taking actually be valued?)
- *Provide resources to support professionalism.* Ideally, these should include training, but where this is not possible, make books or speakers who will address this topic available to your staff. Similarly, providing some administrative support can be very useful in helping people to appear professional to those outside IT. At a minimum, ensure that resources such as document templates, editors, and guidelines for e-mail are made available for staff to use.
- *Grow professionalism in small steps.* People will not develop these skills overnight. Managers should work with individuals in their groups on specific areas of professionalism then provide them with the coaching and support they need.
- *Offer intensive mentoring for staff who are willing to change.* Employees who appear to be more malleable and willing to listen should be given attention from a manager. This can help them develop professional skills more rapidly.
- *Help people find their niche.* No employee (even those who appear to be unwilling to change) should be sidelined; doing so will only leave them increasingly further behind in a rapidly evolving workplace. A better strategy is to help them identify where they feel they can best make a contribution and to help them develop the particular professional skills they will need.
- *Weed out people whose attitudes are destructive.* If people are not willing to change, managers must try to get rid of them or at least contain them in the short term. A longer-term plan must be put in place for dealing with these individuals, or they could risk poisoning their whole team's effectiveness.

Conclusion

"Professional" is a label that many in IT seek but few earn. Unlike the traditional definition of the term, today's professional is a member of any occupational group who behaves in a professional manner. Professionalism can mean different things to different groups and organizations, but there is general agreement that it constitutes a set of behaviors that are expected over and above the technical skills of the job. This chapter has tried to determine what professionalism means for IT workers. By delineating five principles of behavior, it has explored some of the areas in which IT managers should expect to see professionalism displayed. Comportment, preparation, communication, judgment, and attitude are "soft" skills but are often equally as important to getting a job done as technical ability. Professionalism is difficult to teach but easy to *catch* through exposure to exemplars, corporate and team culture, values and standards, and an environment that appreciates and rewards this behavior. As IT work becomes increasingly interconnected with that of the rest of the organization, the professionalism of IT staff will make a big difference in the effectiveness of the IT department as a whole. IT managers would, therefore, be well advised to make professionalism an important value for all IT staff and to recognize and reward it when it is displayed.

References

Belilos, C. "Networking on the Net: Professionalism, Ethics and Courtesy on the Net." CHIC Hospitality Consulting Services, 1998.

Boushka, B. "Business Ethics, Professionalism and the Workplace: Information Systems." High Productivity Publishing, 1998. http://members.aol.com/_ht_a/JBOUSHKA/isethics.htm (accessed January 20, 2003).

Caplow, T. "The Sequence of Professionalization." In *Professionalization*, edited by H. Vollmer and D. Mills. Englewood Cliffs, NJ: Prentice-Hall, 1966.

Chial, M. "Conveying Expectations about Professional Behavior." *Audiology Today* 10, no. 4 (July 1998).

Fryer, B. "Tom Siebel of Siebel Systems: High Tech the Old-fashioned Way." *Harvard Business Review* March (2001).

Gack, G. "Professionalism." Information Technology Effectiveness Inc., 2002. www.iteffectiveness.com/professionalism.htm (accessed January 20, 2003).

Greenwood, W. *Management and Organizational Behavior Theories: An Interdisciplinary Approach*. Cincinnati: Southwestern Publishing, 1965.

Maister, D. *True Professionalism*. New York: The Free Press, 1993.

Myers, C., T. Hall, and D. Pitt. *The Responsible Software Engineer*. Heidelberg, Germany: Springer-Verlag, 1997.

Organ, D. "The Motivational Basis of Organizational Citizenship Behavior." In *Research in Organizational Behavior* 12, edited by B. M. Staw and L. L. Cummings. Greenwich, CT: JAI Press, 43–72. 1990.

Organ, D., and K. Ryan. "A Meta-analytic Review of Attitudinal and Dispositional Predictors of Organizational Citizenship Behavior." *Personnel Psychology* 48 (1995): 775–802.

Podsakoff, P., S. MacKenzie, J. Paine, and D. Bachrach. "Organizational Citizenship Behaviors: A Critical Review of the Theoretical and Empirical Literature and Suggestions for Future Research." *Journal of Management* 26, no. 3 (2000): 513–63.

Scott, W. *Organizational Theory and Behavior Analysis for Management*. Homewood, IL: Irwin, 1967.

Smith, H. "Leading Change at Investco." 1999. www.itworldcanada.com (accessed January 20, 2003).

Texas State Library and Archives Commission. "Small Library Management Training Program." www.tsl.state.tx.us/ld/tutorials/professionalism/IB.html (accessed January 20, 2003).

ACM Code of Ethics and Professional Conduct 1992

(www.acm.org/constitution/code.html, accessed January 20, 2003)

1. **General Moral Imperatives**

   I will . . .

   1.1. contribute to society and human well-being.

   1.2 avoid harm to others.

   1.3. be honest and trustworthy.

   1.4. be fair and take action not to discriminate.

   1.5. honor property rights including copyrights and patents.

   1.6. give proper credit for intellectual property.

   1.7. respect the privacy of others.

   1.8. honor confidentiality.

2. **Personal Responsibilities**

   I will . . .

   2.1. strive to achieve the highest quality, effectiveness, and dignity in both the process and products of professional work.

   2.2. acquire and maintain professional competence.

   2.3. know and respect existing laws pertaining to professional work.

   2.4. accept and provide appropriate professional review.

   2.5. give comprehensive and thorough evaluations of computer systems and their impacts including analysis of possible risks.

   2.6. honor contracts, agreements, and assigned responsibilities.

   2.7. improve public understanding of computing and its consequences.

   2.8. access computing and communication resources only when authorized to do so.

3. **Organizational Leadership Imperatives**

   I will . . .

   3.1. articulate social responsibilities of members of an organizational unit and encourage full acceptance of those responsibilities.

   3.2. manage personnel and resources to design and build information systems that enhance the quality of working life.

   3.3. acknowledge and support proper and authorized uses of an organization's computing and communications resources.

   3.4 ensure that users and those who will be affected by a system have their needs clearly articulated during the assessment and design of requirements; later the system must be validated to meet requirements.

   3.5. articulate and support policies that protect the dignity of users and others affected by a computing system.

   3.6. create opportunities for members of the organization to learn the principles and limitations of computer systems.

IT Professional Standards and Professionalism

Department of Computer Science, University of Virginia

Professionalism and standards should be exercised in the following areas:

- Censorship
- Community values
- Computer ethics and social impact in schools
- Copyrights, patents, trademarks, intellectual property
- Crime
- Disabilities
- Discrimination and harassment
- Ethics
- Fraud and dishonesty in business
- Freedom of speech
- Green machines
- Hacking
- History of computing
- Impact
- Liabilities
- Netiquette
- Privacy
- Relationships
- Responsibilities
- Safety critical systems
- Viruses
- World codes

MINI CASE

Leveraging IT Vendors at SleepSmart

The numbers were in, and Greg Danson breathed a sigh of relief. They looked good. In-stock levels had increased yet again; inventory value per square foot had declined; and sales and general administration costs had come down for the third quarter in a row. "Maybe *now* they'll see we mean business," he said with satisfaction. "They" were the analysts who worked for the leading financial institutions and investment firms. His company, SleepSmart—a leading bed and bedding retailer—had taken a public beating in the past few years. Chief among the criticisms had been the company's outdated technology. "If SleepSmart hopes to compete with retail giants like Sears, Target, and Wal-Mart, it will have to move its technology into the current century . . . and fast," they noted. The result had been a steady decline in the price of SleepSmart's stock.

As SleepSmart's CIO, Greg had always privately agreed with the analysts. Over the years, he had looked longingly at some of the technology other retailers had installed. Although the exact details were secret, he knew that they had databases that gave them up-to-the-minute sales figures, and their systems were integrated with their suppliers and with each other. All of these enabled other retailers to do more (i.e., provide more merchandise and better customer service) with less (i.e., at lower cost). It had been a happy time for him when the other executives had finally been forced to recognize that technology had to be an integral part of SleepSmart's business strategy. This was the first time in his thirty years with the firm that IT had enjoyed serious executive support and investment. Until recently, IT had always been relegated to a supporting role. "We're retailers, not technology gurus," the other executives had explained. "We know what our customers want. We don't need to be leading edge. Just keep our cash registers working."

The company had been in business for almost a hundred years, growing from a small, family-owned mattress manufacturer to a large, national chain store with more than five hundred locations. Growth was essential in the present competitive environment, so in recent years SleepSmart had diversified into all kinds of bedroom furniture, bedding, curtains, and even closet design. Its fledgling BathSmart division was seeking to extend its market reach even further. And its Web site even sold pajamas and nightgowns. But in the rush to diversify, little attention had been paid to streamlining and integrating the firm's technology. Systems did not "talk" to other systems; it took weeks to pull sales figures together from the different divisions; customers were confused. "Why is my SleepSmart Bonus Club statement still coming to my old address when I've already given you my new one, but my charge card bill manages to come to the right address every month?" was a common complaint. Customers didn't realize how many separate systems needed name and address updates. In short, the company's systems had been embarrassingly old-fashioned, and the nudge from the analysts had been a welcome wake-up call, as far as Greg was concerned.

With the company's purse strings finally pried open, Greg had been given the mandate to rebuild the mishmash of systems the company had accumulated into a state-of-the-art technology platform within three years. The first step was relatively simple: draw up a comprehensive "technology blueprint" identifying the desired state of the company's IT platform. After consultation with the business about its current and future needs, followed by an assessment of the current state of the firm's technology (dismal), all of the major technology vendors were consulted for their ideas. Naturally, they all knew how to solve SleepSmart's problem: install their own proprietary software and hire them to implement it! Brushing aside all the hype, Greg had been impressed with the quality of the vendors' presentations and the depth of their retail knowledge. Many had invested substantial amounts in their industry-specific products and brought a breadth of experience to the planning process that his staff didn't have.

This was the fun part. It was a chance to wipe the slate clean of all of the mixed-up, disparate, and overlapping systems and data and really dream big about the future. The new integrated technology blueprint solved all these problems. It called for one financial system, one HR system, and one customer-facing program. There would be one data warehouse and one integrated view of the customer. From this, a three-year plan was developed to help make SleepSmart more cost efficient and to give staff better information for doing their jobs.

But as usual, the devil was in the details. "The *only* way we can do all this work at the same time is by using our suppliers' competencies," he told his chief architect, Stan Bailey, and his other IT directors. "We simply don't have enough staff or skills in-house."

Like most other companies, SleepSmart had worked with a number of different vendors over the years to address their needs and had developed strong competencies in contract development and management. Typically, the IT guys would scour the marketplace to find the product or service they wanted, and they would negotiate with each vendor for the best price. They would then monitor the contract to ensure SleepSmart got value for its money. In the meantime, the vendors were always looking for ways to sell more product because that's how they were compensated. "Doing the deal" was the focus of both groups.

The problem, as Greg explained patiently to his staff, was that this process took time and generated negative energy between the company and the vendor. "We simply don't have the time to do business this way anymore," he stated. "We need another approach to working with our vendors if we're going to get all this work done in time."

And there was another problem. Bailey put his finger on it: the business executives didn't want to have anything to do with their internal "tech guys"—let alone the vendors—even though they were going to be spending tens of millions (or more) with vendor firms. "We're busy enough as it is. Just take the money and fix the technology," was their mantra. "But if we're really going

to achieve the kind of transformational change that's going to affect 'the Street's' view of us, our business executives are going to have to be onside 150 percent," Bailey said. Greg's team considered outsourcing large chunks of the work involved in implementing their plan, but he rejected this idea. "We're betting the company here. We need more control and involvement in these projects."

Bailey and the others agreed. "This can't be a normal outsourcing deal," Bailey noted. "We want access to their best minds. We want innovation, but we want to ensure we're getting business value."

There were a number of large vendors who were interested in helping get the SleepSmart strategic IT plan off the ground. Microsoft, IBM, SAP, Oracle, Cisco, and others *all* wanted to help. Each had something to offer the company. What Greg and Bailey *didn't want or need* was to have to run interference between them. "It's bad enough when we have to deal with two vendors on a single project," groused Bailey. "Whenever anything goes wrong, they end up pointing fingers at each other. Sorting out the problems *always* ends up being our job!"

"*That's* the solution to this whole problem," exclaimed Greg. "We need to create a different environment where we can work more collaboratively with our vendors . . . *and* where they can work collaboratively with each other!" Thus was born the SleepSmart Strategic Technology Alliance (SSTA), although the delivery wasn't easy. No one had ever attempted to get so many different competitors to cooperate. "You'll never get IBM and Microsoft working together," scoffed Bailey. "Their product and service offerings overlap. How are you going to draw the line between them?"

But Greg was adamant that the *only* way SleepSmart could achieve transformational change was if everyone (business and vendors included) worked together on the same plan to achieve a real "win-win-win." The SSTA framework he drew up was both innovative and challenging. Its objectives were designed to create a unique relationship that would deliver *mutual business value*. Its key principles were as follows:

- A commitment to mutual success
- A commitment to favorable price and maximum value

- A commitment to introducing best practices into SleepSmart's technology transformation
- Speed of execution
- A shared governance framework that involved business, IT, and the vendors.

His directors had challenged him at the meeting where he had first presented his idea. "How is *this* strategic alliance different from all the others we've had?" they asked. "Why would any vendor want to do this?"

This had forced him to think more deeply about what he wanted to achieve. "The *key* is that we want to work together to deliver optimal business results for *all* the organizations involved," he said as he paced his office. "It's got to be good for everyone."

Greg's next move was to consult with SleepSmart's potential vendor partners. These had already been identified through the blueprint exercise, but would they be willing to work with other companies (and sometimes rivals) in a more collaborative and less competitive way? Finding out the key leverage points for each one helped him to design relationships that would deliver sustainable benefits to each that were beyond price. For example, he promised each partner a larger part of SleepSmart's "spend" on technology if they would agree to prenegotiated prices and discounts. Covering these in advance with each vendor's executives meant that basic terms, discounts, and volumes of business wouldn't have to be discussed by the lower levels of the business every time they bought new technology. Not only would this save everyone time and effort, but it also meant lower cost of sales for the suppliers, who wouldn't have to invest in any presales activities.

The revised framework won reserved praise from Greg's IT staff. "*If* we can make this work, it will be better for everyone," agreed Bailey. "But there are going to have to be *big* changes in how we work. Getting all these guys in the same room to share information about their products and services is unprecedented. Are you sure you can pull this off?"

Greg went back to the vendors for more talks. As the details were worked out, the process had to move higher and higher in each organization as the individual account executives realized that they couldn't commit to what Greg wanted without higher-level approvals. Greg wanted openness and sharing between SleepSmart and all its vendors. *Everyone* else wanted confidentiality.

As he got further into the details, he also had to go up the ladder within SleepSmart. Just as the vendors needed to be fully committed to collaboration and sharing, so too did the business. Greg made presentations to the firm's CFO, CEO, and finally even the board of directors. "We can't pull this off without full business participation," he said to the executive team. "You're investing millions on these projects. You need to put your best people on these teams to make sure they deliver the kinds of value you want." The businesspeople wanted to know how the SSTA would increase the company's share price. He explained that the idea of the SSTA was to leverage suppliers' competencies to make SleepSmart a retail showcase. SleepSmart would win by getting state-of-the-art technology at lower-than-average prices. Each of the vendors would win by improving their retail offerings, which they could, in turn, sell to others. All members would develop enhanced organizational competencies in the rapid implementation of technology to achieve business value.

The SSTA was announced to "the Street" and in the national press by SleepSmart's CEO and the heads of its five vendor partners. Then the teams got to work. Guided by a technology footprint that clearly delineated which vendor products would be used where and by regular, detailed strategy updates from SleepSmart business executives, Greg and the SSTA began delivering on their promises. Two years later their innovative uses of technology were beginning to win awards for "most influential technology retailer," for "best in show for innovative retail technology," and for "enterprise architecture excellence."

But it was the numbers that told the real story. Greg had watched them slowly turn around, improving slightly at first then significantly every quarter. They were what everyone wanted to see. This last set was the best yet. He allowed himself a moment of satisfaction. He and the SSTA had worked night and day to fundamentally redesign and build the company's entire retailing infrastructure. Cycle time had improved, costs had declined, and technical service quality was at an all-time high. They were seeing results. But would the financial community finally notice?

He got his answer the next week. While acknowledging SleepSmart's efforts to lower its costs, the analysts noted that the company's overall revenues had declined slightly—a bad sign. Now that SleepSmart had all its technical fundamentals right, the analysts suddenly wanted to see top-line growth! So the stock price was still in the dumpster. Greg sighed with frustration. There was only so much a CIO could do for his company. Just how much could IT really be used to generate more revenue? How much was up to the business? How could he get the business to understand enough about technology to see its top-line potential? There wasn't enough time or money to allow them to really experiment with it in a hands-on fashion. Was it really his job anyway? "I can lead them to water, but I can't make them drink," he said to himself. "It's *their* business; I can only offer them effective options."

This was going to be an even bigger challenge than the one they had come through. When they started, there had at least been some clear technical problems that had to be fixed. Integration, single view of the customer, faster information—all these helped reduce costs and increase flexibility. Now they had all these, and the company was ready to grow sales, but that wasn't happening. What could be done to bring in the customers or to increase the amount they spent when they shopped at SleepSmart?

Furthermore, now that they were three years down the road, the SSTA was wearing thin and needed renewing. Most of the players had changed, some more than once. Many of their partners had come out with new offerings and were lobbying to get them included in the technology blueprint, thus disrupting the carefully negotiated balance among them. Competition was rearing its ugly head among the partners. Other suppliers, offering completely new technology, were pressuring him to give them favored SSTA status, but managing the relationships in the alliance was incredibly complicated as it was. Between working with their business partners and working with the different vendors and their staff, Bailey and his small team were going flat out already.

"We've done well, but we can't make money by just winning awards," said Greg to no one in particular. "I'm going to have to refocus and reinvigorate this alliance *and* figure out how to help the business grow revenue." He picked up the phone and called Bailey. "Let's grab a coffee. I need to pick your brain." ■

DISCUSSION QUESTIONS

1. Identify the advantages and disadvantages of the SSTA. Do you think that this sort of vendor partnership can prosper in the long run? Why or why not?
2. Focusing IT on the top line (i.e., growing revenues) is very different than focusing IT on the bottom line (i.e., reducing costs). Explain.
3. Brainstorm some ideas of how SleepSmart could generate additional revenues using IT.

MINI CASE

Desktop Provisioning at CanCredit

"And in conclusion, we feel that there are a number of outsourcing opportunities that would make sense for us at CanCredit. Now that we have consolidated our operations across the country into a shared services delivery model, we are in a position to manage our limited resources more strategically. If you will look at Appendix A of our proposed budget, you will see where these savings will come from. Any questions?"

Monique Lalonde sat down at the large conference room table and prepared to field questions about this important new element in her budget from the IT steering committee. In her three years as CIO at CanCredit, she had worked hard to get to this point. When she had first joined the firm after seventeen years in the finance industry, she had been shocked by how decentralized the firm's IT was and how few technical standards were in place. Every major region across the country had its own IT shop, and the number of technologies and supplier contracts was astounding. And CanCredit, as a business development bank that provided start-up, long-term, and subordinate financing to companies, had offices everywhere.

In those days every IT manager was responsible for dealing with some sort of vendor—whether individual contractors, application software providers, hardware vendors, or service providers. While each tried to make the best deal for the organization, the result was a mishmash of people, contracts, technologies, and approaches to sourcing. She had shuddered at what might happen if any auditor ever looked at the big picture. The costs and duplications involved were huge.

Among her first steps as CIO, Monique had centralized and consolidated her IT organization (over the screams of the users and threats of dire political fallout) and established some common technology standards. It had taken longer than she had planned, but she was now in a position to deliver some serious economies of scale.

"Why have you chosen desktop management and client support as your priorities for outsourcing?" asked Kevin Cheung, Director of Finance. "Don't most companies outsource operations and programming?"

"We feel that desktop management and client support are the most suitable for outsourcing at present because we have well-established standards in these areas, so the risk is relatively low," replied Monique. "By tendering these opportunities first, we can use the lessons we learn to figure out how we might go on to outsource more sophisticated IT activities."

"I certainly like the kinds of the savings you've outlined here," said Jean Girard, CanCredit's CEO. "However, I am concerned about how this is going to affect our flexibility as an organization. Even though we're a relatively small organization, we do business right across the country, which brings us into competition with the major banks. One of our key advantages has been our ability to respond quickly to our customers' needs. It seems to me that any outsourcing arrangement that we enter into must address this issue. For example, if our workers needed to be more mobile, would the outsourcer be capable of rolling out the necessary systems, processes, and training? What if we want to work with other vendors who have an important new technology?"

Monique thought rapidly. Truthfully, she hadn't given much thought to anything other than cost savings. In her experience, organizations always went for the lowest-cost deals. She'd already gone through an extensive bidding process to winnow those vendors that did not have the size and competencies to deal with CanCredit's diverse, national needs. The two who had advanced through this process, IBM and HP, had each come up with very competitive bids, but this issue hadn't been addressed. "I think your suggestion is a good one, sir, and we will incorporate it in the final round of our bidding process."

VP of Operations John McLeod spoke up. "Obviously, anything we can do to save money has my vote, but I'd like to see more on how you are going to ensure a smooth transition from our present service to the outsourcer. This is a major change for us, and we don't want any disruptions to our customers. And what provisions are you making for the IT people who will be displaced or have to move to the outsourcer? We can't afford any negative publicity in either area."

"My concern is that the selected outsourcer provide our users with desktop management and client support that are at least as good as what we have now," stated Helen DeVilliers, VP of Sales and Marketing. "You've done an excellent job of getting us reliable and stable infrastructure over the last three years. But we expect to see this quality of service not only continue, but improve and become more responsive with any outsourcer. In my opinion this is more important than any cost savings we realize."

Monique was rapidly taking notes. "Thank you all for this feedback," she said. "It's given me a much broader mandate for outsourcing than I thought I had. Here's what I suggest that I do now: I'd like to give some serious thought to structuring the final round of bidding to ensure that services we are going to get from our selected outsourcer will support future IT strategies as well as operational considerations. It's clear that our contracts will need some additional clauses to reflect your concerns. And we'll have to come up with a new set of incentives and success metrics and design our relationship to ensure that it is a more collaborative one."

In the follow-up meeting with her direct reports, Monique listed issues that would need to be addressed in the outsourcing deal. "How are we ever going to incorporate requirements like 'flexibility' and 'innovation' in a contract?" she asked. "Whatever we write down is going to change over the life of this contract. We're going to need mechanisms that will allow us to shift gears or directions in response to changing needs and changing technology. Obviously, we need a formal contract, but it seems to me that what's even more important is how we work with the outsourcer we select to ensure that the spirit of the deal is respected. I'd really appreciate your input not only on the qualities we need to look for in our outsourcer, but also what we can do at CanCredit to build a trusting partnership with whichever firm we select." ∎

DISCUSSION QUESTIONS

1. Do you agree with Monique's strategy of outsourcing desktop management and client support?
2. List the issues that CanCredit needs to address regarding desktop management and client support. Can the outsourcer address all these issues?
3. What measurements would you use to assess satisfaction of these issues?

MINI CASE

Project Management at MM

"We've got a real 'warm puppy' here," Brian Smith told Werner McCann. "Make sure you make the most of it. We could use a winner."

Smith was MM's CIO, and Werner was his top project manager. The puppy in question was MM's new venture into direct-to-customer marketing of its "green meters," a product designed to help better manage electrical consumption, and the term referred to the project's wide appeal. The strategy had been a hit with analysts ever since it had been "exposed" to the financial community, and the company's stock was doing extremely well as a result. "At last," one had written in his popular newsletter, "we have a company that is willing to put power literally and figuratively in consumers' hands. If MM can deliver on its promises, we fully expect this company to reap the rewards."

Needless to say, the Green project was popular internally too. "I'm giving it to you because you have the most project-management experience we've got," Smith had said. "There's a lot riding on this one." As he walked away from Smith's office, Werner wasn't sure whether to feel complimented or terrified. He had certainly managed some successful projects for the company (previously known as ModMeters) over the past five years but never anything like this one. That's the problem with project management, he thought. In IT almost every project is completely different. Experience only takes you part of the way.

And Green was different. It was the first truly enterprisewide project the company had ever done, and Werner was having conniptions as he thought about telling Fred Tompkins, the powerful head of manufacturing, that he might not be able to have everything his own way. Werner knew that, to be successful, this project had to take an outside-in approach; that is, to take the end customers' point of view on the company. That meant integrating marketing, ordering, manufacturing, shipping, and service into one seamless process that wouldn't bounce the customer from one department to another in the company. MM had always had separate systems for each of its "silos," and this project would work against the company's traditional culture and processes. The Green project was also going to have to integrate with IT's information management renewal (IMR) project. Separate silos had always meant separate databases, and the IMR project was supposed to resolve inconsistencies among them and provide accurate and integrated information to different parts of the company. This was a huge political challenge, but unless it worked, Werner couldn't deliver on his mandate.

Then there was the issue of resources. Werner groaned at the thought. MM had some good people but not enough to get through all of the projects in the IT plan within their promised timelines. Because of the importance of the Green project, he knew he'd get good cooperation on staffing, but the fact remained that he would have to go outside for some of the technical skills he needed to get the job done. Finally, there was the schedule they had to meet. Somehow, during the preliminary assessment phase, it had become clear that September 5 was to be the "hard launch" date. There were good reasons for this—the fall was when consumers usually became concerned with their energy consumption—but Werner worried that a date barely twelve months from now would put too much pressure on his team. "We've got to get in there first, before the competition," Smith had said to him. "The board expects us to deliver. You've got my backing and the support of the full executive team, but you *have* to deliver this one."

Six Weeks Later

It was full steam ahead on the Green project. It's *amazing* what a board mandate and executive sponsorship can do for a project, thought Werner, who knew how hard it usually was to get business attention to IT initiatives. He now had a full-time business counterpart, Raj Sambamurthy. Samba, as he was known to his colleagues, had come out of Tompkins's division and was doing a fantastic job of getting the right people in the room to make the decisions they needed to move ahead. The Green steering committee was no Mickey Mouse group either. Smith, Tompkins, and every VP affected by the project were meeting biweekly with him and Samba to review every aspect of the project's progress.

Werner had pulled no punches when communicating with the committee. "You've given me the mandate and the budget to get this project off the ground," he had told them. "But we have to be clear about what we're trying to accomplish." Together, they had hammered out a value proposition that emphasized the strategic value of the project and some of the measures they would use to monitor its ultimate success. The requirements and design phase had also gone smoothly because everyone was so motivated to ensure the project's success. "Linking success to *all* our annual bonuses sure helped *that!*" Werner had remarked wryly to Samba.

Now he was beginning to pull together his "dream team" of implementers. The team had chosen a package known as Web-4-U as the front end of the project, but it would take a lot of work to customize it to suit their unique product and, even more, to integrate it with MM's outmoded back-end systems. The Web-4-U company was based in Ireland but had promised to provide 24/7 consulting on an as-needed basis. In addition, Samba had now assembled a small team of business analysts to work on the business processes they would need. They were working out of the firm's Cloverdale office, a thirty-minute drive from IT's downtown location. (It was a shame they couldn't all be together, but space was at a premium in HQ. Werner made a mental note to look into some new collaboration software he'd heard about.) Now that these two pieces were in place, Werner felt free to focus on the technical "guts" of the system. "Maybe this will work out after all," he said.

Three Months to Launch Date

By June, however, he was tearing out what little hair was left on his head. He was seriously considering moving to a remote Peruvian hamlet and breeding llamas. "*Anything* would be better than this mess," he observed to Yung Lee, the senior IT architect, over coffee. They were poring over the project's critical path. "The way I see it," Lee stated matter-of-factly, "we have two choices: we can continue with this inferior technology and meet our deadline but not deliver on our functionality, *or* we can redo the plan and go back to the steering committee with a revised delivery date and budget."

Werner sighed. Techies *always* saw things in black and white, but his world contained much more gray. And so much was riding on this—credibility (his, IT's, the company's), competitiveness, stock price. He dreaded being the bearer of this bad news, so he said, "Let's go over this *one* more time."

"It's not going to get any better, but here goes." Lee took at deep breath. "Web-4-U is based on outmoded technology. It was the best available last year, but *this* year the industry has agreed on a new standard, and if we persist in using Web-4-U, we are going to be out of date before Green even hits the street. We need to go back and completely rethink our technical approach based on the new standard and then redesign our Web interface. I know it's a setback and it will be expensive, but it has to be done."

"How come we didn't know about this earlier?" Werner demanded.

Lee replied, "When the standard was announced, we didn't realize what the implications were at first. It was only in our quarterly architecture meeting that the subject came up. That's why I'm here now." The architects were a breed apart, thought Werner. All tech and *no* business sense. They'd lost almost three months because of this. "By the way," Lee concluded, "Web-4-U knew about this too. They're scrambling to rewrite their code. I guess they figured if you didn't know right away, there would be more chance of you sticking with them."

The chances of *that* are slim to none, thought Werner. His *next* software provider, whoever that was, was going to be sitting right here under his steely gaze. Seeing an agitated Wendy Chan at his door, he brought the meeting to a hasty close. "I'm going to have to discuss this with Brian," he told Lee. "We can't surprise him with this at the steering committee meeting. Hang tight for a couple of days, and I'll get back to you."

"OK," said Lee, "but remember, we're wasting time."

Easy for *you* to say, thought Werner as he gestured Chan into his office. She was his counterpart at the IMR project, and they had always had a good working relationship. "I just wanted to give you a heads-up that we've got a serious problem at IMR that will affect you," she began. Llamas began prancing into his mind's eye. "Tompkins is refusing to switch to our new data dictionary. We've spent months hammering this out with the team, but he says he wasn't kept informed about the implications of the changes, and now he's refusing to play ball. I don't know *how* he could say that. He's had a rep on the team from the beginning, and we've been sending him regular progress reports."

Werner was copied on those reports. Their pages of techno-jargon would put *anyone* to sleep! He was sure that Tompkins had never got past the first page of any of those reports. His rep was a dweeb too, someone Tompkins thought he could live without in his daily operations.

"Damn! This is something I *don't* need." Like all IT guys, Werner *hated* corporate politics with a passion. He didn't understand them and wasn't good at them. Why hadn't Samba and his team picked up on this? They were plugged into the business. Now he was going to have to deal with Chan's problem as well as his own if he wanted to get the Green project going. Their back-end processes wouldn't work at all unless everyone was using the same information in the same format. Why couldn't Tompkins see that? Did he *want* the Green project to fail?

"The best way to deal with this one," advised Chan, "is to *force* him to accept these changes. Go to John Johnson and tell him that you need Tompkins to change his business processes to fit our data dictionary. It's for the good of the company, after all." Chan's strong suit wasn't her political savvy.

"You're right that we need Tompkins on our side," said Werner, "but there may be a better way. Let me talk to Samba. He's got his ear to the ground in the business. I'll speak with him and get back to you."

After a bit of chitchat, Wendy Chan left Werner to his PERT chart, trying again to determine the extra cost in time if they went with the new technology. Just then the phone rang. It was Linda Perkins, his newly hired work-at-home usability designer. She was one of the best in the business, and he was lucky to have snagged her just coming off maternity leave. His promise of flexible working hours and full benefits had lured her back to work two months before her year-long leave ended. "You've *got* to do something about your HR department!" Perkins announced. "They've just told me that I'm not eligible for health and dental benefits because I don't work on the premises! Furthermore, they want to classify me as contingent staff, not managerial, because I don't fit in one of their petty little categories for employees. You promised me that you had covered all this before I took the job! I gave up a good job at LifeCo so I could work from home."

Werner had indeed covered this issue in principle with Rick Morrow, IT's HR representative, but that had been almost eight months ago. Morrow had since left the firm. Werner wondered if he had left any paperwork on this matter. The HR IT spot had not yet been filled, and all of the IT managers were upset about HR's unreceptive attitude when it came to adapting its policies to the realities of today's IT world. "OK, Linda, just hang in there for a day or two and I'll get this all sorted out," he promised. "How's the usability testing coming along?"

"That's *another* thing I wanted to talk with you about. The team's making changes to the look and feel of the product without consulting me," she fumed. "I can't do my job without being in the loop. You *have* to make them tell me when they're doing things like this."

Werner sighed. Getting Linda on the project had been such a coup that he hadn't given much thought to how the lines of communication would work within such a large team. "I hear you, Linda, and we'll work this out. Can you just give me a few days to figure out how we can improve things?"

Hanging up, he grabbed his jacket and slunk out of the office as quickly as he could before any other problems could present themselves. If he just kept walking south, he'd make it to the Andes in three, maybe four months. He could teach himself Spanish along the way. At least the llamas would appreciate his efforts!

MM could take their project and give it to some other poor schmuck. *No way* was he going back! He walked furiously down the street, mentally ticking off the reasons he had been a fool to fall for Smith's sweet talk. Then, unbidden, a plan of attack formed in his head. Walking always did the trick. Getting out of the office cleared his head and focused his priorities. He turned back the way he had come, now eager to get back in the fray. There were some things he had to do right away and others he had to put in place ASAP. ■

DISCUSSION QUESTIONS

1. Some organizational factors increase a project's likelihood of success. Identify these "facilitators" for the Green project.
2. Other organizational factors decrease a project's likelihood of success. Identify these "barriers" for the Green project.
3. Outline the things that Werner needs to do right away.

INDEX

enforcement, effective, as part of governance, 82
enterprise
architecture, 21–22
measures, 30
perspective on IM, 100–101
value, 10
etiquette. See electronic communication
executive information systems (EISs), 174–175
expectations of IT, shifting, 40
expenditures. See budget, IT
experience, defined, 146
"experience" economy, 146–147
experimentation
core business processes, link to, 142
customer value of, 141–142
for diminishing risk, 11–12
management of strategic, 137
as part of innovation, 136–137
prioritizing, 22–23
stages of, 138–139
strategies for successful, 140–142
for testing viability of new concepts/
technologies, 20
transition to innovation, 142–143
venture funding for, 142

F

feedback loops in information delivery, 171
finance specialist position, 95
fiscal IT budget
defined, 87–88
establishing of, 94
fiscal policy, corporate, 92
flexibility
of customer experience, 157–158
as decision criterion for delivery of IT
functions, 238
as leadership skill, 247, 250
of technology, 74
"flow," concept of, in customer interactions,
147–148
follow-up to determine value, 9
framework
for information management, 100–104
for internal controls, 60, 68
"function delivery" profile, 241–242
functional IT budget, defined, 88
functional measures, 30
functions, IT, delivery of
decision criteria for, 238–240

decision framework for, 240–244
delivery options, 234–238
maturity model, 231–233
future of IT
function, 118
governance, 120–121
hardware/software management, 124
internal controls, 121–122
management, 118–119
mission, 116–118
overview, 113–115
self-image, 119–120
staffing, 122–123
standards, 120–121, 123, 124
systems development, 124–125
workplace, 124–125

G

gap analysis, 78–79
global business. See also sourcing
communication issues, 193, 195
consolidating, with technology roadmap, 75
networkcentric operations in future, 170–171
standards-adoption difficulties, 184
goods, defined, 146
governance, IT, 64
architecture governance, 81–82
budget contribution to, 89
of delivery of IT functions, 236
of funding for experimentation, 142
in future, 120–121
skills, for IT leaders, 249
gradual migration strategy, 81

H

hackers, protection against. See security
hardware/software management in future, 124
help desk as business support, 66
holistic orientation to IT value, 11
HR management and training, 64
communication etiquette training, 193
leadership training, 248, 251–254, 254–255
professionalism development, 267

I

identification of potential IT value, 6–7
IM. See information management
immersion and absorption, 146–147, 154